The Saviors of Mankind

THE
SAVIORS OF MANKIND

BY

William Riley Van Buskirk

Essay Index Reprint Series

BOOKS FOR LIBRARIES PRESS
FREEPORT, NEW YORK

First Published 1929
Reprinted 1969

STANDARD BOOK NUMBER:
8369-1432-5

LIBRARY OF CONGRESS CATALOG CARD NUMBER:
71-86790

PRINTED IN THE UNITED STATES OF AMERICA

To My Wife

PREFACE

This is the overlooked and untold story of the world's great prophets and their messages. In a sense it is the inevitable story, for the investigations of scholars and the splendid results from scientific procedure in other fields are rapidly making it certain that religion must be viewed as a social phenomenon, a construction growing out of a social situation and designed primarily to produce a social effect. As it is told within these pages it is necessarily incomplete, now that so many ages have passed and so much priceless evidence has forever perished, but it will serve perhaps to yield a new point of view and to indicate a field for further investigation.

The author wishes to acknowledge his very great indebtedness to Dr. James A. Kelsoe, whose course in Comparative Religion at Western Theological Seminary first called to his attention the profound forces which operate in the origin and development of every religion. The responsibility for the point of view and the opinions expressed in this work is, however, solely that of the author and is not to be assigned to his instructors.

INTRODUCTION

The study of religion from the standpoint of its intellectual form subjects the work of the founders of the world's religious systems to the norm of logical necessity alone. By this method we discover behind the special local manifestations in each religion the presence of common elements which owe their origin to the universal character of the human mind. All religious constructions have these points of similarity—thoughts, doctrines, and devices—which bear upon identical human situations. These indicate that mankind has a set of persistent problems due to the fact that man is what he is. And while there may be some variety in the answer given to each question, the answer is nevertheless universal, as if it were automatic and reflexive. To discover all this may shed some illumination upon human nature, and may show that religion is inevitable, but it can give us very little information about any particular religious system.

The reason for this is not far to seek—the investigation is too general, too abstract. The logical necessities will operate according to the nature of the human intellect, once the proper stimulus is present. But the special character of any religious construction depends entirely upon the source of stimulation and the peculiar way in which it expresses itself. We learn more about a religion, therefore, if we try to discover what the stimulus was than if we catalogue the various points at which it is similar to other faiths. And this follows just because it is the social and personal necessities which have furnished by far the larger portion of every prophet's inspiration.

A study of the theology of any religion is therefore a rather unfruitful procedure and yields little in the way of religious understanding. It omits from the account the intuitive, or mystic, element—the very factor which has constituted the *élan vital* of all great faiths. And it separates religious deliverances from those actual social forces which have always supplied the chief reason for the prophetic voice. When the background which will reveal both the prophet's provocation and the purpose of his utterance is ignored, there is naturally little left except a rather pointless bit of human thinking.

Religions have always appeared in times of national crisis, and are to be regarded as the highest answer of an aspiring soul to the perils and needs of the hour. Aside from the abiding problems which arise from our common humanity, nearly all questions affecting our lot on earth grow out of the social conditions in which we find ourselves. Almost any faith will serve to minister to universal needs, and reformations of the faith are infrequent when society is undisturbed. But when a social order meets with disaster, when the tempo of life increases the centripetal strain, compensation must be found. The prophets of the race have always appeared at such times and have gone about the very practical business of saving the situation. Their problems are perhaps almost always universal, for man's life rises and falls in cycles—emerges from poor and simple conditions to become luxurious, to erect complex societies, and to revert to simplicity and poverty again—but they are concrete and historical problems for all that. The prophet addresses himself to an actual historical peril and his recommendations are designed to remedy the conditions of a people who inhabit this earth.

How inadequate then has been the usual presentation of the religions of mankind. To state a few facts about a world religion, and to call attention to the present-day social depravity of its devotees, is utterly to miss the mark. Such a study gives us nothing of the background which called the faith into being, ignores completely the tendency of all faiths to become formal when the crisis is well passed, and fails in its analysis of the social situation which has resulted more from irreligion than from the vision of the prophet in question. No real knowledge of the founder's purpose can be gained when the historical situation, which he faced and for which his teachings afford relief, is wholly disregarded. And to compare the doctrines of the various world-religions with Christianity is to go just as wide of the mark. It is to substitute pure ideas for the religious values behind the doctrines. The method may have some value as a mental exercise, but it can give us no proper understanding of any of the religions involved.

The science of Comparative Religion so called has proved thus far a very doubtful quantity. Usually it is only comparative theology, or comparative ethics, and, even in its more pretentious moments, is little more than comparative ethnology. Very seldom does it discover a real basis for comparison. It has taken the great leaders and prophets violently out of the only conditions which can explain them, for the purpose of the prophet is always the salvation of his people in a given social situation and at a given period in that people's social development. If we ask, "To what and from what does he try to save them?" we shall come face to face with something more than a sheaf of theological doctrines. We shall discover two forces at war in every conscientious man—the spirit of his group with all its handicaps, and the genius of the individual, pitted against the unfavorable features of society and Nature. This is no abstraction, but a living force struggling against a force no less powerful in the drama of self-expression and survival. Comparative Religion as a study fails largely because it compares doctrinal systems rather than the spirits of historical ages.

The problems of mankind are, to be sure, the same in all ages, yet are ever changing. The thinkers of the world are constantly entering new environments to think upon the old problems, but old problems modified by the exigencies of a new age. It is true that the old humanity periodically renews itself by fresh contacts with the heart of Reality and gains thus a knowledge more mystic than reasoned. But after such moments of personal and mental transfiguration it comes back to lowly everyday affairs and follows the old paths of the race. It looks through the ancient opinions and visions of its seers, and practices the antique habits of departed men. For all its renewed nature it accepts its heritage. It would therefore be utterly impossible for the native Persian to feel and think upon any given question in identically the way a Greek or a Chinese would do. Thus in spite of the similarity to be found in all human thinking the world around, there is a difference, and one that counts heavily against the usual procedure in Comparative Religion. To deprive the several religions of all dissimilar elements is to screen out just the facts which are peculiar to each national group and to lose thereby the very special situation which each religion was designed to meet.

The historical and social approach to the study of any religion is therefore of paramount importance. If any comparisons are to be drawn, they should follow after the historical and social materials have been found and have been well digested. Perhaps only the broadest general statements will be permissible in any case, for it is not easy to compare two widely separated ages within the same nation or to rate the merit of the several leaders involved. One finds it exceedingly difficult to compare George Washington and Ulysses S. Grant; and still more difficult to compare Gladstone and Lincoln. Yet the difficulties to be surmounted by the conventional method of Comparative Religion are even more disconcerting. Religious conclusions based upon an anatomical study of the brains of Confucius and Moses could scarcely be less absurd.

Thus it is clear that environment becomes a profound factor in determining the point and purpose of every religion. It supplies the prophet with his stage of action, it puts a problem to his mind, and it contains within itself the germ of a solution. The prophet sees deeply enough to glimpse the metaphysical principles involved and to read the special force of universal truth as it expresses itself in his time and nation. In other words, he goes to the fount of all truth and finds in the presence of deity the answer he makes to his nation's perplexities. To feel thus a people's afflictions and to find and support a remedy with uncompromising loyalty, is to exercise the prophetic gift. But it is the unfavorable nature of the environment which begins the process of prophet-making and supplies the radius to all prophetic utterance.

The personalities presented in this study are approached from the standpoint of the historical and social problems of their respective nations. In this way it is possible to discover the concrete nature of religion and to determine with greater certainty those factors which contribute to the vogue of a world-faith. By this approach the prophet is rescued from the stigma of impracticability, is permitted to join again the ranks of his fellow mortals, and is allowed to contribute his vision to the totality of human wisdom. We are enabled also to behold the reasons for the prophet's failure when he fails, and to gauge the several devices and forces which have made possible any success he may have achieved. We shall never be able to understand the true nature and function of a religion until we are able to reconstruct the age in which it made its appearance. Nothing so pretentious can be claimed for this story of religion, but it is hoped that the reader will gain from it an inspiration to lift the curtain of oblivion which hides from him the true worth of all his beliefs.

One ought to secure from any correct appraisal of the age of each prophet materials for a new science and philosophy of religion. Such a result should give us new methods for combatting the degeneracy which overtakes all societies. The whole regenerative force of belief may then be presented with greater certainty to achieve deeper and more general results. And a new era of spiritual discovery should replace the feeling that nothing further can now be added to revelation. Scientific procedure, such as characterizes the search for the ideals and purposes of secular education, will replace pious imaginings, and sane and proved methods will supplant those cheap devices which now litter the religious educational field. We shall find the true purpose of religion and set about the construction of an educational procedure which will stamp it indelibly upon the race. This will call for a constant succession of new prophets as the race unfolds its genius and emerges into the light of new ages of the world. It is the purpose of this book only to suggest a way to this lofty enterprise.

CONTENTS

The Saviors of Mankind

CHAPTER I

Lao-Tze

When the Chinese came from Central Asia to China in about 3000 B.C. they found that another race had preceded them. This first eastward moving wave of peoples had penetrated the land between the Yang Tse and the Hwang Ho rivers, and in this latitude which we are accustomed to speak of as "the belt of power" had established those institutions, arts, and views of government which have continued with but slight modification even to this day. The Chinese succeeded in subjugating the territory between the two rivers eastward to the sea, but they were too few in number to enforce at once any considerable basic change in the civilization they had conquered.

The aborigines, variously mentioned by the Annals of the Chinese as the Great Mung, the Lung, the Pu, and the Lao Shan peoples, continued to dwell in the land and to perpetuate their culture and institutions until 1000 A.D. Up to the sixth century B.C. the coming of the Chinese had done little more than to establish a loose confederacy of the native states or kingdoms. The rulers of these states, therefore, continued in office from father to son with but slight embarrassment from the Chinese overlordship.

But somewhere near the ninth century B.C. the Chinese, who had multiplied to vast numbers, began to press eastward and southward and to occupy lands among the aborigines. Three hundred years of this quiet infiltration of the conquerors developed within the native states a tense racial situa-

I

tion. The native princes and peoples resented these encroachments. Friction and bitterness led to frequent armed oppositions on the part of the Lao, but these wars always terminated with the triumph of the Chinese.

When one of the native armies would be defeated it would march out of the country with its possessions and seek a new home. It would conquer the peoples in the territory it was forced to occupy, and thus the Lao in this way came finally to rule all Asia south of the Yang Tse and east of India. Between the Yang Tse and the Hwang Ho several millions of the Lao remained to supply perhaps the largest single element in the present Chinese race-stock. Thus the Chinese became a composite people with institutions and customs very much like those of the peoples they had only apparently absorbed.

It was inevitable that the native princes who saw the fate of their brother rulers, through the encroachments of the Chinese, should attempt to make the most of privileges destined to be of short duration. Those who did not possess the vigor to lead their people forth to find a new home gave themselves up to licentiousness and the effort to live well while they could. They became corrupt, greedy, and tyrannical. This state of vice and oppression naturally outraged the best minds among the native peoples and caused the more courageous ones to demand a remedy.

Thus after the first great migration of the Lao, which took place early in the sixth century B.C., those of the race who remained north of the Yang Tse found themselves in a condition of social turmoil and strife. The self-assertiveness of the native peoples and the oppressive demands of the conquerors made the situation well-nigh intolerable. It was during this period that the great teachers appeared who have shaped the thought and religion of present-day China. There is strong evidence in nearly every case to support the belief that these teachers were

members of the subjugated race. [1] Lao-Tze perhaps reveals his
race by his name; Mencius, or Mung-Tze, is probably a member of the Great Mung race; and Confucius was born in the
little independent kingdom of Lu, a state which was undoubtedly composed of the Lu tribe of the Lao peoples.

Renan in one of his essays calls attention to the Celtic contribution to legend and literature and points out the many
spiritual contributions of the conquered. Greece fell but she
gave to her conquerors the impulse to, and substance of,
philosophy and religion. We encounter the same thing in
ancient China. The conquered Lao supplied to the composite
race the philosophy and religion which it should ever afterwards hold. And what is more natural? That which is truly
indigenous should by right come from that race which supplies the preponderant element to the new stock.

When adversity, strife, cruelty, loss, and defeat overtake a
race the hopelessness of the social condition does not permit
men of genius to enjoy the privileges of external self-realization. The great minds are therefore forced to turn within
themselves and to call upon the intellectual and imaginative
faculties for salvation. The inner harmony and peace thus secured lead naturally to the construction of an imagined social condition in which these inner achievements may be
realized by all. Thus philosophy, religion, and social reformation come to exist. Often, perhaps almost always, the dream
outruns the possibility of even the most remote realization by
society as a whole. A few will accept the dream, but the great
mass of the population will always remain unevangelized.
The teacher may become discouraged because of the ebb and
flow of discipleship attending popular adjustment. He may in
despair go into exile, or, if blessed with much fortitude of

---

[1] Lao is rendered by several writers as meaning "Old," but it probably
means "ancient," "aboriginal." Originally it perhaps meant the Lao people.
Lacouperie suggests that the names have been masked to save Chinese dignity.
A glance at the names will show very little masking if due allowance is
made for Chinese transliteration.

spirit, continue on as the pathetic figure of a lost or impractical cause.

The above is not always, of course, the exact history of the origin of philosophy and religion, but the social condition is, without doubt, the clue which will help us to account for the appearance of practically every great system of religious thought. The prophet appears in the days of decadence. Out of the buoyancy of the human soul in rebellion against its lot, the system comes to be. It is the profound reaction of reason and righteousness, the long-considered answer, to the intolerable condition of spiritual defeat. The recommendations may touch upon the universal facts of life and destiny, but the prescriptions almost always bear marks which show that they are aimed at an immediate social need.

Especially is this true of the teachers who appeared in ancient China during that period of social unrest due to the constant pressure of the conquerors. The immediate situation bulked so large in the minds of these sages that their teachings, while possessing many universal elements, were devised chiefly to meet the affairs of the moment. There is in the writings of each the unmistakable shadow of social policy, and their recommendations are vibrant with life just because they advise an attitude calculated to meet the emergencies of the hour.

One may very properly ask how it would be possible for a member of a conquered race to formulate a teaching that would be acceptable to his conquerors. The answer may be found in the depth and richness of the teaching, the superiority it possesses over any teaching brought by the conquerors. Greek art, philosophy, and religion did make themselves acceptable to the Romans. And Christianity, after many adversities, achieved the same result. If these arts and systems of thought could gain the day by the sheer force of their superiority, how much more would the teachings of the Lao philosophers appeal to a race having souls that were of the predominant Lao stock. The composite Chinese therefore found these teachings more congenial to him than pure Chinese teachings, which could appeal at the most to only a fraction of his being. The long-suppressed Lao nature would rise up with a shout to greet the native voice of its deliverance. A Lao philosopher would be acceptable just because the soul of the new race was a Lao soul.

The first of these teachers was Lao-Tze. Little is known of his acts or of his manner of life. It is generally believed that he was born about 600 b.c., and the date is fixed by some at 604 b.c. Practically all of his biographers include the account of the interview between the aged Lao-Tze and the young Confucius. The account is of great significance in two ways. First, it brings together the system of Lao-Tze and the ideas of Confucius, and shows them to be in conflict. Second, it reveals a weakness in the methods of Lao-Tze, and one that will have a far-reaching influence upon their future as a social force. He is reported to have treated Confucius with an austerity which amounted almost to contempt. This is often the attitude of the ripened wisdom of age to the rather fresh visions of youth. But there is more than a matter of age between these men. Lao-Tze knows something of the views of Confucius, and from his more profound height is antagonistic to what he considers the shallow practicality of Confucius. The truth which Confucius sees supplies its own credential and gives to the younger man an assurance which nettles the old sage. He replies to Confucius' question with the advice, "Put away, sir, your proud air and many desires, your plausibility and ungoverned will. These are of no advantage to you."

This advice is sound enough, but it will not do for this questing age that has stolen upon the old philosopher while he has been preoccupied with the internal matters of the self. There is a social state in which it is advisable to do no more than eat, drink, and walk softly. But that attitude loses its virtue when the customs, arts, and indigenous views of a race are dying with the passing generation. Action for the preservation of native customs may become the better policy, and Confucius for all his shallow doctrines has grasped this truth. The younger man wisely overlooks the scorn of Lao-Tze and finds unerringly the rent in the armor. He turns away saying, "I know how birds fly, fishes swim, and animals run. Yet the runner may be snared, the swimmer hooked, and the flier shot. But there is the dragon. I cannot tell how he mounts on the wind through the clouds, and rises to heaven. To-day I have seen Lao-Tze, and I can only compare him to the dragon." This is no compliment to Lao-Tze. His uncommunicativeness leaves him unintelligible and his philosophical downrightness prevents his acceptance of a wholesome expediency. There has been some doubt as to the authenticity of this interview, but there need not be. This is exactly what would have been said at such a meeting.

We are further told that Lao-Tze was the keeper of the treasury of the imperial court, and that in his old age he resigned and set out for the West. On reaching the frontier, he was asked by the guard to commit his teachings to writing before withdrawing from the world. His compliance with this request resulted in the Tao Te Ching.

This information is meager enough, and at first seems too little to enable us to construct a worthy biography. But with the aid of his teachings it will suffice. Lao-Tze was not a man of action. At his desk in the treasury he performed all the physical action his nature required. The rest of his vital movements may be found in the profound philosophy which he formulated. His story, like that of Kant, consists of the walk every day and the endless staring at a wall.

The first deep stirring of the mind of Lao-Tze began when he noted the amount of taxes collected and saw the items of royal expense. The money he handled had been made sacred by the tears of the people who had been deprived of personal comforts. As he watched the lavish squandering of this wealth by his sovereign his soul rose in protest, and he began to look for a remedy. The prince's will was absolute. Therefore, the first step in reformation must meet the unjust desires of the prince. But there was the conqueror and his demands; he too must be taught to curb his desires.

The more Lao-Tze pondered this principle the more he saw that it was applicable to all men. If the people could be made content with the simple life, they would be happy in their poverty. If they could be taught to be less outspoken, less given to self-seeking, they would not come into conflict with the conqueror. Action and word helped none. Was not a man always himself? Could anything deprive him of his soul except his uncurbed desires and his undiplomatic utterances? Lao-Tze knew that he had kept his position by silence when his soul had been deeply outraged. He had been able to turn within himself and to find there a peace which the prince could not find with all his wealth. If men would get rid of desire there would be peace within and without. Thus originated the social policy and the personal code which made the story of Lao-Tze the briefest of all biographies.

This social policy which seems to grow so naturally out of the broodings of Lao-Tze is not altogether the result of intellectual struggle. If he had been a man of more rash and daring nature, he would have formulated from the same situation a more vigorous policy. In fact, many men had already done so. They had all died in battle against the Chinese, or had gone to join those kindred spirits who had been compelled to migrate south of the Yang Tse. Those who had remained behind in the old home of the race were of docile mold and had arrived at less troublesome conclusions. The teachings of Lao-Tze therefore presuppose the popular decision to stay at home, and are designed to make that decision tolerable.

From the insight afforded by the above set of facts we may

guess with no little accuracy as to the events of the early life of Lao-Tze. Men of quiet temper, who construct quietist philosophies, do not achieve their calm souls. They are born as they are. And we shall not go far astray by filling in the silence of history with the statement that Lao-Tze was a quiet, thoughtful, industrious youth who kept well within the prevailing customs of his people. His dependability, honesty, and industry gained for him very early many positions of trust. And his early life and character were such as to bring him at last to the position of King's treasurer. By the same token his studious habits had prepared him for the rôle of the philosopher, and his mystical nature determined the kind of philosopher he would be.

This view of his youth is confirmed by the events of the middle years of his life. Men who had known him in his student days came to talk with him just because they knew that he had always been a painstaking student. From these quiet conversations grew his later reputation. His friends, who were worthy of him, were amazed at his understanding and began to speak openly in his praise. Students began to flock to him to attend the forums he no doubt conducted after business hours. And during the long years in which this manner of life continued there were thousands of young men to pass under his instruction. It was this practice of teaching which built up the reputation which brought Confucius to interview him.

Thus the years passed quietly and with the sameness which is characteristic of Chinese life to-day. Having learned the story of one day in the life of the sage, we know the story of all his days; for he conducted his affairs with the regularity of a clock. There was nothing to record at great length, just because there was nothing unusual about him except his rare intellectual power.

But there were new forces abroad in the land toward the close of his life. It is the nature of youth to seek for action.

The austere quietism of Lao-Tze ceased to recommend itself to the young, and already the social situation had become so ameliorated that an extreme caution was unnecessary. The young men who were born under the new régime, many of them of mixed blood, were above suspicion. The school of Lao-Tze saw its attendance dwindle until only those who sought philosophy for philosophy's sake were in attendance. And it did not occur to these to think of their master as a great social leader.

Furthermore, the general lukewarmness of the prince toward the views of his treasurer continued to prevail. The monarch showed no tendency toward either repentance or the curtailment of his expenditures. Lao-Tze could see that as a reformer he was losing ground. Either from disgust, or from personal pride, he resigned his post and withdrew from the land. At the border he came up with an official who knew his worth, a man who perhaps had been one of his pupils. This official, being well acquainted with the oral method of instruction that Lao-Tze had used, saw that the great teaching would now be lost. He besought the sage to write out his principles for the good of humanity before leaving the land. There is about this request an irony which shall repeat itself many times hereafter in the world's history. Lao-Tze has been rejected by his people, and, but for the request of this official at the border, the world would have lost all knowledge of him.

The book which thus came to be reveals the primary reason for the master's departure. The man who reads it thoughtfully will be inclined to discredit those speculations which hint at the loss of princely favor. Lao-Tze is not vigorous enough in method to force his way into the fickle heart of his prince. The popularity of the young Confucius at this time is enough to show that the spirit of the times is changing. Men are growing critical of the old philosopher's ideas. The prophet of non-resistance cannot prosecute even a verbal warfare in defense of his doctrines. And when he knows that he cannot continue to teach without strife and arguments, he withdraws in the interest of the public good and his own soul. He is a great failure, but he is a logical one. And of all the philosophers who have ever lived he is perhaps the only one who knew too much to contradict himself.

II

The philosophy of Lao-Tze is primarily monistic. His ground principle is called Tao, a term which has been interpreted as The Way, The Law or The Way of Nature, God, Universal Supreme Reason, The Way of The World, and The Power That Makes for Righteousness. It is a conception which is very closely akin to the term Logos. Perhaps if we use the term The Power That Realizes Design we shall more nearly approximate the sage's meaning. It is a power that originates the universe composed of the actual heavens and the earth. We must not identify it with the term Design, for it is the Power that uses the principle of Design. In and of itself, it is formless and intangible. It is therefore without substance, yet it comprehends within itself all substance. As a power with all material substance to work upon, it is all-producing, all-pervading, all-nourishing, and all-perfecting.

From this description we may surmise that from introspection the philosopher has derived his notion of the Tao. It is of the Self type. The Self is not to be identified with any of its powers. It is behind the material but embraces it, uses it, pervades it, controls it, and perfects it through its action upon it. Self is intangible, invisible, inaudible, and eludes description. From these observations Lao-Tze carried his notion of the self to universal dimensions to become the Tao. This universalized self thus became the nameless, invisible Power which, in its nameless state, may be regarded as the origin of the universe. When we name it, it becomes but the mother of all things. In other words, the name is thought of as degrading the Tao to the level of its functions, as identifying it with its prerogatives. A name is to Lao-Tze a descriptive term, and description is always an account of function. The Tao is that which may function, but it exists apart from its functions. Only when it has produced order, or phenomena, does it become nameable; but when it has become nameable it has lost its eternity. As Lao-Tze puts it, "The Tao which can be named is not the Tao that is eternal."

In this way he draws a distinction between Design and the Designer. As nearly as we can describe the Tao in our language, it is the potential Author of Design. But as soon as it begins to express its authorship it becomes temporal and passing. This is as far as analysis can go. To posit the unmoved and unmoving Mover, the potential Author without authorship, the Power that is as yet unexpressed, is to touch the last big rock.

The visible world is therefore only the perishable expression of the eternal Tao. Men who are subject to their passions can see only this external expression, not the eternal Tao. It is only the man who is ever passionless who may behold the substance of this mystery. The immaterial mystery and the material manifestation differ in name, but they are the same in source. Their unity, however, "is a deep, a deep of deeps, the portal of all mystery."

A clue to Lao-Tze's meaning when he speaks of the common source of the material and the immaterial may be gained from his statements concerning the ideal state. The Tao revolves through the universe to produce order in a mysterious, spontaneous, and effortless manner; but in its eternal form or condition, it is also an ideal state of perfection. Within it, before the visible creation appeared, all things acted harmoniously. It would seem then that the Tao is active-being, in its eternal state. But when this action moves outward it does so in a series of emanations, or rather, in successive stages of the same emanation. This emanation is the visible creation.

And since all things have thus emanated from the Tao of spontaneity, they will regain their ideal state of harmony only by a return to the Tao of spontaneity. Man is but a part of the emanation and must therefore find the state which is above good and evil by a similar return to this state of perfection. Thus "man follows the laws of earth, earth of Heaven, Heaven of Tao, and Tao of spontaneity." That which drew from out the deep of deeps must turn again home.

But man returns to this state, not by death, but by imitation of the action of the Tao; that is, by conforming in all things to the Tao. And since the Tao does not strive, man must be humble, seek the lowest places, and do nothing to interfere with the action of others. Through humbleness, non-interference, and inaction, he may gain a power which is like that of water—a power that wears away the hardest substances. Not to act is, therefore, the secret of power. The unwarlike man conquers.

Such statements depend, of course, upon Lao-Tze's doctrine of opposites. He says that being is the source of not-being, and that not-being is the created world. Being is essence, while not-being is existence. But being and not-being are both contained within absolute being, or Tao. Tao is thus the source of both essence and existence. Lao-Tze is here describing the noumenal and the phenomenal of Hegel at a date nearly twenty-three centuries before Hegel lived.

We can now discern the order of the emanation and can see why man should seek to attain the perfect state of Tao or spontaneity. Out of this state proceeds the creation in its several stages. Therefore, if man would be powerful he ought to identify himself with being, or essence; in this way he will be able to secure all that is not-being. This state is secured through passivity. Thus, by becoming passive, man may receive spontaneously and without effort all the power he requires.

We should give special heed to the nature of the human

objective to be won by a return to Tao. It is not escape from the world; it is not spiritual peace, primarily; nor is it salvation in the sense of immortality. The return is for the sake of power. This objective points directly to the social situation. If we remember that the first great migration of the Lao peoples took place within the time of Lao-Tze, we can discern the reason for wishing to secure this goal. The power of a large portion of the Lao peoples has been broken in battles with the Chinese. This disaster has shown the wiser men of the remaining Lao states that strife can bring nothing but further disaster. The Lao are not at present a warlike people; they have specialized too long in the arts of peace and civilization. The only immediate resource left them is the spontaneous vitality of the Lao nature. If each individual of this race can be persuaded to overcome his desires and combative impulse through an emphasis upon his inner spiritual nature, there will be no further destruction of the Lao peoples. They will be able to dwell with their conquerors and to overcome them by the sheer weight of their numbers and spiritual power. The unwarlike man will conquer.

There can be no doubt as to the wisdom of this teaching. Enough of the Lao remained behind after the immense migrations during the succeeding centuries of conflict to make the Chinese of to-day more like the Lao than the great warriors who first appeared on the border of the Lao country. The millions of the Lao could have absorbed their conquerors and have remained with but a sprinkling of Tartar or Ugral blood in their veins. Finally the victory would have gone to this quiescent, controlled, peaceful, and intellectually undisturbed race. The weakness of the philosopher's vision lay in the fact that it was impossible to win the whole race to an acceptance of his wise policy.

Just what the situation was and how he proposed to meet it, may be learned from one of his utterances: "In a small state with a few inhabitants (I would so order it that) the people, though supplied with all kinds of implements, would not (care to) use them; I would make them look on death as a most grievous thing, but not go away to a distance (to escape it). Though they had boats and carriages, they would have no occasion to ride in them; Though they had buff coats and sharp weapons, they should not don or use them. I would make them return to the use of knotted cords (instead of written characters). They should think their (coarse) food sweet, their (plain) clothing beautiful, their (poor) houses places of rest, and their common (simple) ways sources of enjoyment.

"There should be a neighboring state within sight, and the sounds of the fowls and dogs should be heard from it to us without interruption, but I would make the people to old age, even to death, have no intercourse with it." [2]

Dr. James Legge who quotes this passage from Giles' translation of the Tao Te King remarks: "It would be difficult to suppose that these sentences were written seriously. The thoughts are those of a hermit, and not of a philosopher. Would Lao-Tze really have been glad to abolish writing, and go back to the use of quippos? Would he have had neighboring peoples live all their lives without any intercourse? He was a dreamer, a 'glorious dreamer,' if you like, but after all only a dreamer." [3]

These sentences were not intended, of course, to be taken literally, but Lao-Tze did intend that they should be taken very seriously. It was the habit of small states to become embroiled in quarrels and conflicts with their Chinese and Lao neighbors. Unscrupulous princes often stimulated these unpleasant episodes that they might have excuse to invade their smaller neighboring states and seize both land and people. As the Analects show, the smaller states often abandoned their own territory and sought a new home to avoid

---

[2] Tao Te King, Giles' translation.
[3] James Legge, *Religions of China*, pp. 225-226.

further trouble. At least one of these sentences aims directly at such well-known conditions. And to prevent feudal wars among these Lao principalities and to avoid vengeance from the Chinese, the rest of the passage seems to have been spoken. Any one who studies the special style of the Tao Te King will know at once that the passage advising no neighborly intercourse is not intended to prevent any communication whatever. Only a condition free of senseless meddling and communications with antagonistic intent, is Lao-Tze's real meaning.

It would appear therefore that Lao-Tze's dreams easily become the most sane and practical ones to be met with in his time. This "glorious dreamer" has without doubt seen clearly into the whole ghastly nightmare of social conditions and has made such recommendations as will prevent some of the worst and most dangerous practices. He is certainly not a hermit, and he is a very great social philosopher. In this passage, as well as in a number of others to be met with in his work, Lao-Tze urges a highly practical policy, one that will dispel the turmoil and stop the migrations of this period.

And when Dr. Legge forgets himself for just a moment he says: "Lao-Tze's Taoism is the exhibition of a way or method of living which men should cultivate as the highest and purest development of their natures. . . . Taoism as a discipline for the mind and life has not been without fruit. There have been many who under its influence have withdrawn entirely from the world, and many more who, unable to do that, have endeavored to keep themselves, while in the world, from the vortex of its ambitions and passions, seeking after its three precious things, with the stillness of the soul, the simplicity of motive, and the sympathy with virtue and happiness which it commends." [4]

It was just this latter result, "to keep themselves from the

[4] James Legge, *Religions of China*, pp. 229-230.

vortex of the world's ambitions and passions," which Lao-Tze sought to accomplish as an actual social fact. His words and his own acts may be made to encourage the hermit life, but it is the only alternative after actual effort to produce social reform has failed. The prescription is too austere, not too impractical, for this licentious age.

His hope of reforming society was destroyed through a misunderstanding of his language. He did not dare say openly that his teachings were calculated to save the Lao against the Chinese. The social results must, therefore, be couched in metaphorical terms wherever reference was made to the conqueror. Thus his writings and his public utterances contained a feature which is characteristic of all apocalyptic literature. A missionary told me that the Tai, or Lao, to this day ridicule the European in his presence by seeming to be talking of some animal which is within sight of the company. An example of Lao-Tze's method of talking of the conquerors who may have been sitting with the Lao students in his presence can be seen in the following statement: "The man who knows Tao need not fear the bite of the serpent nor the jaws of wild beasts, nor the claws of the bird of prey. He is inaccessible to good and evil. He need fear neither the rhinoceros nor the tiger. In battle he needs no sword. The tiger cannot tear him, the soldier cannot wound him. He is invulnerable and safe from death."

There is here just enough of the actual interspersed with the figurative to show that the poisonous, tearing fierceness of the Chinese soldier is meant by this description of animals. The Lao will need no sword in battle, and will be invulnerable to wounds, just because there will be no such thing as war. He will remain aloof from both the flatteries and the persecutions of his foe. But he is safe only in a victory over himself.

Stupidity and popular devotion to the old magical religious ideas caused some of his hearers to take him literally.

The results were thus directly opposed to the ones Lao-Tze had hoped to secure. Instead of producing popular humility, non-interference with the desires of the conquerors, and the cessation of hatreds and dangerous conflicts, he actually caused many who heard him to become more haughty than before. His sayings made them believe that they would sweep away all their enemies in battle, and would be able to do so without wounds and death to themselves. Lao-Tze saw that by continuing to teach he was in fact merely hastening the very calamity he was seeking to prevent. Here then was another reason for his withdrawal from the land.

One can now gain a fair idea of the amazement, disgust, and humiliation of Lao-Tze as he turned to leave his people. To explain what was really his aim would serve only to bring him into immediate conflict with the conquerors, something which must be avoided in the interests of the public weal. And, as has already been explained, the younger generation was for action. It was determined to secure its rights and to cleave to its racial worth. Instead of self-suppression it was in favor of self-assertion. Enamored of this purpose, it persisted in reading into the words of the master a way to power, a power which might be used in war or in personal peril. Caught thus between the blind ambition of the coming generation and the danger of openly stating his aims, he could see nothing ahead but exile.

As one watches the retreating figure of Lao-Tze he becomes aware of the holocausts of calamity that are crowding in behind him. The spirit of the younger generation will serve only to revive and crystallize the racial pride in arts and institutions. It will not be able to supply that self-abasement by which alone the Lao will be able to remain in the land. The retreating sage is taking with him the people's salvation, and they are unable to see the things that belong to their peace.

Of course, there is something to be said for the aims of the youth of this period. Suppression can go too far; it can cause irreparable loss. There must be something to save. What a pity that Confucius and Lao-Tze were not more completely contemporaneous! Before Lao-Tze, following the way of time, became dogmatic, set, impervious to the facts of observation, he might have acknowledged the worth of Confucius' point of view. A people, even in a state of Tao, expresses itself in manners and customs that are peculiar to its special endowments. Lao-Tze could have accepted the Confucian revival and have saved it from its worst faults. By a policy of inoffensiveness and a return of good for evil the two men working together might have been able to prevent that rashness and pride which finally caused the Lao to be driven south of the Yang-Tse.

After the departure of Lao-Tze his pupils continued to teach his doctrines, but his words were so emptied of all political significance that the purpose which had originally called them forth was entirely lost. The disciples made of his way to power a selfish individualism having no national or ethical meaning. The more generous minded did not emphasize this aspect of the teaching but turned more to the metaphysical features. Thus, that which the master had intended as a racial policy, designed to meet and overcome the conqueror, was now developed into a mental discipline, or, at most, into little more than an explanation of the Way of Nature.

The most gifted writer and thinker among those who accepted the master's Way was Chuang-Tze. This rather belated disciple erected upon the principles of his predecessor a superstructure which is worthy to stand among the great philosophical systems of all time. His literary style has a quaintness, a humor, and an incisiveness, with now and then a stroke of overwhelming irony, which holds the reader fascinated. He was a contemporary of Mencius, the great disciple of Confucius, and although Mencius is described as being the peer of such men as Aristotle, Zeno, Epicurus, and Demosthenes who lived in his day, Chuang-Tze was in some ways his superior. But for all his gifts and achievements, Chuang-Tze was only a philosopher. He did not aim directly at the social needs of the time. And that lack of social aim, that lack of pointed attempt at national rescue, even though he did much to elevate the thought of all time, will prevent him from being classed as a true disciple of his master.

But, for all his social indifference, what he has said is very significant. His elaboration of the teaching of Lao-Tze, while purely philosophical, reveals the depth of vision which went into the making of the master's great teaching of social redemption. It leads us into the secret of the soul's regimen and declares the substance of that contemplation which Lao-Tze believed would make his people superior to their social lot.

From Chuang-Tze we learn that nothing can produce Tao, yet everything has Tao in it, and continues to produce it without end. In other words, Tao is identified with each stage in the development of all things. Tao is not the thing which unfolds, but is present in it at every moment. It is not identical with anything that is, neither with the form of anything, but it is the ground of all change and development. Thus a man going on from the visible, i.e., the aspect of form in things, comes to know the heavenly. "He knows it as The Great Unity, The Great Illuminator, The Great Framer, The Great Mystery, The Great Truth, The Great Infinite, The Great Determiner. As The Great Unity, he comprehends it; as The Great Illuminator, he contemplates it; as The Great Framer, it is to him the cause of all; as The Great Mystery, he unfolds it; as The Great Truth, he examines it; as The Great Infinite, all is to him its embodiment; as The Great Determiner, he holds it fast." This is the field of contemplation and provides the attitude of the individual toward Tao. This exercise yields complete knowledge; and the harmony of thought and action with Tao as thus understood is intelligence at its best.

It is not difficult to see the object of this discipline. Lao-Tze hoped to cultivate in his people a serenity and poise which would lift them above the possibility of conflict with the lower aims and interests of the conquerors. He sought to put their whole life too high to be captured by the materialistic foe. This exaltation of racial desire was not for him an other-worldliness, but the highest truth and worth of the world we find all about us.

And to prevent the voluble arguments which lead nowhere, and which are the root of all conflict, bitterness, and war, he sought a theory of knowledge which would leave no ground for discussion. In expanding upon the deliverances of his master, Chuang-Tze says: "The explanation of Tao is as if it were no explanation, and the knowledge of it as if it were no knowledge. To have no name and no embodiment—of this one can speak and think, but the more one speaks the further off he gets. Were language adequate, it would take but a day to fully set forth Tao. Not being adequate, we may talk all day and explain only material existences. In that state which is neither speech nor silence (absorbed thought), its transcendental nature may be apprehended." One who possesses a knowledge which is inexplicable, which cannot be put adequately into language, which subtly eludes the very genius of language as soon as one begins to speak, will certainly bring no one into conflict with others. One cannot very well kindle opposition and race hatred by silence.

The attempt to reach this goal is strangely furthered by a statement concerning the brevity of life. "Man passes through this sublunary life as a white horse passes a crack. Here one moment, gone the next. The living creature cries out; human beings sorrow; the bow-sheath is slipped off; and in the confusion the soul wings its flight, and the body follows on the great journey." One who is interested in matters of real importance will therefore look beyond the visible and perishable nature which is his. He will not contend for the merely passing.

Tao is the only thing of real value. But "Tao has no objective value; hence silence is better than argument. It cannot be translated into speech; better, then, say nothing at all. This is the great attainment." Lao-Tze clarifies his position at this point by saying that man has fallen from a primitive state of perfection and must return to this perfection which is in Tao. This is in reality a protest against the social condition as it is, and against the existing government. Chuang-Tze says: "Poh Loh dragged horses from their native haunts, branded them, pared their feet, bridled them, kept them in stables, and one third of them died. Then he kept them hungry, trotted them, galloped, groomed, and drove them, and more than half of them died. In the same way trees and clay suffer at the hands of interfering 'skill.' The Emperors make the same mistake. The people have certain heaven-sent instincts, and interference with these is the cause of human misery."

It is surprising that Chuang-Tze could so accurately interpret his master and yet make no further use of him than to oppose good-naturedly the views of Mencius. But if we remember that Chuang-Tze flourished at least one hundred years after the death of Lao-Tze, we can begin to understand why the disciple should be only an ineffective echo. Even before the death of Lao-Tze public opinion had accepted the more worldly recommendations of Confucius. Chuang-Tze comes on the scene to find Confucius accorded a measure of reverence which, in other lands, would be given only to a patron saint. The views of Lao-Tze are so directly opposed in policy to those of Confucius that no considerable following can be secured. Thus while Chuang-Tze truly and brilliantly sets forth the doctrines of his master, he is content to do little more than to ridicule the Confucian principles.

For this task he is peculiarly well endowed. From his lofty heights he looks down upon the Confucian self-assurance and success with the amused tolerance one is accustomed to accord the statements of a child. "The ruler of the southern sea," he says, "was called Shu (Heedless). The ruler of the northern sea was called Hu (Hasty). The ruler of the central zone was called Hun Tun (Formless). Heedless and Hasty often met on Hun Tun's territory, and being treated kindly by him, sought how they might repay his kindness. They said, 'All men have seven orifices—for seeing, hearing, eating, and breathing. Hun Tun alone has none. We will bore some for him.' So every day they bored one hole; but on the seventh day Hun Tun died." Such is Chuang-Tze's ironical way of describing the futility of the Confucian means of enlightenment. The use of eyes and ears yields only a sensual knowledge, a knowledge of perishable things. Complete knowledge, knowledge of Tao, can be secured only by turning from the senses to pure reason. But the man who emphasizes the use of the senses loses the power to know Tao, the Formless. Chuang-Tze by his anecdote illustrates therefore the utter destruction of the man who adopts the method of Mencius— he loses the power to gain real knowledge.

But Chuang-Tze was himself unwittingly the victim of another kind of irony, the irony of Fate. The philosophical or religious controversialist easily becomes so absorbed in gaining his point against his antagonist that he achieves nothing of note in a social way. He becomes the defender of abstractions. He is betrayed into seeking a triumph on logical grounds, and he fails to realize that the quickening of a vital social hope is finally the only proper vindication of any teaching. The dangers of a false doctrine should be pointed out, but the intellectual strength and the emotional fire must be spent in constructive effort if society is to be saved. Altogether, the program of social redemption visioned by Lao-Tze was grossly mismanaged from the first. It is true that the temper of the times was opposed to a policy of quiescence, just because it seemed to play into the hands of the conquerors. It is equally true that quiescence has its limitations. But an age that requires a reform will of necessity be at variance with the saving truth. The ignorant and unrepentant man is always antagonistic to the views of his savior.

Lao-Tze was so intent upon the achievement of the first step in his nation's salvation that he neglected to make clear to the people the social possibilities of his program. Social action is as inevitable under self-control, non-interference, and inoffensiveness as under self-seeking and the most pronounced aspect of determined nationalism. It is inconceivable that Lao-Tze with his profound gift of analysis should fail to see this. He did see it; his whole teaching is intended to secure the right type of social action. But the action he advocated came so spontaneously out of the attitude of self-effacement that apparently it seemed to him to require no great amount of emphasis. His silence at certain points, and his meagerness of statement at others, contributed not only to the later misunderstanding of his teaching but to the unpopularity of the program even in his own day. Chuang-Tze is not without precedent from his master when he lets the teaching stand or fall by its philosophical character alone.

But even the most abstract and quiescent philosophy has a way of creeping into the actions of men. The disciple will try to live some measure of the truth as he understands it. But in the case of the less discerning of the disciples of Lao-Tze the social ends of the master were misunderstood or wilfully ignored. Doctrines are likely to be judged by the standard of immediate results. Thus Lao-Tze's injunction "love your enemies" could scarcely win popular support when vengeance had always been the rule. And with the growing popularity of Confucius, who taught that it was a duty to reward evil with evil in like measure, there could be no real social expression of non-interference and love toward the conqueror. By the time of the death of Lao-Tze the people had turned their eyes permanently toward the good old days, and it would have taken a more vigorous and positive teaching than Lao-Tze's, and more gifted disciples, to turn the people to a forward look.

Violence always stirs the primitive emotions to life, and "love your enemies" does not become popular during turbulent times.

Thus as time elapsed the philosophy of Lao-Tze passed into the hands of those who sought some means of emphasizing the value of ancient superstitions. The apocalyptic passages seemed ready-made for this purpose and were so used. There could scarcely be a stronger reason than this to show how important it is that a social reformer shall be fool proof in his recommendations. Instead of actually saving his people through an intellectual superiority to the things a conqueror could take from them, Lao-Tze served, perhaps through his vagueness, to encourage their most primitive religious follies. He helped them to face death indifferently, even when misunderstood, but he had meant that they should live, and live more abundantly!

No greater failure ever overtook the memory of a great social leader than this which came to Lao-Tze. His teachings were degraded on the one hand, into a system which was used as a defense of popular magic, and on the other into an elaborately reasoned but socially unfruitful philosophy. His doctrines of quiescence and non-interference, instead of producing the most superior, useful, and dominant members of society, operated through popular misconception toward self-suppression and achieved finally the separation of his disciples from the world. It is bad enough to fail and to know that the wars and destructions of the future cannot be avoided; it is infinitely worse to realize that one's teaching will actually contribute to the debacle one is seeking to evade. All this was well understood by Lao-Tze as he went into exile. It is to be hoped, however, that in the Tao of perfection he now knows nothing of that perversion which has overtaken his theories in modern times.

CHAPTER II

CONFUCIUS

Confucius was born, according to some authorities, at Shang-ping, near the town of Tseuse, in the independent kingdom of Lu, in 551 B.C. The kingdom of Lu then occupied the southern and western part of the present province of Shantung. Whether or not the inhabitants of Lu were then pure Chinese or almost pure Lao cannot now be determined. There are, however, certain facts which would indicate that this section of ancient China was the original home of the Lu tribe of the Lao peoples. First, the name of the kingdom is practically the same as that of the Lu tribe. Again, the Chinese name for the modern Lu is Pa-yi or Shuie-pa-yi, "Water-pa-barbarians." A glance at the map of Shantung shows a peninsula extending out into the Yellow Sea and bordered on the northwest by the Hwang-Ho river. If the people of Lu were anything like other aboriginal communities occupying a similar country, they were a sea-faring folk. The southern shore of the Hwang-Ho and the coasts of the peninsula were dotted with villages of fishermen and sea-going peoples. The situation is enough to give them the name of "Water-pa-barbarians."

Another fact which would seem to confirm the above conjecture is the fact that Mencius was born in the state of Tsou or Chou, a state which was the immediate neighbor of the Lu state. Lacouperie tells us that Kieh, the last ruler of the Hsia dynasty, was exiled among the Tchao or Chao by the new Shang dynasty in 1558 B.C. These Chao lived at a long distance east of Sce-chuan in what is now Anhui province.

This would be directly south of western Lu and bordering it upon the west and south. But Chao is a cognate form of Lao, according to W. C. Dodd.[1] Thus a Lao state bordering on Lu, a name corresponding to that of another tribe of the Lao, would seem to indicate that the Shantung peninsula was early occupied by the Lao people.

That Lu may have been still occupied by Lao peoples in the time of Confucius is not an impossible conjecture. The sage was born in 551 B.C. And we are told that in 338 B.C. a Tsin state conquered an Ai-Lao state, which was locally known as Pa, and caused a gradual migration of the Pa or Lu tribe. But this Ai-Lao state which was conquered by Tsin occupied a position in the northern part of the present province of Sce-chuan, a position almost directly west of Shantung, or a little south of west. The difference in time between the birth of Confucius and the overthrow of the Pa or Lu state in northern Sce-chuan is 213 years, a period of time very close to that of the entire history of the republic of the United States. Did the Chinese who were pressing in from the west and north cross the Hwang-Ho and cause the Lu to migrate to the south and west to establish this second kingdom? Or did the Lu tribe originally occupy all that territory north of the Lao-Shan mountains and bordering the Hwang-Ho from northern Sce-chuan eastward to Shantung? Our present information can give no complete answer to these questions. But from what we know of the movements of the Lao peoples both questions might be answered affirmatively. It was the custom in those days for a ruler of a small principality to move to a new location with as many of his followers as were faithful, and to set up a new kingdom, (Mencius: "Formerly, when king T'ae (Tai-?) dwelt in Pin, the barbarians of the north were continually making incursions upon it. He therefore left it, went to the foot of mount K'e, and there took up his

---

[1] Wm. C. Dodd, *The Tai Race*, p. 8. Chap. I of this work contains a fine summary of the early movements of the Lao peoples.

residence. He did not take this situation, as having chosen
it. It was a matter of necessity with him. . . . The people of
Pin said, 'He is a benevolent man. We must not lose him.'
Those who followed him looked like crowds hastening to
market.") [2]

Much can happen in 213 years under conditions such as
Mencius indicates. The fact that the Lu were still as far north
as northern Sce-chuan in 338 B.C. indicates that the Lu, or the
"Water-pa-barbarians," may have occupied the Shantung
peninsula just previous to or during the time of Confucius.
And if this surmise be correct, the culture, customs, and institutions were prevailingly Lao. This much would be guaranteed under any measure of liberty which could be described
as "independence."

One may, of course, maintain with equally forceful reasons
that the Chinese moved forward in tribes and groups under
various leaders and that Lu was an isolated, independent
group of Chinese who had pushed into Shantung and had
continued the Lao name for the new state. Here, in the midst
of a vast population of barbarians and separated from their
own kindred, they had become careless in the observation of
ancient Chinese customs. This situation Confucius felt called
upon to correct; being himself a cultivated Chinese, he strove
to restore the ancient ceremonies and moralities of his race.
He therefore spent years in travel and study that he might
discover the ancient customs in their purity and introduce
them among the Chinese in Lu. This may very well have been
the case. A similar laxity overtook American Protestantism.
In European churches customs and ritual have persisted practically unchanged since the Reformation, but an itinerant
missionary clergy had no opportunity to practice them in
America. And we are only now seeking to restore the lost
observances in our public worship.

---

[2] Mencius Book I, Part II, Chap. 14.

But this line of argument must meet and reconcile some stubbornly antagonistic facts of history. Confucius never attained in his lifetime any considerable success. If his teaching had been purely Chinese, drawn bodily out of the thought and practices of ancient Chinese life, it is more than probable that he would have received greater encouragement from the princes and barons who ruled the newly erected Chinese states. The austerity and rigid morality of his system may account for the general indifference, to be sure. The elaborate ceremonies may have been ill suited to the newly settled communities, and the high order of morality may have been irksome to the adventurous and licentious princes. But this will scarcely explain why the Chinese Napoleon, Ch'in Shih Huang, who conquered the barons and sought to set up a true Chinese empire, should so bitterly oppose the teachings of Confucius. We are told that he sought out and destroyed all the books of Confucius that he could find. Was it because Confucius was not truly Chinese but essentially Lao in his utterances? Or was it because Ch'in Shih Huang wanted to be known as the founder of the Chinese empire, as some have suggested? Perhaps the last question may be answered in the affirmative just because the record of Confucius was too largely a Lao record. There is, of course, no way of dealing with these questions with any large degree of certainty, but it would seem that the general mildness of Confucius would scarcely provoke such extreme measures if he were presenting ideas that were indigenous to the conquerors. The arguments which make Confucius Chinese are almost as weak as they are strong.

That Confucius may have been of the Lao race and that he was later accepted by the conquerors as their great teacher, is entirely possible. The several tribes of the Lao remained north of the Yang-Tse, and in some cases maintained their independence until 338 B.C., 213 years after the birth of Confucius. Great masses of the native peoples continued in the land, after every migration, to be fused with the conquerors. The Chinese either assimilated them or were assimilated by them. For this age of conflict and turbulence Confucius spoke a message of tranquillity. What is more natural than that the wisest leaders among the conquerors should see that the main object of Confucius was favorable to Chinese supremacy? The tranquillity of the empire—that was exactly the best policy that any one could advocate.

Thus when the warrior Kao Ti (another cognate of Lao?) overthrew the Ch'in dynasty in 195 B.C., he visited the tomb of Confucius and offered an ox. The worth of Confucius as an ameliorating force in the empire, composed of many tribes of the two peoples, was officially recognized. The origin of Confucius did not matter a great deal, if his teachings met the exigencies of Chinese supremacy. In any case, a new empire was being set up. Its problems were not those of the old home of the Chinese, but of the new land and of a newly forming race. Thus a new learning came about—new to the Chinese, at least—and the teacher was officially canonized. Shortly thereafter a temple was erected to him at every center of learning in the empire.

The opposition which may have attended this act of the emperor was very quickly disarmed. The ruling Chinese princes and barons were easily persuaded of the expediency of accepting a Lao teacher of tranquillity. As politicians, and rulers of a mixed people, they saw the wisdom of this course at once. The Lao elements of the population could scarcely object to a teaching which echoed the customs of their forefathers. And if the rank and file of the Chinese immigrants objected? There was the quieting effect of legend to be used— the Great Teacher could be supplied with an impressive Chinese genealogy. Whether or not it was some such emergency which gave rise to the story that Confucius was descended from Hoang-ti, a mythological monarch of China who lived somewhere near 2000 B.C., we cannot say; but it is generally believed that this illustrious pedigree was invented for him, and we know that the myths which collect about a religious leader are something more than the product of an unrestrained imagination.

It may be that Ch'in Shih Huang, the conqueror of the barons and the founder of the new and powerful empire, was a Taoist and that his philosophical convictions led him to burn the books of Confucius, a probability which Principal Soothill merely suggests.[3] But we must remember that it was Ch'in Shih Huang who built the Great Wall to defend China from the hordes of Tartars on the north. Behind this barrier his unusual military genius may have made him feel safe enough to indulge any prejudice which came to mind. But after him the emperors had reason to know that a time would come when China would need to throw all her strength against some powerful leader of the North who would come thundering against her gates. She could then ill afford to have an embittered people within the walls. One enemy at the gate might make it possible for the Tartar hordes to enter the land. Between the Tartar and the Lao she would be caught between two millstones and ground away. Politics has always made strange bedfellows, and in the face of the growing peril from the north the wise Kao Ti may have decided to overlook a little matter of racial difference and to do the expedient thing. The tranquillity of the empire was a matter to be secured at almost any cost. At any rate, peace within is very much to be desired when there is no possibility of peace without.

We shall make a mistake, however, if we overlook the long period of time which intervenes between the birth of Confucius and the act of homage accorded him by Kao Ti. Three hundred and fifty years has seen the rise and fall of a

---

[3] W. E. Soothill, *The Three Religions of China.* It appears that the conqueror was seeking to set up for the first time a pure Chinese empire. It had not been possible before and it turned out to be impossible now.

number of great empires. The social condition in which Confucius was born and to which he addressed himself will without doubt have had time to undergo much transformation in
that time. The steady pressure of the Chinese, due to a steady
pressure of other peoples from behind—a fact which finally
resulted in the erection of the Great Wall—will be able to
change a Lao kingdom in the day of Confucius to an almost
pure Chinese state by 195 B.C. Lacouperie says that during the
Shang-Yu and Chou dynasties (1766-255 B.C.) the Chinese
dominion did not extend more than half the distance between
the Hwang-Ho and the Yangtze, and that this was a territory
much too large for their race, it was interspersed with
aborigines who were kept in check by the power of the
conquerors.[4] The birth of Confucius falls within this period
of time and leaves three hundred years yet to elapse before its
close. The steady pressure of the Chinese had consolidated a
territory extending only some two hundred miles south of
Confucius' home by a date three hundred years after the birth
of the sage. English-speaking peoples have pressed almost two
thousand miles beyond the home of Powhatan in the same
length of time.

A further word from Lacouperie would seem to support
the above position. He says: "One, if not the most striking,
discovery of modern researches is the comparative youth of
the Chinese as a great homogeneous and powerful people.
The Bak tribes, or Peh Sing (name of Chinese immigrants),
were overpowered by the numerous populations which had
preceded them to the Flowery Land. . . . So that, under cover
of Chinese titles and geographical names, large regions occupied by populations entirely non-Chinese were included (in
the historical Annals of China) as homogeneous parts of the
nation, with the effect of concealing the real weakness of the
Chinese Empire previous to the last few centuries."[5] If Pro-

---

[4] Lacouperie, *Early History of Chinese Civilization.*
[5] *Ibid.,* pp. 1-30.

fessor Lacouperie's view be the correct one, we can see why the Annals seem to gloss over the actual social situation as it must have existed in the time of Confucius. The same reasons which would withhold the facts of racial situation would dictate the acceptance of Confucius as a Chinese sage and would supply him with a more unobjectionable pedigree.* Chinese statemen could not afford to admit, even to their subordinates, that they were not an ancient and powerful people in the land. The tribes within the walls were none too securely held together, and the Tartar hordes increased their tumult at the gates. Wisdom would therefore dictate the acceptance of the Confucian policy of tranquillity among the petty rulers.

This acceptance of Confucius by the Chinese came long after the death of the sage, and it may be that he had no real thought of furthering the interests of the conquerors. In his own day he made no headway with the barons, many of whom were undoubtedly Lao. He had seen the Lao princes lose their kingdoms through ill-advised rebellions against the will of their overlord. He had seen them deposed, driven out with a body of loyal soldiers and their families and compelled to find a new home. And he had seen that these princes had suffered because of their tyranny and shameless licentiousness. In the day when their arrogance and pride led them to resist the humiliating terms imposed upon them, they had been deserted by their long-suffering subjects. Justice, benevolence, tolerance, would have made the princes beloved and their subjects a loyal, powerful, and intensely patriotic people. The conquerors would in many cases have been repelled. And if these princes had always sought the peace of the empire after

---

* The cognates of "Lao" mentioned by Dodd, *The Tai Race*, p. 83, if compared with the proper names mentioned in the Analects, The Mean and The Learning, will reveal the Lao race in many positions of importance in Lu and elsewhere. Leao was a musician vitally connected with the ceremonies, Chao was a duke and benefactor of Confucius. Laou was a disciple. Kaou was a name applied to the emperor Woo. Note also Mang, Mung, Shan, and Shang.

they had pledged it their loyalty, they would not have lost their kingdoms. The teachings of Confucius were well-calculated to meet the problem which Lacouperie says existed. If we accept this view we must conclude that Confucius and Lao-Tze were dealing with the same problem. Both were seeking to correct the conditions that were slowly but surely destroying the power of the Lao states. Lao-Tze tried, as we have seen, to secure this end through intellectual superiority, spiritual interests, non-resistance, and a return of good for evil. Confucius turned to the political, practical, and the wisely expedient. Lao-Tze tried to create a self-sufficient and powerful soul, one that would be harmless, irresistible, and perduring in all the welter of change and conflict, one that would not change no matter how much Chinese blood was assimilated. Confucius sought to keep the race intact, independent, pure—an end which was to be gained through a lofty personal morality, a wise and just government, a shrewd and triumphant diplomacy. Under a condition of widespread tranquillity to be achieved by sagacious diplomats, and under wise, just, and benevolent government by Lao princes, the people could maintain their ancient customs and arts. Only a casual glance at the teachings of Confucius will reveal the fact that he was attempting to save the best features of a long-established civilization. This could scarcely be a Chinese civilization which had so recently come into the land, and which had progressed only two or three hundred miles beyond Lu at a date nearly 350 years later.

And how completely the Lao would have triumphed, had they followed implicitly the instruction of either Lao-Tze or Confucius, may be seen from the political emergency which dictated that both these sages be made into well-accredited Chinese teachers. After three hundred years the conquerors were forced to make covert but actual motions of surrender to a people broken, without leaders, disinherited, and in a state of absorption by the dominant Chinese. To be sure, the whole south, and half the territory north of the Yang-Tse, was still securely held by independent Lao rulers when these overtures were made. The situation was perilous enough to a people walled in from their enemies on the north and flanked by more or less hostile peoples on the south. But if the Lao had everywhere remained in the land, maintained their sovereignty at any price, slowly absorbed the conquerors, and had built up powerful and just governments, there would not have been enough Chinese to control the land. Whatever measures would have been necessary to meet the menace of the Tartar hordes would have been carried out by Lao rulers, perhaps by a Lao empire.

It is always interesting to speculate upon the might-have-been, as is done for example by Creasy in his *Fifteen Decisive Battles*. And if it be done by discerning rulers and leaders, there may be some profit in the exercise. It makes for the discovery of those social weaknesses, racial pitfalls, and errors of strategy by both statesmen and military leaders which have changed the course of nations. It may help to prevent a repetition of those steps which have led to destruction. The might-have-been is mentioned here, however, only to show that the saviors of the Lao came to their own and their own received them not. Confucius is not the only true savior of a nation who was rejected by his own and accepted later by strangers.

Governments, however, are seldom saved by the true savior of a people. The saving measure always involves a revolution too far-reaching, a modification in policy too great to be undertaken by short-sighted politicians, a morality and self-discipline too rigid for the flabby will of self-indulgent kings and princes. It requires a stout soul, an invincible will, a tough, untiring, and unconquerable spirit to face the dangers, the exposure to the elements, and the fatiguing duties required to put the vision into effect. The politician cannot believe that there is not an easier way out. He cannot bear to face the opposition and hardship which he must endure to help save the nation. Thus a soft-natured people goes down before the vigor, strength, and endurance of the barbarian. Then lo, the savior is accepted by the barbarian who has the courage and stamina to obey the saving injunction! Later ages make of the sage a god, turn his teachings into a magic or esoteric regimen calculated to save a few individual souls, and thus miss the whole social significance of his life and word. There is cultivation and uplift of the individual here and there, but the nation as a whole is lost.

Whether Confucius was a member of the Lao race seeking to save the sovereignty of the Lao princes, or a Chinese seeking to save China from the turmoil which was hindering her progress and prolonging her national perils, we cannot determine beyond doubt with the meager materials now at hand. The Lao princes were not saved just because they had not the wit or the moral fiber to put his code into effect. The condition of the common people continued to be desperate. We are told that when the sage was once passing Mount T'ai he heard the cries of a woman upon the hillside. He sent a disciple to ask why she wept. She answered, "My husband's father was killed here by a tiger, my husband also, and now my son has met the same fate." Upon being asked why she remained in this dreadful place, she replied, "Because here there is no oppressive ruler." "Scholars," said the sage, "remember this: oppressive rule is more cruel than a tiger." Such rule could not possibly command support in the day of its adversity. Nor would the people follow such heartless princes when they were forced to migrate out of the land.

Just what the conditions were which Confucius attempted to correct are vividly described by Professor Soothill: "Power amongst these barons bred luxury, luxury lust, and lust unrelenting destruction. Princes there were who set all morality at defiance and lived lives of open shame, as witness the acceptance by the sage's own prince, the Duke of Lu, of a present of eighty singing girls, an act which drove our sage to throw up his office, shake the dust of his beloved native State off his feet, and depart to the life of a wanderer and an exile. Men of virtuous character, despairing of reformation, left their portfolios and withdrew from the world, becoming recluses amongst the mountains, or, far from the busy haunts of men, tilling a hard living from an earth kinder and sweeter than the hearts of princes. Some of these recluses, embittered by their sorrows, even poured scorn upon Confucius for his futile attempts to stay the 'disorder which, like a flood,' rolled its resistless torrent through the land. . . . The barons, more powerful than their nominal sovereign, encroached and made war upon each other, at the instigation of ministers even more crafty and ambitious than themselves. The suffering people were ground under the iron heel of the impost-gatherer, dragged from their fields and set to forced labor at and for the pleasure of their rulers, and driven to battles and raids in which they had no interest, and from which they derived no benefit." [7]

The general disregard for law came to the attention of the sage soon after he became the keeper of granaries and overseer of public fields at the age of twenty. His former grave demeanor, his precocious mind, and his careful study of the ancient laws and records had attracted attention, and the reforms he introduced in the discharge of his public duties as an official now won for him the favor of his sovereign. This success, together with the knowledge gained from a further study of the ancient writings, convinced him that the ancient customs were sufficient to correct all existing evils. He began to gather pupils and to teach them the ancient law. His teachings were therefore based upon what he considered to be the doctrines of the best of his predecessors. He was, as he called himself, a transmitter and not a creator.

---

[7] Soothill, *The Three Religions of China*, pp. 23, 24.

Two years later he had already attracted so much attention that many young men came to his house to hear him, and their numbers increased rapidly as his reputation continued to grow. When he was twenty-four his mother died, and this event enabled him to revive an old custom by retiring from office in order to mourn for her three years. This caused him to receive further attention, especially among the official class. For the ten years following he devoted himself to further study and to the instruction of those who came to him. In the meantime one of the chief ministers of Lu had died and on his deathbed had advised his son to join the school of Confucius to learn ceremonial observances that he might the better perform his official duties. The son and one of his near relatives complied with this wish and thus gave much prestige to the already highly respected Confucius. Through the influence of these young men the Duke of Chao was induced to send the sage to the imperial court at Loh-Yang to study the rites in use there that he might introduce them into Lu.

After a year at the imperial capital Confucius returned home only to follow his benefactor, the Duke of Chao, into exile in the adjoining state of Tsi. Tiring of his position in Tsi, he once more went back to his native state. He was now known everywhere as a great teacher. Fitted though he was to advise and rule, he tactfully remained aloof from the rival factions which kept his native state distracted by civil strife. For the next fifteen years he lived quietly, spending his time in study and teaching. Then the brother of the former Duke of Chao came into power in Lu, put down the troublesome factions, and appointed the sage magistrate of the town of Chung-Tu. Confucius introduced such reforms in his administration of the government as to excite the envy of the lords of other states, and they are said to have induced the ruler of Lu to remove the sage from office. Then there were years of wandering from state to state. He met failure at every turn and went home for the last time. The remaining years of his life he spent quietly in Lu teaching and composing his literary works.

His system is, therefore, the fruit of his long years of study and mature thought. He says of himself: "At fifteen, I had my mind bent on learning. At thirty, I stood firm. At forty, I had no doubts. At fifty, I knew the decrees of Heaven. At sixty, my ear was an obedient organ for the reception of truth. At seventy, I could follow what my heart desired without transgressing what was right." [8] He was a great man and the teacher of a high order of morality. Whether or not he was able to desire nothing except that which was right must be left at this late date to private judgment. One thing we learn from the testimony of his disciples—he was not one to treat all desire and appetite as something which would defile a man.

He was inordinately fond of good-fellowship and, like Socrates, spent much of his time wherever men were accustomed to assemble. And he seems not to have given much thought as to whether or not his presence was always desired. Upon one occasion We Shang Mow seems to have lost all patience with him, for he said, "Kew (Confucius), how is it that you keep roosting about? Is it not that you are an insinuating talker?" [9] To this Confucius is supposed to have replied in words which not only explained his habit but which also contained a sufficient measure of sarcasm to save his face. Often we hear him saying that no man receives his teaching, but we seldom hear any complaint that he is either absent or silent.

Perhaps it was his articulate omnipresence which inspired the other slighting remarks which were made of him, although some of them seem to have been aimed at his apparent omniscience. When Tsze-loo, one of his disciples, happened

---

[8] Legge, *Analects*, p. 16.
[9] *Ibid.*, p. 80.

to pass the night at Shihmun, the gate-keeper said to him, "Whom do you come from?" Tsze-loo replied, "From Mr. Kung." "It is he, is it not" said the other, "who knows the impractical nature of the times, and yet will be doing in them?"[10] And there is the rather amusing incident recorded of his encounter in Wei with the man who was carrying a straw basket. The man just mentioned happened to be passing the house where Confucius was staying at just the moment that the sage was playing upon the musical stone. Since any house where a guest had been received was regarded as a public place, the man went in to hear the music. He listened awhile, no doubt thinking that this was quite a come-down for the man who had been a magistrate of a city and who had introduced such famous reforms. Something of the lingering official dignity about the player aroused the antagonism of the man with the straw basket, and he decided to twit the sage over the loss of his office. He said, "His heart must be full who so beats the musical stone." To this Confucius made no reply; how full his heart was because of his failure could not be learned so easily. The man waited a little and tried it again, "How contemptible is the one-idead obstinacy those sounds display! When one is taken no notice of, he has simply at once to give over his wish for public employment. 'Deep water must be crossed with the clothes on; shallow water may be crossed with the clothes held up.'" This was a center shot at the fortitude of the sage who wore at that moment all the garments of dignity he could well put on. The sage with a smile exclaimed, "How determined the man is! But this is not hard to bear."[11]

The manner of the sage was not always so mild, however. There were times when he replied to an antagonist in kind, for he was not one to advocate a soft answer or to reward good for evil. He said that the feelings need not always be spoken,

[10] Legge, *Analects*, p. 81.
[11] *Ibid.*, p. 81.

but his general attitude toward those who injured him may be seen in his answer, "Reward evil with justice, and kindness with kindness." At another time he declared that he was ashamed of the man who concealed his resentment. "Be sincere," was his motto; and he practiced it, often with amusing consequences. Once while on the street he saw Yuen Yang squatting on his heels idly watching the people as they passed. The master drew near saying, "In youth, not humble as befits a junior; in manhood, doing nothing worthy of being handed down; and living on to old age:—this is to be a pest!" [12] With that he lifted his staff and gave Yuen Yang a resounding blow upon the shank. Imagine the indignation of the sage if he should pass the groups about some of our village drugstores to-day!

Usually, however, the sage did not yield to such violent outbursts of sincerity. In the main he was grave, perfectly controlled, and given to whimsical humor which neither the scoffs of his enemies nor the unresponsiveness of his disciples could dispel. When Tsze-kung, one of his disciples, said, "What I do not wish men to do to me, I also wish not to do to them." Confucius answered, "Tsze, you have not attained to that." He then asked Tsze, "Which do you consider superior, yourself or Hwuy?" Tsze was perhaps somewhat suspicious, for he exclaimed generously, "How dare I compare myself with Hwuy? Hwuy hears one point and knows all about a subject; I hear one point and know a second." Confucius very soberly answered, "You are not equal to him. I grant you, you are not equal to him." This question may have been inspired by something the master had heard of Tsze, for it is recorded that Tsze was fond of comparing one man with another. Upon hearing this Confucius had replied, "Tsze must have reached a high pitch of excellence! Now, I have not the leisure for that." Other instances of the

---

[12] Legge, *Analects*, p. 82.

dry humor of the sage are to be found. When he once saw Tsae Yu, another of his disciples, asleep during the daytime, he said, "Rotten wood cannot be carved; a wall of dirty earth will not receive the trowel. This Yu!—what is the use of my reproving him?" At another time, when a messenger came to him from Keu Pih-Yuh, he began to question the man. "What," asked he, "is your master engaged in?" The messenger replied, "My master is anxious to make his faults few, but he has not yet succeeded." He went out and Confucius, after contemplating the secret life of Keu Pih-Yuh for a moment, remarked, "A messenger indeed! A messenger indeed!" [13] And of his errand boy he once said when asked about the boy's progress, "I observe that he is fond of occupying the seat of a full-grown man; I observe that he walks shoulder to shoulder with his elders. He is not one to make progress in learning. He wishes too quickly to become a man."

From his point of view and his own testimony of himself, we discover that his writings are chiefly compilations of selections taken from his predecessors. From his own hand came the Book of History, the ancient Odes, the Book of Changes (Divination), the History of the State of Lu, and the Book of Rites. These writings seem to contain the basic matter for the formulation of his own system, but his oral lectures, while in perfect accord with this body of selected material, give such point and emphasis to it as to impart all the atmosphere of being the original work of the master. For our knowledge of the actual utterances of Confucius we are indebted to his disciples who compiled the Sayings, his discussions under the title of the Great Learning, and his Doctrine of the Mean. These books, together with the one containing the teaching of Mencius, make up the immediate classics of the school of Confucius.

---

[13] Legge, *Analects*, p. 79.

The substance of his teaching falls naturally into two main divisions, for he believed that morality and religious ceremonies would cure all the ills of his age.

His Theory of Morality

Morality is for Confucius the object of true education. He says in the opening sentence of the Great Learning, "The Way of Education lies in elucidating lucid virtues, in the renovation of the people, and in stopping short of nothing but perfection." All things in nature, however, develop in stages, and in the extension of virtue one must begin with the rulers and end with the people. In other words, those at the top must reach down and lift up the lower orders. In pursuance of this view of social reformation the sage continues: "The ancients who wished to cause virtue to shine forth throughout the empire first ordered well their own States. To do this they first set about the regulation of their own families. To do this they first cultivated their external conduct. To do this they first rectified their hearts. To do this they first extended to the utmost their knowledge. Such extension of knowledge lay in the investigation of things."

It is evident that in the time of Confucius no great moral reformation of society was possible without the coöperation of the ruler, for his will was absolute. A perfect moral life on the part of the citizen presupposed a purely conceived and righteous law. This must emanate from the emperor or prince. But before the ruler could issue such a body of law he must extend his knowledge to the utmost by painstaking study and research. Thus with an informed mind he could establish his own heart in righteousness. From this inner state of rectitude would issue a proper external life. Thus he would be able through word and deed to regulate his own household and the State over which he ruled. Others would see his example and would seek to emulate it.

The form of government which Confucius upholds is that of a paternal despotism, but he proclaims the obligation of the ruler to deal wisely and justly with his subjects. The despotism is a limited one, since the people are regarded as being of more importance than their sovereign. The word of the prince or emperor is final, provided it is a just word and does not violate the will of Heaven. In the Book Of History we read that Chou, the last of the Shang dynasty,[14] became an oppressive monster and that the son of Duke Wen led a revolt against him and overthrew him. In his Great Declaration the rebel prince says of his emperor: "But now, Chou, the king of Shang, does not reverence Heaven above, and inflicts calamities on the people below. He is abandoned to drunkenness, and reckless in lust. He has dared to exercise cruel oppression. Along with transgressors he has punished all their relatives. He has put men into office on the hereditary principle. He has made it his pursuit to have palaces, towers, pavilions, terraces, lakes, and all other extravagances, to the most painful injury of you, the myriad people. He has burned and roasted the loyal and the good, and ripped up pregnant women. Great Heaven was removed with indignation, and charged my deceased father Wen reverently to display Its majesty; but he died before the work was accomplished. Shou has no repentant heart. He abides, squatting on his heels, not serving God or the spirits of heaven and earth, neglecting also the temple of his ancestors, and not sacrificing in it. Heaven to protect the common people, made for them rulers, and made for them instructors, that they might be able to aid Heaven, and thus secure the tranquillity of the empire. I now lead the multitude of you to execute the punishment appointed by Heaven. Heaven compassionates the people. What the people desire, Heaven will be found to give effect to." [15]

---

[14] Both Chou and Shang are familiarly Lao in sound. The spelling *may* be Chinese!

[15] *The Book of History.*

Professor Soothill quotes the emperor Shun as saying, "If the sovereign can realize the arduous responsibility of his sovereignty, and each minister of his ministry, government will be well ordered, and the people be sedulous after virtue." [16] In commenting upon the quotation the Professor remarks: "Herein is found that important principle which forms one of the main ideas in Confucian ethics, namely, that the ruler is the *fons et origo* of virtue. From him all virtue proceeds. A highly virtuous ruler conditions a highly virtuous people. A degenerate ruler conditions a degenerate people. There is a power for virtue or vice in the throne of China." Confucius, by recording these statements of the son of Duke Wen and of the emperor Shun, shows that he approves. But elsewhere he declares that the ruler's duty to rule justly and wisely is a Heaven-sent duty and that a ruler who is untrue to his divine mission is worthy of death.

Thus, according to Confucius, reformation not only should come from the top but it must come from the top. It is the first duty of the ruler to renew the life of his people through wise and just government. If he fail in this duty, either by official act or by his manner of life, he is guilty in the sight of Heaven and liable to punishment through some man whom Heaven may raise up for that purpose.

It is not difficult to understand why the self-indulgent princes would not be enthusiastic about introducing the Confucian system into their principalities. It might be the means of their losing not only their sovereignties but also their lives. And we must remember that the times were such that the conditions surrounding these rulers were full of peril to the crowned head. When thrones were kept so precariously it was extremely unlikely that any course would be adopted which might contain an element of added danger. There were enough dangers from without to make the prince think

---

[16] *Three Religions of China*, p. 226.

twice before introducing something which would make his tenure subject to the whim of the people,—an enemy might take this teaching seriously and insinuate himself beyond the ranks of loyal spears.

And we must not lose sight of the practical wisdom involved in the acts of interference by the rulers of other principalities whenever Confucius seemed to be making any real headway for his views. The very success of the sage in securing safety, order, and prosperity made his views the more dangerous. The story of his achievements would travel far and stir up dissatisfaction and rebellion among the peoples of other principalities. Rulers determined that his light of shining virtue should not shine unto them. They prevailed upon the brother of the Duke of Chao to relieve him of his office as magistrate of Chung-Tu. His reforms were too successful and therefore made his general theory of people above prince the more dangerous to slovenly rulers. They did not, of course, come out openly against the honored and successful Confucius. That would draw the lines of controversy, make Confucius and his work an issue, and put the princes in a bad light before the people of their principalities. They took a more subtle step. They sent a present of eighty singing girls to the Duke of Lu. This was blasting the citadel of the Confucian system in Lu, for virtue, according to Confucius, must flow from the prince to the people. The affair was so deftly managed that we feel sure that the outside rulers knew their fellow prince. They had all perhaps been good fellows together times without number.

The prince was not however, the only one who was responsible to Heaven. He must set the example by his own obedience, but every citizen in his realm was also responsible. The divinely felt duty to revolt against the emperor Chou, a feeling which Confucius undoubtedly approves, shows that an obligation to Heaven rested upon every man in the empire. It was certainly the duty of every person to practice virtue, the knowledge of which constituted the best evidence that one knew what the will of Heaven was.

The system of Confucius seems to have made ample room for times and seasons, for temporary duty, for expediency, and for situations that might suddenly arise in human intercourse. Such emphemeral situations and occasions were to be met out of one's experience and general wisdom. But there were, according to the sage, Five Constant Virtues which could be practiced under all circumstances, and must apply to the five relations of life. The Five Constant Virtues were Benevolence, Righteousness, Propriety, Wisdom, and Sincerity.

It is a peculiarity of the Confucian system that it is very free of abstractions. There is no attempt toward formulae, or cut-and-dried definition of a term, as a term. All terms are defined as being essentially a human or a divine relation. Thus when the sage is asked to elucidate any of his terms he turns to actual life for illustration. From the relations of men he points out those items of conduct which contain the virtue in question in its purest form. It is as if Confucius were saying: "Let this act in this particular human relation be your standard. We shall for purposes of convenience make it a pattern, and we shall call this pattern Benevolence, or Righteousness, etc."

As a means of clarifying his ideas and of systematizing the field of human conduct, he divides social life into the Five Relations. These constitute the contacts one should make and preserve. They are, Prince and Minister, Husband and Wife, Father and Son, Brother to Brother, and Friend to Friend. It is evident that some of these terms of relation are more inclusive than their wording would indicate. For instance, Father and Son, manifestly, stands for the broader term of Parental Relation, father-mother to daughter-son. And the relation of Prince and Minister includes the more extensive idea of ruler and subject. The elucidation of the manner in which these relations should be conducted according to virtue constitutes the moral teaching of Confucius.

We have already discussed the first of these to some extent. The Prince has almost unlimited authority over the minister and his subjects, but only when he rules justly. The husband is given a similar authority over the wife. But this authority of the husband does not lessen the influence of the mother with her children; she is regarded as equal to the father in the child's affection and treatment. As a matter of fact, her influence in teaching is superior to that of the father, for the religious ideas she imparts linger with the son long after he has gone out into the world. The high regard in which she is held is revealed in the act of Confucius in resigning his office and in observing the three years of mourning in reverence for his mother at her death.

The relation of father to son comes near to being the core of Chinese religion. The father has absolute control over the son, but that does not mean that a son shall submit without question or reason to the word of the father. Indeed he is no true son who will not expostulate with his father when he knows that a command will bring injury or evil to the family. On the other hand, the son must honor his father by obedience during his father's lifetime, and after the death of his parent must continue to worship him as if he were still alive and present. In fact the well-being of the son, and of society in general, depends upon the discharge of this duty toward the spirits of one's forefathers.

Coupled with filial piety is a respect for one's seniors and superiors. The eldest son takes precedence over the younger. Confucius said: "When a youth is at home, let him be filial; when abroad, respectful to his elders; let him be circumspect and sincere, and while exhibiting a comprehensive love for all men, let him ally himself with the good. Having so acted, if he have energy to spare, let him employ it in study." Filial piety consists in making provision for the material needs of the parents—in actually anticipating their needs before they are spoken—and in the sincerest affection. Humanity, brotherhood, and sympathy represent the sum of virtue. It is virtue and not material wealth which makes a people rich and a neighborhood desirable as a place in which to live. Valor had its worth because it was the natural outcome of a proper regard for one's prince. There were three persons for whom one might readily die—his parent, his teacher, and his prince. Lust is condemned; and honesty, good faith, courtesy, modesty, are emphasized. Confucius does not see how a man can get along without virtue, for without it no man is fit to engage in religious worship.

The Confucian morality has also its metaphysical side, its ground, or divine relation. This feature is discussed in the Doctrine of the Mean, a book composed by Tzu Ssu, one of the disciples of Confucius. On the teachings of his Master, Tzu Ssu has this to say: "That which Heaven has conferred is called the Nature, accordance with this Nature is called the Tao (the Way), the regulation of this Way is called Education. The way may not be left for an instant. If it could be left it would not be the Way. Therefore the wise man is cautious about the invisible, and is apprehensive in regard to the inaudible. For there is nothing more open than the secret thing, and nothing more manifest than the minute. Therefore the wise man is watchful over himself." This is an attempt to establish morality on the acts and design of Heaven. There is a Way which Heaven intended us to pursue. It is peculiar to our Heaven-given nature, and is the only way by which we may realize in ourselves the purposes of Heaven. The regulation of our conduct, in accordance with this Heavenly purpose, comes through education.

The achievement of this moral end is furthered by a dispassionate approach. Tzu Ssu says: "While there are no emotions of pleasure or anger, sorrow or joy, it is called the Mean of Equilibrium. When the emotions act in their due degree, it is called a condition of Harmony. The Mean is the radical cosmic principle. Harmony is the pervading cosmic Tao, or Law. Let the states of the Mean and of Harmony exist perfectly, and universal order will result and all things be nourished." Confucius probably means, according to this statement, that there is an all-pervading Law, or Tao, which may be felt and consciously appreciated from within, and it is not inconceivable that the sage is speaking of the Conscience. When one acts in complete harmony with this felt inner Law, or Way of Nature, and does so without emotion, he approximates the Mean of Equilibrium. When emotion is present, but controlled and allowed only its due place, he attains a condition of Harmony. And in the final statement of the sage, "Let the states of the Mean and of Harmony exist perfectly, and universal order will result and all things be nourished," he is probably making a plea for the perfect balance of the two states—conscience as intellectually observed, and conscience as felt. In other words, a purely intellectual code of conduct would be cold and at times unjust. Living according to conscience without controlling one's emotions would be equally improper. Confucius says by way of elucidation, "When one cultivates to the full the principles of his nature, and exercises them on the basis of sympathy, he is not far from the path." Not a pure rationalism, not a free emotionalism, but mercy seasoning justice. To conclude in his words, "Do not do unto others what you would not like yourself."

In the above quotations we must remember that Confucius is not engaged in a discussion of metaphysics as such, but in an attempt to set forth the inner workings of the nature of man in relation to others. The sage has no real interest in metaphysical speculations for their own sake and is here led into it momentarily only in an attempt to set forth his theory of conduct in relation to its source in thought and emotion. Because of his practical aim and his consistency in sticking to his purpose, we do not get from him any clear-cut meta-physical system. He seeks to tell us that we are certain creatures by nature and that we must achieve a harmony of all our faculties through education and control that we may discover and perform true justice toward all men.

APPROACHING THE DIVINE

The second part of the social program of Confucius was the observation of religious ceremonies. In this field he was not an innovator. The religion of China in his day embraced the noblest thoughts of the ancients, the purest conceptions of deity, the most impressive and elevating ceremonies, imbedded in a mass of popular animistic lore and the practices of super-stition and magic. Into this jungle of faith and practice the sage went boldly, making it his chief concern to seek out the best and purest. While he appears not to have introduced anything new, his discrimination and selection had the effect of a new teaching. He cut away much superstition, fruitless theology, empty speculation, and the impractical in the hope that he might leave only that which would lead the nation into reverent, thoughtful, and noble living in the present world.

The ideas of God which he encountered in his researches show that the best thinkers had already achieved a very ad-vanced religion. There was a Supreme Ruler who was called Shang Ti, and there was T'ien which was their word for Heaven, but which was very probably a personalized term. Professor Soothill thinks that T'ien was an impersonal term, but it would seem that the Chinese used this word very much as we use the word Heaven; at times the term is substituted for the Supreme Ruler. However, as Professor Soothill re-marks, "The 'term question' is a very old one." . . . When the Emperor K'ang Hsi in the seventeenth century A.D. would have settled the dispute between his friends the Jesuits on the one hand, and the Franciscans and Dominicans on the other, by the adoption of the word T'ien for God, the impersonality of the term was strenuously objected to by the Franciscans and Dominicans. The Pope, to whom an appeal was made over the Emperor, supported their view, with the result that personal 'T'ien Chu,' or 'Lord of Heaven' has been the Roman designation ever since. This claim of the Pope to override the decision of the Emperor was one of the causes which, by Roman Catholic writers, is said to have prevented the conversion of the Emperor, and through him of all China, which they think was then imminent." [17] Just how much the Emperor's action was influenced by political pride we cannot say, but it is conceivable that linguistic considerations and caution may have had much to do with his action. He probably felt that the idiomatic use of T'ien for the Supreme Ruler was the only allowable word on grounds of propriety. And perhaps the failure to identify God with T'ien made him feel that he would be looked upon as departing from the customs of the fathers and as worshiping a foreign God.

Professor Soothill goes on to say that a close examination proves that all the qualities attributed to Shang Ti are attributed to T'ien, and that some qualities attributed to T'ien are not attributed to Shang Ti. This, Professor Soothill thinks, would indicate that Shang Ti is more of a sovereign ruling the world than a person having a paternal relationship toward humanity—that Heaven is looked up to not only as a sovereign but also as having a more intimate relationship with men. There can be no doubt that an important distinction is drawn between Shang Ti and T'ien, but, in spite of Professor Soothill's very great knowledge of things Chinese, I venture to think that the cause of all the confusion regarding Shang Ti and T'ien lies in a failure to recognize the force of a point of etiquette. Only the Emperor was privileged to

[17] Soothill, *Three Religions of China*, pp. 141sq.

worship the Supreme Ruler by His name Shang Ti. The people could not approach Him in that degree of familiarity which would permit them to speak His *name* in worship. Their relation to Him was too detached and impersonal. The two terms for the Supreme Ruler would seem therefore to express an earthly distinction rather than a heavenly one. The Pope, of course, was not particularly interested in Chinese etiquette.

And it is just possible that the failure to appreciate the force of this point has led Dr. James Legge to say that Confucius was unreligious, if not atheistical. Many differ with Dr. Legge and supply abundant quotation to substantiate their position. I shall not go into the debate here. Dr. Legge has further stated that the religion of China was originally monistic, and that Confucius by his frequent references to Heaven, instead of using the phraseology of the older sages, gave occasion to many of his followers to identify God with a principle of Reason and the course of Nature. But it seems to me that one would need to note the social position of these "older sages" before deciding that Confucius has made any radical departure in using T'ien rather than Shang Ti. If Dr. Legge is referring to the "sages" mentioned in the Book of History, we may properly remark that they were either emperors or were addressing emperors, and were therefore privileged to use the personal term for the Supreme Ruler. Confucius, being only a private citizen, would in conformity to the law of propriety use the term T'ien, or Heaven, in lecturing to his classes. And as to causing his followers to identify God with a principle of Reason and the course of Nature, we may call attention to the fact that the doctrine of the Tao existed in some form long before the appearance of either Confucius or Lao Tze. It is an idea inseparable from the original monism which Dr. Legge mentions.

The religion of China does have a monistic source which was early separated into a dualism, consisting of two orders of subordinate gods and spirits. Long before Confucius' day men were making offerings to the spirits of departed great men. Kings offered sacrifices to their illustrious predecessors, and the kingly example was quickly imitated by the common people. Confucius, who had for his purpose the establishment of virtue and the tranquillity of the empire, selected from the mass of thought and practice only that which conformed to his aim. He took therefore from various sources the materials he required, but he seems to have favored the regulations of the Chow dynasty as incorporating the best in both moral and religious practice. He says, "Chow had the advantage of viewing the two past dynasties. How complete and elegant are its regulations! I follow Chow!" [18]

The method of delimitation pursued by Confucius makes him a very potent force against his nation's superstitions. The great number of objects feared and worshiped by the people had become burdensome; toward these Confucius was antagonistic. He would not talk about the spirits, and advised that they be avoided, saying, "To sacrifice to a spirit not one's own (of one's family circle) is sycophancy." In his book, Ritual of the Chow dynasty, we find the order of sacrifice, or religious worship, set forth as follows:

"The Son of Heaven sacrificed to heaven and earth; to the four quarters; to the hills and streams; and offered the five sacrifices, all in the course of the year.

"The feudal princes sacrificed to the four quarters (their territories); to the hills and streams; and offered the five domestic sacrifices; all in the course of the year.

"High officers offered the five domestic sacrifices.

"Minor officers sacrificed to their forefathers."

While thus limiting the nature and number of sacrifices made by the several classes, Confucius was not irreverent toward any of them. He felt it his duty to be present even at

---

[18] *Analects*, p. 22.

the great sacrifice (to Heaven and Earth), and at all times he advocated sincerity and exactness in sacrificial observances. An instance which shows his attitude is related in the Analects: "Tsze-kung (one of the disciples) wished to do away with the offering of a sheep connected with the inauguration of the first day of each month. The Master said, 'Tsze, you love the sheep; I love the ceremony.' " [19]

The limitation of the common people to the sacrifices made to their ancestors served two purposes: first, it prevented extravagant attempts to emulate the expensive offerings made by the upper classes; and second, it prevented the adoption of an overwhelming number of gods, spirits, and objects through superstition and fear. While this was a move in the right direction, and very beneficial at the moment, its force was destroyed when, after a few centuries, the number of ancestors equaled the number of objects which might conceivably have been adopted. The only real benefit gained by the limitation was in the purity of religion—the people ceased to create spirits. Instead of an ever pyramiding polytheism to overload the family pantheon, the additions came in the course of nature.

But the function of worship in the development of the worshiper is apparently the keynote of the Confucian system of sacrifice. The Master is quoted as saying, "How greatly filial was Shun! His virtue was that of a sage; his dignity was the imperial throne; his riches were all within the four seas. He offered his sacrifices in his ancestral temple, and his descendants preserved the sacrifices to himself.

"Therefore having such great virtue, it could not but be that he should obtain the throne, that he should obtain those riches, that he should obtain his fame, that he should attain to his long life.

"Thus it is that Heaven, in the production of things, is

---

[19] *Analects*, p. 22.

surely bountiful to them, according to their qualities. Hence the tree that is flourishing, it nourishes, while that which is ready to fall, it overthrows." [20]

The term "filial" in this passage is unquestionably a technical expression used to describe the religious faithfulness of Shun who offered his sacrifices in his ancestral temple. This in a very large measure constituted his virtue; and his virtue was of such excellence that it inevitably brought him the imperial throne, all the lands between the four seas, the very great fame that was his, and the long life he enjoyed. All this could come inevitably just because the spirits "enter into all things, and there is nothing without them," and because he was faithful to his Heaven-sent gifts. Thus it was that Heaven could be bountiful to him and bless him according to his qualities.

The link between virtue and sacrifice seems to lie in the exercise of sincerity in worship. "Sincerity is the end and beginning of things," says Confucius, "and without sincerity there would be nothing. It is only he who is possessed of the most complete sincerity that can exist under heaven, who can give its full development to his nature. Sincerity is that whereby self-completion is effected. The possessor of sincerity does not merely accomplish the self-completion of himself. With this quality he completes other men." A sincere expression of the Heavenly within the worshiper, as he approaches Heaven in his acts of worship, presents no barrier to the power of Heaven. This approximates our idea of the unity of the worshiper and the Worshiped: they met on holy ground and on the side of their common nature.

The idea of reward and punishment for moral or spiritual delinquency was an accepted teaching from the very earliest times. And although Confucius, because of his special social interest, does not mention rewards or punishments in the here-

[20] *The Mean* xviii. 1sq.

after, it is in his record of the ancients that we learn of the existence of such beliefs. The calamities of his day were so great and the punishments for evil-doing so severe that moral reformation could be secured without dwelling upon the future state if it could be secured at all. Confucius tells us that the man who lives an evil life will come to a bad end, but he does not tell us where or how. In a state of society where wars between rival princes were of almost daily occurrence the tranquillity of the empire was of immediate and consuming importance. Employed with his great earthly undertaking, Confucius, no doubt, was inclined to leave the hereafter as he had found it in the writings of the sages before him. At any rate, the labor to build up a virtuous, sincere, and peaceful nation would help to save his people in time and eternity.

But selfishness, mutual distrust, and fear kept the whole empire in a state of constant warfare. Even the heads of families, or tribes, within the state of Lu strove with one another for the lands and villages near their borders. Even the disciples of Confucius upon occasion were not above winking at the greed of their chiefs. If Professor Lacouperie's view be interpreted so as to make Confucius live in a Lao state, there is one incident recorded in the *Analects* which mirrors, as nothing else can, the real reason for the downfall of the Lao peoples. There were three leading families in the state of Lu—the Ke-Kang, the Mang (Mung?), and the Shuh-sun. We are told that the head of the Ke-Kang family contemplated an attack upon Chuen-yu which belonged to the Mang family. "Yen Yew and Ke Loo (disciples of Confucius and ministers to the chief of the Ke-Kang) had an interview with Confucius, and said, 'Our chief, Ke, is going to commence operations against Chuen-yu.' "

This so outraged the Master that he revealed not only his loyalty to his ideals but perhaps his racial background as well. He said in reply: "K'ew (Yen Yew), is it not you who are at fault here? Now, in regard to Chuen-yu, long ago a former

king appointed it to preside over the sacrifices to the eastern
Mung (the word is Lao); moreover, it is in the midst of the
territory of our state, and its ruler is a minister in direct
connexion with the emperor. What has your chief to do with
attacking it?"

Yen Yew said, "Our master wishes the thing; neither of us
two ministers wishes it."

Confucius had no notion of allowing his disciples to thus
shift the responsibility for the situation. He said, "K'ew, there
are the words of Chow-Jin—'When he can put forth his
ability, he takes his place in the ranks of office; when he finds
himself unable to do so, he retires from it. How can he be
used as a guide to a blind man, who does not support him
when tottering, nor raise him up when fallen?' And further,
you speak wrongly. When a tiger or wild bull escapes from
his cage; when a tortoise or gem is injured in its repository
—whose fault is it?"

Yen Yew said, "But at present, Chuen-yu is strong and near
to Pe; if our chief do not take it now, it will hereafter be a
sorrow to his descendants."

Confucius said, "K'ew, the superior man hates the declin-
ing to say—'I want such and such a thing,' and framing ex-
planations for the conduct. I have heard that rulers of states
and chiefs of families are not troubled lest their people should
be few, but are troubled lest they should not keep their several
places; that they are not troubled with fears of poverty, but
are troubled with a fear of a want of repose among the peoples
in their several places. For when the people keep their several
places, there will be no poverty; when harmony prevails, there
will be no scarcity of people; and when there is such contented repose, there will be no rebellious upsettings. So it is
therefore, if remoter people are not submissive, all the influences of civil culture and virtue are to be cultivated to
attract them to be so; and when they have been attracted, they
must be made contented and tranquil. Now, here you are,

Yew and K'ew, assisting your chief. Remoter people are not submissive and, with your help, he cannot attract them to him. In his own territory there are divisions and downfalls, leavings and separations, and, with your help, he cannot preserve it. And yet he is planning these hostile movements within our state. I am afraid that the sorrow of the Ke-sun family will not be on account of Chuen-yu, but will be found within the screen of their own court." [21]

It is not difficult to see what has happened. The rule of the chief of the Ke-Kang has been oppressive and his people have been migrating to the more inviting government and happier conditions of Chuen-yu. He has not been able to attract his people just because neither he nor his advisers were willing to take the steps that would make for good government. But he is jealous, covetous, and is planning to proceed against Chuen-yu which by its wisdom and justice has been able to attract many members of other tribes to its territory. He is, therefore, with the help of the disciples of Confucius, seeking to destroy the city of Chuen-yu which has become an actual example of the very truth which Confucius has always taught. It is small wonder that the sage indulges in this biting reproof of the two ministers of Ke.

Then occurs the utterance which makes a prophet of Confucius and which no doubt explains the fate which overtook the Lao peoples: "When good government prevails in the empire, ceremonies, music, and punitive military expeditions proceed from the emperor. When bad government prevails in the empire, ceremonies, music, and punitive expeditions proceed from the princes. When these things proceed from the princes, as a rule, the cases will be few in which they do not lose their power in ten generations. When they proceed from the *great officers* of the princes, as a rule, the cases will be

---

[21] Legge, *Analects*, pp. 88sq.

few in which they do not lose their power in five generations. When the *subsidiary ministers of the great officers* hold in their grasp the orders of the kingdom, as a rule, the cases will be few in which they do not lose their power in three generations." Chief Ke was one of the *great officers* of the prince of Lu, and Yew and K'ew were the *subsidiary ministers* of this great officer. Confucius is predicting the downfall of the state of Lu in from seventy-five to one hundred years! As an explanation of how it was possible for the united but greatly outnumbered Chinese to displace the rulers of the millions of Lao peoples and to convert the land into a nominal Chinese empire, nothing could be more accurate. With the great officers and their advisers in actual revolt against the authority of the Prince of Lu and the friends of the emperor, it required only the acceptance of the eighty singing girls by the Prince to show Confucius that there was no hope for his native state. The prophecy was, however, delayed somewhat in its fulfillment. After the death of Confucius it was clear to all that "the mountain had fallen" and a reform set in. When Mencius visited the principality of Lu in his later years, about one hundred and fifty years after the death of Confucius, he praises the prince of Lu for his love of goodness. But the lack of widespread reform caused the downfall of the power of the Lao princes and chiefs on every hand, and thus the tide of Chinese empire pushed steadily southward to the Yang-Tse.

A final word concerning the contribution of Mencius to the work of Confucius will not be amiss. Confucius advocated benevolence, but Mencius added to benevolence the virtue of righteousness; Confucius spoke of the importance of the will, or mind; Mencius dwelt upon the nourishment of the passion nature. These additions were made because Mencius believed in the goodness of human nature. Man's nature came from Heaven and was therefore instinctively good. That nature must be kept good, or righteous; and if it was to be expressed with vigor, it must be seconded by strong feeling and a strong physical nature. Han Yu says, "Mencius did great service to the world by his teaching the goodness of man's nature."

In practically all other particulars Mencius adopted the views of Confucius with very slight modification. He advocated the importance of virtue, the reformation of society through the example and will of the prince, and the interests of the people as being superior to those of their rulers. His courage and sincerity are attested by the answer he gave to his sovereign when asked about the relative duties of king and people. He said, "If the prince have great faults, they (the people) ought to remonstrate with him, and if he do not listen to them after they have done so again and again, they ought to dethrone him." The king was moved to anger and changed countenance when he heard this, whereupon Mencius hastened to add: "Let not your Majesty be offended. You asked me, and I dared not answer but according to truth."

The chief service of Mencius was in the perpetuation of the Confucian tradition. We are told that there were teachers who were stopping up the way of truth when Mencius appeared to confute them, scattering their delusions without difficulty. And when the Ts'in dynasty sought to destroy the classical books, and put the scholars to death, the work of Mencius ended but his writings were preserved on the ground that they were "philosophical." It was thus in combating error and in giving to the teachings of Confucius a philosophical form that he was able to preserve the teaching of the master in its purity. It was this method, together with his outstanding ability as a thinker, which has won and maintained the loyalty of the educated and cultivated classes of China for Confucianism.

Students and scholars have usually been international in their outlook. In thus commending himself to this class in China Mencius served to make himself and his master immortal. Though both Confucius and Mencius were very probably of Lao stock and wrote primarily for the benefit of the Lao people, the fair-minded Chinese intellectuals, as well as the advocates of expediency, gave the teaching their support and thus enabled it to weather the narrow-minded policies of the conqueror, Ch'in Shih Huang. When it became the way of life to this class, its future was safe until some loftier way might be proclaimed.

CHAPTER III

GAUTAMA

About five hundred years before Christ the Sakiya tribe of the Aryans was situated near the city called Kapilavastu. This tribe had doubtless been a part of that first invading host which had swept down upon India from Central Asia. When the territory first occupied by these conquerors became too densely populated for comfort, a number of the tribes, among them the Sakiyas, turned eastward, made further conquests, and established new homes. The Sakiyas had kept well to the front of this second forward movement and now held a somewhat precarious position between the Licchavis, who were building to the east of them the powerful kingdom of Magadha, and that tribe which had founded the kingdom of Kosala to the west. Northward were the hill tribes of Mongolian extraction who made frequent forays into the land. There was a strong rivalry between Magadha and Kosala, and this turned out rather to the safety of the Sakiya tribe, for its territory became a buffer state. As to the hill tribes, the Sakiyas were able to repel their sporadic incursions and to maintain a precarious independence. The chief occupation of the people was agriculture, the water necessary for this pursuit being taken from the Rohini River.

The king of the Sakiyas had married two daughters of his neighbor, the chief of the Koliyans, a tribe closely related to the Sakiyas. To one of these women Siddartha, or Gautama the Buddha, was born. The prevailing uncertainty with regard to the future of the Sakiyas, and the lack of an adequate popular religion, produced a state of anxiety and unrest among all classes of the people with the possible exception of the priests, or Brahmans. General depression, therefore, superseded the vigor and enthusiasm of the former tribal life. Gautama grew up in this atmosphere and absorbed its poison and its hunger. Being a man of unusual intellectual ability he quickly saw the nature of the trouble: the priests had taken to themselves the exclusive right to administer the religious hope, and they had failed the people. Like many another member of the Kastriya, or warrior class, he realized that the remedy could never come from the priests. The task of restoring the ancient spirit of the Aryans must come from another quarter. To this undertaking he dedicated his life, and Buddhism was the result.

Gautama's teachings have been styled, with some reason, the Protestantism of India.[1] But the nature of Buddha's protest, and the character of the religion against which he protested, are so dissimilar to anything with which we are acquainted that such a term is very misleading. In fact the whole technique of religious method is in India almost the exact reverse of that encountered in the Occident. We seek for self-expression, for the liberation of sin-bound faculties, that we may assume the privileges of a free nature, one that may go on unimpeded to better things. But in India, even before Gautama's time, all religious thought and practice looked toward silence, inactivity, and the merging of the self in the Self of the Absolute. Desire, ambition, self-attainment had become discounted, controlled, and finally completely overcome. The individual ceased all self-expression and became identified with the life and being of the Overself.

Furthermore, our religion is still young and is therefore an exploring and adventurous faith. Our Protestantism has rebelled against conditions which it believes would prevent it

---

[1] J. F. Clarke, *Ten Great Religions,* p. 139.

from achieving the best life for the individual. Each generation continues to make further protest and to assume larger freedom. In India, however, long before Gautama's appearance, all these protests had been made. Religion was very old —mature in both theory and practice. Many agnosticisms and reforms had contributed to systematic effort, and within the inner circle of the priests the development had reached the limit. The ripe theological fruit had hung so long upon the tree of time that it had acquired the bitter taste of vanity. The protestantism of Gautama comes, therefore, at the end of this process rather than as a part of the development, as does our own. Not perhaps for another thousand years will our pagan interests and vigor be depressed enough for us to know the world-weariness and spiritual gloom which had settled down upon the official religious thinkers of India before Gautama appeared. The old living faith had yielded to a secretly held, or esoteric, philosophy.

The Aryans, a vigorous, barbaric race, were very different when they left their ancient home in the north and west. They had come with a singularly hopeful, free, and happy faith. All around them were "the bright ones," the shining beauties of nature, the stars, the sun, the clouds, the rivers, and the fire, all of which bestowed a magic blessing, a deific favor, upon this optimistic people. They had already achieved that division of labor and organization which made them an effective and powerful nation. One class kept the wisdom, the religious traditions, the songs and poems of the bards, and performed at the altars the function of sacrifice. Another fought the battles, set up the government, and executed the civil laws in the interests of peace and order. A third class carried on trade and commerce, while still another tilled the soil and kept the flocks and herds. This specialization which descended from father to son enabled the members of each class, later, caste, to perfect the arts of its own group. Thus the Aryans swept the aborigines out of the valleys, pushed down the rivers to the east, set up a number of powerful kingdoms, and in time established an enormous empire. They created a great literature and a profound theological and philosophical religion. And they prospered in flocks and herds and in lands and houses until they attained a security from economic pressure which few peoples have surpassed.

It is with the religion of the Aryans, however, that we are chiefly interested, for when it had reached its highest development and had come to decadence Buddha appeared with his protest and gospel of reformation. The Vedas, the literature of the time, which were not a written literature but one carried in the memory of the Brahmans, tell us incidentally the whole story of the early spiritual development of the Aryans in India. From this source, and the Vedanta, we discover that there were three phases, or distinct advances, in religious thought.

First, those who observed the beauty of nature applied to its luster the term "deva," a word which meant originally "bright," and nothing more. The word deva, or bright, was thus always used of the stars, the sky, the dawn, the sun, the day, the rivers, the spring, and the earth. Then the poets appeared to personalize the several aspects of nature and to describe all the brightness so personalized as "the bright ones." [2] By this simple process, the devas, the bright ones, became the Heavenly, the beneficent, the powerful, the immortal. These bright presences derived from generalizing and personalizing the beauty of Nature came in time to be very like the early gods of the Greeks.

"In this way," says Max Muller, "one Beyond, the Beyond of Nature, was built up in the ancient religion of the Veda, and peopled with Devas, and Ashuras, and Vasus, and Adityas, all names for the bright solar, celestial, diurnal, and vernal powers of nature, without altogether excluding, however, even

---

[2] Cf. Brinton, *Religions of Primitive Peoples*, pp. 112-118. Brinton makes poetry and mythology religious from the first. We know from Zoroastrianism that the devas were brought to India.

the dark and unfriendly powers, those of the night, of the dark clouds, or the winter, capable of mischief, but always destined in the end to succumb to the valor and strength of their bright antagonists." [3]

This is a religion of naturalism, a kind of animism. And yet, there is evidently a distinction to be drawn between nature and the devas. All the brightness of nature, when referred to in a collective way by the poets, was described as the bright ones. But in the religious thought of the faithful the bright ones were something more than poetical personifications. They were the immortals, the gods, the helpers of man, who revealed their presence in, or were best revealed by, the bright aspects of nature. The poetical personifications were not, however, the devas of the faith; the bodily persons, or devas, undoubtedly originated, or became conceived, as a result of such poeticisms. Thus the simile takes on bodily shape and immortality, just as an "old wife's tale" becomes an article of faith.

The second step in the development of religion was the conception of a region of departed mortals. It arose spontaneously out of the inability, or unwillingness, of the people to believe that anything which had existed could cease to be. Thus it was thought that the fathers existed somewhere, in the East from which the devas came, or in the West where all the devas seemed to go.

In time this belief in the immortality of the departed ones came to exert its force upon the laws and customs of each family. Each household sought to perpetuate the will which had ruled it, and in seasons of confusion or of danger the absent fathers were appealed to in prayer for counsel and protection. Thus the dead came to possess all the qualities of the devas in their relation to their living offspring, so that the

---

[3] *India: What Can It Teach Us?* p. 237.

living might pray, "May the rising Dawns protect me, may
the flowing Rivers protect me, may the firm Mountains protect me, may the Fathers protect me at this invocation of the
devas." [4]

. The above quotation places the fathers on an equality with
the devas. In fact, so far as man's needs are concerned, the
fathers *are* devas, to all intents and purposes, yet differing
from them in point of origin and appearance. The great men
of the nation, those who had lived in remote times and had
thus become legendary, were nearer the exalted state of
the old devas than those recently deceased. The reason for this
is easily understood. The ancients were more indistinct and
ethereal than the fathers who had but recently departed. They
did not exhibit to the eye of memory a bodily form, or the
works of their hands; nor could one hear the sounds of their
words in decree and counsel. This actual difference affected the
rank or position of the dead in the second beyond; the recently
departed had not yet attained to the region of the bright ones.
But this difference between the fortune of the ancients and the
late deceased was only a temporary one—those who had but recently passed away would in due time make their way into
the presence of that immortal company which dwelt with the
gods.

There was still a third region called the Rita. Muller [5]
thinks that it originally meant no more than "a straight line."
He points out that the word is used in referring to the straight
line of the sun in its daily course, to the straight line followed
by day and night, to the straight line that regulates the seasons, to the straight line which runs through the whole realm
of nature. As applied to the world, the Rita corresponds to
the Law of Nature; as applied to human behavior, it is the
Moral Law. It is, therefore, as the law of man and nature, the

---

[4] Rig-Veda VI. 52, 4, Muller's translation.
[5] *India: What Can It Teach Us?* p. 263.

law of the Creator which expresses itself outwardly in cosmic order and speaks in man as conscience.

It is this last advance in religious thought which gave rise to the philosophical movement in India. The unity of all things under one fundamental law implies the existence of a highest deva or Law Giver. He is not described often as the Creator, or Supreme Ruler, but as Atman, the Self. This Atman, or Self, is presented in many ways and praised according to each manifestation or name assigned to him; but the later writers of the Vedas believed that "the other devas are but so many members or phases (masks, illusions) of the one Atman, or Self."

To determine how the several devas are related to the Atman, or Self, will call for a review of the principles of Vedanta philosophy. How completely this philosophy of the Vedanta (the end, or goal, of the Veda) was systematized before the day of Buddha we do not know, but from certain passages contained in the later Vedic hymns we can distinguish ideas which indicate that the faith has been rationalized to a very high degree.

The Vedanta philosophy is based upon the Vedas and is contained in the Upanishads, or commentaries upon the Vedas. But such commentaries would have had little point, or connection with the Vedic hymns, had not the Vedas themselves contained certain passages of a philosophical nature. These portions of the hymns, which are cosmological in form, naturally represent a later period in Indian religious history, and indicate that already (before the composition of the Upanishads) theologians had begun to seek to systematize the Vedic faith. As Ragozin observes, "all the cosmological and metaphysical portions of the Rig-Veda may already be entitled Upanishads, as they certainly form the transition to the Upanishad period and literature." [6]

---

[6] *Vedic India*, p. 422.

Perhaps the most outstanding cosmogonic hymn (X. 129) contains more than the germ of the systematic thought which appears in the Brahmanic Upanishads. Already before the Veda was completed, a definite system of thought had been achieved which here reflects itself in outline. The gradual passage from the Vedas to the Upanishads indicates that the philosophical venture had begun long before the Vedas were completed and thus determined the character of the thought contained in the later hymns. At any rate X. 129 presents something more than inchoate poetic inspiration:

1. Nor Aught nor Naught existed then; nor the aerial space, nor heaven's bright woof above. What covered all? Where rested all? Was it water, the profound Abyss?

2. Death was not then, nor immortality; there was no difference of day and night. That One breathed breathless in Itself (existed, but without exerting or manifesting itself); and there was nothing other than It.

3. In the beginning there was darkness in darkness enfolded, all was indistinguishable water. That One, which lay in empty space, wrapped in nothingness, was developed by the power of heat.

4. Desire first arose in It—that was the primal germ of mind, which poets, searching with their intellects, discovered in their hearts to be the bond betwen Being and Not-Being.

5. The ray of light which stretched across these worlds, did it come from below or from above? Then seeds were sown and mighty forces arose, Nature beneath and Power and Will above.

6. Who indeed knows? Who proclaimed it here—whence, whence this creation was produced? The gods were later than its production—who then knows whence it sprang?

He from whom this creation sprang, whether he made it or not, the All-Seer in the highest heaven, he knows it—or he does not.

Of this hymn Ragozin remarks: "Startling indeed are the last lines—most startling the last words. The despondency, the hopelessness of them, is like the sudden relaxing of a superhuman tension. It also seems to foreshadow the cloud which was to fall on the spiritual life of the Aryans of India, after altered conditions of life, and especially the physically enervating climatic influences of their new abodes, had changed the joyous, somewhat belligerent, nature-worship, utterly untramelled with laming self-consciousness, of the first settlers of the Sapta-Sindhavak into introspective brooding, so destructive to action and single-hearted enjoyment, of the dwellers of the Ganges." [7]

It is possible that Ragozin has merely overlooked the fact that the startling last words may be a later addition, one provoked by the very despair he has so well described. The rest of the hymn sounds well enough, and easily expresses that triumphant tone which must have characterized the thinkers who began the philosophical venture. But he may be right in viewing the entire hymn as the work of a single author. It is just possible that the whole dates from a time when doubt, both of the authority of the Vedas and of human reason, was the prevailing spirit. When philosophy had done its work, the effect of climate and of further thought may have led to the belief that all is vanity. If the hymn originates in such circumstances, the whole perhaps exists just for the sake of that last startling phrase. The doubt is placed over against the orthodox philosophical position for purposes of emphasis.

Such a view would of course put the first philosophical attempts far back of the date when the last of the Vedas were written. And this must quite naturally have been the case, for even the first hymns must have provoked many questions among those who heard them sung. It would be strange indeed if such a considerable body of literature covering such an extended period should produce no questioning whatever. It is therefore very likely that almost from the first the Vedic hymns awakened the speculative side of the Aryan mind. By the time X. 129 was written philosophy had made its first

---

[7] *Vedic India*, p. 428.

great constructions and had passed into its first period of skepticism.

Another hymn, X. 121, seems to indicate, even more forcefully, that the theologians and philosophers had arrived at systematic fundamentals and had begun to make their results felt:

1. In the beginning there arose the Golden Child. He was the one born lord of all that is. He established the earth and this sky:—Who is the god to whom we shall offer our sacrifice?

2. He who gives breath (i. e. life), He who gives strength; whose commands all the gods revere; whose shadow is immortality, whose shadow is death:—Who is the god to whom we shall offer our sacrifice?

3. He who through greatness is the one king of the breathing and awakening world; He who governs man and beast:—Who is the God to whom we shall offer our sacrifice?

4. He whose greatness the Himavat, the samudra, the Rasa (the snowy mountains, the sea, and the distant river) proclaim; He whose these regions are, as it were his two arms:—Who is the god to whom we shall offer our sacrifice?

5. He through whom the sky is bright and the earth firm; He through whom the heaven is established,—nay the highest heaven; He who measured out the aerial spaces:—Who is the God, etc.

6. He to whom the two battle-hosts, sustained by his support, look up trembling in spirit, there where the risen sun shines:—Who is the God, etc.

7. When the mighty waters pervaded the universe, holding the germ and begetting fire, thence He arose, who is the sole life of gods:—Who is the God, etc.

8. He who by His might looked even over the waters which gave strength and lit the sacrifice; He who alone is god above all the gods:—Who is the God, etc.

9. May He not harm us, the Creator of this earth; who, ruling by fixed ordinances, created the heaven; who also created the bright and mighty waters:—Who is the God, etc.

However polytheistic the religion of the earlier Vedas may be, and however polytheistic the later ones may seem to be, it is quite evident that we have here, as the ground of the being of all the gods, one divine person or principle which contains all things—earth, sky, man, and the gods. Somewhere between the earlier and the later Vedas a great theological and philosophical system has been achieved. Ragozin [8] argues from hymn I. 64, verse 46, that the one god is Agni (fire) and that the Aryans were originally fire-worshipers. If his contention be correct the philosophical system must have grown up simultaneously with the hymns, and, it might be urged with some reason, may have antedated them. Ragozin quotes, "Wise poets make the beautiful-winged, though he is One, manifold by words." "O Agni, many names are given thee, O god, immortal ruler." "Agni is all the Gods." He has this evidence and the fact that the Indo-Iranians seem to have been fire-worshipers, to support his conclusion. This would indicate that fire-worship among the Aryans preceded the invasion of India. If that be true, the first philosophical system among the Aryans of India must have grown up along with the composition of the Vedas. The many personifications of the poets which came to have deific significance were attached to and absorbed into the being of Agni. The more conservative party of the Aryans would thus be forced to philosophy to save the ancient religion.

Ragozin may be right, but he has overlooked a peculiarity of the Vedic writers who exalt each god in turn to the position of Supreme God. Muller says: "The hymns celebrate Varuna, Indra, Agni, etc., and each in turn is called supreme. The whole mythology is fluent. . . . It would be easy to find, in the numerous hymns of the Veda, passages in which almost every single god is represented as supreme and absolute. Agni is called 'Ruler of the Universe;' Indra is celebrated as the Strongest god, and in one hymn it is said, 'Indra is strongest of all.' It is said of Soma that 'he conquers every one.'" [9] Ragozin admits that "there is one divine person who attracts

---

[8] *Vedic India*, pp. 434-435.
[9] Cf. *India: What Can It Teach Us?* Chap. VI.

and absorbs the others somewhat as a globule of quicksilver does any number of smaller ones. And as that globule, at the slightest jolt, breaks up again into an elusive bevy of smaller ones, so that divine entity, just when we think we are fairly grasping it, suddenly vanishes, and the polytheistic host confronts us in full array." [10]

The truth is, the original monotheism (only a local deity perhaps) has been enriched with many personifications which are not easily absorbed into the one god. The most thoughtful no doubt believe that the one god possesses all these manifestations, wears them as garments, carries them to the highest possible height. But the hard and fast conception of system has not yet been attained; the personifications swim freely in the sea of the concept of the divine. Unity of attribute and expression has not yet been wrought out, or focused, But it will come!

This loosely constructed philosophical theology could not continue when thinking grew more acute and when problems of the group pressed for solution. The lines of the thought had to be drawn clear and bold. Thus attention naturally shifted from the parts, which were found to be as supreme as the god, and centered itself upon that One whose nature embraced each supreme part or quality. In other words, the Vedas spring from the poetic, pluralistic, particularizing phase of thought; philosophy comes from the unifying, constructive, and generalizing faculty. Every mind possesses both powers at the same time. There will therefore be no real break between poetry and philosophy—an epoch devoted to one and an epoch devoted to the other; they will exist simultaneously. We must therefore expect to find several types of constructive thinking imbedded in the Vedas.

This is exactly what we do find. And yet, there is such a thing as a fad or fashion in intellectual pursuits. Poetry will

[10] Ragozin, Vedic India, p. 433.

be the chief interest at times; philosophy will be the chief thing at some other time. Thus after the Vedas had been composed as almost pure poetry, we find the poetry being supplanted by philosophy and the later Vedas containing more philosophy than poetry. Then the poetry gives place to prose works in which the interest is expository, frankly philosophical or theological.

It is not an easy matter to erect a clear-cut system from the earliest philosophical utterances of the Vedas; and this we ought naturally to expect, for thinking is nebulous at first— one main idea which is only gradually clarified and made explicit in its details. That main idea is clear enough, however. It is a sense of the Oneness of the god-head. The other gods, or all the gods, are but so many members of the one god. How long it took the thinkers of India to determine that this one god was of the nature of the self, we do not know. But by the fifth century B.C. this idea is well established.

Muller places this achievement in the interim between the first and second periods of the Vedic literature: "In the second period of Vedic literature, in the so-called Brahmanas, and more particularly in what is called the Upanishads, or the Vedanta portion, these thoughts advance to perfect clearness and definiteness. Here the development of religious thought, which took its beginning in the hymns, attains its fulfilment. The circle becomes complete. Instead of comprehending the One by many names, the many names are now comprehended to be One. The old names are openly discarded; even such titles as Pragapati, lord of creatures, Visvakarman, maker of all things, Dhatri, creator, are put aside as inadequate. The name now used is an expression of nothing but the purest and highest subjectiveness—it is Atman, the Self, far more abstract than our Ego—the Self of all things, the Self of all the old mythological gods—for they were not *mere* names, but names intended for something—lastly, the Self in which each individual self must find rest, must come to himself, must find his own true Self." [11]

In the Katha-Upanishad not only the character of the godhead but also the way of salvation for man is definitely stated. We learn from this source that there is a world of delusion. The man who has not found the true source of wisdom goes round and round, staggering to and fro, thinking, "This is the world," seeking wealth, influence, power, but utterly lost. In a state which knows neither joy nor sorrow the mortal, after meditating on his Self, recognizes the Old man within, the Self hidden in darkness, and recognizes his Self, as God. But it is not meditation which lays hold upon this Self. The power to recognize the Self as God comes by the grace of God. "That Self cannot be gained by the Veda; nor by the understanding, nor by much learning. He whom the Self chooses, by him alone the Self can be gained. The Self chooses him as his own. But he who has not first turned away from wickedness, who is not calm and subdued, or whose mind is not at rest, he can never obtain the Self, even by knowledge." The value of self-denial, self-control, meditation, discipline is seen to lie in the fact that *it may render the man an instrument which God may choose.*

This is a fairly correct statement of the nature of the knowing process. We are always receptive. The recognitions dawn upon us. No amount of effort or discipline can enable us to reach out and take any item of knowledge. What we are to learn, or seize, by knowing must first dawn upon us before we can take it; but when it dawns, lo, we already have it. Attention, meditation, is therefore, but tuning the self for these dawnings or revelations. Thus the Vedantists who explored the knowing process saw the situation just as it is. The accidental arrival of knowledge to a receptive agent is looked upon as being divinely controlled, extra-individual at least;

---

[11] *India: What Can It Teach Us?* pp. 266-267.

and whoever knows the Self as God is thought of as being chosen to this event. The brooding, the fixing of attention, which we regard as turning the mind toward the source of new facts which we hope will dawn upon us, the Brahman regarded as a necessary qualifying step.

The difference between us and the Brahman at this point is a difference in the interpretation of the nature of the knower. We think of him as having certain powers, limitations, gifts, and tendencies, or habits of mind. These he brings with him as a part of the intellectual lens which he turns toward the Source. What dawns upon the knower will be determined by the nature of the mind so gifted and limited. The Brahman thought of these gifts and limitations under the general term, the divine choice. God determined what we should know or not know. By meditation and discipline we might prepare ourselves to be chosen, but how much or how little we should know was divinely determined. A strict application of our concept "Creator" will amount in the end to the same thing. We have set the divine agency only a little further back, perhaps; and perhaps not. Every system has its points at which it presses its logical and divine determinisms and at which it relaxes them. At any rate, the difference between our account of the origin of knowledge and the Brahmanic account is more apparent than real—just a matter of mental and lingual habit; we each cover the same ground with the same tools.

Salvation of the individual consisted in recognizing the Old man within, the identification of the Self with the Atman, the Self of all things. In this identification man reaches his true being, his highest nature, his immortality. In this achievement man escapes from the desires and sorrows of the world and gains peace.

This situation is possible because the Self-of-all-things is the true nature of all things. The Self expresses himself differently in each thing he enters and according to the nature of that thing, but he exists also apart from each thing. This Self is never contaminated by the impurities of the world which man beholds or engages in. Man does not thus destroy his highest nature by an evil life; he simply misses it. He lives in delusion; never lives his true nature, but leaves it hidden from him. The power of delusion must be broken, negated, undone. Then one is in a position to be elected to the knowledge of the Atman, or Self of all things.

It is evident at once that such an interpretation of the way of salvation will greatly lessen the power of the priests and the whole sacrificial system. Not sacrifice but mental and moral discipline is the true means of approach to a saved life. The consequences of this position were met by the priests in their theory of revelation. They held that the Vedas were not inspired! Thus the whole philosophical system built upon them was greatly weakened in its appeal because it lacked the essential element of authority.

Ragozin says: "It would seem to the unbiased mind as though the Rig-Veda alone, being the corner-stone and fountain-head of India's entire spiritual life, would be entitled to be enshrined in it as Shruti (i.e. that which was heard, or) revealed, repeated from 'what was heard' by the Rishis who were the chosen vessels of the divine message to men. This would be logical, but would not have suited the Brahmans at all. This most ambitious and crafty of all priesthoods made such exorbitant, nay monstrous demands upon the credulity, docility, and liberality of the people over which they claimed —though they may never have quite established—absolute power, both spiritual and temporal, that not even such a contemplative, indolent, physically enervated race as the once vigorous Aryans were changed into by a long sojourn amid the relaxing, debilitating influences of semi-tropical Eastern Hindustan, would have submitted so tamely and unresistingly, had they not become imbued with the conviction that they were obeying the will of Heaven. Now all these things that the Brahmans claimed for themselves were not in the Rig-

Veda—to begin with the claim of revelation itself, which the old poets did not put forth for their hymns, of which, indeed, they emphatically speak as their own creation, boasting that they made this or that new song, 'as the carpenter fashions a wagon.' It had all to be spun out of embryonic hints contained in scattered texts, meanings made out, twisted, and made to fit where needed. The text was nothing, the interpretation everything." [12]

In this way the priests, who were losing the sacrifice, managed to secure the exclusive right to philosophize. Rhys Davids declares that there is abundant evidence to show that the grand generalization upon which the Vedanta philosophy rested did not originate with the priests or in the priestly schools: "Precisely as regards the highest point of the generalization, the very keystone of the arch, the priestly literature has preserved the names of the rajput laymen who thought it out and taught it to the priests." [13] But this of course happened in the first blush of confusion after popular thought had turned from the older priestly theology. How completely the new philosophy had won its way by the time Buddha appeared is not clear. Many of the priests were ignorant, superstitious, and bigoted. There were some who were sincerely thoughtful and others who were men of great philosophical ability. Perhaps only among the men of unusual ability had the Vedanta philosophy in its various aspects gained a foothold. If that be true, we can understand how Buddha would seek out the leaders of the philosophical schools for the true enlightenment.

The evidence seems to indicate that in the time of Buddha's young manhood the priests had again succeeded in getting control of religious thought. The work of the brilliant laymen had been taken over by brilliant priests and their disciples. Wanderers—priests and lay teachers—traveled from place to place engaging one another in argumentation before popular

---

[12] *Vedic India*, pp. 123-124.
[13] T. W. Rhys Davids, *Buddhist India*, p. 257.

audiences. It was a time of great liberty of thought, and yet it was the priest who broke the bread of life. No lay teacher could ever enter that inner circle of the Brahmans or secure the precious privileges supposed to be conferred upon this special sacerdotal class.

The spirit of the times was naturally one in which great philosophers vied with one another at the expense of the authority of the Vedas, the efficacy of the sacrifice, and the value of the thinking process itself. Certain men turned to the ascetic life, to tapas, to secure satisfaction and spiritual peace. Faith in any means, sacrificial, philosophical, or ascetic, gradually waned. And man's soul does not rest in negation and doubt, in purely intellectual gymnastics, and in an unproductive union with deity. The soul must get somewhere; its greatest need is to go on. Unless there is an inviting prospect ahead the goal is despair.

The Aryans of India were amazingly well endowed for philosophical speculation. They reasoned with such subtlety, and at such length, that they could not be deceived by false hopes. A few, by temperament, could rest in spiritual union with the Atman. But very few, probably, knew anything of this source of consolation. The Wanderers also were divided into numerous groups who no doubt found their spiritual panaceas in their own way. The whole trouble with the times was just the fact that all India was spiritually ill. Climate had its enervating effect; unprecedented simplicity of life had given little to occupy the mind; the decay of faith in the authority of the Vedas had left no foundation for the soul to rest upon, or to poise for new adventures; and the philosophy of the Vedantists was very probably an esoteric doctrine reserved only for the edification of a few. The common people were thus without faith or future. And a society which is wedged in between delusion on the one hand and futility on the other must be rescued.

If we remember the progress of Gautama in his quest we

shall be able to understand the spirit of the times and the utter hopelessness of the social condition from the standpoint of the common man. From the outside, as a member of the warrior class, he saw all too clearly the insupportable character of Indian life. Upon almost every face was the utter despair of psychic sickness. And before the people remained the old, old tragedies of mortality—age, sickness, and decay. Surely there must be some balm for himself and his people. But where? Then he caught sight of the peaceful face of a hermit. Here perhaps might be a way. He would see. He would follow that way. He would find the secret if possible. He would bring it back to this perishing people. He went out from his palace; he turned to the Vedantist philosophers, but saw in their teaching nothing that was to him good news—all was the arid, exhausted field of the seeking spirit; he tortured his flesh unto fainting and got no relief and no inspiring light. Within himself he knew that, for his generation, salvation must come from some great new source of inspiration, some new country which could claim the whole of the energy of the human spirit. He had not found it in either popular philosophy or asceticism. Along every path he took he reached the limit of human energy and faced only the barren wastes before the soul. The quest along the conventional lines of salvation brought him to the brink of a bottomless pit.

And this seems strange indeed when we compare the "enlightenment" which he finally declared with the philosophies which we have reason to know were already in existence. Oldenburg states, "There was nothing in Buddha's attitude generally which could be regarded by his contemporaries as unusual; he had not to introduce anything fundamentally new." [14] And Ananda Coomaraswamy says: "All writers upon Buddhism are faced with the difficulty to explain in what respect the teaching of Gautama differs from the higher

---

[14] *Buddha* (English Translation), p. 119.

phases of Brahman thought. It is true that the distinction appeared clear enough to Gautama and his successors; but this was largely because the Brahmanism against which they maintained their polemic was after all merely the popular aspect of Brahmanism. From the study of the Buddha's dialogues it would appear that he never encountered a capable exponent of the highest Vedantic idealism, such a one as Yajnavalkhya or Janaka; or if Alara is to be considered such, Gautama took exception to the Atmanistic terminology rather than its ultimate significance." [15] All this seems just enough. The goal of the rational process according to Buddha and the Vedantists *is* indistinguishable.

We may well wonder, then, why he did not accept the highest Vedantic idealism. If we agree that he could not have known of it, we have ample reason for the whole career of Gautama. The older religion had lost its authority and therefore its power to console. India was without a god and without hope in the world—not all Indians, to be sure, for the Vedantists had a philosophy which revealed a redemption almost identical with the one Gautama discovered, but the people as a whole had nothing. An examination of the teaching of Gautama will reveal a marked correspondence with the system of Samkhya which was formulated by a sage named Kapila, from whom the name of Kapilavatthu, Gautama's native city, may have been derived. It is therefore quite certain that Gautama favored the teachings of Kapila above all other systems, but it is almost equally certain that its provision for salvation—the fact that almost no one could be saved by it—caused Gautama to turn from it in despair. He, undoubtedly, had already come to feel that the "Soul" was the seat of all continuous rebirth and that any who escaped from retelling the story of human misery must deny the existence of the "Soul." This may be why he was antagonistic to Alara when

---

[15] *Buddha and the Gospel of Buddhism*, p. 198.

he later sought him for wisdom, and why, because of his impatience he never learned the highest signifiance of Vedantic thought.

At any rate, we may be sure that Gautama believed that he had explored the philosophical systems of his day and that he had found in them nothing that could provide peace to the thoughtful soul, now more thirsty for all its philosophizings than ever before. He then taxed his flesh and mind to the verge of extinction and met with nothing on this road but the mad shapes of illusion and despair. And his experience must have been that of the thousands of India who were seeking the way of peace. A salvation which is so esoteric as to be almost unapproachable, which is kept only for the elect, needs to be popularized. Practically there was a place for Buddha, a service for him to perform for the people.

This is undoubtedly the situation in India when Gautama came on the scene. His people had made too much intellectual advancement, and had lost too much physical energy in this trying climate, to return again to barbaric pursuits and modes of thought. These were delusions, the mere ease of the flesh and nerves born of healthful bodily function. The simple manner of life of the common people required little physical labor, there was no healing forgetfulness to be had in the round of daily tasks. And the worth of a higher and more luxurious standard of living did not appeal to the nation as a whole; there were too many ascetics, hermits, and Wanderers who taught the inadequacy of wealth and the earthly career. Furthermore, approximately the same position was the national heritage from those first invaders of India who put true life above possessions. Very little enthusiasm could be worked up for a luxury-loving, materialistic society; barbaric energy was too low and history and life had too long discounted such an ideal. Philosophy also had had a long development. Three great systems had mined the whole region about the mountains of deity and around the little hill of human personality. Even Buddha found nothing really new. In the cool caves of the hermits a few rested in the salvation derived from various philosophies; but nothing had come to the common people except the backwash of agnosticism. The popular statement of these systems could not appeal to the subtle, inquisitive, profound thinkers outside the Brahman class. As for asceticism, it was looked upon as a necessary evil, the natural accompaniment of all truth-seeking; but its product was but an echo of ancient truth, the old exhausted ways the nation had already traveled.

Moral evil always produces social incompetence and cuts short the social experiment. Those who have sought to save the people from social inertia and decay have therefore always found it necessary to stress the cardinal virtues and to point out the fact that the better future must rest upon righteousness. But when a people imagines that it has tracked righteousness to its source in delusion; has examined exhaustively the social venture and found it to be vanity; has explored the nature of deity as creator, master mechanic, vast bosom of embracing rest; and has reviewed all attempts to penetrate man's gifts and destiny, and in each investigation has found no escape from mortality—age, disease, and death—it will demand of its deliverer a new technique of salvation, one that saves the mortal from these roads which seem to lead nowhere.

There is ample proof to show that practically everything embraced in the highest aspects of Buddhism had already been attained by the philosophers; that Gautama never made an exhaustive study of Vedantism, never knew its profound solution of the problem of rational peace, never explored to the limit its offerings to life here and hereafter. But it is equally true that we shall never understand the popularity of the gospel of Gautama unless we recognize that he addressed himself to a skepticism which could see no value in popular religion. Nothing short of this can explain Gautama's vogue or account for the success of Mahavira, another reformer who flourished at the same time and who sought to meet the spiritual aridity of the times in another way.

We behold, therefore, in the rise of both Buddha and Mahavira a significant fact: The truth which was put in the Occident in the form, "No bishop, no king," and expressed by the Hebrew Prophet in the memorable phrase, "Where there is no prophet the people perish," was fully appreciated by the Ksatriya, or warrior (ruling) class. All true statesmen, whether of Europe, Israel, India, China, Egypt, or of Periclean Athens, have realized the importance, nay, the necessity, of the thing which we call religion. They have seen that it is absolutely necessary to the contentment and progress of mankind, that without it rulers cannot keep the scepter or the privileged classes enjoy their rich possessions. It is, therefore, no very great cause for surprise that the warriors, or ruling class of India—those accustomed to rule and who were the only students of government in the nation—produced the reformers who sought so profoundly to find a way of authority and peace. Least of all should we be surprised that sincere men of this class, men who conscientiously looked to the welfare of their subjects, should feel themselves in duty bound to find a new touchstone of inspiration and hope. To every right-thinking and noble-minded man of this class the spiritual chaos of the times could not help furnishing an abiding challenge, no matter how incompetent he might be to find a remedy. It is therefore to be expected that the philosophical systems of India should originate just where they did.

Gautama the Buddha was a member of this governing class. His father was the king of Oude, with Kapilavastu as his capital city. The king was married to two daughters of a neighboring ruler, and one of these, Maya, was the mother of Siddartha, who became Gautama the Buddha. Maya died seven days after the birth of her son, and the prince was brought up by his maternal aunt, the other wife of the king.

Legend has supplied us with a number of miraculous events

concerning the birth, childhood, and youth of Gautama. Few of these, however, seem to have any real foundation other than the desire of his followers to impress upon others the exalted character of the Teacher. Even the four events connected with his call have no doubt come to wear a religious and theological significance, a sacredness which they could not have had at the time. There is no reason to question the validity of the account, but the place of these facts in the rationalizings of Gautama, as he struggled with the spiritual problems of his people, is far more important than to regard them as events upon the street of Kapilavastu. In fact the whole situation was such that they need not have actually happened. When Gautama came to weigh the value of the religion taught in his day, when he saw its inadequacy before the abiding tragedies of human existence, he would pass these four scenes in review. And as abiding events in human life, he put them into that rational view of humanity which called him to the rôle of savior as no external event could ever do.

There is a truth in the story that it was the sight of an aged man, of another who was ill, and of one who had died, that caused him to meditate upon the lot of man. These are the permanent puzzles of mankind. Any complete truth concerning humanity must solve these riddles of the race. Naturally the prevailing religion, which purported to be the truth, ought to give some sort of an answer to these persistent problems. But it had given no satisfactory reply, as we have already seen. Men were saved, but not saved from these horrors. Despondency and futility settled down upon the nation; the prospective young ruler might well be concerned with the state of the people he was soon to govern. Then he caught sight of a hermit with contented, glowing face. Here was one man who had overcome the depression of the times. Here was a man who was truly saved, for he had escaped out of the power of that terror which was crushing the nation. This man must have an answer—a complete answer—to the very intellectual problems which confronted the prince. Peace must rest on truth, reasoned Gautama. As one responsible for the welfare of the nation, it was his duty to seek out that truth.

The Buddhist account of the call of Gautama states that one day when the prince was driving through the city he saw an old and decrepit man before him. He turned to Channa, his charioteer, and asked, "What kind of man is this?" Channa replied, "Sire, it is an aged man, bowed down with years." "Are all men then," said the prince, "or this man only, subject to age?" The charioteer said, sadly, that age came to every living being. "Shame, then, on life," cried the prince, "since the decay of every living thing is notorious!" Again the prince drove forth to visit the pleasure-gardens. On the way he met a sick man, thin, weak, and scorched with fever. When the charioteer explained the condition of the man, Gautama exclaimed, "If health be frail as the substance of a dream, who then can take delight in joy and pleasure?" Unhappy, he turned the chariot and drove back to the palace, his thought of the pleasure-grounds put from him. A third time he went forth, and this time he met a corpse. He looked upon the mourners who were weeping and tearing their hair. "Why does this man lie on a bier," said the prince, "and why do they weep and beat their breasts?" "Sire," said Channa, "he is dead, and may never more see his father or mother, children or home: he has departed to another world." "Woe then to such youth as is destroyed by age," exclaimed Gautama, "and woe to the health that is destroyed by innumerable maladies! Woe to the life so soon ended! Would that sickness, age, and death might be forever bound! Turn back again, that I may seek a way of deliverance." A fourth time the young prince left the palace, and this time he met a mendicant. The Bhikkhu was self-possessed, serene, dignified, self-controlled, and with downcast eyes, dressed in simple garb and carrying a beggar's bowl. "Who is this man of so calm temper?" said the prince, "clothed in russet garments, and of such dignified demeanor?" "Sire," said Channa, "He is a Bhikkhu, a religious, who has abandoned all longings and leads a life of austerity, he lives without passion or envy, and begs his daily food." The prince replied, "That is well done, and makes me eager for the same course of life: to become religious has ever been praised by the wise, and this shall be my refuge and the refuge of others and shall yield the fruit of life, and immortality."

There are at least a dozen reasons against the possibility that this conversation ever took place, and probably only one in its favor. The prince was married at sixteen and continued on at Kapilavastu for the next ten years. No man twenty-six years of age is unacquainted with the fact that people become ill, grow old, and die. Furthermore, the Bhikkhu represented a class of people that wandered from city to city lecturing at certain shelters before the people who resorted thither to hear them. The class was numerous, the shelters were many and provided at public expense; and it was the general custom to announce in the city that certain famed Bhikkhus had arrived at these shelters and were ready to teach. The prince could not possibly have been so ignorant of the affairs of the kingdom as the account of his questions implies. It is possible, of course, that he took this way of announcing his intentions; but this explanation is highly improbable. The whole story bears the marks of the literary craftsman, the maker of legends, and for that reason must be taken with considerable discount.

But there is much behind the story, as we know. Gautama had been well disciplined in all that comprised an education in his day. And from his later achievements we know that he was a man of force and of great intellectual ability. In his conversations, perhaps with Channa, and with others also, he revealed that he had struggled with the very evils that were destroying the vigorous, buoyant spirit of his people. His thought, long focused upon the facts of illness, age, and death, had amounted to a brooding which attracted the attention of all and which had caused the king much concern. We are told that the father resorted to a number of expedients to divert the prince from his dark obsessions. All this has been told by the maker of legends according to his own taste, and thus we have it as related above. The young prince no doubt had been in the habit of attending the lectures of the Bhikkhus when they came to the capital city. His eagerness to hear them had further alarmed the king; for the prince might at any moment join the Wanderers, leaving no one to take the throne. Perhaps Gautama may have said in the presence of his charioteer that he would prefer to become a religious. In the main, then, and thus modified, the report of Gautama's call and the sorrow and anxiety of the king are authentic.

There were a number of things to prevent the prince from taking immediate action in his desire to become a Bhikkhu. He was the heir to the throne and his father would be made very unhappy. He was married, and would be compelled to give up his wife and his home. He debated long with himself and became more certain that he must go; but he recognized the claims of father and wife and waited. When his son Rahula was born, he is reported to have said, "A bond has come into being, a hindrance to me." The next day after the birth of the son the prince drove through the city and heard his cousin, Kisa Gotama, singing in celebration of the birth of his child:

Blessed indeed is the mother, blessed indeed the father,
Blessed indeed is the wife, whose is the Lord so glorious.

The word "blessed" struck upon his attention and caused his heart to leap within him. "Blessed" meant "happy," but it also meant "freed." "Delivered" is the person burdened by sin and the fate of transmigration.

This naturally intensified his constant thought and desire. He took off his necklace of pearls and sent it to the singer as a token of his gratitude. "Let this be her fee as a teacher," he said. That night he decided to leave his palace and to become a mendicant.

He sent his charioteer to get his horse, and while the servant was gone he went to the door of his wife's room. In the dim light he watched her sleeping, surrounded by flowers, one hand resting upon the head of their child. He had come with the thought of taking the babe in his arms before going away, but he saw now that he could not do this without awaking the mother. Realizing that should she awake his resolution might not be strong enough to support him against her tears and pleading, he tore himself away and went out to mount his horse. Accompanied by Channa he left his home, his wealth and power, his young wife and only son. At the end of that night's ride he would take the road as a penniless wanderer.

When the two had crossed the river Anoma, Gautama alighted from his horse and said: "Good Channa, the time has come for you to return, and take with you all my jewels together with my horse (Kanthaka), for I am about to become a hermit and a wanderer in these forests. Do not grieve for me, but mourn for those who stay behind, bound by longings of which the fruit is sorrow. It is my resolve to seek the highest good this very day, for what confidence have we in life when death is ever at hand? And do you comfort the king, and so speak with him that he may not even remember me, for where affection is lost, there is no sorrow." Channa protested and sought to prevail upon his master to take pity upon the king, his deserted wife, and the city of Kapilavastu. Gautama answered: "Even were I to return to my kindred by reason of affection, yet we should be divided in the end by death. The meeting and parting of living things is as when the clouds having come together drift apart again, or as when the leaves are parted from the trees. There is nothing we can call our own in a union that is nothing but a dream. Therefore, since it is so, go, and grieve not, and say to the people of

Kapilavastu: 'Either he will soon return, the conqueror of age and death, or he himself will fail and perish.' " Then Channa expressed the wish to become a hermit and remain with his master. "If your love is so great," said Gautama, "deliver my message, and return."

Nothing could more clearly reveal the intellectual and spiritual despair of India in the time of Gautama than this answer to Channa's appeal to remember the affection of wife and father. "The meeting and parting of living things is as when the clouds having come together drift apart again, or as when the leaves are parted from the tree. There is nothing we can call our own in a union that is nothing but a dream." Surely no greater indictment of popular religion could be found than this bitter estimate of the most precious human ties.

The account of Gautama's life from now until he appears as a teacher of enlightenment is glossed with legend until it is almost impossible to discover the truth. And yet, the main facts, perhaps all we need for our purpose, can be discerned. First, he sought out Alara Kalama, a sage who enjoyed a considerable degree of popularity in that day. Alara taught the doctrine of the Atman. He said to Gautama that the sage who is versed in the Supreme Self, "having abolished himself by himself, sees that nought exists and is called a Nihilist: then, like a bird from its cage, the soul escaping from the body, is declared to be free: this is that supreme Brahman, constant, eternal, and without distinctive signs, which the wise who know reality declare to be liberation." But Gautama declared that a liberated soul is still a soul, and, in whatever condition it arrives, must therefore be subject to rebirth: "Since each successive renunciation is held to be still accompanied by qualities, I maintain that the absolute attainment of our end is only to be found in the abandonment of everything." Gautama evidently fails to see that the Supreme Self is without any of the distinguishing marks of personality and that the "soul" (self of the individual) unites with the Supreme Self only when it has escaped all distinctive marks of personality. Perhaps Alara did not know of this highest triumph of Vedantic thought—the neuter Brahman in which the "soul" of the man becomes neuter also and therefore subject to no qualifying force whatever. The failure here is evidently Alara's, for he had his opportunity to explain the true Vedanta position.

Gautama left the hermitage and began an investigation of the methods of the Wanderers. For six years, we are told, he practiced the austere rule of fasting and of mortification. He ate only the very smallest amount of food, a sesamum seed or a grain of rice. One day, either from illness or extreme weakness, he fell fainting. His companions believed that he would die, but he recovered and decided that mortification was not the road to enlightenment and liberation. He took his begging bowl and went into the towns and villages to secure food. This action caused his friends to leave him in disgust, for they felt that if he could not gain enlightenment through mortification there was no chance now of his doing so while eating ordinary food.

During all this period of mortification he had been dwelling in the forest of Uruvela. The daughter of the village headman, by name Sujata, had been accustomed to make a daily offering of food to the Brahmans who resided there. And during the next fifty days she supplied Gautama with food while he struggled to gain his enlightenment and found it. Legend tells us that he won it before the dawn of the second day, and that he continued on in thought for seven weeks thereafter to determine the scope and details of his scheme of salvation.

The fancy of the maker of ascetic formulae has done a curious thing to this period of normal reflection. Gautama, now enlightened, remained seated and motionless for the next seven days realizing the bliss of Nirvana; he arose and stood for the succeeding seven days regarding the spot where he had just been sitting; then for seven days he paced to and fro between the spot where he had been sitting and the spot where he had been standing; this completed, he sat for seven days in a god-wrought pavilion composing the Abhidhamma Pitaka and his doctrine of casuality; then for seven days he sat beneath the Nigrodha tree of Sujata's offering, and meditated upon the sweetness of Nirvana. Some hold that it was at this time that he met and overcame the threefold temptation of Maya. Then for seven days more, while a storm raged, he was sheltered by the sevenfold hood of a serpent; and for a final seven days he sat beneath a Rajayatana tree and enjoyed the sweetness of liberation.

It is easy enough to see that this account of Gautama's meditation has been considerably doctored—a normal fact has been turned into a regimen. The man who makes a philosophy must think until he thinks through; but sanctimonious claptrap easily forces upon the normal experience a regularity, significance, artificiality of stages, and the discovery of truth in sections. When meditation becomes an instrument of religion, a means to holy revelation, it cannot retain its normal character; it will not be holy enough in its natural state, to discover anything holy. It is this type of reasoning which has drawn up the regimen of religious meditation. Thus it forces upon that which is only the normal and natural use of the human brain an impossible account of forty or forty-nine days of fasting and of a threefold temptation. There is only one way in which the human mind can work in arriving at a system of thought; but we have abundant evidence that it can work in quite another way when it sets out to turn human functions into divine ones. And this work of Indian imagination has produced amazing repercussions in various regions, all of which proves that ideas had a tendency to drift about freely in the ancient world.

As soon as he had thought his system through he went to Deer Park in Benares to find his former companions, that he might reveal to them the truth he had discovered. There he began preaching; his first sermon was on The Foundation of The Kingdom of Righteousness.

There are two extremes which he who has gone forth ought not to follow—habitual devotion on the one hand to the passions, to the pleasures of sensual things, a low and pagan way (of seeking satisfaction), ignoble, unprofitable, fit only for the worldly-minded; and habitual devotion, on the other hand, to self-mortification, which is painful, ignoble, unprofitable. There is a Middle Path discovered by the Tathagata (the name used by Buddha for himself),—a path which opens the eyes, and bestows understanding which leads to peace, to insight, to the higher wisdom, to Nirvana. Verily it is this Ariyan Eightfold Path; that is to say Right Views, Right Aspirations, Right Speech, Right Conduct, Right Mode of Livelihood, Right Effort, Right Mindfulness, and Right Rapture.

Now this is the Noble Truth as to suffering. Birth is attended with pain, decay is painful, disease is painful, death is painful. Union with the unpleasant is painful, painful is separation from the pleasant; and any craving unsatisfied, that, too, is painful. In brief, the five aggregates of clinging (that is, the conditions of individuality) are painful.

Now this is the Noble Truth as to the origin of suffering. Verily it is the craving thirst that causes the renewal of becomings, that is accompanied by sensual delights, and seeks satisfaction, now here now there—that is to say, the craving for the gratification of the senses, or the craving for prosperity.

Now this is the Noble Truth as to the passing away of pain. Verily it is the passing away so that no passion remains, the giving up, the getting rid of, the emancipation from, the harboring no longer of this craving thirst.

Now this is the Noble Truth as to the way that leads to the passing away of pain. Verily it is this Ariyan Eightfold Path, that is to say, Right Views, Right Aspirations, Right Speech, Conduct, and Mode of Living, Right Effort, Right Mindfulness, and Right Rapture.[16]

This first address is an introduction, the preliminary statement to the more complex ideas of Buddha's system. In the

---

[16] Rhys Davids, *Early Buddhism*, pp. 51, 52.

main it is clear, terse, direct. Suffering is established as a fact; its origin is revealed in the craving thirst for continuence and gratification; Pain can be made to pass away; and the Way of escape from Pain is declared. Quite enough for one lecture, since pain has always been in all ages the stumbling-block of philosophers and theologians. On the fifth day Gautama preached again, and this time upon "The Non-existence of Soul."

The body, O Bhikkhus, cannot be eternal soul, for it tends toward destruction. Nor do sensations, perceptions, the predispositions, and consciousness together constitute the eternal soul, for, were it so, it would not be the case that the consciousness likewise tends toward destruction. Or how think you, whether is form permanent or transitory? and whether are sensations, perception, and predispositions and consciousness permanent or transitory? "They are transitory," replied the Five (Gautama's former companions). "And that which is transitory, is it evil or good?" "It is evil," replied the Five. "And that which is transitory, evil, and liable to change, can it be said that 'This is mine, this am I, this is my eternal soul?'" "Nay, verily, it cannot be so said," replied the Five. "Then, O Bhikkhus, it must be said of all physical form whatsoever, past or present or to be, subjective, or objective, far or near, high or low, that 'this is not mine, this am I not, these are not my eternal soul.' And in like manner of all sensations, perceptions, predispositions and consciousness, it must be said, 'These are not mine, these am I not, these are not my eternal soul.' And perceiving this, O Bhikkhus, the true disciple will conceive a disgust for physical form, and for sensation, perception, predispositions and consciousness, and so will be divested of desire, and thereby he is freed, and becomes aware that he is freed; and he knows that becoming is exhausted, that he has lived the pure life, that he has done what it behooved him do, and that he has put off mortality for ever."

From these addresses we begin to see that Gautama believes that all mortality—becoming that continues, all immorality, all the vast round of temporality and illusion, all suffering, pain and death, have their origin in "aggregates of clinging," the craving thirst arising from the conditions of individuality.

But individuality is only another aggregate, just as the chariot is nothing but a group of qualities associated. If we overcome the spell, the dominance of these aggregates, we escape the illusion of individuality. The soul does not really exist. All is transitory, evil, and changing, which we associate and style, in the lump, a soul. Whoever thus subdues the elements of this aggregate, such as sensations, perceptions, predispositions and consciousness, and physical form, becomes free of the illusion of soul, or of individuality. In this way also he becomes free of mortality with all its pain, disease, and death.

The third sermon was the famous "Discourse on Fire":

All things, O Bhikkhus, are on fire. And what, O Bhikkhus, are all these things that are on fire? The eye is on fire, forms are on fire, eye-consciousness is on fire, impressions received by the eye are on fire; and whatever sensation—pleasant, unpleasant, or neutral—originates in the impressions received by the eye, is likewise on fire.

And with what are all these on fire? I say with the fire of lust of resentment, and the fire of glamour (raga, dosa, and moha); with birth, old age, death, lamentation, misery, grief and despair they are afire.

And so with the ear, with the nose, and with the tongue, and in the case of touch. The mind too, is on fire, thoughts are on fire; and mind-consciousness, and the impressions received by the mind, and the sensations that arise from the impressions that the mind receives, these too are on fire.

And with what are they on fire? I say with the fire of lust, with the fire of resentment, and the fire of glamour; with birth, old age, death, sorrow, lamentation, misery and grief and despair, they are afire.

And seeing this, O Bhikkhus, the true disciple conceives disgust for the eye, for forms, for eye-consciousness, for impressions received by the eye, and for the sensations arising therein; and for the ear, the nose, the tongue, and for the sense of touch, and for the mind, and for thoughts and mind-consciousness, impressions, and sensations. And so he is divested for desire, and thereby he is freed, and is aware that he is freed, and he knows that becoming is exhausted, that he has lived the pure life, that he has done what it behoved him to do, and that he has put off mortality for ever.[17]

The significance of this sermon is understood when we realize that Nirvana, the blessed state, is secured when we have extinguished this very fire and all that feeds it. Nirvana means "to blow out," to extinguish, as one blows out a candle, as one extinguishes a fire. And from this sermon we learn what is to be blown out or extinguished. Here is declared the way of salvation as well as the nature of the salvation to be sought.

This fire may be likened to a consuming fever, since we have already said that the real trouble with India was to be found in the fact that all her people were spiritually ill. On this point Coomaraswamy says: "The whole of the doctrine (dhamma, Sanscrit dharma) of Gautama is simply and briefly capitulated in the Four Ariyan Truths, or axioms; That there is suffering (Dukkha), that it has a cause (Samudaya), that it can be suppressed (Nirodha), and that there is a way to accomplish this (Magga), the 'Path.' This represents the application of current medical science to the healing of the spiritually sick. The good physician, seeing Everyman in pain, proceeds to diagnosis: he reflects upon the cure, and commends the necessary régime to the patient—this is the history of the life of Gautama. The sick soul knows its sickness only by its pain; it seeks the cause of its suffering, and the assurance of a remedy, and asks what shall it do to be saved—this is the history of those who take refuge in the Law of the Buddha." The remedy for the disease thus diagnosed is the Eightfold Path.

The cure—the deliverance of Everyman, the patient, from his fever—involves a spiritual journey along the Eightfold Path. The least travel along this way is productive of relief; and the farther one goes and the more completely he gives

---

[17] Warren, *Buddhism in Translations*, p. 351.

himself to this way, the more nearly perfect is the cure. But there are many who take only a part of the cure. Thus the eschatology of Gautama has been carefully and intricately conceived to accommodate itself to all these degrees of cure. By means of the accompanying graph (see page 98), we may be able to trace the career of the individual through all the possibilities which can result from an application of the cure.

It is interesting to note that Gautama views no man as being completely devoid of antecedent existence and of merit or demerit. When a man is born this quantum from the past attaches to him, and it becomes a powerful agent of pre-destination. It may even determine his career completely unless superseded by a good or bad choice. We are told that this quantum, which passes from a life that is ended to a life that begins, is no *thing*. In other words it is not a soul, but that which we would describe as character, or as personality with-out person. It operates like the lighting of one candle from another—the flame is the same but the candles are different, distinct. Or to use a favorite illustration with those who seek to explain Causality, it is like the transference of force from one billiard ball to another. The force transmigrates about the table from one ball to another, determining the direction and speed of each in turn. The first ball does not pass over beyond its dead-point; it stops and yields its force to another. But it is just this speed, force, direction, momentum, i.e. its *Karma*, which is transmitted. This force, however, does not operate as mechanical determination, for we have intelligence, will, the power of choice. The dice may be cogged but not so completely as to invalidate human effort and responsibility. And the force, Karma, may in time be invalidated by another and a stronger force—by the force or momentum picked up along the Eightfold Path. This acquired force is, of course, also Karma, but a Karma of another kind. Thus we see the one essential of the Buddhist system, it is discipline, right effort according to right views. The Buddhist ideal is, there-

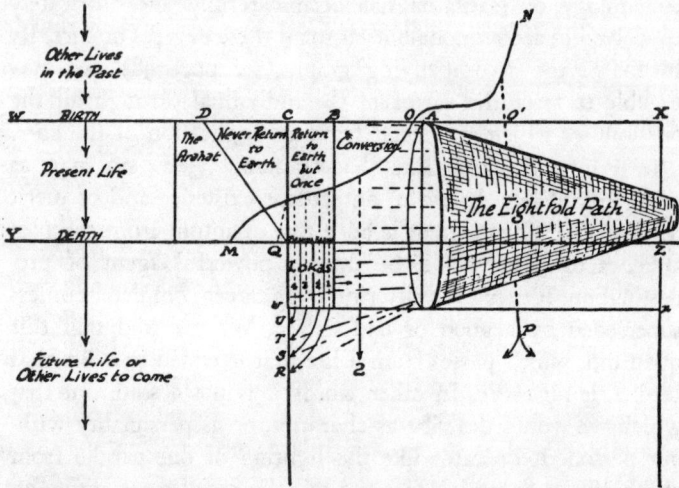

Line W to X separates past incarnations from the present life.

Line Y to Z separates present life from future incarnations if any.

Line w to x separates Buddhist heavens from reincarnations.

Line N to O or N to O' marks course of karma.

Line O' to P marks course of life uninfluenced by Eightfold Path of Buddha's system.

Lines O to M, O to Q, O to R, O to S, O to T, O to U, mark course of a life influenced by Eightfold Path of Buddha.

Beginning at O a convert may either live only as a convert, die, pass through the Lokas (Heavens) and return to earth at Q by rebirth; or he may cross the line B to the next stage leading to perfection,—the stage of those who return to earth but once. In the second stage he may seek only a limited degree of merit and, dying, pass through the Loka marked by the figure 1. Or he may according to merit enter any one of the other Lokas marked 2, 3, and 4. Thus he returns to earth by rebirth, but is, by his merit, determined to escape rebirth a second time. The last possibility is that he may cross the line C to enter the third stage; once here he is destined to cross the line D to Arahatship before he dies. Arriving at Arahatship his story ends at death,—beyond this Buddha chose not to think.

The Trumpet represents the Eightfold Path and the scope of its power.

fore, an ascetic and ethical one. Man must use the power that will deliver him from a force he has received at birth. "Man is born like a garden ready planted and sown." His task is to destroy the weeds and to cultivate the crop; also to replant it where it is too meager.

It is very difficult to see how there can be true transmigration, or rebirth, according to Gautama's system. If the Karma is handed over from one life to another, and these lives are not identical in any way, except in the single quality of character, where is the rebirth? The Karma is non-personal; it is not the soul and not the individual. The moving cause in the destiny of one life simply becomes the dominant moving cause in another life. It is merely this non-personal force of character which is handed over—which is reborn, if anything is reborn. Karma is thus inherited habit.

Coomaraswamy says: "Brahmanical schools avoid this difficulty by postulating an astral body, a material complex, not the Atman, serving as the vehicle of mind and character, and not disintegrated with the death of the physical body. In other words, we have a group, of body, soul, and spirit; where the two first are material, complex, and phenomenal, while the third is 'not so, not so.' That which transmigrates, and carries over karma from one life A to another life B, is the soul or subtle body (which the Vedanta entirely agrees with Gautama in defining as non-Atman). It is this subtle body which forms the basis of a new physical body, which it moulds upon itself, effecting as it were a spiritualistic 'materialization' which is maintained throughout life. The principle is the same wherever the individual is reborn, in heaven or purgatory or on earth." [18]

Gautama, if he is consistent, must be opposed to this view. In denying the survival of soul, the astral or subtle body, he would need to deny the survival of personality. But such seems

[18] *Buddha and The Gospel of Buddhism*, p. 109.

not to be the case, chiefly because according to Gautama's system personality is no thing, but an aggregate with a certain character, just as the parts of a chariot lead to the use of the word chariot. The karma is a character which supplies all the conditions which would cause us to use the word "personality," but the personality is no thing. It is this "no thing" which depends upon the karma, or character, for its being, which is perpetuated in all who have not attained Nirvana. It is therefore possible that the same "no thing" may reappear in the next birth just because the karma determines both the existence and the nature of the "no thing." In the attainment of Nirvana the evil karma is vitiated and with its disappearance goes that delusion which Gautama defines as soul, or personality.

It is clearly taught by Gautama that all who do not attain to Nirvana in this life will be reborn again somewhere, either on earth, or in other worlds or heavens. These heavens are of two great orders: the higher order is called the Brahma-lokas, which consist of two Planes, the Planes of Form, and the Planes of No-form. The Planes of No-form are composed of four heavens, free of sensuous desires and not conditioned by form. The Planes of Form contain sixteen heavens, free of sensuous desire but conditioned by form. The Kama-lokas, the Planes of sensuous desire are also grouped into two divisions: they are the six heavens which are to be secured by good works; and the five worlds of men, demons, ghosts, animals, and purgatory. In one division of the six heavens secured by good works it is said on the authority of the Payasi Sutta that the life of a person who reaches this place is thirty-six million years. If one were compelled to reach Nirvana by taking each of the heavens in turn and by proceeding thus through all the Kama and Brahma Planes, the process would be infinite. And yet, Gautama was reborn into this world from the heaven I have just described and reached Nirvana in one lifetime. If one is fortunate enough to return to earth after he passes a certain mark in a previous earthly life, he may reach Nirvana without any further return to earth.

Nirvana, the goal of the Buddhist discipline, is a state in which the fire of lust, of resentment, of glamour, of thirst for life, or Becoming, has been completely extinguished. The person seeking this salvation acts rightly and in accord with right views for the purpose of extinguishing the evil karma, which is the root of all becoming or transmigration. The salvation consists also of the suppression of the delusions of karma, especially the delusion of the "I," the individual. This is not a condition to be secured at death, but can be and is attained by the living. Coomaraswamy says: "The emancipation contemplated in early Buddhism is from *manna*, the conceit of self-reference, the Samkhyan ahamkara. Of him that has attained, we can truly say that nothing of himself is left in him." [19]

This is the summum bonum of Gautama's teaching. To one who has attained it, death can make no difference. There can be neither joy nor tragedy. As to a life after death, there is no positive teaching and no tendency to think upon the possibility. Gautama said: "I have not revealed that the Arahat exists after death, I have not revealed that he does not exist; I have not revealed that he at once exists and does not exist after death, nor that he neither exists nor does not exist after death. And why, Malunkyaputta, have I not revealed these things? Because, O Malunkyaputta, this is not edifying, nor connected with the essence of the norm, nor tend to turning the will, to the absence of passion, to cessation, rest, to the higher faculties, to supreme wisdom, nor to Nibbana; therefore have I not revealed it." [20]

Such is the explanation of Gautama's silence with regard to the future state of the Arahat. And yet the system would imply a future in a state of not-being. The Arahat is left ab-

---

[19] *Buddha and the Gospel of Buddhism*, p. 119.
[20] Majjhima Nikaya, Sutta 63.

sorbed in not-being. Gautama says that he has not revealed that the Arahat does not exist; but he precisely does not reveal that the Arahat does *not* not-exist. It is the individuation which is submerged. The thing thus submerged must be somewhere in the solution, or embracing medium, which is not-being. But all this is unprofitable speculation, for Gautama's purpose is a spiritual utilitarianism. When he has achieved the thing he sets out to do, he has no logical reason to go further. And besides, to think further would tend to frustrate the achievement he hopes to gain. One cannot dwell upon a future after death and at the same time gain a condition which is the negative of such a desire.

The person thus submerged has not lost his faculties, he has only come to the proper use of them. He sees things as they are. "To say of a Brother thus set free by insight—'He knows not, he sees not'—that were absurd." Thus the man, with all his powers of observation cleansed, sees all things as empty, void, as not-being. This is the position of mysticism in all lands and all ages of the world. Buddha has escaped from mortality—age, disease, death, sorrow, and the will to live—by negating it, or by submerging the individual in the Absolute, in not-being. And this position is, for all practical purposes, in no way to be distinguished from the Brahmanical result, "Not so, not so." If Gautama really knew nothing of the highest Vedantic thought, his system affords a strong support for the contention in some quarters that philosophies are a temperamental matter, a thing peculiar to certain types of mentality, and to be accounted for on the basis of one's nervous organization and health, as well as one's race.

This salvation is not for the mentally incompetent but for those gifted with the power of concentration and with sustained attention. Mrs. Rhys Davids says: "The mass of good average folk, going, with the patience and courage of all sane mortals, through stage after stage of green immaturity, through the joys and sorrows that have recurred and will recur so infinitely often, heaven and purgatory and earth itself await their future." [21] Only the man who has turned from the world to pursue the ascetic life has the time and the favorable condition which will enable him to engage in those contemplations which achieve Arahatship.

This goal is won directly by a discipline of attention and by an abstraction identical almost with the discipline which leads to the goal of all the mystics. The individual must force his mind to cease from self-willing and self-thinking. His imagination and senses must be insulated and stilled. The mystic seeks in this way to immerse his being in the One Reality, a state in which all differentia disappear and the finite self and all things become One, and that One such that the individual is supreme. It is the mental position in which the individual self loses all selfhood, yet is made all embracing, containing all things. The Arahat reaches the same position, but to him the self disappears in the infinite. In this position he sees things as they are: all distinctions, forms, shapes, things, worlds, individuals, are merged into No-thing, or a Void, which is all containing. This is also the Vedantist "Not so, not so."

The value of this position according to Gautama lies just in the fact that all distinctions, things, shapes, and individuals, together with the world and the gods, are changing. No aggregate exists but must separate, disappear, and with it must go the delusion which rests upon it. In fact, there is only the vastness of infinity beneath the passing world; and this vastness containing all, this great emptiness about which nothing can be affirmed, is the only abiding fact. Pure Being, then, both of the cosmos and of the individual, is the goal for the mystic as well as the Buddhist. The mental realization of this concept is Nirvana. The individual by this means escapes all changes, all delusions, all bitterness of sorrow, for he has

---

[21] C. A. F. Rhys Davids, *Buddhist Psychology*, quoted by Coomaraswamy, p. 127.

found the Unchanging, the Eternal, and in identifying himself with it has achieved enduring Peace.

Gautama knew, of course, that this salvation could not be
reached by all men in their present condition. He admitted
frankly that there are diversities of gifts, and he shaped his
system to meet the several abilities of men. Only certain
favored ones could in this incarnation attain to Arahatship,
but there were crumbs about his table for even the most lowly.
In other worlds to come conditions would be better. Through
continued faithfulness the most poorly endowed would be able
to build up such a momentum of favorable karma that
Arahatship would finally be secured. This, according to our
notion, is not a highly inviting redemption. We are too impatient for immediate results to see in a hope delayed thirty
five thousand years a ground for exultation. But such a faith
was able to secure a considerable following during Gautama's
lifetime, and, within a century after his death, was able to
compete with its opponents and rivals upon more than equal
terms.

That such an abstract faith, and one having so little to offer
of immediate blessing to the common man, should attract so
much attention from all classes is a strong indication that
there was ample need for religious reform. Surely no one can
doubt that the acceptance of Gautama's meager hope is proof
enough that the common people were not being reached by
the mendicants and Vedantist philosophers. The opposition
of Gautama to the Vedantists and Sankyas, an opposition not
warranted by careful examination of the three systems of
thought, would indicate that only a few had access to the
consolations of the prevailing philosophies. If a man of
Gautama's standing, a royal personage and heir-apparent,
could thus fail to know what the philosophers were about,
we can imagine how utterly without hope was the great mass
of the people. And while the chief motive for Gautama's
action in abandoning his home and in seeking enlightenment

is pictured as a purely personal one—his own great despair—
we may feel reasonably sure that the lot of his people weighed
heavily upon him.

Gautama of course reveals his limitations in both message
and method. He refused to accept the current belief in the
existence of the soul. On the other hand, he did accept the
popular belief in the transmigration, or rebirth, of all that
constitutes the delusion of personality. This latter position
was no doubt dictated by the very nature of the salvation he
advocated and by the simple-mindedness of the common
people. People who were unlettered and who had only average intellectual ability could not hope to command the saving
genius of the philosopher. If there was to be any help for
the common man he must be reborn into more favorable conditions, given a second chance under more propitious circumstances.

Here we encounter the weakness of Gautama's whole theology. Can a delusion ever be worth saving? And when we
have saved it by destroying the forces upon which its existence
depends, and have called into being a no less pronounced delusion through the assumption of favorable karma, just what
have we actually saved? Can a delusion which depends upon
unfavorable, or evil karma, ever be identified with a delusion
which depends for its existence upon a karma of righteousness? Is there not a cleavage here which amounts to the
severing of the thread of identity? In practice apparently not,
for the followers of Gautama speak of memories drawn from
a future existence, and by the same token one may reasonably
remember events of this present life when he has passed to
other worlds. But it does not appear to be rationally established
by the fundamental positions of the Buddha's teaching. Where
inchoateness, or lack of concatenation, exists, the imagination
always steps in; and here as in all such cases it is an imagination backed by previous training and superstitions. The gaps
are filled with Vedic and Vedantic notions, and that which

denies the existence of the soul is made practically to support it. Just what it is that abides and remembers from incarnation to incarnation is therefore very difficult to describe.

And as to method, Gautama adopts the institutionalism and disciplines which had prevailed from time immemorial. Here is nothing new, or as Oldenburg would say, "nothing to startle any one of that day" who was well acquainted with his India. The procedure of Gautama in giving his teaching to the world is not therefore to be regarded as any departure from the method of the religious leaders of his day. He selected the ascetic ideal and followed it with a singular devotion, appropriating all the disciplines in meditation, all the restrictions with which conventional institutionalism surrounded the members of the Brotherhood, and all the exclusiveness and apartness, both physical and mental, which characterized the holy men of his time. There is, then, in the régime of Gautama, no turnover of accepted social expression. The teaching may give place more freely to the spiritual life of the common people—all men may share to a degree its consolations—but, as heretofore, there is a premium upon the religious technique which has been in vogue for centuries.

This would seem to constitute a considerable limitation of both Gautama's originality and his capacity for actual service to the cause of the spiritual life. He is thus more contemporary than timeless, more Indian than universal. His gospel, as well as his conception of its social expression, is only another facet of the life of that spirit which is India. In a way this is no small limitation, for it deprives the individual of those horizons beyond the selected one; it excludes the rest of the map and shuts the soul up to those regions which the Indian had already so long inhabited. But we must never forget that Gautama in this way remains indigenous to the soil which produced him. He is introducing no foreign modes of thought, no hated innovations in manners and customs, no unfamiliar paths of destiny, and no great break with those values which the past centuries have refined. Gautama is not a tornado sweeping away all customs and institutions; he is a great, clean, vigorous wind blowing along the old road and bearing his people, all of them, to their own native uplands.

Naturally there will be little opposition to Gautama's preaching; it is too national, too conventional, and, for all his claim of originality, not so new in its discoveries. Opposition developed later, of course, which excluded Buddhism from India, but it grew out of political rivalries and the fact that the Buddhists were hostile to Vedantism where no logical antagonism ought to have existed. The zeal for its political dominance, and its illogical opposition to the highest Vedantic thought, put Buddhism in the position of appearing unjust and intolerant. Thus powerful enemies arose to seize the government and to persecute the Buddhists until they fled from the country. But, at first, there was only the heartiest of welcomes to attend the preaching of Gautama and his disciples.

This very correspondence between Buddhism and the existing institutions, modes of thought, and ethical and philosophical ideals, constituted in time a ground for attack. No doubt many Vedantists, actuated by jealousy, sought to minimize the whole Buddhist movement. The exclusive, esoteric group saw that it was losing its position of honor and influence; it came out of its shell and began to make a fight of it. It sought to show that Gautama had made no contribution superior to its own. In one way this was true; but in another it was not, for Gautama had at least adapted his thought and regimen so that there was something in the way of blessing for every one. To defend itself against this threat Buddhism developed those traditions and homilies which present Vedantism being overwhelmed by the superior mind and enlightenment of Gautama.

All this is very human, and just what we might expect from a situation in which Buddhism is supplanting Vedantism in the popular regard. It is too much to expect that the Vedantists will submit without a struggle. And we should realize that the Buddhists will attack Vedantism at its strongest point, however unfair the attack may seem, if only for the purpose of creating an issue and drawing the lines. The opposition to the Vedantic system would seem, therefore, not to have originated with Gautama himself, but with his later disciples who found it necessary to make a defense of the faith.

What Gautama's real attitude toward Vedantism was we can easily surmise both from the fact of his quest and the provisions of his teaching. The Vedantists had developed a salvation for the intellectuals and had nothing for any one outside of its circle of the elect. It advocated the doctrine of the "soul" which appeared to Gautama to be the chief factor in continuing the tragedy of mortality and misery. He perhaps had no real objection to the philosophical redemption which the elect secured—no doubt he regarded the saved condition thus attained good enough, if it could be attained. But he was opposed to the doctrine of the "soul" that quantum of being which could not be prevented from carrying over to the next life the whole force of karma intact. He felt that there must be a certain fluidity and plasticity at this point. Was it not there in the man? By analysis he found much to support his philosophical need, and much with which to oppose the Vedantists. He therefore denied the existence of the "soul" and formulated the regimen and the elaborate cosmology which enabled every man to escape, at some time, that delusion which intensified the power of evil karma.

It would seem, then, that Gautama's chief service lay not in discovering the saved state, but in devising a new means to secure it. The only practical difference between his saved state and that of the Vedantists was, after all, just a matter of getting there. Gautama destroyed the power of evil karma and allowed each person to sink without distinction or difference into the bosom of the Void. The Vedantists refined the soul until it merged without distinction or difference into the being of the Atman, the Self of all things. Here, manifestly, the two systems differ only in the names applied to the various stages of the process. To be sure, man ends in a Void, according to Gautama, and in unqualified Being, according to the Vedantists. But in either case the goal is the same—one of negation, of not-Being, for man. Perhaps the system of Gautama lends itself more readily to a lucid account of Change and Causality, principles which are everywhere apparent. This enabled him to make himself clear to the average man and to thus give his gospel a popular appeal.

It is always dangerous to attempt to name a single task as the work of any man; the social conditions in which his life is lived are too complex for that. And yet, some one achievement will stand out above all the others. In the life of Gautama we find no exception. He so interpreted man's nature that salvation was put within the reach of all men. It does not matter that philosophically and institutionally his salvation was not new. He found the people without hope. The interpretation of human nature then prevailing among Vedantists presented an interminable process to those who had not the intellectual endowment to achieve salvation in this life—and even that process was practically unknown to all except the Brahmans. Gautama has at least the merit of taking his way of life to the people; he gave hope where no hope was. And by doing this he was able to force a reform among the advocates of other religions. Both directly and indirectly, then, he was constructive.

His life after his enlightenment did not differ from that of the Wanderer. During the winter months and rainy season he would go into seclusion at some station and instruct his disciples. As soon as weather conditions would permit he would travel about from place to place, preaching to the people and establishing schools and centers for the Order which he had established. As a teacher and organizer he was very successful, and, in conflict with controversialists from other orders, proved himself to be a highly resourceful antagonist. His influence increased rapidly and, long before his death, grew to such proportions that his views were accepted throughout all northern India.

His success was due chiefly to the fact that it was given to him to live long enough to guide his disciples through those differences of opinion and doctrine which almost always beset the path of a new teaching. He lived long enough to become a legendary personage before his death, long enough to be able to correct the legend whenever it was on the point of going astray. He thus preserved the purity of his teachings and guaranteed that they would be accurately transmitted. He guided his disciples with safety and honor, preserved them from political entanglements, and, when he left them in his eightieth year, saw them a stable community. Had he been followed by a great leader at a later time there is little reason to doubt that Buddhism would have remained to this day the consolation of many millions in India. From events during his lifetime we know that Gautama would have steered clear of the ambitions which resulted in exiling his followers from India.

Thus closes the episode of Gautama. He began with the hope of securing for all men an enlightenment that would enable them to live with hope and courage in a world of illusion and pain. He achieved his purpose, becoming through his services the great leader of his race. Opinions differ as to the actual value of his contribution to religious thought, but, even if we can assign to him no new philosophical discovery and no original religious practice, we must admit his inestimable achievement in reawakening popular faith. In any complete story of the development of religion in India, he must be given a place of the foremost importance. And this must be granted because he forced the Brahmans to unlock the rich intellectual treasure-house which contained the store of Aryan genius, and contributed no little himself to its total wealth. Not even the fact that religion again lost its power to serve and gave sanction to the caste system and other social abuses can detract from his glory. It is a depressing fact that all religions become overlaid with formalism, lose their fire, and decay within and without. After so many centuries India would in all probability be very much as she is to-day. The prophets must keep coming if the world is to be saved and kept safe. It is the business of the great religious genius to lead his own generation into the light; it is the business of the rest of mankind to tap the springs of truth which will save their own. And by such a norm of judgment the labors of Gautama place him easily among the greatest of the prophets of mankind.

CHAPTER IV

ZOROASTER

The Aryan Indians and the Persians together compose the Indo-Iranian branch of the Aryan peoples. Zoroaster was a member of the Iranian division of this group and was therefore closely related to those tribes which made their way into India to set up the Aryan civilization which we have encountered in our study of Gautama. In language, cultural inheritance, religon, and blood the two peoples were very similar; but there were a number of differences, many of them of great significance for our purpose, which separated them. In some cases these items of demarcation are easily explained; they came naturally as the expression of growth, tribal consciousness, and seclusion, or lack of social intercourse. Others, however, can be accounted for only on the basis of strong antagonism. A proper interpretation of the significance of these antagonisms will therefore go far toward reconstructing some features of the lost history of both the Indians and the Iranians.

Zoroaster, as an Iranian, inherited the common background of the whole Indo-Iranian race, but that background with the peculiar modifications it received from the preferences and prejudices of his Iranian ancestors. He inherited the modes of thought, the practical and theological religious habits, and the tastes and temperament of his people. When he begins his labors there is no great overturning of Iranian life in any particular. He takes his people as he finds them and builds upon their beliefs and manner of life. We may, therefore re-

gard his work as an expansion in both thought and practice—
a logical and normal development—of religious history begun
we know not how long ago.

There can be little doubt that the Aryan peoples originated
somewhere in Central Asia. The first Fargard of the Vendidad
speaks of a good country, Aryana-Vaejo, which was created
by Ahura-Mazda (Ormazd) and made a garden of delight.
We are then told what happened to this good land: "The
evil being, Anra-Mainyu (Ahriman), full of death, created
a mighty serpent, and winter, the work of the Devas. Ten
months of winter are there, two months of summer. Seven
months of summer are (were?) there; five months of winter
were there. The latter are cold as to water, cold as to earth,
cold as to trees. There is the heart of winter; there all around
falls deep snow. There is the worst of evils." [1] J. F. Clarke [2] believes that this passage is intended to describe the ancient
home of the Aryan peoples and the result of those geological
convulsions which affected it. The climate of the good land
was changed from an almost tropical nature to one that meets
the conditions of central Siberia. Such a change would explain
many things, the migration of the Aryans southward, perhaps
the migration of the Lao peoples eastward, and the general
movement of the peoples of Aryan origin away from Central
Asia. Clarke says: "Thus in the very first verse of the Vendidad appears the affectionate recollection of these emigrant
races for their fatherland in Central Asia, and the Zoroastrian
faith in a creative and protective Providence. The awful con-
vulsion which turned their summer climate into the present
Siberian winter of ten months duration was part of a divine
plan. Old Iran would have been too attractive, and all mankind would have crowded into that Eden. So the evil Ahriman
was permitted to glide into it, a new serpent of destruction,

---

[1] Fargard I:3.   [2] *Ten Great Religions*, pp. 184, 185.

and its seven months of summer and five of winter were changed to ten of winter and two of summer." [2]

Clarke speaks of the *permission* operative in the case, but the religion of Iran conceives the two forces, Ormazd and Ahriman, as too evenly matched for events to happen by "permission." It is significant, however, that the Fargard mentions winter as the work of the devas. The devas are of course the gods of Aryans who settled in India. The gods of the Vedas, therefore, drove the Aryans out of their ancient home, Aryana-Vaejo, by means of winter. The Indians and the Iranians must, therefore, have set out southward together. But somewhere upon the road a disagreement arose which had far-reaching consequences. It separated the two peoples. It made the gods of the Indians the devils of the Iranians, and the gods of the Iranians the devils of the Vedic hymns.

How could all this come about? The "devas," as we have already learned in our study of Buddha, were the bright ones, and expressed themselves in the bright sun, clouds, stars, waters, and trees. The splendid semi-tropical country, Aryana-Vaejo, is well calculated to be the home of such divinities—they had made this good land. But what had changed the land from prevailing summer to almost endless winter? No doubt the two peoples were very greatly puzzled by the calamity. For a few years they would seek to remain in the land, hoping that next year, or the next, there would be a seed-time and a harvest. Then on the verge of starvation they would go out of the country in search of a new home, realizing that if there had been no other regions favorable for habitation all men would have pressed into Aryana-Vaejo. But they would not be likely to go out without much bitterness and complaining. This calamity was undoubtedly brought about by divine power. It did not seem reasonable that the gods would turn against them, but in what other way could it come?

---

[2] *Ibid.*, p. 185.

In each of the tribes there were priests who looked after the religious interests of the whole people. To these were referred all questions concerning the gods. During the days most adjacent to the calamity, confusion and perplexity would naturally be the prevailing mood of all men,—priests and laymen alike. Many conflicting answers would be given, and perhaps a number of views concerning the recent disaster would appear. At least two such opinions must have gained a considerable following among the priests, thus dividing the whole body of the priesthood into two parties. The priests, of course, at once divided the people, and the antagonisms thus originated, caused the Aryans, somewhere on the southward trek, to drift apart. The end of the matter was the division of the Aryans into the Indians and the Iranians; the gods of the one people became the devils of the other, and vice versa.

Whether or not this interpretation of the circumstances hinted at in the first Fargard be the right one, or whether some other must be substituted, we cannot know. But the fact of a common culture and religion behind the Indians and the Iranians, together with the strange opposition among the deities which we have noted, indicates that the two peoples parted over some natural holocaust which sorely tried their faith. One party naturally continued its loyalty to the "bright ones," even when everything was covered with snow; the other did not. The loyalists in religion made their way into India; the rebels turned southwest into Persia, or Iran. The more we ponder Clarke's interpretation the more we become convinced that the first Fargard itself contains more fact than fancy. There was a great national disaster of some kind; and there is no reason to doubt that it was just as it is pictured.

Nothing could more effectually divide a people in that age of the world than a quarrel over the nature of the gods. And it must have been very alarming to the Iranian party to find the Indian group worshiping as gods the authors of the national disaster. There would be a speedy separation and a considerable distance placed between the contending theologians. All the dramatic color and profound hate and fear of this momentous occasion have been suppressed in the Fargard under discussion, and nothing remains of them but the simple statement that the devas caused the change of climate in the old home of the race. It will, no doubt, be a happy time for all concerned when some other theological differences can be as completely buried.

But if the pantheon suffered among the Iranians a complete revision, or reversal, habits and customs were not changed with such ease. The people perpetuated their civil and social traditions. Many items of belief remained the same—the theory of man's nature, his religious obligations, his philosophical notions, and his whole set of ideals. These could not be changed except by a long period of teaching and practice. On the whole the Iranians remained just as they were and followed those ancient walks of life which made up the daily occupations of the people in old Iran. They had introduced only a new interpretation of their history and its causes by calling the deity by another name.

But the incident reveals a fact which is worthy of our attention. The gods of the Indians became, as we have noted, the demons of the Iranians. Have we here entered upon the threshold of an idea that may help us in clearing up the whole substance and point of the teaching of Zoroaster? Were the gods of the traitors, the oppressors, the enemy, always demons? If so we can put solid fact behind many of the statements of the Zoroastrian writers; we can transpose a confusing other-world expression into a mannerism, a literary vehicle, a way of describing actual history. And when we thus stand face to face with facts instead of fancies we can see the social significance of Zoroaster's work.

A great deal of information can be secured upon this point if we examine the profession of faith which was required of the Mazdayasnian convert. It shows us how firmly Zoroaster drew the lines, and, incidently, it contains materials which give cause for the firmness.

I curse the daevas. I confess myself a worshipper of Mazda, a follower of Zarathushtra, a foe of the daevas, a believer in Ahura, a praiser of the Amesha-Spentas. . . .
I believe in the good, holy Armaiti, may she abide with me. I forswear henceforth all robbing and stealing of cattle and the plundering and destruction of villages belonging to worshippers of Mazda.
To householders I promise that they may roam at will and abide unmolested wherever upon earth they may be dwelling with their herds. Humbly with uplifted hands to Asha I swear this. Nor will I hereafter bring plunder or destruction on the Mazdayasnian villages, not even to avenge life and limb. . . .
I confess myself a worshipper of Mazda, a follower of Zara-thushtra, professing and confessing the same. I profess good thoughts, good words, good deeds.
I profess the Mazdayasnian religion which, while girded with armor, resorts not to weapons, and the righteous marriage among kindred; which religion, as established by Ahura and Zarathush-tra, is the highest, best, and most excellent among those that are and are to be. . . . This is the profession of the Mazdayasnian religion.[4]

The firmness alluded to appears to arise from the fact that the old Aryan religion has greatly decayed and has lost sight of the obligations of justice and fair dealing. Aryans are plundering Aryans, driving off their cattle, destroying their villages on one pretense or another, and making impossible the existence of an agricultural society. Against these enemies of an advancing civilization Zoroaster aims his blows. His followers must keep the social and tribal lines intact, must sustain the wholesome, fair, and constructive type of mind and conduct, and must become the supporters of the house-hold type of society wherever it is to be found.

This condition against which Zoroaster arrays himself is not the original state of the Aryans. They were already the

---

[4] Yasna, A. V. W. Jackson's translation.

founders of villages and households. A study of comparative philology reveals the fact that all the Aryan languages contain words of similar formation for the various objects of the householder's manner of life. We may be sure, therefore, that this form of society was in existence before the several Aryan peoples were separated. The purpose of Zoroaster was, then, not an attempt to lift society from a nomadic or savage condition to the level of the household and the agricultural state, but an effort to preserve the ancient Aryan form of society from destruction at the hands of brigands and plunderers. He was so zealous in this undertaking that he required of all his followers a promise not to plunder or destroy Mazdayasnian villages "not even to avenge life and limb."

This promise reveals much regarding the state of insecurity then prevailing. Ayrans were plundering Aryans, but the followers of Zoroaster were not permitted to plunder their fellow religionists. That this requirement did not extend protection to the Aryans who worshiped other gods than Mazda is indicated by the first requirement, "I curse the daevas." The devas were the deities of the Indian branch of the Aryan peoples, the protectors, no doubt, of those Aryans who were plundering the Iranians. Further light on the situation is revealed in Chapter XXX of Yasna, verse 7. "The daevas," we are told, "also made not the right choice (between good and evil), for, as they were debating, folly overcame them, so that they chose the Worst Mind (ako-mano, opposed to vohu-mano). And they assembled in the house of violence (aeshma) to destroy the life of man" (i.e., they joined with the enemies of the Zarathustrians, the plunderers and destroyers of their settlements, farms, and cattle).[5] We do not require further evidence to prove that the Aryan-Indians were plundering the Iranians and appeared to be doing so under the protection of their devas. Undoubtedly the above quotation refers to the people under the name of their gods. Perhaps this situation

---

[5] *Arische Forschungen*, II, Bartholomae's translation.

may be the holocaust which turned the Iranians from the devas rather than the one recorded in the first Fargard. It is interesting to note, in any case, that the devas were not regarded as originally evil. They became evil through the evil choice they made.

If we remember that the Iranians were an intensely practical people, little given to the construction of a world of the imagination, we shall have no difficulty in seeing the fact behind the utterances of Zoroaster. He has seen the Indian Aryans, and perhaps some Iranian Aryans as well, join themselves to the Turanians that they might plunder the villages and settlements of the Iranians. With these peoples go their gods. Their deeds are indefensible, utterly evil in the sight of man and Ormazd. Such gods are no gods, but demons. Thus the whole of Zoroaster's authentic teaching is undoubtedly aimed at an actual historical situation which his words but thinly conceal, and which, in his own day, he did not conceal from any one.

This practical aspect of the prophet's work is revealed in the Avestan account of Zoroaster's temptation:

> From the region of the north, from the regions of the north, forth rushed Anra Mainyu, the deadly, the Demon of Demons. And thus howled the maleficent Anra Mainyu, the deadly: "O Fiend, rush on and kill him," O righteous Zarathushtra! The fiend rushed then along, the demon Buiti, the secret moving pestilence, the deceiver. . . .
> Up started Zarathushtra, forward stepped Zarathushtra, undaunted by Evil Thought, by the hardness of his malicious questions, and wielding stones in his hand, stones big as a house, having obtained them from Ahura Mazda, he the righteous Zarathushtra.
> Whereat in this broad, round earth, whose boundaries are far distant (asked the Demon), dost thou wield (these stones), thou who standest upon the high bank of the river Drej (Dareja), at the abode of Pourushaspa?"
> And Zarathushtra responded to Anra Mainyu: "O maleficent Anra Mainyu! I shall smite the Nasu (demon of Death), who is

created by the Demons. I shall smite the enchantress (Pairika Khnathaiti), until the Savior (Saoshyant), the Victorious shall be born from the waters of Kasava, from the region of the dawn, from the regions of the dawn."

Thereupon to him howled back Anra Mainyu, the Lord of Evil Creation: "Do not destroy my creatures, O righteous Zarathushtra! Thou art the son of Pourushaspa; I was worshipped by thy mother. Renounce the good religion of the worshippers of Mazda, so as to obtain a boon such as Vandaghana obtained, the rule of a nation."[6]

The reference to the prophet's mother is enough to show us how this passage is to be interpreted. Zoroaster is confronted with an actual earthly situation. His temptation comes from the fact that his proposed program of reform will oppose the religion of his mother. His mother had been born at Rhai,[7] probably in the vicinity of the modern Teheran. His father's house was on the bank of the Drej river (Dareja) in the region of Lake Urumiah. Following the principle of substituting the gods for the people, the Demon of Demons from the north is the Chief of the Aryan tribes to the north, or conceivably the Chief of the Aryan and Turanian confederacy, which has been plundering the Iranian settlements. This great chief sends an envoy to confer with the Prophet; the account says, to kill him. But Zoroaster meets this representative with such firmness and with such a following that the extreme measure cannot be carried out.

The ambassador of the Great King (Demon of Demons) haughtily demands of the prophet an explanation of his purposes: "Whereat in this broad, round earth, whose boundaries are far distant, dost thou propose to strike?" But Zoroaster is not to be overawed. He declares without the least hesitation that it is his chief aim to put an end to the raids, and that he will continue to labor until his people are victorious over their

---

[6] Vendidad 19:1-7.
[7] Cf. Jackson, Zoroaster—Prophet of Ancient Iran, p. 205.

enemies. Before such resolution the envoy decides upon a change of tactics. He points out that Zoroaster's mother was a worshiper of the devas, and, while the prophet is indeed the son of his father, it is not the part of a true son to attack his mother's people.

Apparently Zoroaster is impervious to the appeal to sentiment, and the ambassador of the Great King is compelled to try another plan. He decides to bribe the prophet to give up this undertaking which is sure to stir up Iran against the oppressor. "Renounce the good Religion of the worshipers of Mazda," he urges, "so as to obtain a boon such as Vadhaghana obtained, the rule of a nation." One of the liberators of Iran has already succumbed to the lure of wealth and power and has given up his mission. He has been bought at a great price; but the Great King of the north can easily pay traitors with territory which will be lost, in case the traitor should be true to his own nation and liberate it. The envoy mentions the present prosperity of Vadaghana and implies that the prophet shall have an equal reward if he will but remain silent.

But Zoroaster is of sterner stuff than Vadhaghana. "No!" he replies, "I shall not renounce the good Religion of the worshipers of Mazda, not though life, and limb, and soul should part asunder!" The king's representative wishes to know by what means Zoroaster will achieve his purpose. "By whose word wilt thou vanquish, by whose word wilt thou withstand, and by what weapon will the Iranian people oppose the Great King?" This is a very telling argument, for Zoroaster is alone except for an inconsiderable group of personal admirers. How can he hope to repel the harrying squadrons of the Great King's horse? What king will come to his relief? What trained soldiers can he muster to his defense? To this reminder of his helplessness Zoroaster replies that he will oppose his truth against his enemies. Truth is enough. It will be equal to any emergency.

The whole account is considerably overlaid with the religious phraseology and theological conceptions of a later time, but the main facts of the historical event are still visible under the veneer. The Great King realizes that Zoroaster will become a source of no little trouble to him. Perhaps the prophet has already succeeded in producing disturbances that the king cannot afford to ignore. He therefore goes to the source of the trouble, the teacher himself. He instructs his envoy to use every means to win the prophet, and, failing in this, to put him to death. Evidently the ambassador fails to do either.

But it is just as clear that it is unsafe for Zoroaster to remain in his native province. He has thrown down the gauge of battle and he knows that the Great King will have him assassinated sooner or later. He decides therefore, in the interests of personal safety and the success of his mission, to leave the West. And herein we have an explanation of the situation that has so long puzzled the student of Zoroaster's career. A considerable amount of evidence shows that Zoroaster was born in the West, and some writers have sought to maintain that his life work was prosecuted there. There is also no small amount of tradition which states that his chief work was done in the East (in Bactria, in modern Khorassan). The two bodies of tradition have been blindly weighed against each other when it is abundantly clear from the account of the prophet's temptation that he could not possibly have continued in the West. He had defied the Great King, rejecting all overtures toward a practical understanding between the two. The only possible course for the prophet to pursue is to find a new field for his activities.

Zoroaster now goes into hiding with his disciples, none of whom has as yet fully accepted his teaching. But success is not far off. The manner in which he withstood the threats and bribes of the Great King has attracted the attention of all true Iranians, no matter how feeble their own resolution. They flock to him in his places of concealment and hear him gladly and with great respect. Finally his own cousin, Maidhyoi-maonha, is converted. This important event takes place "in the forest of reedy hollows, which is the haunt of swine of the wild-boar species." [8] Why was this wild region the scene of Zoroaster's ministry? The nature of the Temptation will account for it; the prophet is a fugitive, a political exile in the wilds of his own country, an outlaw hiding from the authorities.

This condition is not conducive to the rapid growth of the new order which the prophet is seeking to establish. It is now clear that he may in time win the West; but there is Bactria, or the provinces to the east which later became Bactria. He must seek to win it also if he would present a united Iranian front to the combined Confederacy of Aryans and Turanians. He becomes a wanderer and transfers his activities to the East. He goes to the court of Vishtaspa, a ruler who is "in the toils of evil religious influence and fettered by the false belief that was rife in the land." A. V. Williams Jackson says: "Iran, or the court of Vishtasp, is dominated by scheming and unscrupulous priests, the Kigs and Karaps, or Kavis and Karpans of the Avesta. Especially powerful among these is one Zak—a name that seems to occur only in the Dinkart, and his ill reputation has destined him otherwise to oblivion." [9] At the court of Vishtaspa Zoroaster encounters the antagonism and persecution of this group and is through its plotting cast into prison.

The plan the priests used to bring about his arrest finally became the very means to his liberation. They bribed the porter of his lodging and "concealed in his room the hair, nails, and heads of cats and dogs, together with other objects of witchcraft and sorcery." [10] On this evidence they were able to convict the prophet of being a wizard and necromancer. Shortly afterward the king's black horse, his

---

[8] Selections of Zat-sparam 23:8 from *Sacred Books of The East.*
[9] *Zoroaster—The Prophet of Iran,* p. 57.
[10] *Ibid.,* p. 62.

favorite charger, became ill and was unable to stand upon its feet. In his cell Zoroaster learned what had happened— very probably because the king wished him to hear of it. The prophet declared that he would restore the horse upon the fulfilment of certain specific conditions. The king pledged himself to fulfill them and the horse was completely cured.

This account is also dressed up in all the superstition and magic of the later phase of Zoroastrianism. A great deal of hocus-pocus therefore attends the healing, but in the main the conditions are practical enough. Vishtaspa must become a convert to the prophet's teaching; Isfendiar, the king's son, must lead a crusade in defense of the true faith; the prophet is to be given the privilege of converting the queen, and the culprits who bribed Zoroaster's doorkeeper and secured his arrest and imprisonment must be discovered and punished. In view of the dangerous position in which the prophet finds himself, there is nothing inconsistent about any of his exactions. He has already had one encounter with the Great King's envoys and he knows quite well that there will be another. If Vishtaspa accepts the faith, he will be called upon to fight for his convictions.

The real force of Zoroaster's conditions is plain enough when we study the events which immediately follow the conversion of Vishtaspa. The Dinkart says: "For the sake of daily and visibly showing to Vishtasp the certified victory over Arjasp and the Khyons, and his own superior position, unceasing rule, splendor, and glory, the creator Auharmazd sends, at the same time, the angel Neryosang to the abode of Vishtasp, as a reminder for the archangel Ashavahishto to give to Vishtasp, to drink of that fountain of life, for looking into the existence of the spirits, the enlightening food by means of which great glory and beauty are seen by Vishtasp." [11] Vishtaspa is at this moment a subject prince ruling

---

[11] Dinkart 7.4.84.

under Arjasp, the probable Demon of Demons in the north. His conversion amounts to treason against his sovereign. The account reads as if he were so uneasy about the step he has taken that he required daily instruction by the prophet to steady his conviction and to regale him with the prospect of national independence. The rest—the angels and the archangels—are the product of a later age.

Outwardly at least there was no break with the Turanian overlord. The king Vishtaspa continued to send in his tribute and to maintain a semblance of obedience to his master. Meanwhile, under royal influence conversions were the order of the day. Thousands flocked into the ranks of the faithful. Practically all the territory ruled by Vishtaspa was at least nominally brought under the new religion. In addition to the widespread growth of Zoroastrianism in Iran a number of the Turanians became believers. One of these, Isvant, son of Varaza, is styled "Isvant, son of Varaz, from the countries of Turan, 'who shall officiate at the final resurrection.' " [12] Fryana of Turan is mentioned as "This man who among men did propitiate Spitima Zarathushtra by his generosity." [13] According to certain traditions, the teachings of the prophet made a profound impression among the Hindus. One of these, Cangranghacah, a famous philosopher and teacher of Jamasp, minister to King Vishtaspa, wrote a letter to the king remonstrating with the monarch for accepting the teachings of the upstart Zoroaster. Vishtaspa invited Cangranghacah to visit "Balkh" and to debate with Zoroaster.[14] Of course the Hindu was defeated in the argumentation and became a disciple, one who actually carried the prophet's teachings to India.

There can be little doubt that Zoroaster or some of his followers made missionary journeys to foreign lands and throughout all the territory of Iran. Nothing definite can be

---

[12] *Ibid.*, 9.33.5.
[13] Yasna 46.12.
[14] Anquetil du Perron—Zend-Avesta i. Pt. 2, pp. 47sq.

stated regarding this work other than to say that within a reasonably short period Zoroaster felt himself strong enough to openly oppose the sovereignty of Arjasp, the Turanian. This confidence came from two things: first, all Iran was practically united under one faith. Second a number of crusades conducted against the most stubborn portions of the Iranians and the conversion of these regions by the sword had given Vishtaspa a considerable army of trained men. As we have already seen, national independence and freedom from tribute, from lawlessness, and from plunderers, was always the social part of the prophet's mission. It was inevitable that he should strike at the Turanian conquerors just as soon as he felt himself able to do so.

If the account of the temptation and the story of the outbreak of the so-called Holy Wars are reliable, we have abundant proof of the fact that the prophet could work and wait. He gave ten years to preparation and teaching before he secured a single convert. Then, just as it began to appear that he might be successful, the authorities waited upon him to threaten him, thus making it unsafe for him to teach openly. For the next two years he was probably a fugitive in his own country. In the depths of the wild forest regions he gathered about him the most daring men of his province and taught them. Among these was his cousin, who was his first convert. The apparent hopelessness of this type of labor caused the prophet to migrate to the East and to make a new beginning at the court of King Vishtaspa. After meeting with many oppositions and dangers he succeeded in winning the king. Then followed seventeen years of missionary work at home and abroad. Throughout all this period of perhaps twenty years, he was very careful not to enter into open conflict with the Turanian authorities. Zoroaster is as much to be admired for his later quiet tenacity and diplomacy as for his youthful boldness against the envoy who sought to bribe and intimidate him.

We are told that the real cause of the war is to be "found in Vishtaspa's refusal to continue the payment of the tribute to Arjasp and in the latter's consequent and persistent pressing of his demand." A. V. W. Jackson continues: "So much for the pretense. The actual ground for difficulty, however, seems to have been the religious difference; for Vishtasp's adoption of the new Faith really lies at the basis of the trouble. The religious question is certainly mixed up with the tribute matter. Perhaps one could hardly expect the two to be separated. The affair of the tribute is recorded in the Pahlavi Dinkart as well as the Shah Namah. On the other hand, the Yatkar-i-Zariran makes the religious issue the main one. In the Shah Namah, when the question comes up, Zoroaster appears practically in the position of a cardinal vested with regal power and wielding a vigorous hand in matters of state. He urges Gushtasp (Vishtaspa) absolutely to refuse payment of the tax. The great priest's personal interest in the political situation and the problem to be settled is evidently largely governed by religious motives; Arjasp, it is known, had declined to accept the true Faith." [15]

As a matter of fact, there has never been for Zoroaster any separation of the religious and civil question. In his own mind righteousness must operate from top to bottom of the social structure. From the first he has seen clearly that there can never be any social justice for the Iranians under Turanian rule. His people have been robbed, slain, and plundered. Whole villages have been burned by marauders from Turan. The only way to relief is through national independence, in a trust in the justice of Heaven and in the right arm of every Iranian warrior. The only reason there has been no opposition to the payment of tribute before this is to be explained by the fact that Zoroaster wished to make sure that he would be strong enough to meet the enemy.

---

[15] *Zoroaster—Prophet of Iran*, p. 106.

Nor was the real cause of the trouble unknown to Arjasp. The Dinkart says: "When Vishtasp, accepting the religion, praises righteousness, the demons in hell are disabled; and the demon Aeshm rushes to the country of the Khyons and to Arjasp, the deadly one of the Khyons, because he was the mightiest of tyrants at that time; and the most hideous of all, of so many of them in the country of the Khyons, are poured out for war." [16] Zoroaster by his success with King Vishtaspa has no doubt aroused the jealousy of some priest or official who has turned traitor and has hurried to the court of Arjasp to report all that has taken place. In this way the traitor hopes to accomplish the overthrow of Zoroaster and secure his own return to power. Arjasp accordingly sends Vishtaspa an ultimatum. Vishtaspa must abandon the new faith or be prepared to have his country (Iran) invaded within two months. Two envoys bore this letter to Vishtaspa and, when it was read, its insolence so moved Vishtaspa's warlike brother Zarir that he stepped forward and hurled defiance at Arjasp's messengers. He dictated a letter which the king approved, and war was at once declared.

The prophet was not wrong in believing that Iran now possessed a feeling of nationality and a sense of social worth which would make her sons invincible warriors. He had carefully superintended the formation of this great ideal, for he had spent almost ten years in giving it birth in his own mind. He had done all in his power to give it currency among the people. He had been outlawed, exiled, and persecuted for it; but he had known from the beginning that it was the highest social and moral level to which his nation could attain. And he had felt in his own heart that it was the deepest interpretation of the aspirations of the Iranian soul. In twenty years he had watched the spread of his truth throughout the land and had seen that, no matter by what means conversions

---

[16] Dinkart 7.4.87.

had taken place, it had produced lasting results. He knew better than any one else when his teaching had become an integral part of the nation's very existence. And as he saw the splendid divisions of the army of Vishtaspa march by to engage the hosts of Arjasp, he must have felt that, in very truth, he was a man of destiny, a prophet of the Lord.

In the battle which followed, the first of this war, the leaders fought bravely and so inspired their men that the engagement, though threatening to prove a disaster to the forces of Iran, turned out with honors practically even on both sides. This result was actually a moral victory for the Iranians, for they had been for long tributaries of the Turanians. To withstand such a fierce foe and to come off so well, filled every one with enthusiasm. The tide of this first battle was turned by the personal courage of Garami, the son of the prime minister and chief counselor of Vishtaspa. In the most critical moment of the battle he rescued the Iranian standard from the hands of the enemy by an act that inspired his countrymen to redoubled effort. With the imperial banner held in his teeth he continued to fight until he fell.

The second trial of strength was just as glorious for Iran. Her nobles would not be turned back, but fought until they drove the enemy before them or died in the attempt. In this battle Zarir, whose reply to the envoys of Arjasp had begun the war, was the principal hero. The *Yatkar-i Zariran* describes the part he took in this battle: "The dashing leader Zarir began the fight as fiercely as when the god of Fire bursts into a hay-rick and is impelled onward by a blast of the storm. Each time as he struck his sword down, he killed ten Khyons; and, as he drew it back, he slew eleven. When hungry and thirsty, he needed only to look upon the blood of the Khyons and he became refreshed." Zarir was no doubt much less miraculous in his blows than this account records and far more the shrewd and gallant general. That he was careless of his personal safety is proved by the fact that he was killed by an enemy from behind. With a few followers he had perhaps dashed far into the enemy's lines. When he had fallen, his youthful son, Bastvar, almost a child in years but a stalwart man in strength and courage, put himself at the head of his father's command. Accompanied by Isfendiar, his uncle, he killed the man who slew his father and sent Arjasp in defeat and humiliation back to his capital.

A stipulation in favor of the new religion of Iran was imposed as a part of the terms of peace. Vishtaspa marched back to Balkh to celebrate his victory and to plan a number of crusades into foreign countries on behalf of Zoroastrianism. Isfendiar as Crusader was everywhere highly successful. Many nations hastened to send envoys and to request that they be given a copy of the teachings of the prophet. It is apparent, of course, that such eagerness was only simulated, a matter of good diplomacy, for it would avert an invasion of their country by the Iranians. But the fact that ambassadors from various countries were sent to the court of Vishtaspa shows what the teachings of the prophet had done for a harassed and tributary people. After only a little over twenty years of labor he had quietly undergirded them and made them into a conquering world power, one feared and respected by all the surrounding nations.

There is now a considerable period of peace, perhaps twenty years, and Vishtaspa is free to carry on his missionary crusades among the nations. Isfendiar is given one of his sisters in marriage and is promised the throne as soon as his conquests have been completed. In due time the hero returns to the capital expecting to receive the promised throne. But his brother has been plying the king with lies until he distrusts Isfendiar so that he has him immediately imprisoned in a fortress on Mount Spendtodata in Khorassan. During the next two years Vishtaspa leaves his capital and visits Rustam in Seistan and Zabulistan. While he is away affairs begin to assume a different aspect in Iran. Arjasp takes advantage of his absence from his kingdom to collect an army for the purpose of retaliation upon his conqueror. Isfendiar, the only great general among the Iranians, is in prison and his genius cannot be opposed to Arjasp. It is just the situation most favorable to the possible success of the Turanians. Vishtaspa's absence from the capital leaves it weakened, or unprotected. The city is stormed; the aged general, Lohrasp, falls in battle; the temple is destroyed; and Zoroaster is slain. One account says that a Turanian soldier entered the prophet's oratory and struck him down with a sword. News of this disaster was carried to Vishtaspa in Seistan. The king of Iran hastened to join forces with his son, Farshidvard, who had been made Suzerain of Khorassan. Thus reënforced, he hastened toward Balkh to meet the armies of Arjasp.

In the battle which follows Farshidvard is slain, and Vishtaspa is routed and forced to seek refuge in the mountains. The Iranians are besieged and all seems lost, when Jamasp decides to seek the help of Isfendiar. He secretly visits the imprisoned leader and prevails upon him to forget his wrongs and to do all he can to bring about the defeat of Arjasp. Isfendiar promises to lead the army and hastens to take complete command. Under his inspiring presence the battle terminates victoriously for Iran. Arjasp flees to Turan; but this time his country is invaded, his capital is stormed and taken, and he himself is slain. The Zoroastrian faith is now everywhere triumphant, even though the prophet has not lived to see it.

II

But what of the teachings which achieved this result? A study of the great social and national reformations in history will show that they spring from a body of truth which has behind it the voice, or character, of deity—to speak philosophically, truth which is metaphysically founded. Nothing short of this can claim the loyalty of thinking men, for such men will not lay down their lives for a chimera. Zoroaster succeeded because he was intuitively wise enough to obey this principle. He did not, of course, consciously ferret out this fact about human nature and build his message accordingly; he did not need to do that. Already certain fundamental ideas of religion and of life were well established—especially this one: truth to be truth must have its source in deity, in the created order of this world. Zoroaster's good sense told him that this was the true road to social achievement.

And as we shall see hereafter in our study of the great saviors of the race, he had to observe the true worth of all the religious development which had gone before. Religions are never created outright; never do the reformers completely overturn the altars of the people. A reformation could not possibly succeed if it undertook to do that. It is therefore interesting to see just how the Prophet of Iran squared with the religious convictions of his people on the one hand, and with the metaphysical necessities on the other, and yet at the same time developed a successful social corrective, one that met adequately the social problems of the Iranians. On all sides—religiously, philosophically, and socially—he was sound.

As we have already observed, a schism had developed between the Iranians and the other Aryans. And we may be sure that it was of comparatively long standing. It is just possible, of course, that the division in question grew out of the antagonisms of this troubled period, but the probabilities are somewhat against it. Religious differences probably dictated the hostilities, for peoples of the same faith seldom turn against each other. The schism, therefore, probably occurred where Clarke placed it, at a time before the separation of the Iranians and the Indians. Some of the Aryans outside of India continued to champion the older racial theology and came thus into conflict with the Iranians. The raids which these worshipers of the devas conducted against their kinsmen, the

Iranians, served to widen the breach. Zoroaster did not leave his people under the stigma of the thought that they were traitors and corrupters of their ancient religion, a charge that is very frequently hurled at religious reformers by the conservatives; he so grounded his views that the Iranian policy of secession—if indeed they were the seceders—became justified as the inevitable step in a divine plan. He thus rescued his people from any self-blame for the schism, and made them proud of their doctrinal position.

He did this by declaring that there were two orders existing simultaneously and in direct opposition the one to the other. The strife between Aryans, which was so much in evidence and which must have been a source of secret shame before the nations, was not a light matter, something on the surface and which ought to be and could be easily removed. It was in the very nature of things that this difference should arise. It grew out of the fact that from the beginning two almost equally powerful gods had entered the lists against each other. The Aryan situation was therefore the reflection of the celestial or spiritual warfare. It was not altogether a preventable matter and one arising only from Aryan perversity; it was foreordained, and would exist until the better God should win against his opponent and set all things right.

It is interesting to note also how cleverly Zoroaster goes back to that ancient debate to put his own people in the right and his enemies in the wrong, to see how he grounds human responsibility and establishes the necessity for Iranian coöperation with the God of Right against the Champion of Evil. He says that the devas *chose* their evil ways. And since it was, perhaps, a matter of history that the Iranians had chosen Ahura-Mazda as their God, this statement implies that the prophet's people had just cause to be proud of their own choice. They have selected the Good and were on the side of Right.

But the warfare between the two divine Forces is everywhere apparent from top to bottom of the Universe. There is growth and decay, life and death, darkness and light, good deeds and evil deeds—all in practically equal proportion. The whole army of the Right must battle this strong enemy which is seeking to overcome the world and to subject it to the power of Evil. Thus the wrongs of the Iranians which have resulted in so much suffering and sorrow have come from this warfare. Shall the Iranians submit without a struggle? Shall they now desert their God when He is most sorely pressed, when so many of the Aryans have gone over to the enemy? Shall Iran continue stupidly under the yoke of the foe when it is in her power to hasten the final triumph of Ahura-Mazda?

It is almost impossible to present adequately the social reaction from such a gospel unless we review in detail all the triumphs of Iran. The national cause is transported from one weakened by self-accusation to one which is marked by a sense of self-respect and righteousness. The people are therefore set free of the stigma of divine condemnation for their supposed apostasy toward the devas, and appear in the light of true champions of the God of Right. Their present miseries are not, therefore, to be thought of as coming from punitive measures on the part of the gods, but only from their own ignorance and lack of loyalty. The battle is not lost as yet, however. If Iran will awake, gird herself, trust in Ahura-Mazda, and fight bravely, she will be able to turn the tide and change the whole character of the Universe. Perhaps at no other time in all the history of the world has a gospel been conceived which could put so much divine power in the right arm of the warrior. Every stroke of a sword in the hands of an Iranian was a divine blow for a divine end. The foes of Iran could not hope to subjugate this people or keep it in bondage until they had slain the last man to hold this faith.

The literature of Zoroastrianism may seem to us to be artificially elaborate, and almost silly in its miraculous claims, but we may be very sure that such simplicity was not the essence of the message of the Prophet. His thoughts burned their way into the heart, for his words were a flame of fire. Through the medium of popular beliefs he poured the white-hot metal of a new sword of the spirit. And we may be very sure that behind the obscure popular religious terminology that sword was gleaming in all its glorious length and arousing Iran to the pitch of frenzy. The prophet's real message was not the desiccated web which we possess to-day, but a living faith bravely conceived and boldly declared. Only when we read this literature discerningly do we catch an authentic breath of his spirit and feel a little of that thrill which shook all Iran to its core and toppled emperors from their thrones. No subject people has ever suddenly swept away its oppressors when fed exclusively upon philosophical speculations and theological elaborations. There must be conviction to produce new men and a new national spirit. And we shall not find the secret of this reform until we realize that all reformations follow the law of contagion and are communicated from man to man. We must look, therefore, for the living firebrand behind the rather tame Zoroastrian documents if we are to discover the cause of all that took place in Iran.

Clark in delineating the spirit of Zoroaster erroneously makes him contemporary with the cataclysm of nature which we have already discussed: "Amid these terrible convulsions of the air and ground, these antagonisms of outward good and evil, Zoroaster developed his belief in the dualism of all things. To his mind, as to that of the Hebrew poet, God had placed all things against each other two and two. No Pantheistic optimism, like that of India, could satisfy his thought. He could not say, 'Whatever is, is right'; some things seemed fatally wrong. The world was a scene of war, not of peace and rest. Life to the good man was not sleep, but battle. If there was a good God over all, as he devoutly believed, there was also a spirit of evil, of awful power, to whom we were not to yield, but with whom we should do battle. In the far distance he saw the triumph of good; but that triumph could only come by fighting the good fight now. But his weapons were not carnal. 'Pure thought' going out into 'true words' and resulting in 'right actions'; this was the whole duty of man." [17]

We shall go astray regarding both the spirit of Zoroaster and the force which liberated Iran if we look upon the teachings of the prophet, as favoring a conquest by the magic of passive worth and placid self-assurance. He precisely does not depend upon pure thoughts, true words, harmless actions. The celestial and the terrestrial are one with him—Ahura-Mazda clothed himself with this world which he himself had made. Here all the battle must be fought and the sword in the hand of the man who has chosen good is not an evil but a powerful constructive force for righteousness, if he fight bravely. We must not forget that Zoroaster advocated the crusade as a means of spreading the faith.

There could, therefore, scarcely be a greater contrast between the words such a leader must have spoken and the religious books which are derived from his teachings. Clark says: "If, in taking up the Zend Avesta, we expect to find a system of theology or philosophy, we shall be disappointed. It is a liturgy—a collection of hymns, prayers, invocations, thanksgivings. It contains prayers to multitudes of deities, among whom Ormadz is always counted supreme, and the rest only his servants." [18] And we shall be equally disappointed if we seek for public addresses which must have had a pronounced place in Zoroaster's ministry. Much that we find is indeed the product of a later time and has thus been gratuitously supplied, but these supplements never attain the hortatory excellence of those orations which the Babylonian

Jews put into the mouth of Moses.[19] And yet there can be little doubt that both Zoroaster and Moses were orators of no mean ability and spoke with such force as to electrify their peoples.

The prophet's most significant public address occurs in the Avesta in Chapter XXX of Yasna:

> Now shall I proclaim unto you, O ye all that here approach me, what the wise should lay to heart; the songs of praise and the sacrificial rites which pious men pay the Lord (Ahura), and the sacred truths and ordinances, that what was secret until now may appear in the light.
>
> Hear with your ears that which is best, and test it with clear understanding, before each man decides for himself between the two teachings. . . .
>
> The two Spirits, the Twins, skilfully created, in the beginning, Good and Evil, in thought, in speech, and in deed. And between these two, the wise have made the right choice; not so the senseless.
>
> And when these two spirits had agreed to institute the springing up and the passing away of all things, and to decree that in the end the lot of the followers of Lie should receive the worst life, and that the followers of Truth should have the happiest mental state. . . .
>
> Then of these two Spirits the lying one elected to do evil, while the holiest Spirit (Spenta-Mainyu), he who is clothed with the solid heavens as with a robe, elected the Right (asha), and with him all those who wish to do right in the eyes of Ahura-Mazda.
>
> And to his side came with Khshathra, Vohu-mano and Asha, and Aramaiti the eternal, who made the earth her body. In these mayest thou outdo all others in wealth.
>
> The daevas also made not the right choice, for as they were debating, folly overcame them, so that they chose the Worst Mind. And they assembled in the house of violence to destroy the life of man;
>
> But when the vengeance comes for their deeds of violence, then O Ahura-Mazda, surely the sovereignty will be given by thy

---

[19] Cf. Deuteronomy i-iv, v-xxx, xxxii.

good mind to those who will have helped truth to overcome Lie.

Therefore will we belong to those who are in time to lead this life on to perfection. Grant us then, O Mazda, and ye gods, your assistance, and thou also, O Asha, that every man may be enlightened whose understanding, as yet, judges falsely.

For then the blow of destruction shall fall on the liar, while those who keep the good teaching will assemble unhindered in the beauteous abode of Vohu-mano, Mazda, and Asha.

If, O men, you lay to your hearts these ordinances which Mazda instituted, and the good and the evil, and the long torments which await the followers of falsehood, and the bliss that must come to the holders of the true teaching, it will go well with you.[20]

This address begins with an appeal for attention that those who hear may be able to understand the nature of the two teachings and may be able to judge for themselves as to the merit of each. It has been suggested that this address may have been delivered at the court of king Vishtaspa upon the occasion of the defeat of the ruling priests and the cure of the king's favorite steed. If this surmise be correct the teachings of Zoroaster must represent a considerable advance upon the religion then in power. And if, as often happens, the ancient religion succeeded in injecting into the new teaching a considerable portion of its own doctrine at a later time, we have here perhaps the simplest statement of the prophet's real gospel. It is clear in any event that Zoroaster means to rid the people of the lying teaching of the Karpans or court-priests. And as time passes and progress is slow, we hear him exclaim in a moment of near despair: "When, O Mazda, shall the men of perfect mind come? And when shall they drive from hence this polluted drunken joy whereby the Karpans with angry zeal would crush us, and by whose inspiration the tyrants of the provinces hold their evil rule." [21]

---

[20] Bartholomae's translation in *Arische Forschungen*, II.
[21] Yasna 48.10.

The details which the address omits are here somewhat supplied. The Karpans, as the tools of the tyrants in all the provinces, have turned the use of the sacred haoma, an intoxicating beverage, into a means of corrupting and destroying the people. Conditions of life are hard, and no doubt many prefer to drown their sorrows in this popular religious practice. The result is poverty, degradation, tyranny, and the loss of healthful energy. It would appear that Zoroaster is a strong advocate of temperance and a foe to the priests who are hand in glove with corrupt officials and tyrants in perpetuating the traffic.

The reference in the address to the two Spirits, the good and the evil, and the statement that the devas made not the right choice, very probably is another thrust at the court-religion. This view is strengthened when we remember the state of the government. All Iran with her many provinces and petty tyrants is but a tributary of the king of Turan. And what is more natural than that the several courts of the tyrants should imitate the religious and social life of the court of their sovereign? This would introduce many foreign elements into the native religion, if, indeed, it did not transplant a foreign religion to become the court religion of each province.

Here again we are face to face with the old question: Did Zoroaster introduce the teaching which created a schism in the old Aryan religion, or was it already in existence previous to this time? If Zoroaster brought it about, the native Aryan priests, the representatives of the ancient religion, had chosen to make terms with the conquerors and had introduced those innovations which had corrupted the ancient faith. Furthermore, they had given themselves body and soul to the support of the tyrants and were no longer the spiritual guides of the Iranian people. If the schism already existed there has been an attempt to root out the views of Iran. At each court priests have been brought in to minister who are advocates of the ancient faith in its pre-schismatic character. These men are more anxious to further the interests of Turan and the tyrants than to serve the Iranians. No matter which view we take regarding the origin of the schism, the results for Iran are practically the same. Zoroaster is opposed to this foreign interference in matters of faith. And when he becomes the dominant influence at the court of Vishtaspa, the Karpans report to Arjasp in Turan with the result that the Turanian monarch demands that Vishtaspa give up his faith and return to the Karpans.

Zoroaster speaks of the violence of the Karpans in his address and declares that there will be a day of vengeance. In that day the sovereignty will be given to those who will have helped the truth to overcome the false régime of the Karpans. There can be no mistaking the real object of the prophet from these words. He has come to set his people free of their oppressors. He has come to preach temperance, sanity, righteousness, spirituality, faith in the good God, and the duty of every man to be frugal, industrious, right-minded, constructive, brave, and the foe of the oppressor. In other words, he has come to regenerate his people and to give them the strength to overcome evil with good. And he does not hesitate to point out that all the woes of his nation originate in the fact that it is subject to Turan.

It is worth noting, finally, that from this one address we learn that the prophet is an eloquent and pious man. Religion has seldom had a more powerful advocate. Suddenly, in the climactic moments of his oratory, the speaker turns from his audience to address the deity in a prayerful appeal for the triumph of the cause. It is apparent at once that such an oratorical device would be worse than useless unless the God appealed to were native to this people. These prayers interspersed within the oration are therefore the most conclusive proof that Ahura-Mazda is no god unknown to the Iranians until Zoroaster appears upon the scene. The prophet is making an appeal to his nation to return to its native faith and institutions. Thus his teaching, for all its novelty, is Iranian to the core. And with his gifts of personal charm, his eloquence, his lucid utterance, his sincere piety, and his downright courage, he creates a profound impression among those who hear him. It is small wonder that the Turanians hunted him out of his native province and dogged his steps wherever he went, for he was raising up a powerful foe in Iran.

As to the two Spirits which were coexistent from the beginning, it is apparent that Zoroaster is establishing from all eternity the main features of the schism which has divided the Aryan peoples. Anra-Mainyu with the subordinate devas, the gods worshiped by the Aryans other than the Iranians, constitute the hierarchy of Evil Spirits. Ahura-Mazda with the archangels, or subordinate deities under him, constitute the hierarchy of Good Spirits and are the recipients of the worship of all true Iranians. The prophet needs no better proof of the correctness of his classification than the testimony of Iranian history. The other Aryans have opposed the gods of Iran and have called upon their own gods to help them against the Iranians. The division he observes is a fact. The two hierarchies are actually worshiped by different families of the same people and have, for the people of Iran, just the character which Zoroaster assigns to them.

But there is another order of proof. The subordinate gods of each hierarchy are nature gods who preside over different aspects of nature. In the natural world there is life and death, growth and decay, the favorable and the unfavorable forces, right and wrong, good fortune and evil fortune. The antagonism is represented by a complete cleavage which runs through all things. The division is fundamental, metaphysical, as eternal as the existence of the gods. The Zoroastrian literature does not present in detail a philosophy or theology as such; but it is all there by implication, and when the prophet taught the people he must have presented the main features of his system in clearest outline. Thoughtful patriots everywhere gained from him a very convincing theory of life and nature, so much so, in fact, that they accepted his teachings enthusiastically and were willing to die for the hope they contained.

The chief work of Zoroaster was, therefore, that of bringing order out of the chaos and confusion of the nation's religious heritage. He convinced his people that the conflict between Iran and the other Aryans was inevitable—it was a reflection of the two orders of nature to be seen everywhere. He explained adequately the reason why a religion which had been common to the whole Aryan race had become inherently evil —this had come about by choosing evil. This accounted also for all treasons, betrayals, and evil practices either at home or abroad—the individuals who did such things had chosen to do evil. Again, he explained the reason Iran had continued so long in her present miseries under her conqueror—all existence was a battle against destruction, and man must fight with the gods to achieve a good and benevolent social life. Iran had remained inactive while her enemies had never ceased to be vigilant. If Iran would be free she must choose the Right and actively fight on its side against the encroachments of Evil. With understanding and devotion she must assist the good forces of Nature, the archangels, in reconstructing the prosperity and happiness of the nation.

The main features of the hierarchy of Good must have been an article of faith before Zoroaster began to teach. The archangels did not perhaps have their functions marked out for them until the prophet determined the work each should do. Just as in the case of the devas of the Vedas there must have been much overlapping of function and frequent exaltation of each in turn to the position of supreme god. In his seven visions the prophet entered into an understanding of the distinctive character and work of each of the archangels, and thus brought about the end of the overlapping of function which had been the chief source of confusion and the lack of a true national spirit in Iran. None of the local deities was

denied; each was assigned his place in the national pantheon. Thus definiteness and clarity became a powerful factor
in welding the several communities together for the great
enterprise of national independence.

In his first vision Zoroaster conferred with Ahura Mazda.
He was instructed in the great cardinal doctrines of the faith,
and was initiated into the secrets of Heaven and the gods. In
the second he conferred with Vohu-mano and learned the
sacred care and keeping of useful animals. The third vision
was of Asha Vahishta, who enjoined upon him the care of the
Fire and the guardianship of all fires, sacred and secular.
Khshathra Vairya appeared to him in the fourth vision and
assigned to him the care and keeping of metals. The fifth of
the visions was of Spenta Armaiti, who instructed the prophet
as to the boundaries of the countries upon the earth and the
care of the earth. Haurvatat in the sixth vision presented the
manner of the care and propitiation of water. And the seventh
vision enabled the prophet to learn from Ameretat the care
and protection of plants.

After the first vision the young prophet, now about thirty
years of age, began to preach. We are told that Ahura Mazda
had taught him the true Wisdom and had initiated him into
the divine secrets. He went immediately to the Kigs and
Karaps, or the Kavis and Karpans, to instruct them in the
true religion. These were the priests and provincial governors
of the land who had become blind and deaf to law. The
teaching was rejected by these agents of the conqueror, and
the prophet, seeing the reason for their action, decided to go
to the source of all the trouble. He accordingly hastened to
the king of Turan and presented his message. The king gave
him protection and shielded him from the priests and nobles
who clamored for his death. The teacher was quick to see that
nothing could be done in this atmosphere of intrigue where
the ruler was swayed by the hostile influence of the courtiers.
He therefore decided to approach one of the richest of the

Karpans to secure patronage. His proposal met with a vigorous refusal and he was compelled to flee from the country.

A. V. W. Jackson says: "Such rebuffs could not but produce times of despondency and distress, an echo of which we hear lingering in these Hymns (Zoroastrian Psalms). Zarathushtra more than once breaks forth with a cry against such rulers and powerful lords who use not their sovereignty for the protection of the righteous and for the advancement of virtue." [22] The situation was discouraging, to be sure, but that which is of greatest interest to us is the method of the prophet. He goes to the fount of authority and seeks there to produce the needed reforms, among the priests, the tyrants, and the wealthy. Failing in this he returns to his home. He has become aware at last that he cannot do it by approaching Turan.

Then follows a period of meditation and the six visions. From their character it is apparent that the prophet has decided upon an appeal to the people. To do this he must make some concession to popular beliefs. He now fixes the place and function of the several archangels in the hierarchy and no doubt takes over many existing practices of the popular religion, items which could scarcely have been a part of the message he has been proclaiming in this first unsuccessful missionary enterprise.

What was the nature of this earlier message? It was probably a pure dualism with emphasis upon a lofty and austere virtue, upon social righteousness, sincerity and honesty in the administration of religion, and the protection of the people in their peaceful occupations. The prophet has tried this gospel and has found that those who have the power to put it into effect will not accept it. Having thus failed at the top of the social structure, he must begin at the bottom. But to do this with any hope of success he must reconstruct his theology. And while he is about it he does so at the expense of the

---

[22] *Zoroaster—The Prophet of Iran*, p. 44.

Karpans, identifying them with the Spirit of Evil who is at war with all that is Good. This new doctrine is so revolutionary, so uncompromisingly direct, so dangerous to the continued sway of the Turanians, that he is asked to cease his activities. As a fugitive he surrounds himself with a few choice spirits and continues his labors. But, as we have seen, his success is so small that he decides to go back to his original plan and to seek again for a royal patron.

Another feature of interest in the teachings of Zoroaster is Messianism. In the Vendidad account of the temptation [23] the agent of the Turanian monarch wishes to know the prophet's intentions. Zoroaster replies: "O maleficent Anra Mainyu! I shall smite the creation of the Demons, I shall smite the Nasu who is created by the Demons. I shall smite the Enchantress until the Savior (Saosyant), the Victorious shall be born from the waters of Kasava, from the region of the dawn, from the regions of the dawn." This Messiah (Savior) was to be born of the seed of Zoroaster, according to a later account, and was to come from Seistan, the principality of the Kayanian family.

This legend may be entirely the product of a later age. After Zoroaster had been exalted by his followers to a position but little below that of Ahura Mazda, it was not difficult for them to believe that he knew beforehand that he would win King Vishtaspa. Thus he was presented as defying the agent of Turan and as predicting at the same time his final triumph through a Deliverer in the East. Still later the tradition was made the basis of a permanent expectation of the faithful. Legends are very frequently, however, supported by a strand of historical fact. And it is just possible that Zoroaster may have told the agent that he would never cease to labor until he had been able to arouse someone to deliver the nation. This declaration, his journey to the East, and his final complete triumph, would afterward take on the color of a prophecy and

---

[23] Vendidad 19.1.10.

its fulfillment. Still later, after Iran had once more become a conquered country and the Zoroastrians were being persecuted, this same material would form the basis of a hope of future deliverance. Defeat is the historical circumstance behind the Messianism in any religion.

But perhaps the most thrilling doctrine for the soldier of Iran was that of the resurrection. In warfare on earth many would be slain, and the probabilities were very great that any soldier would come to this fate in battle. But the soldier fought in a cause that was destined to be victorious. Right would eventually overcome Wrong. In the period following the triumph, when the two phases of the kingdom—the earthly and the spiritual—were established in prosperity and glory, those who had defended the Good would be resurrected to enjoy the blessing. It mattered not, therefore, whether a man lived or died in the struggle; whatever his fortune, he would be present to receive his reward. This doctrine of the immortality of the individual had an inestimable effect upon the morale of the soldier. He went into battle without fear and without reserve; and when he or his companions were mortally wounded, there was no quailing or regret before the great Change.

The general nature of this religion has perhaps given rise to those analogies which have always figured in homilies on the resurrection. Everything alive, or that has substance, enjoys the special attention of the two opposed hierarchies which war over it. When Evil, darkness, winter, decay have won a victory, it is only temporary. The Good, light, summer, creation always bring back the life and beauty of living things again. Just as the plant goes down to its cold winter death and emerges with the coming summer, so man goes down to death to rise again. When Mithraism (a faith derived in part from Zoroaster's teachings and partly from the more ancient Aryan religion) had made its way West after the Alexandrian conquest, or perhaps earlier through the medium of the Greek philosophers, it took with it its eclecticism as well as its faith. Behind the argument of Saul of Tarsus, "There are celestial bodies and bodies terrestrial. One bears grain—it may chance of wheat"[24]—there is a long history of the very figure he used in explaining his Christian doctrine of the resurrection. In fact, he was employing it with people who were perfectly acquainted with its use for this same purpose. And by using it this Apostle of the Gentiles was able to present clearly the distinctive and perhaps superior character of his own teaching.

This doctrine of immortality and the resurrection must have been in existence among the Aryans long before the Zoroastrian reform, and doubtless long before the Iranians were separated from their brethren. As we have already seen even the Vedas contain a belief that the dead finally make their way to the abode of the gods in the West and the East. One of the most ancient elements of the Aryan religious heritage would therefore seem to be a belief in personal immortality. Zoroaster now vivified it by identifying human existence with the striving order of the cosmos,—strengthened it by uniting man organically to Nature which dies to rise again. He put faith where it could be seen in operation—"If a corn of wheat fall into the ground." To the Iranian the resurrection was a metaphysical and cosmic fact; the only thing that could delay it was the temporary success of the powers of Evil. Thus the soldier who went into battle against his country's foes hastened his liberation from the bands of Death with every successful stroke against the enemy. The doctrine therefore made brave men and great fighters.

When the success of Iranian arms had brought safety and prosperity to give a season of relief from the Great Warfare there was freedom for theological speculation. Great masses of the people had been forced to give allegiance to the Zoroastrian faith who possessed practically no religious information except that which composed the common heritage of the

---

[24] I Corinthians xv. 36-55.

Iranians. And this, as we have reason to know, was not fundamentally different from the ancient Aryan faith except in the matter of the names of the deities worshiped. Much of this ancient material was perpetuated by being engrafted upon the loftier stalk which Zoroaster had planted. Myths, legends, even the haoma, thus became well accredited within the body of Zoroastrian teaching. The master himself became unduly exalted among the gods; the qualities of Ahura Mazda, which he personalized only to meet the facts of popular religion, were substantialized into actual deities which played their part in the drama of human life; the facts of history—events which took place on earth and between men—were given a celestial character so that the history of this period reads like the actions of gods and demons (the flesh and blood agent of the king of Turan becomes a demon sent by the Demon of Demons); and the private meditation of Zoroaster as he struggled with the actual, earthly social situation until he hit upon a gospel, was made into a conference with the celestials in the heavenly land. To be sure, there is always the possibility that the prophet may have employed this highly figurative terminology to impress his hearers with a sense of awe and to awaken in them the conviction that he was proclaiming a divine body of truth. But we ought to be able to fathom Oriental modes of expression sufficiently to make due allowance for the style—to find the historical fact behind the figure. And we ought to be able to see the times of the prophet clearly enough to fix the main items of his teaching. Within the Zend-Avesta itself there is enough to enable us to trace the glorious drama of Iranian political life.

In approaching Eastern religious books we Westerners are usually in bondage to two habits which utterly disqualify us for a proper understanding of their true contents: a literal-mindedness which makes us miss the significance of the narratives, and a theory of authorship which makes us take the stories as they read or not at all. Our histories are usually so downright as to be superficial, so true to the seen as to miss the more important unseen, so full of the pagan noise of battle as to be empty of philosophy—in fact so truthful as to be worthless for the cause of Wisdom. The Eastern mind approaches history from the abode of the spirit and thus sees the wars and strivings of men in a totally different light. Small wonder that they alone have given us the great theological philosophies of history.

When we have become somewhat more emancipated from our infirmity and have come to find the historical data behind these ancient philosophies, we may be able to trace a philosophy of mankind for ourselves. Even the most stupid man of any race realizes that things and acts have both being and meaning. But just what meaning any thing or act may have will always depend upon the needs and ideals of the men who interpret it. As to language—well, that is is only a means of presenting, of describing—a figure and a farce—a reflection of a reflected deed or thing. When we are less stupid we shall have loftier philosophies, and be able to read them with less error.

It has been the divine gift of the prophet to have by nature or by accident a vision of the meaning of history. He has seen through the web of events to the forces that make the tragedies and triumphs of men. He has read it in the light of deity and destiny, has seen the place of ethics in the consummation of spirituality—the least deed of the doer in the pattern which God weaves—the inevitable reaction of an ordered world, and a Will which leads the stars in their courses and determines how far the maker of history may go. Thus he has been able to sound solemn warnings in the face of approaching danger and to give great counsel to the rulers of men. But he has so completely acclimated his deities to our earthly scenes that the literal-minded have at times imagined they could see the celestial shapes go by and hear the great voices crying down the world. And this last state can be ever so much worse than the first. Woe to us when imagination possess neither art nor wisdom!

As A. V. W. Jackson truly remarks: "Great men are the children of their age. Heirs to the heritage of the past, they are charged with the stewardship of the possessions to be handed down to the future. Summing up within themselves the influences of the times that call them forth, stamped with the impress of their day, their spirit in turn shows its reflex upon the age that gives them birth. We read them in their age; we read their age in them. So it is of the prophets and sages, religious teachers and interpreters, which have been since the world began. The teaching of a prophet is the voice of the age in which he lives; his preaching is the echo of the heart of the people of his day. The era of a prophet is therefore not without its historic significance; it is an event that marks an epoch in the life of mankind. The age of most of the great religious teachers of antiquity is comparatively well known; but wide diversity prevails with regard to the date at which Iran's ancient prophet Zoroaster lived and taught; yet his appearance must have had its national significance in the land between the Indus and the Tigris; and the great religious movement which he set on foot must have wrought changes and helped shape the course of events in the early history of Iran." [25]

That is just the social function of the true prophet in every age—"to shape the course of events in the history of his people." But very often it is not the spirit of his age that produces him; the age has only provoked him. It is antiquity which composes his brain and nerves and understanding; and it is for antiquity that he speaks and writes. Not antiquity as it was, to be sure; but antiquity as it can be, as it ought logically to be, and as, by the help of all the gods, it will be. The prophet is a reformer in an age that has become perverse

---

[25] *Zoroaster—Prophet of Iran*, p. 150.

and has lost its soul. He is its product only in the sense that he has grown up in it and knows it through and through; he has been bored, antagonized, outraged, suppressed, until, in the interest of liberty, justice, and the life he craves, he turns upon it with holy indignation; it is then that this product of antiquity breaks out of the jail of his own time and builds a temple.

Thus it happened that Zoroaster, who lived somewhere near the seventh century before the Christian era and who had been well trained in the ancient virtues of his nation, became so embittered by oppressions and religious hypocrisies that he determined to find a remedy. He pondered long the meaning of the religion of his fathers, he studied the powers that held his nation by the throat, he suffered with his people in the afflictions which came to all Iranians, and he saw at last the way to deliverance. Elaborately he worked out his gospel, modifying it no doubt as experience in preaching showed him the way; and when it was complete it was "the echo of the heart of the people of his day," for it awoke the slumbering soul of Iran to arise and take its rights and its desires.

CHAPTER IV

AAKHNATON

We now come to Amenhotep IV of Egypt. He became ruler when the empire established by Thutmose III was at its height. From the fourth cataract of the Nile and from the Euphrates in the north the length of his dominions, like a river with two sources, flowed in a stream of gold to Thebes. Practically the whole of this region had been Egyptianized. The tribes of negroes in the south now wore Egyptian clothing, worshiped Egypt's gods in Egyptian temples, supplied troops for the Egyptian army, and sent to Thebes each year their allotment of tribute consisting of cattle, grain, gold, feathers, and precious stones. In the north the dynasts of Palestine and Syria were loyal and cultivated princes, who had been brought to Egypt for their education and had been sent back to administer the government in the name of the Pharaoh. So completely Egyptianized were these rulers that they now entertained no thought of revolt. A word from their overlord was sufficient to bring any one of them to Thebes to protest his utter devotion and loyalty. And if some prince delayed the payment of tribute the appearance of an Egyptian commissioner was enough to hasten action. Law and order together with a strong feeling of solidarity prevailed from one end of the Empire to the other.

Furthermore, all the rulers north and east of Syria were very anxious to be on good terms with Egypt. The Pharaohs for over a hundred years had been prompt to put down all revolts and to bring the guilty to swift justice. There had been many tests of the Egyptian power, but the strategy, great courage, and persistence of each of the Pharaohs had sooner or later overwhelmed all opposition and had established the supremacy of Egypt. Nothing could withstand the will of these rulers of the Nile valley except their own failure to consolidate their conquests. And when this had been done they had always pushed on to other lands. Treaties, however, were sacredly kept, and the rulers of the nations soon learned that it was not the way of Egypt to break an agreement made with other peoples. Thus the kings of Babylon, Mitanni, and Kheta hastened to make terms that the Egyptian armies might not come knocking at the doors of their palaces.

As soon as it was learned in any of these nations that the emperor had died, embassies were dispatched to Egypt immediately to confer with the new ruler and to call attention to the long-standing friendship and treaties. Political marriages were arranged between the emperor and the daughters of these rulers, new pledges were made, costly gifts were exchanged, and coöperative policies formulated to meet the emergencies of revolt. Even extradition treaties, covering criminals and the transfer of property, were drawn up and faithfully observed by all parties. The victories of Ahmose, Amenhotep I, Thutmose III, and his successors, all bore evidence to a will in Egypt that could not be regarded lightly. The dynasts who ruled for the Pharaoh, and even the surrounding despots, were very careful to keep any hostile intentions to themselves and to do everything in their power to keep the peace in Asia.

So well established was the sovereignty of Egypt by the time Amenhotep III came to the throne that it was unnecessary for the Pharaoh to visit his vassals in the north. His lieutenants, together with the native princes, could put down all sporadic revolts among the subject peoples there. The monarch had merely to make his will known and it was done.

Under such conditions it has always been the custom of emperors to give their whole attention to social, economic, and building enterprises. Amenhotep III was no exception to the rule. Trade was now developed as never before in Egypt's history. Breasted tells us that the "Nile from the Delta to the cataracts was alive with the freight of all the world, which flowed into it from the Red Sea fleets and from long caravans passing back and forth through the Isthmus of Suez, bearing the rich stuffs of Syria, the spices and aromatic woods of the East, the weapons and chased vessels of the Phoenicians, and the myriad of other things, which brought their Semitic names into the hieroglyphic and their use into the life of the Nile-dwellers." [1] A Mediterranean trade, no less in magnitude and quality, kept vast fleets of Phoenician galleys coming and going by sea. All this trade was regulated, protected by police on land and by navies at sea, taxed by reasonable tariffs which added large sums to the public treasury, and given every opportunity free of discrimination and subsidized opposition. The borders were patrolled and all persons who could not explain their business satisfactorily were turned back.

The most outstanding result of such wealth was the immense building enterprise of the Pharaoh. With his vast sums of money, and with a constant stream of slaves from Syria, he was able to bring about what Breasted styles "a new and fundamental chapter in the history of the world's architecture." Amenhotep was surrounded by men of the highest gifts, and these brought a new spirit into the older forms of architecture and imbued them with a grace and beauty not heretofore attained. The temples constructed at this period, whether large or small, have an impressiveness of line and mass, a gorgeousness of detail in some cases and an exquisite simplicity in others, and are, even in ruins, impressive in their grandeur and artistry. These men of sensitive, creative temper embodied the spirit of Egypt in works of "beauty, dignity, and splendor."

The sculptors of this period brought to their work an

---

[1] Breasted, *A History of Egypt*, pp. 337sq.

originality and freedom which carried out the possibilities of
the older standards of art. There must have been many who
complained against the conventional restrictions and who
stretched these rules as far as conservatism would permit. At
any rate, there was a pronounced movement toward refined
realism in both sculpture and painting which, as we shall see,
had far-reaching consequences. It ushered in a new way of
looking at both art and life and prepared the mind to dis-
criminate between the true and the false on esthetic grounds.
There was also a tendency to import into the conventional
composition new subject matter and more pronounced loyalty
to the facts of actual life. Battle scenes celebrated with elaborate details the actual events, glorious and humorous, of the
Pharaoh's conflict with his enemies. And the results of wisdom
and of matured observation took the place of bare repetition
of the conventional figures as heretofore. There was no
decided break with tradition, but there was put into the pos-
ture and countenance of the several figures the mood and
thought which experience and observation had discovered.

As to the residence of the Pharaoh of this period, we shall
turn to the description given by Breasted: "On the left (of
Amenhotep's avenue of sculptured jackals), behind the temple and nearer the cliffs, appeared a palace of the king of
wooden architecture in bright colors; very light and airy, the
façade adorned with flagstaves bearing tufts of parti-colored
pennants, and having over the front entrance a gorgeous
cushioned balcony with graceful columns, in which the king
showed himself to his favorites on occasion. The art which
adorned such a palace was as exquisite in its refined aesthetics
as in its technical skill. Innumerable products of the industrial
artist which fill the museums of Europe indicate with what
tempered richness and delicate beauty such a royal chateau was
furnished and adorned. Magnificent vessels in gold and silver
with figures of men and animals, plants and flowers rising
from the rim, glittered on the king's table among crystal gob-

lets, glass vases, and gray porcelain vessels inlaid with pale blue designs. The walls were covered with woven tapestry of workmanship so fine and color and design so exquisite that skilled judges have declared it equal to the best modern work. Besides painted pavements depicting animal life, the walls also were adorned with fine blue glazed tiles, the rich color of which shone through elaborate designs in brilliant gold leaf, while glazed figures were employed in encrusting larger surfaces. All this was done with fine and intelligent consideration of the whole color scheme. In all the refined arts it is an age like that of Louis XV, and the palace everywhere reflects the spirit of the age." [2]

In spite of the statement of Sir Ernest A. Wallis Budge [3] that the Egyptian mind was too concrete and practical to be philosophical, we may be very sure that a people which has made such advancement in the arts of civilization which is evidenced by the above description, and by the organization and administration of an empire, is not unfamiliar with ideas profound enough to supply the meat of a very great philosophy. There may not be any systematic statement, and the sense of system may not be present, but the ideas are there, and we may be sure that the mind of such a people took all the mental steps by which the profoundness was attained. An argument against the existence of philosophy which is based upon a lack of written evidence is too precariously supported to command our respect. The philosophy may be present without statement, without the realization of its presence. Philosophy always far outruns the conscious systematizer. It is not difficult to sense and understand the spirit of an age or a people, especially if one be born there; and there have been numerous ages and peoples who are the despair of the thinker who toils at the task of systematizing them. Have we any person who has yet stated the philosophy of the American

---

[2] Breasted, *A History of Egypt*, pp. 348-349.
[3] Budge, *Tutankhamen, Amenism, Atenism*, pp. 95, 96.

people, the living philosophy which constitutes the source of
our life and achievement? Yet we all sense it and coöperate in
its inner and outward expression with a high degree of certainty and efficiency. Excavators will in the future perhaps
declare that we were too concrete in our thinking to possess a
philosophy. They will see clearly the inadequacy and irrelated-
ness of our present philosophizing and will see at once that it
is not indigenous. They will trace it all to Germany and leave
us a backward and rather simple-minded nation—enterprising,
skilled in arts and mechanics, builders, inventors, but not of
philosophical temper. No, the Egyptians had a philosophy.

Arguments based upon the songs or hymns of a people are
perhaps even more precariously established. Some of the theology does get into the lines, but by no means all. We have the
spectacle of a Protestant church guided in many cases by the
most modern gospel, still singing the fragments of a medieval
theology. Sir Wallis Budge should not think too little of either
the ethics or the purpose of Aakhnaton from the mere evidence of the hymns. Sermons still have a "thirdly"; prayers
are still built in both language and idea upon an ancient pattern; and in some cases at least, the ritual of worship harks
back to pre-historic practices. We ought not to demand that
Aakhnaton make a more complete cleavage with the past than
we are willing to make. He may not have been as enlightened
and consistent as we think we are.

There is, however, something to be learned from the presence of ancient elements in the Aton hymns. These echoes do
not indicate that no new leaven was present, but only that
the past is so hard to exclude. Habits, customs, ritual, modes
of worship, these are the most stubbornly conservative forces
in the life of any people. The bended knee, before God—how
old is the practice! And who can say that it is not more reminiscent of the palace than of the temple? Things were carried
over into the Aton worship from the past devotional life of
the people; not intentionally, but unconsciously, the inconsis-

tent element was not noticed, or it was considered unimportant. And when Aakhnaton died he may have left many religious statements that fared no better than his fine temples. All this in spite of the fact that reformers of religion in all ages have seldom spoken their whole mind in the public ear. There is a great untold story behind the public acts of Aakhnaton, the king. And we can guess some of it from the universal facts of human nature. But we shall say more of this later.

Aakhnaton came to the throne when Egyptian arms had secured the greatest empire Egypt was ever to possess. Egyptian architects had filled the Nile valley with the most splendid palaces, temples, obelisks, and tombs. All the wealth of the world flowed into the valley. Perhaps never before or since has any monarch possessed such security and treasure.

As we have already seen, there was a silent and powerful spirit of reform abroad in the land, especially among the architects and artists and sculptors. Such revolts do not begin in a corner. They are the surest barometer of an age. All the thoughts, the desires, the antipathies toward convention, and the impact of youthful buoyancy against tradition, congeal now and then into a force which begins to make itself felt in all creative work. Unless something violent occurs to stamp it out, this force will become the prevailing fashion and thus produce a new epoch in the story of man. Aakhnaton could not help knowing his time. He was a youth, and of his time. Nor could he wholly misunderstand the meaning of the revolt or fail utterly to see where it was going. Being a youth, he was naturally sympathetic with the interests of the younger generation; and being the pharaoh also, what is more natural than that he should occupy a prominent position in some department of the movement? Monarchs have seldom stood by as mere observers of such spectacles.

And if this generation had wearied of the conventional restrictions to its art, who more than Aakhnaton had an opportunity to feel the galling weight of custom? As the prince-royal, all his life, even to the most trivial details, was determined for him by hoary precedent. And as each generation added to the list of things he must or must not do, it is small wonder that he decided to assert his independence.

But independence was not to be had by a mere declaration. The pharaoh was as much a rôle to be played upon the stage of Egyptian history as it was a position calling for courage and initiative. There was, for instance, the mask of deity. The pharaoh upon all state occasions was remote, haughty, unapproachable, a god to whom all must bow in adoration. Never outside of his palace was he to know one moment of relaxation from this godlike pose. If he had felt the need of it, and had selected it for himself, it might have been supportable. But this was not of his doing. The conventions were the creation of others who had gone before him, or were the fictions prescribed for the advantage of those who stood to profit by them. Aakhnaton must have heard his father lament bitterly that he was thus only a lay figure exhibited in public for the profit of the Amonite priestly party. And as the young ruler began himself to experience the iron hand, he resolved to break with such play-acting forever. Why live this impossible farce? He would destroy the necessity for it. He would live a life according to the dictates of nature and common sense. He would lead his people back to the truth.

To understand the significance of Aakhnaton's position, and the revolt he proposed in the interest of "truth," we must go back an hundred years or more to the coronation of his great-grandfather, Thutmose III, founder of the empire. Thutmose I had no legitimate claim to the throne but came to power only through his marriage to a princess descended from the old Theban rulers who had expelled the Hyksos from Egypt. When his queen died, he was old, and was probably forced to give way before a challenge from the party of legitimacy. His queen had given him four children, but only one, the princess Hatshepsut, was alive. Thutmose I, however, had two sons by other queens. One of these, afterwards Thutmose II, was the son of a princess; the other son, who later became Thutmose III, was born to the pharaoh by a concubine of no particular rank. The fact that Thutmose I was to leave no male heir by his queen had early raised the question of the succession, and the party of the legitimacy had forced the king to designate his daughter Hatshepsut as his successor. But there had always been a strong sentiment against being ruled by a woman, and the leaders of the conservative popular party rallied to the support of the son of noble lineage, although he had no claim to the throne through his mother. The party of the legitimacy, however, won the advantage by the marriage of Hatshepsut to the king's second son, who afterward became Thutmose III. This son had no real claim to the throne and had been placed in the temple of Karnak as a priest with the rank of prophet. By his marriage to Hatshepsut, who had been legally declared successor, he had as much right to the throne as his father had had.

It is not difficult to see what has taken place. The party of the legitimacy has called in the aid of the Amonite priesthood, probably with the understanding that Hatshepsut shall be the real ruler. The priests, being anxious to further their own interests, were not averse to lending a hand, for they no doubt saw an opportunity to deceive the party of the legitimacy and to make Thutmose III ruler in fact. By a skillful coup d'état they placed Thutmose upon the throne. Thereafter the terms of the bargain seem to have been ignored, for Thutmose III took over the government with a strong hand and accorded his queen no greater title than "chief royal wife." This displeased the party of legitimacy, who now succeeded in forcing the king to make his queen co-regent. With this entering wedge they were able to go further; and knowing that they could not trust either the priests or the king, they did not stop until they had pushed Thutmose III aside.

But the party of the legitimacy had gone too far. They had no doubt been aided in their efforts by the conservative party, one now composed of Thutmose I, the ambitious Thutmose II, and those who were secretly averse to the rule of a woman. This could be easily brought about because of the high-handed procedure of the priests in displacing Thutmose I, and later Hatshepsut, with Thutmose III as king. But the party of the legitimacy had called in powerful men and had given them positions from which they could not be dislodged. These men together with Thutmose I and Thutmose II made good use of their position. And it is not inconceivable that, with the Amonite party neutral under the circumstances, they very quickly regained the throne with Thutmose II as co-regent. This advantage they held until the death of Thutmose I, when Thutmose II called in Thutmose III as co-regent. The co-regency established between the two brothers lasted until the death of Thutmose II three years later. Amon and the old royalists were too strong for the party of the legitimacy. But the party of the legitimacy, after the death of Thutmose I, forced the recognition of Hatshepsut as co-regent, and later secured sufficient power to force Thutmose III into the background. This was done by special agreement with the Amonite priesthood. The priesthood of the whole land was reorganized under Hapuseneb as high-priest; the position of grand-vizier was given to him in addition. Thus when both the civil government and the religious control had been turned over to the priests of Amon, the party of the legitimacy had secured its ends. But it had created a situation that would dominate Egyptian affairs for centuries. Hatshepsut continued to reign long enough for the Amonite priesthood to become thoroughly entrenched in both religious and civil affairs. When the queen died in the twentieth year of her reign, Thutmose III was called to the throne by the priests. And while he was a strong man and one of the greatest military geniuses of all time, he could not dominate the priestly party because of his lack of legitimate claim to the throne.

He did, however, take belated vengeance upon all who had originally aided in depriving him of his kingship. These, no doubt, had all died and had been succeeded in office by others. But Thutmose hacked their names from their mortuary temples and tombs that no trace might be left of their works. The new generation of priests who had aided him in securing the throne, he advanced in every way possible. And when he returned from his first great campaign in Asia he gave to Amon three towns which he had captured in Asia, together with an immense number of gold and silver vessels and precious stones. To maintain the temple according to this standard of sumptuousness large tracts of land in both northern and southern Egypt were turned over to the temple. These lands were supplied with great herds of cattle and slaves for shepherds and farmers. Thus began that immense fortune which enabled the priests of Amon to become in many respects even more powerful than the pharaoh himself.

Thutmose we may be sure had a perfect knowledge of the character of the priests. He was one of their number and had taken part in the political manipulations which had placed him upon the throne to succeed Thutmose I. He had lent himself to the duplicity which had thwarted the desires of the party of legitimacy. And he knew all too well the terms of that bargain which had enabled Hatshepsut and the party of legitimacy to thrust him aside. He now profited by the wisdom the priests had taught him. Since these men could be bought, he bought them with gifts and endowments and thus made his position secure.

But perhaps even he did not realize the full consequences of his policy. He had in accepting the kingship at their hands practically admitted that a king must receive their favor. It was equivalent to a recognition that priestly blessing outweighed the right of inheritance. No such question of theory came up during his term of office, to be sure; but the priests were not slow to realize the significance of events and to make the circumstances of his second coronation a precedent. Thus as time· went on it became a matter of course that a pharaoh must receive divine approval if he were to enter upon his career as ruler with all parties satisfied.

The language of Thutmose III in describing his victories served only to further buttress the priestly contention. It was Amon who had chosen him to be ruler, and it was Amon who gave him his great victories in Asia. In thus attributing all his success to the god, and by his lavish gifts, the pharaoh was able to combat any adverse criticism from the party of legitimacy. There was no other person who had a better right to the throne than he, but there may have been others who were better born. A defeated party will, however, seldom balk at measures of compromise if it can find no other way to secure an advantage. But in reënforcing the popular impression of his divine right to rule, the emperor forged the chain of slavery about his neck. Thus the fiction which he must have been quite willing to advance for popular effect served only to strengthen the hands of the ambitious Amonite party. Then, as the full implication of the king's action became more and more accepted, the priests had abundant opportunity to force the hand of the king in securing their wishes.

From this point onward we behold the priests encroaching upon the kingly prerogatives, consolidating their positions of influence, enriching their estates, pyramiding their vast fortune of silver and gold, and establishing the public appearances and acts of the king as religious functions. The life of the ruler becomes more and more conventionalized, solemnized, given a significance as hallowed as the various stages of a religious ceremony. In both act and cast of countenance he becomes the austere vicegerent of the god. In private, away from the eyes of his subjects, or in the company of the most powerful members of the priesthood, he is at most only a man. And as we move farther away from the capable Thutmose III and come to his weaker successors, we shall expect to encounter more and more dictation from the priests. How much of this may be imposed upon a spirited man will depend altogether upon his temperament, courage, and desire to rule.

That the Egyptian character was more tractable, or more congenial, to this farce of magnificence and austerity than that of other races seems borne out by subsequent events. As long as the pharaohs were of pure Egyptian blood they accepted the rôle. But when the descendants of Thutmose had become preponderantly Asiatic, perhaps preponderantly Aryan, through several generations of foreign marriages, the priests were confronted with a more pronounced liberty-loving personality. The pharaohs were not content to fit themselves into the mold of royal solemnity which precedent had dictated for them. They inwardly rebelled, perhaps grumbled a little. Furthermore their wives and mothers were daughters of kings who made their every whim the law of the land. Naturally the daughters of such kings would be inclined to hostility toward the Egyptian customs as undue restriction of the royal will. Feminine nature suffers no great change through the ages, and we may be very sure the king heard his queen's opinion of such court regulations. Ridicule is a powerful weapon when used against a nature already convinced of its follies. Thus we notice the kings beginning to assert themselves. They become more human in spite of their continued conformity to regal etiquette. Amenhotep III took liberties, and became more like the despots of Asia than his forefathers in Egypt. He became a hard-driving, vigorous hunter of wild beasts. He celebrated his successes in the chase by having scarabs struck recounting the results of the royal prowess. Even in selecting this medium of announcement he was going against all previous custom. Three or four generations of feminine rebellion has had its effect upon the kingly nature.

As we have seen, it was also an age of freedom. Culture, education, and great wealth had aroused the native genius to seek its destiny. The crudities and smug unreality of convention in art and architecture were readily seen, and there was a pronounced desire to emancipate, refine, and develop, the creative impulse. The rebellion was aimed primarily at the criterions of art, but we may be sure that the movement met with opposition from the same party which had so effectively congealed the whole field of life and morals. The young king, Amenhotep IV, encountered much unpleasantness in seeking to become a man of his age and at the same time wear the insignia of the pharaoh. And as his difficulties increased he more and more took refuge in the dictates of desire and common sense.

It was precisely in this direction that the movement for reform was tending. Amenhotep III and his group had shown the way. They had introduced here and there the ripe fruit of observation and thought, and had evidenced a strong tendency toward naturalness—toward fidelity to life as it was actually lived everywhere except in the court-circle. The king had stretched his privileges of human nature as far as he could without shocking the public mind. He came just short of stepping out of his character of a lay figure of priestly creation to become a personality. His circle followed him with eagerness. The artist added a line of reality to his design. The architect groped for verisimilitude and natural dignity. And the human soul began to look out of the windows of its prison at the world and to pronounce it good. Once these visions dawned upon the mind nothing could hold in check the excited will. The bars had to come down.

History reveals a gap just here which may with some show of reason be bridged with Aakhnaton's word "truth." The history of all reforms has brought to light the fact that they all develop according to a pattern. There is the weariness, the antipathy, and the inner revolt which provoke a mischievous perversity. The new is stealthily added to the old, or is unconsciously put there when the enlightened soul expresses its true nature. Ideas permeate the body politic as water makes its way through the soil—a silent, hidden ooze that touches everything. No one can be made culpable at first, for the new is too slight to be detected by any except the probationers, the gropers after the light. The new is indeed like leaven; discipleship adds many adherents. The movement grows strong, waxes bold, speaks out, enters into controversy, never fails to give a good account of itself because it takes its adversaries unawares and attacks their weaknesses, wins public opinion, and finally takes over the power and the glory. The new which has been styled "the truth," by its advocates, is now in a position to watch the old error die among its worshipers. We do not need the record of Aakhnaton's time to tell us what took place. We know the law.

The young pharaoh Amenhotep IV was inducted into office in the conventional manner. Outwardly, at least, he appeared to be in full sympathy with the proceedings and docile enough in his manner to leave no doubt in the mind of the Amonite hierarchy that it was making another ruler who would do its will and guard its sacred interests. The master of ceremonies, the high-priest of Amon, may have detected in him a more wilful nature than that possessed by Amenhotep III. But he would scarcely have any premonition of the antogonism that would soon exist between him and this new king. Amenhotep III had been somewhat unconventional, but in all that really mattered he had been quite circumspect. This new king could be forgiven much, for he was still very young—young enough to serve Amon all the better, for if he needed advice it would be given.

Nor is it likely that Amenhotep IV was contemplating the extreme measures he afterwards put into effect. Was he not pharaoh? The pharaoh had the power to follow his own wishes very largely. There were certain foolish customs that had vexed his father and that would undoubtedly prove tiresome to him, but he would conform to them. He was doing so now. Youth is very tolerant, very likely to yield easily to the popular will until it is opposed in something it really desires. Then if, in addition to chiding, it feels the iron hand, it is likely to assert itself rashly. And if it possesses the power to have its way, it may do so with an utter disregard for consequences. Amenhotep IV could not know of course that he would be opposed in any desire until he began to issue those royal commands that were so essentially a part of his youthful and modern spirit. Even then he did not break at once with the priests of Amon; he did not realize the gulf that actually existed between him and them.

But he was not to remain in ignorance for long. His father, no doubt, had permitted him to come and go at will. The young prince had seemed to have every liberty to form associations with the youth of his day; and the father perhaps secretly enjoyed seeing his son do things that might have shocked the priests had they known of them. A father who throws aside the mantle of austerity upon occasion, and who celebrates his deeds in an unheard of way, will not be too strict in his son's upbringing. Thus the young prince was permitted to grow up with such habits of thought and conduct that he could not quickly comply with the demands of his position. And if greater demands were made of him than were made of his father, it is easy to see how the breach came about between him and the priestly hierarchy.

The probabilities in the case are that the young pharaoh found the many restrictions of his position very irksome. He loved sunlight, warmth, freedom, and people. He could not bear to be on parade at every moment that he was beyond the doors of his palace. He liked to roam about in his gardens, bathe in the lagoons, talk with all kinds of disreputable people, and wear the simplest clothes. And he decidedly did not like to be nagged by the priests who were determined to exhibit him as an incarnation of deity. A drive through the streets with his wife shocked all Thebes, and brought down upon his head the thinly veiled displeasure of the priests. He was the pharaoh! Such things were unheard of! Surely the dignity of his office, his sublime and exalted character, the customs of royalty, the necessity to command the adoration of his people, his position as a representative of Amon, and much more in the same vein, touched the tender pride of this youth and awoke his resentment. Yes, he was the pharaoh. And as such he would order his own steps. Let them go back to their altars and their incense. If he had needed any coaching for this reply his wife and mother could have supplied it—they had never felt too kindly regarding the gratuitous help of these priests in matters of public conduct. Back in Matanni a king was a king.

The priests of Amon had of course not the slightest knowledge of the resourcefulness and daring of the man they thought to control. He was to them only a spoiled, petulant child. They would bring him around safe enough in good time. Responsibilities, a few mistakes, a few weighty problems of statesmanship, and he would be seeking for help. If only they could keep him from scandalizing his people in the meantime, all would be well. Thus while they were waiting, very sure of themselves, the young king began to formulate one of the most daring schemes ever attempted in the history of the world.

He saw his position very clearly. He was the creature of the priests. They were the real rulers of his country; and he, the descendant of the greatest soldiers, must account to them for his every action. And what were they? Had not his grandfather given them all their power and wealth? And was he to allow them to rule the son of such a powerful king? By no means! If his grandfather could create a priesthood and raise it to such prominence, the thing could be done again. He would create his own priesthood and build temples according to his own heart.

The young pharaoh could not possibly know the magnitude of the task he was proposing to undertake. To have extracted the sovereignty from the firm hand of the hierarchy would have been enough for one lifetime. To have founded a religion would have been enough to keep at least two generations of powerful leaders working full time. Christ had his St. Paul; Confucius had his Mencius. And to have caused a faith as deep-rooted in the life of a people as that of Amon to wholly disappear would have taken the missionary zeal of a half-dozen generations. But Amenhotep IV was not amazed, partly because he had no conception of the difficulties he would encounter, and partly because he was after all a descendant of Thutmose III. Something of the will, if not the wisdom and experience, of the old conqueror had continued to live in this boy. And there were ghosts of others present also, men who had kept their thrones in all the turbulence and bloodshed of that political cauldron of Western Asia. And but for the ignorance and superstition of other men, this daring youth would have succeeded! His failure came not from the odds against him, but from the deep fears so long cultivated in the popular mind by kings and priests alike.

It must have produced a great deal of consternation among the priests of Amon when orders were given to the architects for the erection of a temple to Aton on ground very close to their own temple. The young king was certainly carrying the war to them, granted that they knew there was a war, and he was making it a war to the hilt. At first the hierarchy very probably was inclined to treat the matter lightly. They were no longer dependent upon the bounty of the monarch for the continuance of their worship. With their vast holdings of lands, their herds and slaves, and their wealth in silver and gold, they could sit quietly and smile at the young man's folly. The matter was, of course, a distinct misfortune in one way, for there would very probably be no more state celebrations in their temples. But they had the people, unless the king should compel every one to worship at his shrine. And they had influence, for many of their number held secular offices in the government and could be relied upon to be loyal to their faith. The priests reached out and tightened up their lines. They decided to make this upstart feel their power.

But they reckoned without their king. When they drew upon their power and influence to discomfit him and to make the city of Thebes secretly hostile to him, he was equal to the situation. Realizing as he did that no lasting headway could be made within a city so hallowed by tradition and memories of the old order, he decided to build a new capitol. This of course required immense sums. The state revenues alone were not sufficient to erect and maintain the new palaces and temples. The hierarchy may have congratulated itself over its apparent success; but if so, its exultation was very brief. At a word from the pharaoh all the lands of Amon, his herds and slaves, and his immense private fortune were confiscated to Aton! The worship of Amon had to be suspended because of insufficient revenues to maintain it.

There were convulsions immediately afterwards, riots led by the priests in protest of this action, but they were promptly quelled and the culprits soundly punished. And when trouble broke out a second time the young ruler avenged himself upon the priests by sending men to chisel the name of Amon from every inscription in the land. Thebes became but an empty house, a city of departed glory and of fearful, despairing people. What would become of them? Their temples were empty, their king had gone, the priests were sent to work or were begging from door to door, and there was now no proper burial of the dead. Amenhotep IV had taken from them everything except the fear of the underworld and the judgment to come.

The stranglehold of the Amonite hierarchy was broken at

last. The young ruler had accomplished it with a swiftness
and thoroughness worthy of a descendant of the great Thutmose III. In flesh and blood he was almost wholly foreign;
but in heritage, in ideas, in will, he was Egyptian. We must
not look upon Amenhotep IV as a mere fanatic nor as a
dreamer of impossible dreams. He had his faults, and one of
them—the chief one to prove his undoing—was the fact that
he was mortal; he could not live long enough to thoroughly
establish his reform. But neither in the conception of his God
nor in these first steps of royal policy did he move as dreamers
and fanatics move. He understood the whole social and religious aspect of his nation too well to be that sort of person.
He struck too surely, with a fine sense of expediency, and
with a political penetration found only among true statesmen.
Of course, it is entirely possible to argue that necessity dictated the pharaoh's policy—there were no revenues to be had
without plundering the Amonites, there was no possibility of
success in Thebes. But is it not just the way of great statesmen to keep their feet on the ground and to recognize the
social facts as they exist? And is not this action, which seems
forced by the facts, the highest proof of the statesman's
ability? And if we examine the hymns to Aton and the
political policy of the king as aspects of the same unified procedure, we discover a shrewd practicality which no mere
fanatic could have achieved except by the most happy accident.
Thus we may be sure that none of these early steps is accidental; they smack too much of malice aforethought for that. The
young king sees his way, and he has the courage to follow his
insight.

If it be argued that a sane man would have hesitated because of the popular horror his measures would arouse, we
have only to reply that a sane man would have lost the struggle before he had begun it. The Amonite hierarchy was too
well entrenched, too wealthy, too popular, and too shrewdly
directed to be easily defeated at a game of political chess. The

only way to defeat it was to see that it had no real opportunity to play. To have dallied would have added to the popular horror all the intelligence, political acumen, and financial resources of the priests. And the pharaoh had enough history before him to know that unless he made it impossible for the hierarchy to buy its way it would not hesitate to corrupt his officials and to put some one else upon the throne. Had not this powerful organization used even Thutmose III as a pawn in its game? And it had not hesitated to remove him from his position of power and to cast him aside when its interests were better served thereby. There is too much calculation in the policy of Amenhotep IV, too much consideration of past history, too much shrewdness in the blows he aimed at the foe, for us to believe long that he was only an unprincipled fanatic or an irrational dreamer. His head was clear; he had the heart of a fighter; and his blows in consequence were deadly.

And he had a great cause. Aside from all religious considerations—if they can ever be left out of the reckoning in the Orient—there was his duty toward the creative impulse of his people. When the least departure from the stereotyped patterns and modes of expression were regarded as religious heresy and culpable before priestly tribunals, or civil ones dominated by priestly influence, how could Egyptian art, science, and morals become other than a conformity to artificiality—one vast social and artistic falsehood? How could such a people work out its true destiny? Insincerity always breeds license, lawlessness, corruption, and political death. But the worst feature of the situation, as it existed, was the lack of stimulation, the absence of any prod to the popular imagination. And without this there can be no great national enthusiasms, no true nationality in the vital sense, and no guides except those who lead to the ditch and destruction. The young pharaoh saw whither the hierarchy was leading— saw the whole great untruth which had so long blighted the highest life of his people—and he had reached the conclusion that, as the pharaoh, it was his solemn and divine duty to end this national curse. It was now time for "the truth" to be declared. He would proclaim it, establish it as a permanent way of life by royal policy, and give to all true minds that liberty which would permit them to toil and create without fear. And it is this king who has been described by some in language which implies that he was only a short-sighted fool!

Amenhoptep's political acts supply the key that unlocks all the meaning of his reforms. To look for it in the hymns to Aton, and in the prayers, can supply but a poor insight into either the times or the religious genius of the king. A comparison of the best Babylonian, Hebrew, Vedic, and Zoroastrian hymns will reveal little of the political situation or the problem which the times have created for the reformer. And one will find that it is possible to substitute the name of his own god for all the others without doing violence to the creed of his system. The chief reason for this lies in the fact that people are very much alike in all ages. The man in despair, no matter where he lives, has a very simple request to make—he wants help. And when his deliverance comes, he can voice no greater praise than touches the humanity he shares with every other human being. Thus prayer and praise are probably the ground upon which all religions may be harmonized. Beyond this crying out to God humanity thinks in every direction with all sorts of theistic imaginations and distinctions. There will, therefore, be no great difference in the prayer of an Amonite and an Atonite. How could there be when all men everywhere want the same things from God? How little point there is then to Sir Wallis Budge's statement that the hymns to Aton are too conservative in tone to indicate that Amenhotep IV was a profound religious thinker and reformer. It is not a man's prayer but his deeds which reveal his genius or his deviltry. And when we look at the deeds of Amenhotep IV in the light of previous history and the social conditions then existing, we behold behind them a brave, keen-witted, profoundly penetrating youthful mind which has felt the value of liberty and justice and which has a courage seldom associated with great understanding. A few more men with his gifts would add materially to the list of the world's outstanding names.

Nor should we too quickly assume the worst about Amenhotep IV from the later disintegration of his empire. People quite often suffer from their stubbornness in ignoring their leaders, perhaps almost as often as from the so-called impractical policies of their leaders. And it is equally true that impractical methods are often only unpracticed methods. At any rate, to argue from social solidarity and inertia that one is rash and unwise to pursue measures of reform, is to reveal that one has a very low ideal of social duty. And to brand a man with terms of derision such as fanatic and dreamer because he pits himself against great odds, is to put the most serviceable human qualities in ill repute. The sane man thus becomes one who maintains his place without regard to principle and who draws no distinction between right and wrong. His chief virtue is that he continues to do business. Is it always right to play safe? Is it always wrong to fail? There are some who think so, but they will never become great leaders of mankind.

The young pharaoh determined to do all he could for his cause. Some have surmised that he met with such opposition in Thebes that he found it more pleasant to withdraw, but one who could deprive the Amonite hierarchy of its revenues would very probably be able to surround himself with whatever degree of adulation he desired. Others have felt that there were too many associations with, too many reminders of, the old order. This is very probably nearer the truth. We know that it was the custom throughout the world of that day to associate the god with some place which was his city

or his province. Amon's seat was at Thebes; Re's seat was at
Heliopolis. Aton had to have a seat like the others. And since
many generations had been accustomed to think of Thebes
as the seat of Amon, time would be gained and all theological
controversy avoided by founding a city which would be the
home of this god. Such a step would minimize opposition, for
no one would be likely to deny that a distant region might
be the home of some god other than Amon. This is probably
the sole reason for leaving Thebes and for establishing the
new city of Akhetaton. But whatever may have been the
cause for the king's departure, he at least had a free hand at
Akhetaton and constructed there his capitol city according
to his most advanced ideas of artistic creation.

We are now able to see the situation which Amenhotep was
called upon to face. The character of the king and the spirit
in which he set about his task can also be understood. The
pharaoh now selected the site for his capital, a plain notched
in the hills along the Nile at a point about half way between
Thebes and Memphis. This territory, occupying both sides of
the Nile, was marked off by stelae which proclaimed that the
region was the property of Aton. Here were situated the
palace of the king, the state and individual temples, the seat
of civil government, and the home of that new movement
which had left its traces upon the architecture and sculpture
of the previous reign. The rich nobles who wished to stand
well with the king built luxurious villas and surrounded
them with beautiful lawns dotted with palms and shrubs and
flowers. The capitol was called Akhetaton, Horizon of Aton,
and was one of the most beautiful cities of any time.

The king was not only the sponsor of the new spirit, which
he sought to establish as the highest expression of Egyptian
genius, but he must have played a far more intimate part in
the undertaking. The chief architect tells us in his tomb inscriptions that he was taught his art by the king. Whether
this was only a motion of honor to the king or a record of

actual fact cannot be positively determined; but we may be
very sure that as chief prophet and founder of the Aton faith,
Amenhotep IV, now Aakhnaton, would give very minute advice regarding the construction of all religious edifices. Again
we may discover the influence of his "truth" as the force which
supplied the substance of all creative work. That there was a
new philosophy, a new point of view, or a new way of approaching life and art cannot be doubted. It may not have
been stated in such detail as we moderns would put it, but it
was very clearly understood by the leaders of the movement.
And its relation to art and conduct was carefully considered,
and as carefully taught to all officials and artisans.

Something of the character of the new teaching, or new
point of view, may be gained from fragments of the artistic
achievement and from the inscriptions and reliefs of the time.
It was moral and artistic naturalness, for one thing. The
carved figures lose their accustomed stiffness of pose and take
on a freedom and reality never before found in Egypt. The
work of the sculptors, especially the figures in the round, reveals a grace and realism which make us wonder if here is
not to be found the chief source of later Greek art. It is entirely possible, however, that the stimulation may have been
the other way about. The immense trade of this period of the
empire brought to Egypt the best work of all the gold and
silversmiths, wood-carvers, workers in bronze and ivory, and
the sculptors of all lands. It did not require a finished Greek
art to inspire the artists of the Nile valley. They would detect at once in the foreign workers a tendency to naturalness
entirely unknown to the frozen conventionality of their own
schools. And having discovered the tendency, they would
very probably react to it as we moderns who are the creators
of fads and movements. Thus the knowledge of the unfettered
artistry of other lands may have helped to arouse that desire
for freedom which caused the revolt of the youth of Egypt.

At any rate, Amenhotep IV must have had abundant opportunity to know much of the manners, customs, art, and government of other lands. For two generations, at least, a not inconsiderable foreign influence had been present at the court of Egypt. The foreign queens had been accompanied by a large retinue of servants, companions, and teachers when they came to Egypt. And we may be sure that they were richly supplied with the wealth and works of art of their own people. In addition to this, the trade regulations of Egypt allowed all articles destined for the use of the emperor to come in free of all duty. These articles were in many cases gifts from kings, princes, merchants, and high officials of Egypt in Asia, and were no doubt for the most part works of art, carved vessels of silver and gold, statuettes, miniature houses, temples, ships, religious processions, and whatever else the artists and sculptors of foreign lands chose to represent. The young king and his companions could not help being familiar with these presents. And since it is the way of kings to discuss art with artists, sculpture with sculptors, architecture with architects, in fact, to know something of the theoretical side of every occupation and interest in the land, we may be sure that the young prince and his group had weighed the merits and superiorities of these foreign achievements; especially would this be true when already the foreign influence had begun to show its effect. Such is the way of all progress—it comes by comparison, by noting tendencies, by an exchange of ideas, by following the hint left by one's predecessors and contemporaries. And so it happened in Egypt. There is no other way for it to happen with the human mind as it is.

The close association of religion and art in Egypt, and in all lands of that age, for that matter, make religious and artistic revolution one and the same movement. Art naturally reflected the religious customs, and conduct was prescribed by religious sanction. Thus a reform in either art or morals required a modification of the popular religion. Amenhotep's desire for freedom for himself and his people, therefore, dictated his action in conceiving a new deity, in changing the names of himself and his associates to conform to the new god, in leaving Thebes the seat of Amon, and in building Akhetaton the seat of the new god and the capital of the nation. Thus as Aakhnaton we shall know him hereafter.

What was the nature of Aakhnaton's God? From the hymns and inscriptions which have survived we have all too little with which to attempt any complete answer. In fact there is, as Sir Wallis Budge [4] points out, very little that would indicate that Aton was far and away superior to the gods already worshiped in Egypt. The hymns might be sung of Amon if one should make but a slight modification of his nature, if one should identify Amon with the energy that emanates from the sun. And almost no modification is necessary in order to insert the name of Re in these hymns, for Re was the sun-god of Heliopolis. It is not therefore in external and objective nature that Aakhnaton made his great departure. Nor can we say that the deity differed in the matter of his general benevolence. Only when we realize that Aton was first of all the result of the social situation do we begin to find the outstanding qualities which separate Aton from all other gods, for, after all, Aton was the divine phase of the answer to the social need.

As we have already seen, freedom in both art and morals is the primary need. It will therefore be the task of the ruler to supply this need. But since both art and morals must proceed from religion, i.e. be the expression of religious teaching and have religious sanction, the king must so conceive his god that the social need will be met. Furthermore, the reform must begin, not in the heavens but on the earth; deity in its relation to humanity must so act that freedom is possible. This explains why it is not necessary to make any profound revolution in conceiving the external nature of deity. Almost any

---

[4] Budge, *Tutankhamen, Atenism, Amenism*, pp. 115, 149-151.

god then existing in Egypt might have served, if only there were a way of coupling his benevolence with humanity in a way that would secure the desired liberty. What is wanted is a divine ground, or sanction, for moral and artistic freedom. This must be rationally accounted for,—even though some writers rather minimize the rational necessities of the Egyptian. How was all this to be worked out in convincing and systematic detail?

The first step was to take the freedom wanted, and to make it seem reasonable afterward. This will explain perhaps the gradual enrichment of the conception of Aton and the detailed development of his providence. Aton instead of being merely the disk of the sun was also the heat of the sun. Thus the deity with his rays could touch every living thing and give it life. So far there is no great advance upon the doctrines of other religions. But the advance may begin just where this energy is conceived of as penetrating the living being and supplying it with warmth and breath. The life of the living thing is a divine quality! Let us see how that effects the situation. Life will be holy; its natural desires, hopes, thoughts, and works will be the expression of the divine quality which is life. To curb these, to suppress them, to condemn them to conventional forms, is to hinder the deity. It is to fight against God! Man is not merely created by Aton,[5] but awakened daily by him, filled with new energy, warmth, breath, life, and joy;[6] moved by him to perform the tasks of art and life; sustained until the work is done. Then, as duration,[7] Aton lingers in man until the night is past and the god returns in the heavens. Man lies in slumber near the verge of death until the long rays of the sun touch him and raise him to his feet. There is here all the sanction for human freedom that any one could desire.

---

[5] Breasted, A History of Egypt, p. 374.
[6] Ibid., p. 372.
[7] Ibid., p. 375.

But art is also rescued. Aton has made every living thing on land or sea. He has made every creature as it is, and has divided the nations into races and colors. [8] He has made the beauty of form, [9] has designed all things. [10] Thus it is no sin to be true to the natural form in artistic labors, for the form is holy and beautiful. And even if the origin of such naturalness be but an imitation of the works of foreign races, there is still no sin committed. Aton has made the nations of men, given them their possessions, differentiated their speech, their forms, and even the color of their skins. [11] It cannot be wrong to attempt to represent the works of deity.

Budge and Breasted [12] have both pointed out that from the hymns we get no great elevated religion—that there is here a weakness in the absence of any demand for individual righteousness. This is quite true in a way, and also very easily accounted for. When the natural is truth and human freedom is the goal, no large emphasis can be put upon restrictions to human action. The blessing of Aton descends upon the just and the unjust, for the sun shines upon the evil and the good alike. Sin, according to Aakhnaton's religion, would seem to consist in a failure to be oneself,—a failure to act naturally and normally. This may be the reason that little is said of judgment and why the whole gloomy, intricate underworld is omitted in the Aton religion. With no logical necessity for judgment on the one hand, and with Aton as the only god, it would be rather incongruous to introduce an underworld peopled with so many gods and so many stages of examination as existed according to the Amonite creed. If there be a weakness here, as the hymns would indicate, it

---

[8] Ibid., p. 374.
[9] Ibid., p. 375.
[10] Ibid., p. 375.
[11] Ibid., p. 374.
[12] Budge, Tutankhamen, etc., p. 115; Breasted, ibid., p. 377.

follows logically from the universal character of Aton's nature and work.

Budge remarks: "We look in vain for the figures of the old gods of Egypt, Ra, Horus, Ptah, Osiris, Isis, Anubis, and the cycles of the gods of the dead and of the Tuat (Underworld), and not a single ancient text, whether hymn, prayer, spell, incantation, litany, from the Book of the Dead in any of its Recensions is to be found there (on the walls of the tombs of Aakhnaton's officials). To the Atenites the tomb was a mere hiding place for the dead body, not a model of the Tuat, as their ancestors thought. Their royal leader rejected all the old funerary Liturgies like the 'Book of Opening the Mouth,' and the 'Liturgy of funerary offerings,' and he treated with silent contempt such works as the 'Book of the Two Ways,' and the 'Book of Gates.' Thus it would appear that he rejected *en bloc* all funerary rites and ceremonies, and disapproved of all services of commemoration of the dead, which were so dear to the hearts of all Egyptians. The absence of figures of Osiris in the tombs of his officials and all mention of this god in the inscriptions found in them suggests that he disbelieved in the Last Judgment, and in the dogma of rewards for the righteous and punishments for the evil doers. If this were so, the Field of Reeds, the Field of the Grasshoppers, the Field of Offerings in the Elysian Fields, and the Block of Slaughter with the headsman Shesmu, the five pits of the Tuat, and the burning of the wicked were all ridiculous fictions to him. Perhaps they were, but they were ineradicably fixed in the minds of his subjects, and he gave them nothing to put in the place of these fictions. The cult of Aten did not satisfy them, as history shows, for right or wrong, the Egyptian, being of African origin, never understood or cared for philosophical abstractions." [13]

Budge shows a proper British antipathy for Aakhnaton's

---

[13] Budge, *ibid.*, pp. 94-96.

high-handed rule all through his book, and we suspect that he takes a great deal of pleasure in making Aakhnaton as he wants him before shooting at him. That, of course, is his right under present literary conventions and the guarantee of free speech. But one finds it difficult to muster much sympathy for people deprived of their precious under-world, their cycles of the gods of the dead, their liturgy of funerary offerings which must have impoverished many a family of moderate circumstances, their Block of Slaughter with the headsman Shesmu, and the five pits where the sinners were burned. And we are inclined to believe that this whole subterranean maze was not so "dear" to the Egyptian heart after all. Was it not fear rather that perpetuated this whole gloomy prospect? Aakhnaton probably knew more about its objectionable social reactions than any modern can even imagine, for did he not have reason to guess rather accurately as to how it all came about? He tried to rid the Egyptian of this cause for fear, along with all the other ills they suffered; and it is just possible that, if he had succeeded, the temporary loss of an empire and the withdrawal of a certain amount of individual liberty would not have been too great a price to pay. A religion which enslaves a people, blights its creative power, intimidates government, takes one fourth of all the land for its private maintenance, and puts the pall of fear over the nation, ought to be supplanted by a better faith. And perhaps almost any measures are justified if they have the least chance of loosing the grasp of such a curse.

Aakhnaton's religion was of course not devoid of a belief in the immortality of man. But it just happens that his view of deity and of man's life requires no such long-drawn-out and hazardous means of getting to heaven as the old faith provided. The life in man, which was his personality, was the gift of Aton.[14] No doubt it returned to its source at death—

---

[14] Budge, *ibid.*, p. 128.

the spirit returned unto the god who gave it and the body returned unto the earth as it was. And that may explain much that is omitted in the way of righteousness and judgment to come. It begins to appear that Aakhnaton did not leave his people entirely without hope.

And in his guarantee of human freedom, of divine sanction for man's work, and of a measure of immortal hope Aakhnaton achieved no mean system of philosophy. It was just in the concatenation of religious ideas that philosophy was accustomed to express itself in ancient times. Religious thought contained the substance and system of the first metaphysic and in this field of vital interest the rationalizing genius of the ancient world was expended.[15] If we keep this fact in mind we shall be able to understand the force of Aakhnaton's ideas. They were a very close-knit and rationally satisfying answer to the whole question of origins and contained also the remedy for the fears, errors, and restrictions which blighted the human spirit in his kingdom. We admit that the hymns and inscriptions are very meager materials with which to reconstruct the rather profound religious thought of Aakhnaton, but when we remember the social problem which he was seeking to solve we are not dependent upon the hymns and inscriptions alone. The various statements, and even the silences, become clothed with a significance which is highly fruitful for our purpose.

In this connection, note please that despite Wallis Budge's statement that Aton and Aakhnaton become one in the king's thought,[16] there is a high probability that Aton always remains apart from his creatures. The god sends down his rays and revives, gives life, and leaves the creature free. In no other way could the freedom of man be grounded in religious

---

[15] Cf. Shastri, *The Essentials of Eastern Philosophy*, p. 16. The same was true of all religions of the Semitic peoples also—religion, philosophy, and practice were one, and more profound than we can imagine.

[16] Budge, *ibid.*, p. 82.

or metaphysical fact. And we have very good reason to know that freedom is a primary interest with Aakhnaton on several counts. There is of course a high degree of dependence or control at this point—when the god goes to rest in his horizon (the west) man lies down and is very much like a dead man. But he does not die—the energies of the god remain in him until at morning he may be again awakened. And yet, in spite of the large degree of control which the god exerts over man— an item which is preserved and magnified to sanctify all life and form—it has yet to be proved that Aakhnaton conceived a complete determinism. In fact, Aakhnaton is not one to escape the slavery of Amon only to bind himself with a worse bondage. The phraseology of the hymns may not say all this, but the social situation shows us how the phrases should be interpreted.

In thus tracing personality to Aton as its source—in making human personality a divine energy in man—the king is not far from the modern philosopher and religious teacher who makes human personality an image of God's personality. And Aakhnaton has given an answer to something that has long puzzled us—a theory of the depression, if not the suspension, of personality in sleep. To be sure, the answer, when taken literally, in no way satisfies the modern student of this problem; but Aakhnaton saw the problem about as clearly as any of us, and he made an attempt to solve it. The *divine energy* subsides in man when the rays of *divine benevolence* are toned down through the night. Death, therefore, would be but the final and complete suspension of the gift of this type of divine energy to man. Why the suspension took place, resulting in death, is one of the silences we encounter, but we may be sure that the silence is only our misfortune; Aakhnaton filled in the gap in his teaching. He could not possibly set aside the whole funerary liturgy, the underworld, and the stages of the soul's progress in the final judgment, and the final rewards and punishments of the Amon system, and give no compensation for his action. And we may feel reasonably sure that the arguments he offered were satisfying enough to some people, for they cause the continuance of the Aton worship for some years after the death of Aakhnaton.

What was the answer? We cannot be sure, but the intimate relation of the god to all men—the giving of thoughts and words, the dividing of mankind into various races, the implication of intelligence as a divine attribute which expresses itself in design and form—argue that the creator and sustainer of man had something to do with man's demise. At any rate, the divine energy—shall we say man's personality—was withdrawn by the god. Whether man's soul merged into the being of the god and was lost, we do not know. There are many possibilities running all the way from reincarnation and transmigration to happy individual existence in the bosom of Aton. As we have already seen, there was no painful progress in the underworld—man was taken immediately to his god. And the silence indicates that man did not return to earth again to seek for his body. Final destiny was in the presence of the god, perhaps in some heavenly land, for there was at least a Nile in the sky.

Thus the divine energy which constitutes the human personality, and which dwells so precariously in the human body, could not be given or taken away except at the will of Aton. Man lives and moves and has his being only with the energies thus bestowed, and without them he departs and his body is but dust. Here is revealed a fidelity to the actual observed facts of human life, the very essence of the teaching of Aakhnaton, for we have reason to know that "truth" according to his view was an acceptance of the real and simple facts of daily life. To restrict the natural impulses was to restrain the divine energies, to oppose deity, to live falsehood, and to miss the true ends of earthly existence. Breasted says: "For him what was was right, and its propriety was evident by its very existence. Thus his family life was open and unconcealed be-

fore the people. He took the greatest delight in his children
and appeared with them and the queen, their mother, on all
possible occasions, as if he had been but the humblest scribe
in the Aton-temple. He had himself depicted on the monuments while enjoying the most familiar and unaffected intercourse with his family, and whenever he appeared in the
temple to offer sacrifice the queen and the daughters she had
borne him participated in the service. All that was natural
was to him true, and he never failed practically to exemplify
this belief, however radically he was obliged to disregard tradition." [17] This statement from Breasted must not be interpreted to mean that there were no standards of morality, no
norm of judgment in the field of the natural. The very revolt which Aakhnaton carried out implies the presence of a
standard and its application in arriving at a determination of
the truth in both art and morals. Aakhnaton did not end in
chaos. Falsehood existed also; and Aakhnaton detected it,
pointed it out, fought it with all his regal power. In what
way the standard was applied we are not told. But the results
of his reform may be seen in the art of the time, in both
technique and subject matter. We find the artist exerting a
fine sense of selection, which shows that he has gone into
the field of Nature to discover ideal form, to find there in all
the varied life the highest approximation of the truth. Breasted
says: "Thus the artists of his (Aakhnaton's) court were taught
to make the chisel and the brush tell the story of what they
actually saw. The result was a simple and beautiful realism
that saw more clearly than ever any art had seen before.
They caught the instantaneous postures of animal life; the
coursing hound, the fleeing game, the wild bull leaping in
the swamp; for all these belonged to the truth which Ikh-
naton lived." [18] We discover, however, that selection is not
carried to the point that the ideal becomes idealizing. Always

---

[17] Breasted, *ibid.*, pp. 377-378.
[18] Breasted, *ibid.*, p. 378.

the concrete fact holds sway. It is as if the king had said: "The universal does not exist apart from the particular, and we must express the particular which embodies the universal. Get as much of the universal in your particular as you can, but be sure that your particular is a particular."

There are some who will continue to declare that such an idea could not have entered the mind of Aakhnaton. And they will maintain it in spite of the fact that intelligence belongs to all time. However, a study of Egyptian life, from the battlefield to the boudoir of the queen, will reveal that life ever since has been little more than imitating the ways of the Egyptians. The appointments, the necessities and luxuries, the whole conduct of the business of daily existence, even the follies, wisdom, and vanities, have not changed fundamentally. And we search in vain for any biological reason why a brilliant mind in Egypt should not think as straight and as swiftly as any mind of equal caliber to-day. The fact that the wisdom of that day was not clothed in our terminology is no argument against the existence of a knowledge which had a systematic excellence of high degree. If in their performance they acted as if they possessed such understanding, we will do well to conclude that they did not daily perform better than they knew.

And when we encounter an art that exhibits a truth, a proportion, a fidelity that rivals our most advanced understanding of the proper relation between the ideal and the real, we must admit that at least the teachers of this art have done some thinking. And whether the thought is put into word or is expressed only by line and form, the thought is there in the mind. Will a mentality which attains this power of penetration fail to grasp the values of that higher but very similar art,—the construction which depends upon logic and forms of thought? The probabilities are such that one ought not to decide too quickly that the Egyptians could not think this or that. And if philosophy be put almost wholly into religion there is far more to be said for Aakhnaton than the following: "He tried to force the worship of 'Horus of the Two Horizons in his name of Shu (i.e., Heat), who is in Aten' upon his people and failed. When he found that his subjects refused to accept his personal views about an old, perhaps the oldest, solar god, whose cult had been dead for centuries, he abandoned the capital of his great and warlike ancestors in disgust, and like a spoilt child, which no doubt he was, he withdrew to a new city of his own making. Like all such religious megalomaniacs, so long as he could satisfy his own peculiar aspirations and gratify his wishes, he was content." [19] Such comments are of course ridiculous to any person who studies the social consequences of the Horus who has been dead for centuries and compares them with the spirit and achievement of Aakhnaton. One might as well try to identify twentieth-century United States of America with Athens because both may be described with the word "democracy." If Aakhnaton were as stupid as the above quotation would imply, he would have been a slave to his model; he would certainly never have achieved that surprisingly modern spirit which shows in everything connected with his "reform."

And it is too easy to brand the man, who is truly great, and who fails, with a word of infamy. It makes our own lack of understanding less noticeable, perhaps, but it is a term which can bring the investigation to a close at almost any point. And we need not hesitate to believe that Aakhnaton thought and acted with a subtlety which will not be grasped by one who merely compiles the events of his reign. The more profoundly individual a man is, the more will he escape the understanding of every other man. In just his measure of individuality will he always remain a mystery to the rest of us. He may seem to be a selfish megalomaniac, a spoilt child, or even a mad-man, but his worst fault may be that he is alto-

---

[19] Budge, *ibid.*, p. 106.

gether too complex for our conventional wits. And are we not all blinded somewhat with our own conceits, the private opinion that wisdom never existed in high degree except in our generation? Perhaps if we try long enough to put ourselves back into Aakhnaton's time we shall be able to understand something of the tragedy that overtook him.[20] And it may turn out that his failure is but another crime which can be charged to those who are too stupid to be worthy of great men.

But before we attach to Aakhnaton the final word of dismissal, "He failed," it may be well to review the facts in the case. Those who pass this judgment upon him keep their eyes upon the empire conquered by Thutmose III and read the Tell el Amarna letters. The hostile critics of Aakhnaton seldom think of describing Thutmose III as a failure, and yet the very evils which Aakhnaton sought to correct had their inception in the political juggling which took place in Thutmose III's day. The problem goes much deeper than a question of a rather superficial imposition upon personal liberty. It involves political and social precedents together with the economic distress which the precedents have brought about. With the whole civil, social, industrial, and agricultural life of the people centered in the Amon worship, the people were reduced to a state little better than that of temple slaves. And the king was powerless to remedy the situation without challenging the power of the Amonite hierarchy. Thutmose III built a great empire, but at the same time he nourished a viper in his bosom and it coiled about the whole life of the nation, ready to strike at the least hostile move. There are thus two ways of regarding the work of Thutmose; and from the point of view of the social results produced, we discover that Aakhnaton was trying to correct another man's failure.

---

[20] If some one more Oriental had excavated Egypt we might be far richer in our knowledge of Egyptian thought; the West has imagination, but lacks philosophical understanding of the East.

The Tell el Amarna letters in one way make the case look very bad for Aakhnaton. If it can be proved that the emperor made no reply to the appeal of his vassals in Asia, or that he did not attempt to send them relief, he may be made to appear negligent of the tasks of government. But was it not the compromises which Thutmose made with the hierarchy that added all these lands to Egypt? And which was better, a great empire stretching from the fourth cataract to the Euphrates but existing only to feed the greed of Amon, or a free, intellectually progressive, and comfortable people bounded by the fourth cataract and the Isthmus? Asia was always reconquered when Egypt became strong, and lost when she was weak. Seventeen years is a short time in which to reform a nation, free its long restricted genius, help it to find its true life, and make it again into a world power. And seventeen years was all the time Aakhnaton had. Who knows but that he had the wit to take one step at a time—to move surely so that when Asia was again conquered a new civilization could be given to the world? To be sure, the loss of Asia meant the loss of Egypt's greatest source of revenue. There can be no minimizing the calamity. And yet it is equally true that in her present condition Egypt was at a standstill; there could have been no going forward no matter how tight she held to her vassals. How much should a nation pay to save its soul? When we consider all this, the apparent silence to the cries of the dynasts in Asia is not the accusing thing it was before.

It has been said that Aakhnaton may have been averse to war and, on that ground alone, neglected his dependencies. But his religion bears quite distinctly the marks of imperialism. It is not merely the religion of a province; Aton has made all the nations of men and divided them into races. He rules over them, blesses them—in fact, he seems not to have chosen one nation more than another. Surely this is the religion of an empire such as Egypt was at that moment—Ethiopians, Soudanese, Egyptians, dwellers of the Oases, Arabs, Phoe-

nicians, men of the Orontes valley. It embraced all of them.
And it is not likely that a man who knew how he had been
compelled to strive with the priests of Amon would imagine
that Aton could conquer the world without the aid of Egyptian arms.

And perhaps the calamity which came to Egypt as a result
of the loss of Asia was not the distressing misfortune some
have thought it was. There could scarcely have been much un-
employment among the artisans who formerly had been kept
busy building the temples and tombs of the worshipers of
Amon, for there were new temples to build in Akhetaton and
employment among the artisans who formerly had been kept
case under the old régime. The resources and revenues of the
Amonite hierarchy were enough to support the new order
as fast as it was established. Then there was an entire new
capital city to be erected, and its size and and luxuriousness
rivaled that of Thebes; it could not very well be inferior.
There were also the usual number of tombs; perhaps even
more, for Aakhnaton had them built at his own expense to
be given to his most loyal supporters. The employment situation was perhaps far better under the rule of Aakhnaton than
under the preceding pharaohs. The usual agricultural pursuits of the valley would not be interrupted—there would be
plenty of food. The demands for materials for the new buildings of the capital would afford an unusual stimulation of
commerce with the Phoenician cities, and the regular tribute
of Ethiopia came in. Surely in all that could possibly comprise
a legitimate prosperity there was no vital loss.

It is true that the king did not make costly gifts to the
monarchs of Babylon, Mitanni, and Kheta as his fathers had
done.[21] But that does not mean that he was niggardly or short-
sighted in his policy.[22] With the immensity of his new building venture there would be abundant need for this gold at

---

[21] Budge, *ibid.*, p. 102.
[22] *Ibid.*, pp. 106-107.

home to pay laborers, to purchase materials, and to decorate the splendid buildings. Aton, who was the light and energy of the sun, must have a gleaming city. Aakhnaton did not plunder Asia, to be sure, but neither was he compelled to support and provision a large army of mercenaries which, when all is said and done, with the gifts to other monarchs and to the god Amon, must greatly have reduced the actual amount which could be used to better the condition of the common people. Altogether, the economic policy of Aakhnaton seems about as sound as that of any preceding ruler. And it may have been sounder, for immense sums must have gone into the pocket of the wage earner and agriculturalist.

It would appear, then, that we must look for other causes than those of the economic situation for the failure of the Aton worship. As long as Aakhnaton lived the cause of Aton made headway, and creative power increased under the new freedom. If the reformer had been followed by a strong ruler who was equally devoted to the new régime and as qualified to direct its destiny, there seems little reason not to believe that the Aton worship would have been, in time, the dominant religion of Egypt. But Aakhnaton was followed by men who made the new liberty their worst fault and who possessed none of his profound understanding and political sagacity. When we add to the weakness of the rulers the natural conservatism of the Egyptain and his fear of the underworld which is so hard to purge from the mind of any people, we have a sufficient reason for the failure.

Sir Wallis Budge tells us that "it was impossible to overthrow the great and wealthy priesthood of Amen, to say nothing of the social institutions of which Amen was the head. The monotheism of Amenhotep (Aakhnaton) from a religious point of view was not new, but from a political point of view it was. It consisted chiefly of the dogma that Amen was unfit to be the national god of Egypt, the Sudan, and Syria, and that Aten was more just, more righteous, and more

merciful than the upstart god of Thebes, and that Aten alone
was fitted to be the national god of Egypt and her dominions.
When Amenhotep tried to give a practical form to his views,
his attempt was accompanied, as has frequently been the case
with religious 'reformers,' by the confiscation of sacrosanct
property, and by social confusion and misery. It was fortunate
for Egypt that she only produced one king who was an individualist and idealist, a pacifist, and a religious 'reformer' all
in one." [23]

It is of course unnecessary to indicate all the points at which
Budge contradicts his own thesis by the above statement. The
power of the wealthy priesthood and the confiscation of
sacrosanct property will serve as a sample of the reasoning he
urges in criticism of the policies of Aakhnaton. It is naturally
extremely difficult to reform the faith of any people which
has once been thoroughly grounded in a certain type of religious thought. Witness the result in both England and
America of recent attempts to reform certain parts of the
phraseology of the Episcopal Prayer Book. How few priests
are required to hold the lines! The laity will do that without
much encouragement. This is a universal law of human
nature and was pointed out by Jesus of Nazareth: "No man
having drunk old wine straightway desireth new: for he saith,
The old is better." This is undoubtedly the rock upon which
the Aton reform struck and was dismembered after the
death of Aakhnaton.

Only one more portion of Budge's statement requires our
notice. He dwells upon the idea that the monotheism of Aakhnaton was not new, although he has previously stated that it
did not favor the elaborate underworld so "dear" to the Egyptian. If the reform of Aakhnaton had involved nothing more
than the substitution of the name of Aten for Amon, it is
inconceivable that the new order would have produced the

---

[23] Budge, *ibid.*, p. 151.

"social confusion and misery" which Budge mentions as a
reason for believeing that Egypt was fortunate to have but one
Aakhnaton. Perhaps the very fact that an unsympathetic
treatment of the acts of the "reformer" involves one in so
much contradiction is the best evidence that his "truth" was
the solution of the social and religious problem.

The power, therefore, which defeated Aakhnaton's reformation was the fear of personal annihilation in divine judgment. Closing the temples of Amon could not insulate the
heart from the virus of the old teaching nor the old teachers.
The common people, and even the fanatical members of the
higher orders, would never escape the spell of uneasiness. Religious enlightenment does not always go hand in hand with
intelligence. Great soldiers, scientists, lawyers, and men of
affairs may be the veriest children before the prospects of
the world to come. Fears are as deep-rooted as the foundations
of the soul, and dogmas are as hallowed as the instinct to
pray, often by the prayer itself. It was precisely the fact that
the reformation of Aakhnaton advocated freedom from fear,
and the ground for fear, that caused it to fail in the hands of
less courageous kings. Those who were themselves a little
fearful could not cast out fear.

It therefore requires time to secure the full step in religious
reformation, especially if an escape from fear be the chief portion of the advance. The older generation must pass away
with all its errors and superstitions, and the new one must
have escaped the control of the old teaching during the
formative years. How little of the task requiring at least seventy years of enlightenment and most intensive instruction
could be accomplished in seventeen years! And yet, without
doubt, a strong successor to Aakhnaton, and one privileged
to have a long reign, could have brought it about.

The only point, however, which needs to be determined to
establish the noble character of the purposes of Aakhnaton is
whether or not his reform could have secured more happiness,

comfort, safety, and spiritual satisfaction for the people of Egypt than could the faith of Amon. This question cannot be answered categorically because the Amonite hierarchy was reëstablished and was enabled to blot out almost all of the records of Aakhnaton's work. But some light may be gained from the later history of the Amonite priesthood which will go far toward exonerating the "reformer." Under the reorganized empire of the Rameses the priests of Amon had their opportunity. They secured their reëstablishment and the return of their property.

Breasted tells us that under Rameses III the political power wielded by the Amonite priesthood because of its vast wealth became a force which no pharaoh could ignore. "Without compromising with it and continually conciliating it, no Pharaoh could have ruled long, although the current conclusion that the gradual usurpation of power and final assumption of the throne by the High Priest of Amon was due solely to the wealth of Amon is not supported by our results. Other forces contributed largely to this result, as we shall see. Among these was the gradual extension of Amon's influence to the other temples and their fortunes. His high-priest had in the Eighteenth Dynasty become head of all the priesthoods of Egypt; in the Nineteenth Dynasty he had gained hereditary hold upon his office; his Theban temple now became the sacerdotal capital, where the records of the other temples were kept; his priesthood was given more or less supervision over the administration, and the furtive power of Amon was thus gradually extended over all the sacred estates in the land.

"It is a mistake to suppose, as is commonly done, that Rameses III was solely or even chiefly responsible for these conditions. However lavish his contributions to the sacerdotal wealth, they never could have raised it to the proportions which we have indicated. This is true of the fortune of Amon in particular as of the temple wealth in general. The gift of over seventy miles of Nubian Nile shores to Khnum by

Rameses III was but the confirmation by him of an old title; and the enormous endowments enumerated in the great Papyrus Harris, long supposed to be the gifts of Rameses III, are but inventories of the old sacerdotal estates, in the possession of which the temples are confirmed by him. These long misunderstood inventories are the source of the above statistics, which reveal to us the situation and they show that it was an inherited situation, created by the prodigal gifts of the Eighteenth and Nineteenth Dynasties, beginning at least as far back as Thutmose III, who presented three towns in Syria to Amon." [24]

If we recall the fact that Thutmose III punished the memory of the priests of Amon who set him aside in favor of Hatshepsut we shall begin to see that the story of Amon is the same from beginning to end. In addition to other elements of power they exercised under Hatshepsut the civil power also, and it was only the vigor of Thutmose III that partially loosened the hold of the priests upon the royal prerogative. But with the complete reëstablishment of Amon under the Ramesoids they were able to set to work again and did not stop until they had taken over the office of the pharaoh. Under Rameses III they had become so powerful that he dared not make a stand against them. [25] In fact, Breasted tells us, he was in need of sacerdotal support to keep his position as pharaoh.

The actual situation is vividly presented by Breasted, who records the painful struggles of a band of necropolis workmen in their endeavors to secure the monthly fifty sacks of grain due them. "Month after month they are obliged to resort to the extremest measures, climbing the necropolis wall and driven by hunger, threatening to storm the very granary itself if food is not given them. Told by the vizier himself that there is nothing in the treasury or deceived by the glib promises of some intermediate scribe, they would return to their daily

---

[24] Breasted, *ibid.*, pp. 494-495.
[25] *Ibid.*, pp. 495-496.

task only to find starvation forcing them to throw down their work and to gather with cries and tumult at the offices of their superior, demanding their monthly rations. Thus while the poor in the employ of the state were starving at the door of an empty treasury, the store-houses of the gods were groaning with plenty, and Amon was yearly receiving over two hundred and five thousand bushels of grain for the offerings at his annual feasts alone." [26]

And yet Aakhnaton is the only one who dares to challenge this power which so many pharaohs had reason to know was gradually and systematically entrenching itself through the centuries. The priests of Amon extinguished the power of the pharaoh, but their greed and selfishness caused at last the downfall of Egypt. And the purpose of the hierarchy was the same from the beginning to the end of the chapter,—as clear in Aakhnaton's day as ever it was. The young and brilliant leader who figures in the later Egyptian annals as "the criminal" saw where the hierarchy was leading, and, with noble courage and with a selflessness worthy of a great leader, he did all he could to set his people free. He has been styled by some as the first individualist and idealist, a ranking which is of course a debatable matter. But that he was almost the only true statesman that Egypt ever had will perhaps become increasingly clear as the long story of Egypt and Amon are unfolded. And if that be the final judgment of the scholar, it will be seen that the early death of Aakhnaton was of infinite loss to Egypt and to all mankind.

---

[26] Breasted, *ibid.*, p. 496.

CHAPTER VI

Moses

The contribution which Moses made to religious development in Israel is similar to that which every other great religious leader has performed for his people. Israel's religion did not begin with him. Before he appeared there had been many generations of believers and a long history of worship. Moses took the loftiest implications of the faith as he found it and developed them into his own peculiar message. In this way he made possible the spiritual and political future of his people. A study of the conditions attending every great constructive religious movement would have led us to make this inference concerning his work, but fortunately we are not compelled to depend upon inference alone. We have enough knowledge of the customs, beliefs, and institutions of his time to say with certainty that he revised a faith already accepted.

This should not seem at all strange to anyone who has traced the story of some great religious movement or has watched the modifications of creeds in his own time. Great religious advances are possible only because they are actually implied in the faith already established. Racial and social inertia are too stubborn to permit the creation of a faith which has no connection with the past. And even when the forward step is made, no matter how legitimately it may flow out of the past position, the old persists for a long period of time. Thus in the religion of Israel we discover existing side by side all of the several stages of the brilliant unfolding of the sublime story of Hebrew monotheism. We find the customs and religious practices of Bedouin persisting in the worship at "holy places" long after the central sanctuary has been established. We encounter tribal jealousies expressing themselves in the political parties and feuds of a well established Hebrew nation. And we find that this nation was finally disintegrated, after centuries of establishment, through the recrudescence of the ancient tribal spirit—the northern nation went back to the days of the Exodus, and perhaps much earlier,[1] for the religion it established when it seceded from the kingdom of Solomon.

These survivals, however much they were condemned by the writers in Israel, are very fortunate for the student of religion, for they are historical documents of the highest rank. They reveal the imperfect establishment of the ideas of the prophets and leaders of the nation on the one hand, and on the other, the precise nature of the contribution each leader sought to make. Thus it is to these documents, rather than to the fanciful and often prejudiced literary productions, to which we should turn for trustworthy information regarding the early history of Israel. As one studies these writings, he meets, however, with so many contradictions, so many evidences of the modification of fact through the influence of the authors' peculiar purposes, and so many signs of historical romancing, that he may doubt that he has any record of the past worthy of consideration. But if he will look at the conditions of religious life as mirrored unconsciously by these writers, he will probably be forced to conclude that in the main these scriptures trace the true story of Israel. And if proper allowance be made for the literary peculiarities and conventions of Semitic authors, and for the time element which always figures in religious growth, he will be able to reconstruct with some accuracy the age in which each of the great leaders lived. Such, in any case, must be the method used in the effort to

---

[1] Cf. Hastings, *Dictionary of the Bible*, art. "Golden Calf," Vol. I, p. 342.

arrive at a correct appraisal of Moses and his influence upon Israel.

And such a procedure brings to light some startling results. First, we find the figures of the patriarchs retreating into a dim past and in their places are the vast movements of kindred tribes fighting their way into Canaan and leading a precarious existence among the peoples who already hold the land. We discover that our writers are seeking to present, according to the acceptable customs of their day, an explanation of existing feuds, of geographical location, and of the similarities of race and language of the various Semitic tribes in and around Canaan. Back of each tribe there was at one time an actual personality, but the late composition of our narratives precludes the possibility of our authors having more worthy materials for their stories than legends.[2] In other words, Abraham, Cain, Jacob, Ishmael, and Esau had long been names applied to actual or to legendary tribes. And even the stories the writers record of these personalities reveal groups or tribes of such magnitude that the original founders could not still have been alive. We are thus forced to two possibilities: we must admit either that the patriarchal names are applied to powerful leaders who have inherited their position over the tribes they lead, or that the names refer to tribes. There is no possibility that the leaders described could also have been the founders of their tribes; the exploits of the so-called patriarchs demand too many fighting men for that.

A proof of this is found in the account which tells of Abraham's battle with the kings (Gen. xiv). Abraham is pictured in this narrative as a general with a considerable body of retainers. Four Mesopotamian kings assault five towns of the plain, plunder them, and carry Lot and his family away as a part of the booty. Abraham hears of it. He pursues the marauders, overcomes Chedorlaomer, rescues Lot, and returns

---

[2] Cf. Preserved Smith, *Old Testament History*, pp. 34-40.

with the spoil. The mention of "kings" gives us surprise when we have been thinking of Abraham as the head of a family of no great size. But when we realize that these "kings" are probably no more than desert sheiks and that Abraham is just as great a "king" as any one of them, perhaps greater, we find the account only a mirror of the daily life of the time. Abraham is here no more than a leader of a clan of nomads, a desert tribe of pastoral people, hardened by their occupation and the skirmishings of almost constant warfare. Thus Abraham must have been a person, if he bore the name of his tribe, who was equivalent to that member of the MacGregor clan who is styled "*the* MacGregor."

If our surmise regarding Abraham's occupation of Canaan be correct—an incursion of numerous and vigorous Aramean tribes upon the weakened settlements of Palestine—the historicity of the sojourn of the Abrahamic peoples is fairly well attested to by the Tell el Amarna letters. There is, however, one point of difference between the Amarna letters and the Genesis account: Genesis would seem to indicate that the several tribes of Israel originate from Jacob after the first invasion of Palestine; but the Amarna letters distinctly mention the Khabiri under the leadership of Abd-Ashratum (Asher).[3] Abd-Ashratum may be the father or leader of Asher who is assisted in his forays into Canaan by the other Khabiri (Hebrew) tribes.

It is impossible to be sure of the movements of these early Semitic peoples in Western Asia, but we are forced to recognize their magnitude by the historical data afforded by the Tell el Amarna letters. From Genesis we gain the impression that Abraham sojourned in the land, meeting with but very slight opposition. From the Tell el Amarna letters we learn that Canaan was occupied long before this time by a powerful

---

[3] Ab-Asheratem, or Abed-Asheratem: the leader of the Asher clan, or peoples; or the Asherite destroyer, an Asherite leader of extremely cruel tendencies. Note that Abd-Ashratum has the early form of the pronominal.

Hebrew people who were quick to take advantage of any weakness in Egypt to assert their independence. No small group of pastoral peoples could have maintained itself in the land against the wishes of the Canaanites. And from this same well-accredited historical source we learn of the magnitude of the assault of the Hebrew, or Aramean, tribes upon the cities of Canaan; and we find out at the same time why this movement could be successful against the power of Egypt.

From the Egyptian background, and from the Tell el Amarna letters which indicate its nature, we learn that it became possible for the Aramean tribes to enter Canaan with impunity because of the pressure of the Hittites on the north and the lack of Egyptian aid to the Canaanite dynasts at the proper time. The cities of Canaan had been practically disarmed and garrisoned by Egyptian mercenaries. No native force had been trained that could repel an invasion in great strength. The Egyptian garrisons were very probably only large enough to hold the native populations in hand. Thus an invading foe might be able to overwhelm the cities unless the mercenary troops were given strong reënforcements from Egypt. No considerable reënforcement was sent so far as we know, for the king of Egypt, Aakhnaton, had enough to do to keep order at home in view of the great religious reform he was prosecuting.

The origin of these tribes is difficult to trace. They were perhaps Kaldaic in language and blood, although it is just as easy to believe that the Kaldeans, Arameans, and the Bedouins all came from a common stock of shepherd tribes. The Kaldean peoples wandered into the fertile region of the Tigris and Euphrates delta and became permanent dwellers—in time, an agricultural people. The Arameans pushed out from the desert or migrated down the river from the delta. The Bedouin tribes were wandering shepherds from time immemorial, and went where their swords could command a way. There is no real reason for denying that the Abrahamic tribes came from the region of Ur and reached Palestine by way of Aramea. The fact that common ties of blood and language extend along this route would afford very strong evidence for the historicity of this part of the story of the Hebrews. But the Moabite stone,[4] and other evidences, would indicate that the whole region from the Euphrates, south and west, was occupied by peoples who were also closely related to the members of the Abrahamic confederation. Perhaps the only thing that divided them was the rite of circumcision—the sign of the covenant, the seal of the worshiper of Yah.

That the cleavage between these various Semitic peoples was religious, rather than racial, is now established almost beyond doubt. The language was the same, or at most revealed only varying dialectical differences. Perhaps the only thing which could have kept them apart was religious customs. And if the tribes outside the covenant had wished to become a part of the league it could have been managed by the acceptance of Jehovah and the fulfillment of the proper rite. There were dialectical differences even in Israel—some could not frame to pronounce the word Shibboleth.

Beyond the mere fact of kinship and the worship of the same God, there was, however, no spirit of coöperation nor sense of solidarity. Two or three tribes might unite for raids against other peoples, but when the venture had been carried out they separated and kept to their own regions. Intercourse must have been considerably restricted because of the very nature of the occupation and the general ruggedness and barrenness of the land. It is this lack of unity plus the nomadic occupation which prevents the permanent settlement of the Hebrew tribes in Canaan in the days of Aakhnaton, king of Egypt.

Genesis mentions the occurrence of a drought in Canaan as the reason for the migration of the Hebrews into Egypt. Such

---

[4] Any person acquainted with Hebrew can read the inscription which the King of Moab put on this stone.

an event would naturally produce prompt action on the part of a nomadic people. The inviting plains of the Egyptian district of Goshen would, however, be quite sufficient to cause these tribes to continue the line of their trek beyond the Isthmus. And during the days of political corruption and disorganization immediately after the death of Aakhnaton they would very probably meet with little opposition from the Egyptian border patrol. In the days of Thutmose III and his immediate successors in Egypt these nomads would have been turned back, and it is extremely unlikely that they would have produced any disturbance in Canaan without meeting with swift retribution. If in addition to the circumstances as outlined the Abrahamic peoples had strong influence at the Egyptian court, the shepherd immigrants would be welcomed and assigned to a locality favoring their occupation.

That some of the Hebrew tribes would make their way into Egypt at this time is naturally to be expected, for it was only by the most vigilant watchfulness that the country was kept free of them at any time. Previous to this the Hyksos [5] had invaded the land from Palestine, had conquered lower Egypt, and had held their conquests for nearly two hundred years. Under the weakened condition of the Egyptian government the pharaoh might deem a peaceful arrangement with the Hebrews a far wiser step than a trial of strength against the men who had smothered the combined opposition of the Egyptian mercenaries and native troops in Canaan. It was a way of making friends who would defend Egyptian soil against the possible invasion of the country by more ambitious nations. Again a possible representative at court may be inferred.

It is not likely that all of the Hebrew tribes entered Egypt either at this or at a later time. The Kenites at any rate went

---

[5] Cf. Breasted, *A History of Egypt*, pp. 211-229.

into the South and occupied the regions of the upper Sinaitic peninsula. These migrations, however, left Canaan free to the native occupants who took advantage of the respite to provide themselves with adequate defense. Contact between the kindred tribes in Egypt and Sinai was not lost completely at any time. And when a rehabilitated Egypt made slaves of the Hebrew immigrants, the tribes in Sinai must have sympathized deeply with their unfortunate brethren.

This in brief is the story of the wanderings of the Hebrews of the patriarchal age. Details cannot of course be ascertained, but the surviving historical data, the testimony of the monuments, and the persistence of Hebrew tradition indicate that the Hebrew migrations were approximately as here set forth. Along with what must have been an oral tradition handed down by the tribes from father to son, the religious development of a later time has been incorporated into the record of Hebrew history. The result is great confusion, and the task of dissecting the religion of the patriarchs from the mass of material, historical and otherwise, which makes up the Pentateuch, is therefore extremely difficult. But unless we can do this with a fair degree of accuracy it will be impossible to set forth the nature of the contribution which Moses made to the religious thought of his nation.

Certain parts of the record dealing with the life of Moses reflect the internal condition of Egypt and show us why the Israelites were enslaved. The opening chapter of Exodus says, "The children of Israel were fruitful, and increased abundantly, and multiplied, and waxed exceedingly mighty; and the land was filled with them. Now there arose up a king over Egypt who knew not Joseph." "And he said unto his people, 'Behold, the people of the children of Israel are more and mightier than we: Come, let us deal wisely with them; lest they multiply, and it come to pass that, when there falleth out any war, they join also unto our enemies, and fight against us, and get them up out of the land.' Therefore he set over them taskmasters to afflict them with burdens." [6] The account of Joseph relates how he accused his brothers of being spies who had come to spy out the land.[7] Details are not clear owing to the late date of the composition of the Pentateuch, but something of the suspicion and fear of a weakened Egypt is preserved and is a correct mirror of the times.

The enslavement of Israel was an imperial policy which naturally sprang from the uneasiness and fear of Egypt's rulers. It was a provision against the possibility of invasion by a powerful foe which might enlist its kindred, who were already in Egypt, to its standard. Exodus no doubt relates accurately the fears of the king, but it misses the point when it tells us that there was an unwillingness at this time to allow Israel to depart. If Israel could have been dispossessed and sent away peaceably, it would have been done. But to drive her out would have increased the hostile strength in Canaan. Fear, dictated by knowledge of Egyptian weakness, made the king take the only course left open to him. By enslaving the Israelites he added to his resources without augmenting the power of his foes.

We learn also that the Israelites were set to building the great store cities which would in case of war enable the king to maintain a large army in the vicinity of the Isthmus. With this large foreign population at work in the fields and upon the buildings, the Egyptians could maintain themselves and use their own people for military purposes. The account of the rigor of the Israelitish bondage is an indication of the thoroughness with which the pharaoh moved, and is a further proof of the prevailing alarm.

It was probably during the earlier years of Israel's misfortune that Moses was born. Extreme measures would be used, at first, especially during the lifetime of those who had

---

[6] Exodus i.9-11.
[7] Genesis xlii. 9-15.

known liberty and who still remembered their successful warfare in Canaan. It would be during these earlier years that every precaution would be necessary in handling large groups of this fierce and warlike people now deeply outraged by the injustice and humiliation of forced labor. No doubt there were almost daily pitched battles between the taskmasters and the Israelites. And as time went on and even the more docile slaves became embittered and desperate, it would be clear to the Egyptian authorities that there was a limit to which this rebellious population could be increased with safety. It was then that the decree went forth for the slaughter of all Hebrew male children.[8]

The shadow of the pharaoh's decree lends a dramatic intensity to the account of Moses' birth. The simple, straightforward style of the chronicler achieves a clarity and charm to be found only in the work of the greatest compilers of myths and legends.

And there went a man of the house of Levi, and took to wife a daughter of Levi.

And the woman conceived, and bare a son: and when she saw him that he was a goodly child, she hid him three months.

And when she could no longer hide him, she took for him an ark of bulrushes, and daubed it with slime and with pitch, and put the child therein; and she laid it in the flags by the river's brink.

And his sister stood far off, to wit what would be done to him. And the daughter of the Pharaoh came down to wash herself at the river; and her maidens walked along by the river's side; and when she saw the ark among the flags, she sent her maid to fetch it.

And when she had opened it, she saw the child: and, behold, the babe wept. And she had compassion on him, and said, "This is one of the Hebrew's children."

Then said his sister to Pharaoh's daughter, "Shall I go and call to thee a nurse of the Hebrew women, that she may nurse the child for thee?"

---

[8] Exodus i.15-22.

And Pharaoh's daughter said to her, "Go." And the maid went and called the child's mother.

And Pharaoh's daughter said unto her, "Take this child away, and nurse it for me, and I will give thee thy wages." And the woman took the child and nursed it.

And the child grew, and she brought him unto Pharaoh's daughter, and he became her son. And she called his name Moses (drawn out): and she said, "Because I drew him out of the water." [9]

The detailed vividness of this story furnishes a strong proof of its historicity. It could scarcely be the result of accumulated legendary material growing out of the fact that Moses' name has in some respects an Egyptian sound. Nor is it likely that this story has its foundation in a modified form of a section of the legend of Osiris. The Israelites would remember their sufferings too keenly to adopt anything Egyptian into their folklore. They might imitate, but the probabilities are that all supposed imitations have their origin in customs common to both peoples. It would therefore appear that Moses was born, educated, and given every liberty at a time when the very fact that he lived was a violation of a royal decree. In the days of Israel's bondage the pharaoh's commands were executed with studied thoroughness, for the ruler took upon himself the duty of inspecting the public works and the conduct of his officials. That a Hebrew, a member of an enslaved race, could enjoy the privileges of a free citizen, and even a noble, is inexplicable without the aid of unusual circumstances. In any case nothing short of powerful influence at court could guarantee his personal safety at a time when the worst cruelties and the most bitter revolts marked the enforcement of the decree which enslaved Israel. The story of his being set adrift among the reeds near the spot where the princess bathed is true to the nature of the times. And the fact that the princess must have seen through the ruse, and yet took measures to

[9] Exodus ii.1-10.

preserve the child, is a stroke which can scarcely be due to the artistry of the maker of legends. The story is too evidently a human document for that.

Later writers have sought to explain the compassion of the princess. She has been described as a married woman without children and as being very unhappy because of her childless state.[10] This may be true; but she was a woman, and that is perhaps enough explanation. When the circumstances surrounding the discovery of the child were understood, pity touched her heart. And if there was any need for royal permission to save the child she would prove a very effective advocate. The adoption of Moses as the son of the princess would evade the strict letter of the law and secure for him the privileges he later enjoyed.

The way in which the deliverance was conducted indicates that the leader of the Exodus was familiar with Egyptian and Sinaitic conditions and that he had been over the route he took in bringing the people safely out of the country. Again circumstances support the main features of the life of Moses. He knew Egypt, its customs, policies, language, and territory. He knew Sinai—the rugged mountains, the dry valleys, the watering places, the spots where food might be obtained; and he knew the safety the region afforded for those who wished to avoid Egyptian authority. If we do not accept the story which accounts for Moses' possession of this knowledge, we shall be compelled to give him an even more romantic and adventurous life. The deliverer of the Israelites knew the country through which he passed before he began his journey with a mob of slaves at his heels.

Since the facts attending the actual deliverance thus support the account of his early life as it has come down to us, it will be well to review the story in some detail. At some time after his education had been completed, he went out and looked

---

[10] Ap. Eusebius *Praep. Ev.* 9:27 and Philo *Vit. Mosis* 1:14.

upon the sufferings of his people. He saw that they were being destroyed by the exposure and hardships of their bondage. Herodotus tells us that Necho caused the death of 120,000 men in an attempt to reopen the canal between the Nile and the Red Sea.[11] And it is said that ten thousand men perished under Memet Ali during the construction of the canal at Alexandria. The conditions of great heat, of constant toil under the vigilant drivers, the poor houses assigned to the slaves, and the prevalence of pestilence, all contributed to make the bondage of Israel only a means of race destruction. All this could not escape the observing eye of Moses, even if he had been wholly insensible to pity.

The language used to describe his means of securing a knowledge of the condition of Israel bears the stamp of official-dom. Moses was acting in an official capacity, perhaps making the rounds of a royal inspector, when he looked upon the afflictions of his race. What he saw must have been a very shocking sight to his sensitive soul. He was grieved, outraged, and deeply angered. And seeing at once that such cruelty could not exist except by the express will of the pharaoh, he realized, perhaps for the first time, how precariously he lived. The least sign of disloyalty, or the loss of his friends at court, would cause him to be sent to drag out his life in bondage.

There can be little doubt that he protested against the intolerable conditions of his people, and little doubt that the protest was useless. Again he went from quarry to brick kiln and from canal to field inspecting the public works and noting always the same merciless treatment of the Israelites. His soul within him burned with rage. And one day, when he saw an Egyptian strike a Hebrew, he interfered. We are not told what was said upon this occasion; but it is conceivable that the Egyptian replied with scorn, perhaps lamenting that the pharaoh's uniform offered protection to Israelitish scum. The

---

[11] Herodotus ii.158.

driver struck the slave again after Moses had protested, and
the future liberator slew the Egyptian.[12] Then looking about
hastily and finding that his deed had not been detected by
other Egyptians, he made a place quickly in the sand and
buried the slave-driver. This event could not have happened
until Moses had seen enough of Egyptian cruelty and indifference to know that there was no other form of redress.
The very hopelessness of the situation made him a temporary
madman and he struck out in the rage of despair.

But his precautions were futile, for the abused Israelite had
seen the deed.[13] Had Moses taken time to reflect he would
have known that his act of murder was not the first to mark
the bitter hatred of Israel for the oppressor. And he would
have known that an investigation would be instituted as soon
as night came and the driver did not appear. Every Israelitish
slave under the supervision of the unfortunate Egyptian would
be subjected to horrible tortures until the truth was told. But
fortunately for Moses, his work took him to the same vicinity
the next day and he learned that his crime was known. Without waiting to ascertain whether his deed had been reported
to the pharaoh, he fled and thus escaped the wrath of the
king.

"But Moses fled from the face of Pharaoh, and dwelt in the
land of Midian," says the writer of Exodus. This sentence
leaves untold a thrilling chapter of the life of Moses, for it
was not easy to flee successfully the face of the pharaoh, and
flight to Midian was especially difficult. From the days of
Thutmose III, the builder of the empire, the border between
Egypt and Asia was as tightly held against all comers as is the
port of New York in our day.[14] Every person approaching
Egypt from Asia was subjected to careful questioning. And,
except under the weak kings immediately following Aakhna-

---

[12] Exodus ii. 11-12.
[13] Exodus ii. 13-15.
[14] Breasted, A History of Egypt, pp. 338-339.

ton, there was no passing the border patrol without meeting Egyptian requirements. In the day in which Moses took to flight there had been a careful reorganization of the border forces because of a fear of invasion. All persons belonging to the Abrahamic tribes would be sure to be turned back just because it was felt that any increase in the number of these peoples would be extremely dangerous to Egypt. And any person who approached the border from the Egyptian side would be subjected to an even more rigid examination, for the fear of spies now controlled the procedure. It would be practically impossible for an Israelite of any rank to pass. Moses we may be sure would not try it, for he would know that he would be held a prisoner until his identity could be determined.

How did he get into Midian? There must have been a way of avoiding the patrol, a way well known to a few Israelites on both sides of the border. It was over this secret route that communication between the Abrahamic peoples in Egypt and Sinai was effected. And no doubt many runaway slaves followed this secret path in making good their escape out of the land. The secret was carefully guarded, so much so that it seems not to have been known to the Egyptian authorities. It was along this route that Moses escaped when he left Egypt; and his return was undoubtedly by the same way. The strange line of march by which he conducted the Exodus is a revelation in itself. At a certain point on the highway to the Isthmus the fugitive turned aside into the desert, made his way to the Red Sea, and when the wind and tide were favorable traversed the sea-bed over to the other side.

This was probably a nightly occurrence. The east wind blew from the cool mountains westward toward the desert and the tide rushed out of the arm of the sea leaving a long winding bar covered by shallow water. It was a precarious road for any one not acquainted with its every turn. Here, as always, however, there must have been those who made it a business to smuggle men and goods in and out of the country. By the aid of the services of these men Moses escaped. And the route he followed when he struck boldly into the desert with Israel in the march of deliverance indicates that he knew well what he was about. Here was a way which enabled him to avoid the army posts at the border. He was not guessing; he was not taking the measures of desperation, hoping against hope that something favorable might happen; he knew what would happen, for he knew the path to the ford.

When he arrived in Midian after his flight, he would think long upon how comparatively easy had been his escape. If by some ruse the pharaoh could be persuaded to allow Israel to assemble and to get far enough on the road, all the Israelitish slaves in Egypt could be brought safely out of the land! The thought was so daring, so nearly impossible of fulfillment, that Moses tried to put it from him. But it would not stay out of mind. And in the months and years that followed the idea became the consuming subject of his meditation.

He settled down in the tribe of Midian and became as one of them. Exodus records the act of chivalry by which he attracted the attention of Reuel, the priest of Midian.[15] The fugitive, out of gratitude for his act of kindness, was made a member of the household, for that is exactly the significance of the invitation to eat bread in Reuel's tent. He now shared the joys and labors of the family into which he had been adopted, and took his place with the others in tending the flocks. In time he married Zipporah, Reuel's daughter, and seemed outwardly to be content with his surroundings and the daily scenes of his wandering nomad life.

But he had not the temperament to forget Egypt and his brethren. Every pleasure of his present life served by contrast to bring back the miseries of his kinsmen in bondage. This quiet, peaceful land with its bright, cool uplands and its se-

---

[15] Exodus ii. 16-21.

cure and sheltered valleys, how delightful it was after the somber flatness and scorching heat of the Nile valley! And here at night, when the day's toil was over and the flocks were safe in the fold, the shepherds would gather about a fire under the clear stars and talk and sing in happy contentment. Could he forget his brethren in Egypt who crawled with groanings and curses into their heated hovels of filth each night? Could he forget their wounds and tears so long as he knew there was a road by which a courageous man might bring them away safely? The man who struck down a cruel Egyptian slave-driver and who drove back the shepherds who imposed upon Reuel's daughters has in him a quality that will never give him peace until he comes to the relief of all Israel. He may delay action, but the action is sure to take place at some time.

The delay ended one day when he was with the flocks upon the mountain. We are told that he led the flock to the backside of the desert and came to the mountain of God, even to Horeb. [16] The story is evidently of very late date, and appears to possess a number of marks common to Zoroastrianism, but we know that long before this it was the custom of Semites to worship God in high places and to associate Him with sacred trees and groves. Under a great tree on Horeb Moses communed with Jehovah—that much is true to the religious customs of the Semitic peoples of that age. Here to the holy place Moses had come to lay before God the great problem of his soul, and we can scarcely doubt that he made this journey expressly for the experience which followed. He saw the shekinah and heard the voice of his God saying: "I have surely seen the affliction of my people which are in Egypt, and have heard their cry by reason of their taskmasters. I know their sorrows." [17]

It is not difficult to discover the background of Moses' thought from these words of God. He has come protesting

---

[16] Exodus iii. 1.
[17] Exodus iii. 7.

against the apparent slowness of divine relief in answer to the many years of prayer and sorrow of the enslaved Israelites. We can almost hear Moses saying: "Lord, have you not seen the afflictions of Israel? Have you not heard her cry? Do you not know of the endless cruelties of her taskmasters? Why do you delay to deliver her?" This line of thought is quite natural enough, for it is the problem which grows out of every extended period of human misery. But the immediate cause of Moses' prayer is an event which has perhaps taken place only the night before. Another fugitive has made his way out of Egypt to sit by Reuel's fire. He has told during the evening of the death of the old pharaoh and of the even more cruel practices of the young man who has succeeded to the thone. And whereas the condition of Israel was almost intolerable before, it has now become but destruction. The man who slew an Egyptian taskmaster knows what the condition was formerly, and now he listens silently, his eyes burning with a deep, smouldering anger. At daylight he is up and away with his flock to the mount of God. He will present this outrage before the Lord.

He arrives at last and pours out the bitterness of his heart in prayer to God. While he prays he is aware of a light and God is speaking to him. And as he listens the delay is made clear; God has been waiting for a man who can lead the deliverance.

"I know their sorrows," saith God. "And I have come down to deliver them out of the hand of the Egyptians, and to bring them up out of that land unto a good land and a large, unto a land flowing with milk and honey. Now therefore, behold: Since the cry of the children of Israel is come unto me, and since I have also seen the oppression wherewith the Egyptians oppress them, come, therefore, and I will send *thee* unto Pharaoh, that *thou* mayest bring forth my people, the children of Israel, out of Egypt." [18]

[18] Exodus iii. 7-9.

Moses protests that he is not the person to go, but there is no escape from God and the voice of his own heart. He knows that success is a possibility, that if he can once get Israel far enough upon the road he can bring her safely out of the land. His own chivalrous soul will not permit him to refuse to try. And when he has admitted this much, it is only a question of how to gain the confidence of Israel and get her far enough on her way out of the country to make good her escape. How shall he go about it? What shall he say to Israel and to the pharaoh?

There are two problems to be met in securing full leadership of Israel. First, the scattered condition of the Israelites, owing to the different kinds of work and the widely separated localities in which they are employed, make concerted action extremely difficult. It is a part of the pharaoh's policy to divide and rule. Thus the enterprise which Moses is undertaking is just the thing the Egyptian authorities all along have sought to prevent. It will be no small task to reach each group effectively and secretly—to restore confidence, to create the belief that the plan will succeed, and to do it all without the knowledge of the authorities. No one could possibly do this unaided. The writer of Exodus tells us that it was done through the elders who were in charge of each of these groups; through them the Deliverer communicated with all Israel.

The second problem was that of restoring Israel's faith in God. The people must be persuaded that God had not forgotten them all these years, and that He had witnessed their afflictions and had heard their many prayers to Him. This was no easy task in that day. When one people conquered another it was believed that the result was obtained because of the power of the conqueror's god. A people won or lost a battle because its god was stronger or weaker than the god of the enemy. Again, gods were regional in their jurisdiction. No favor could be secured from the gods unless one were able to prevail with the gods of the district in which he lived. Jehovah had not been able to prevail against the gods of the Nile valley. The best proof of this was the long bondage of His people. They had called upon Him, but He had done nothing; the only rational conclusion, according to the prevailing religious thought of the time, was that He could do nothing for them. To circumvent this article of popular religion is one of the first steps the Deliverer must take.

From the account given in Exodus of this phase of the work of Moses we cannot see clearly just how the step was taken. If we adopt the premise that no profoundly philosophical conception was possible among the Hebrews, we shall meet with only a renewed emotional contact between the Hebrew and his God. Any idea will serve, if it be able to produce the emotional ferment that will secure faith and action. And yet the situation is precisely one that demands a philosophy of profound depth and scope. While it is true that the average Hebrew slave will not be equal to a highly abstract religious philosophy, we will do well to remember that a conquered people never remains "average" for long. The iron enters the soul and produces powerful thought reactions. Up to the limit of individual capacity the tortured spirit explores the whole realm of philosophy. And there is no reason to suppose that the Hebrew of that period was on the average any more stupid than he is to-day. There must have been many minds of unusual capacity which groped at the whole problem of man and God, and especially employed themselves with trying to fathom the ways of a deity who would prosper Joseph and forget them.

It would seem, therefore, that Moses is talking about something of more importance than a question of identity when he asks, "Behold, when I come to the children of Israel, and shall say unto them, 'The God of your fathers hath sent me unto you'; and they shall say to me, 'What is his name?' what shall I say unto them?" [19] We already know that a name to the Hebrew was an expression of the character of the person named. And what is more natural than the question Moses puts in the mouth of the Hebrew slaves? Surely that is just the crux of the religious thinking the bondage will produce. What about this God of our fathers? How do you reconcile his conduct toward Joseph and toward us? What sort of character does he possess? Explain this terrible predicament? Moses must have an answer, and we may be sure it could be no shallow one. Philosophical or not, if it explores the whole metaphysical realm in seeking the nature of deity, a few tags of terminology have little to do with the case.

The writers who have assigned a limit to the philosophical capacity of the Hebrew and the Egyptian of this period will do well, therefore, to reconsider their conclusions. To be sure, no such depreciation of the intelligence of the men of the ancient world would have appeared if proper attention had been given to their achievements, their capacities, their intellectual intercourse, and the true function of their religions. And yet, perhaps it is not ignorance of these facts but the determination to support a thesis which has caused all the trouble. The attempt to support the evolutionary theory of the development of man from materials to be found in historic times is probably the root of this error. If we had all looked upon our historic data as only the record of human experimentation in certain directions we should have kept our feet more firmly upon the ground. The intelligence was there, as brilliant as any to be found to-day; but it expressed itself by a different tongue, put its achievements in another mold.

When we come to the question of Moses and the answer of God, we face a profound intellectual solution of a problem of deity. What kind of a God must Moses take to the oppressed Israel? Surely no other God than the god of the

---

[19] Exodus iii. 13.

fathers, for no other God will be accepted. But how can this God be trusted to deliver the people after all these years of neglect, or of apparent inability to relieve their sufferings? The problem of Moses evidently becomes one of re-interpreting the being and purposes of God, a matter of reading history in a way that will preserve the honor of God and stir the loyalty of Israel to fever heat. This task may not be an exercise in logic and metaphysics, but it will be the creation of a practical theism and the development of a theory of politics. And perhaps the belief that God speaks great, illuminating thoughts to us is as true a description of the origin of truth as any our modern psychology has brought to light. At any rate, it gives to truth a solemnity which proves of immense value to morality and progress. It is hard to see wherein we have outstripped the ancients. In fact, it appears that we have yet to profit by their example—they reformed the philosophies and creeds which failed to meet the problems of life.

The question of Moses is, therefore, a solemn confession, not of the sins of Israel, but of the inadequacy of former beliefs. There is no masking the fact that Israel will no longer follow a preacher of an ancient theology. They will follow the God of their fathers, provided He is considerably and sufficiently modified. But they have lost all confidence in Him in His ancient rôle. To go to them with all the old doctrines intact is to invite their most bitter scorn. It is not that Israel is not religious, but that she is no longer to be commanded by a conception of God that has failed them at every point. They will ask of this new preacher very searching questions: "What is the name of your God? Tell us about this God of our fathers. What kind of a character has He? How does He meet the problems of life and history?" And unless the preacher can make his story sublimely convincing there will be no deliverance.

The answer calculated to meet this situation of legitimate agnosticism is rather obscure. God said to Moses: "I am that

I am. Thus shalt thou say unto the children of Israel, I am hath sent me unto you. The Lord God of your fathers, the God of Abraham, the God of Isaac, and the God of Jacob, hath sent me unto you: This is my memorial name for ever, and this is my memorial unto all generations. Go, and gather the elders of Israel together, and say unto them, 'The Lord God of your fathers, the God of Abraham, of Isaac, and of Jacob, appeared unto me, saying, I have surely visited you, and seen that which is done to you in Egypt. And I have said, I will bring you out of the affliction of Egypt." [20] Here from the language one might surmise that Jehovah has made a flying trip to Egypt and has personally inspected the condition of his people. Such does seem to be the meaning of the reference to the patriarchs and the statement, "I have surely visited you in Egypt." One may with some reason conclude that all this goes back to Mt. Zion as the place where God dwells, and is therefore the view of a later time. But the statement is also true of this time. Even Jehovah very probably had his territory where he held exclusive jurisdiction.

There have been a number of attempts to extract the substance of the Mosaic reformation from God's declaration of His name. Some of the exegetes have engaged in a debate regarding the possibility of assigning a metaphysical content to the statement, "I am that I am." A Greek or Hegelian conception of being has been wielded by the affirmative; the evolutionary hypothesis demonstrable in historic times has been the chief infirmity of the negative. Naturally the debate has ended without profit to anyone. A little more light has been liberated by the group which has translated the imperfect tense employed in the Hebrew by an English future tense, "I will be what I will be," "I will be has sent me unto you." Aside from the fact that the translation has the highest probability of being the correct one, we have gained little real in-

---

[20] Exodus iii. 14-17a.

sight into our problem. It is urged, of course, that this translation puts a future into Israelitish life, something which Israel
needed very much indeed at the moment. The phrase is
reminiscent of the wording of all covenants and promises
during this period and is completely harmonious with the
new rôle of Jehovah as Deliverer and Covenant Maker. A very
good case is thus made for the opinion that the name sets
forth a Covenant Maker declaring His character. But, while
all this is quite reasonable enough, we are not overwhelmingly
convinced that this would be sufficient to electrify an agnostic
and embittered Israel. Surely protection and keeping are the
function of any God of a people, and a few more promises
are not likely to make a very great impression upon a people
long neglected and enslaved. They will surely ask: "How can
we be sure that He will at last come to our relief? Is this
promise any more likely to be fulfilled than the natural obligation a deity owes to his people?"

Perhaps we shall make more progress in our understanding
of the nature of the Mosaic contribution to religion if we
center our attention upon the immediate religious needs of
Israel rather than upon the results of exegesis. After all, religion is never popular unless it ministers to the actual social
and spiritual life of a people. Moses will have the advantage
over some religious leaders—he will not need to combat a
religious creed deeply entrenched in powerful institutions.
Israel has no institutions other than her primitive tribal ones,
and even these have become greatly discredited. But, as we
have seen, the very forces which have weakened the older
faith will provide a powerful test for the new. The exegesis
of Jehovah's name may reveal Him to be no more than a
Maker of Promises, but the agnosticism which the years of
affliction have produced will demand infinitely more. And
Moses supplied all that the situation required, exegesis not-
withstanding. There was no possibility of successfully reviving
the weakened morale of race and religious consciousness without

it. The colorless ghost of deity which so many writers have exhibited would have been laughed to scorn. Thinking men in Israel would not have accorded Him even the dignity of being brushed aside. Moses supplied a tremendously stimulating and reviving hope. We may never know just what it was, but we do know what it did.

The most essential thing demanded under the circumstances of Israel's condition is powerful proof of the deity's presence among them. After so many years of prayer and suffering there must be a little divine action. The "I will be" must begin to get busy with His program of "being." The appearance of Moses to the elders with the statement that the God of the fathers has sent him to deliver Israel will excite only a mild curiosity at best. Not until Jehovah stalks through the land with a mighty tread will He attract the attention of a doubting and despairing Israel. Then come the plagues which a few writers have regarded as only so much legendary clap-trap, not realizing that nothing short of the moving of heaven and earth could have awakened Israel to life and faith.

Whether Moses appeared during the plagues and merely took advantage of their presence as they occurred is wholly beside the point. His situation demanded just the interpretation he gave them. And that he had a God to communicate who commanded the forces of nature and struck His blows with flood and pestilence is very fortunate for the venture of deliverance. When this feature of the nature of deity is found to be so admirably fitted to Israel's actual need, we may be inclined to wonder whether the recorded conversation on Horeb between Moses and Jehovah is just what took place. Perhaps the exegetes will be able to smooth matters out somewhat in the future, but just now it appears that there is a disjointed relation between Egypt and Horeb. The Covenant Maker becomes too suddenly the Whirlwind in Egypt. To a certain type of mind there is, of course, perfect harmony all along the line; but another kind of mind will be prone to infer that a later generation has supplied the thunders and the flaming tree of the Serbal range.

We shall spend no time with the question as to which mind will be nearest the truth, for we have the suspicion that the real message of Moses can be studied best from the west side of the Red Sea. Sinai and Israel's later history will of course furnish to this message further details. The Jehovah of the Deliverance was in turn also the Covenant Maker, the God of Hosts, the resident of Mount Zion, and finally the God of the Whole Earth. But what he was in Egypt is the real message of Moses during the Exodus and was the power behind the Covenant for long years thereafter.

And note, please, that in Egypt Jehovah spends no time in making covenants with Israel or with anyone else. His emissary informs the elders of Israel that he has been sent to conduct them and their people out of the land. Then with a dignity to be expected of the representative of an all-powerful God, he makes his way to the palace and formally presents a demand to let the Hebrews depart. Here again the extra-Isthmian character of Jehovah is revealed. He dwells outside of Egypt, like a powerful Asiatic despot or emperor, and has sent his plenipotentiary to arrange with the king of Egypt for the departure of Israel. And who is so qualified as Moses to play the part of such a representative? Moses is thoroughly familiar with the etiquette of the Egyptian court. He speaks the Egyptian tongue as well and perhaps better than the language of Israel. He will know exactly how to conduct himself as the emissary of Jehovah—his manner will be such as to leave the impression that here is the representative of a power the pharaoh will do well to placate.

The first interview, however, is not such as would contain a challenge to the pharaoh's authority. Moses makes a simple request that the people be allowed to go on a three days' journey that they may make a feast to Jehovah in the wilderness. The pharaoh haughtily declares that he knows no such

God as the God of the Hebrews and that he will not grant the request. Moses then repeats his petition and states that he makes it in order that Jehovah may not come and fall upon them with pestilence and sword. But the pharaoh cares nothing for Israel and has no fear of Jehovah. He has held Israel in bondage for years in spite of the God of the Hebrews. Why should he fear their God now? Furthermore, the slaves have ceased their labors and have become a clamoring mob. The situation is such as to demand a strong hand to control it. He will send Israel back to work. And to make sure that no such insubordination shall recur, he gives command that the tasks shall be performed under worse conditions than heretofore. The will of the pharaoh is obeyed. The cruelties of the taskmasters are such that the elders of Israel appear before the pharaoh to protest. The result of the interview only further increases the rigor of the already intolerable burden.

So far it would seem that Moses has simply acted upon the old plan that has so long haunted his thought. He would by a ruse secure permission to allow Israel to get far enough on the road to make good her escape from the land. To strengthen his petition he has first approached the slaves and has aroused in them much dissatisfaction, the equivalent of a popular uprising. He has found that the pharaoh is not to be duped nor easily awed. And to make matters worse, the situation has become such as to threaten the success of the project of deliverance. He has antagonized the pharaoh and has practically lost the confidence of Israel. When the elders come out from their conference with the pharaoh they turn upon Moses and Aaron in solemn condemnation: "The Lord look upon you and judge; because ye have made our reputation to be abhorred in the eyes of the Pharaoh, and in the eyes of his servants (taskmasters), to put a sword in their hands to slay us." [21] A worse situation could scarcely be imagined.

---

[21] Exodus v. 21.

Now occurs the actual fulfillment of the phrase, "I will be." Moses at his wits' end turns to God, saying: "Lord, wherefore hast thou done evil to this people? Was it for this that thou didst send me? Since I came to Pharaoh to speak in thy name, he hath done evil to this people, and thou hast not delivered them." [22] Note the reply of the Lord, for it is perhaps the key to the interpretation of the whole Mosaic message: "Now shalt thou see what I will do to Pharaoh: for with a strong hand shall he let them go, and with a strong hand shall he drive them out of this land. I appeared unto Abraham, unto Isaac, and unto Jacob, as God Almighty, but as Jehovah was I not known to them." [23] Under the standard of God Almighty the Hebrews marched through Canaan to Egypt. The Almighty was the Mighty One in only one particular, as God of Hosts. He has never revealed Himself to any one heretofore as All-Embracing Might. Now He will be what He can be. He will use the powers of Nature and show that He is truly the Almighty. He is not to be, therefore, a Maker of Promises only; He is to be the Covenant Fulfiller. That is precisely the need of this hour. In no other way could Israel be delivered. For the successful revelation of Himself in this new rôle it is hard to see how the first interview of Moses with the pharaoh could have been more auspicious. Moses with even the least hold upon Israel must have shared with Jehovah a part of the glory. Now the honor shall belong to God alone.

Thus we are enabled to see the exact relation between the past and the future of Israel's faith. God, the Almighty, has been the same from of old, but He has never yet proved it fully in the life of Israel. He has, to be sure, proved to be equal to the needs of His people prior to this, but that was done without bringing in the weapons of pestilence and Nature. Now He will fight with these for His people. What He was

---

[22] Exodus v. 22-23.
[23] Exodus vi. 1-3.

capable of being all along, He will now reveal Himself to be. Just whatever the situation may demand, He is competent to become. And in thus unfolding the latent power of His ancient character, He ushers in that advance in religious thought which hushes all human doubt and electrifies His people.

We have happened here upon a strange fact—the nature of deity keeping abreast of the social and spiritual needs of a people. And perhaps that is all that God can ever be to any age or nation. People do not usually understand sufficiently to pray beyond their actual wants; neither do they frame situations and stretch the nature of deity to cover them. In fact, they do not often comprehend the full significance of the little light they possess. They see God as sufficient for to-day, and never realize that in so seeing Him they have found also the source of their help for the new perils of to-morrow. Here is the cause of practically all agnosticism—the failure to read the larger meaning of one's present creed. The religious genius comes along, makes an adequate distribution of the middle term, ties the future to the past, and humanity resumes its amazement and worship. Human thinking, and not God, is thus expanded to saving proportions.

This is all Moses did, for it was all he could do. To reëstablish himself with Israel he must preach a delivering God. And since human agency is powerless before the will of the pharaoh, he and Israel must wait until the God of Might has wrought His wonders in the land. But Moses must apprise the people of the fact that mighty things are to take place, that God shall begin to show His power, else the "natural" weapons will be regarded as only another phase of their calamity. Thus the message of Moses to Israel now becomes, "Do not lose heart. God will redeem you with a stretched out arm and with great judgments." [24] Israel, of course, does not believe him "because of anguish of spirit and

---

[24] Exodus vi. 6b.

because of the cruel bondage." [25] But that is to be expected at this stage of the proceedings. When the Whirlwind and Destruction begin to stalk through the land they will remember his words.

A still further phase of the situation is worthy of our attention. Moses is himself much confused. He has no idea how he ought to proceed, now that his prearranged plan has come to naught. Nor has he any notion of the manner in which the arm of Jehovah shall be stretched out or the way in which the mighty judgments shall express themselves. We hear him protesting against a second interview with pharaoh: "The children of Israel have not hearkened unto me, and how then shall Pharaoh hear me?" [26] Did Moses expect to intimidate the pharaoh by reason of the turmoil and ferment of the Israelites? If so, his protest has a meaning we can understand. And there can be no doubt that religion is developed in exactly this way—the leader finds his creed in rationalizing the events of nature and history. He discovers the ways of God in the events as they transpire. A great religious teacher must therefore be something of an opportunist at all times; he must interpret the events of life and nature, must set forth their religious significance. At this particular moment, before the judgment begins, Moses has no need for anything more than a belief that God will deliver His people. The very difficulties in the way will show him that the deliverance will be wrought by mighty acts. Perhaps he too is impatient for the judgment to begin, for he seems to feel that the time for conferences is at an end.

How much of the calamity of the plagues is foreseen by Moses, we cannot know. It is not inconceivable that he could see that the millions and billions of frogs would perish because of the lack of food, that there would be flies and murrain and boils as a result of the filth and putrefaction. Any one else

---

[25] Exodus vi. 9.
[26] Exodus vi. 12.

might have foreseen it, but the fact that Moses was present to deliver his people, and that from first to last all these plagues were universally regarded in that day as a sign of the deity's displeasure, affords a coincidence strongly favoring the interpretation of their origin which finally prevailed. As calamity followed upon calamity and the people became more and more panic stricken, this view of the source of Egypt's affliction would be inevitable. Moses, because of his convictions, would be perhaps the only person unamazed. His manner, his warnings, and his repeated demands, always followed by further distress after each refusal, made him a dreaded figure wherever he went. His creed therefore had such immediate illustration that both Israelites and Egyptians came to accord his every word the highest respect.

The change in the pharaoh's attitude toward Moses and Aaron as the calamities increased is an interesting study, and perhaps affords a strong proof that we are on fairly sure historical ground. At first the pharaoh's advisers reflected the haughtiness of their king, but at length, after many afflictions had taken their toll, they were surprised at their ruler's stubbornness. And when Moses was withdrawing with another threat upon his lips they conceived a compromise, one that would save the pharaoh's dignity but which would acquaint him exactly with the state of his people. "How long shall this man be a snare to us?" they asked. "Let the men go that they may serve the Lord their God. Do you not know yet that Egypt is destroyed?" [27] There may have been more tact in their advice, and there may not have been. A ruler is not very formidable when his subjects are storming at his gates for redress. In the day of an uprising the menial always becomes possessed of the courage to speak his mind.

The very bluntness of the counsel had its effect. Moses and Aaron were recalled. It was the first time there had been such

---

[27] Exodus x. 6, 7.

prompt action and was to the two leaders a sign that the pharaoh was weakening. They were greeted with the command, "Go and serve your God; but who and who shall go?" The pharaoh was not yet completely reduced. He had known all along that once out of the land the slaves would not return. He tore away the mask. At last the situation had to come out. The reply of Moses confirmed his conclusions, and he, after threatening them, commanded that only the male Israelites should depart. With a great show of bluster he drove out of his presence Moses and Aaron. But the Liberator knew the bluster was meant to save the face of the king. Only a little more of this and Israel would be free to leave the country.

Locusts came upon the fields, and then three days of sandstorms that darkened the sky and left the land in night. In haste the pharaoh sent for Moses and commanded him to leave, taking with him all of his people. But Moses refused to depart without the means of offering sacrifice. In anger the king ordered him to go, saying, "Take heed to thyself, see my face no more; for in the day that thou seest my face thou shalt surely die!" [28]

It was as far as the pharaoh could go and keep his dignity as a ruler. But all the force of his threat was lost by the counterthreat of Moses, "Thou hast spoken well. I will see thy face again no more!" [29] There was just enough of suppression and mystery in this defiant retort to throw the whole court into a panic. And to make matters still worse Moses made his first appeal to the pharaoh's subjects.[30] The man in the palace had lost his scepter for the moment and the man from Horeb was lord of the land. He went up and down making his arrangements for the Exodus. Jewels of silver and gold were exacted, flocks and herds were collected, and the people were commanded to be in readiness to depart. Then a pesti-

---

[28] Exodus x. 28.
[29] Exodus x. 29.
[30] Exodus xi. 2-3.

lence came to practically every household in Egypt. The pharaoh sent to Moses in haste begging him to get him, his people, and his flocks out of the land at once. During the confusion that followed the Israelites took what spoil [31] they could of gold and silver, of jewels and raiment, and of flocks and herds, and began their march toward the Isthmus.

The line of march cannot be accurately determined, but at some distance inside the Isthmus the Israelites turned aside into the desert and marched toward the Red Sea. An interesting comment on the march states that they went five abreast on the road.[32] This is undoubtedly a military term and indicates that a considerable number of the Israelites must have been soldiers in the army of the pharaoh. No doubt they were armed, and against any except the best trained troops could have given a good account of themselves. The organization of the march must have been well conceived. There were shepherds and herdsmen who drove the large flocks—cattle and sheep and goats equal to the number that had originally belonged to them and which had been confiscated by the pharaoh when he had enslaved the people. Moses in demanding that the flocks be taken along was doing no more than require that the people's property be restored to them. Divisions or companies of the quickly devised soldiery guarded the front and rear and either side.

Progress must have been slow, for such an immense number of people and cattle could not have made many miles during the actual marching time of each day. The pharaoh's captains kept a close watch, no doubt hoping that the Israelites would be turned back dismayed at the border. But when Moses led them eastward into the desert they were surprised and hastily reported to the king the turn the march had taken. Quickly inferring that the eagerly hoped for dissension had occurred, and that Israel had turned aside into the desert

[31] Exodus xii. 30-36.
[32] Exodus xiii. 18 and xii. 51.

to settle her quarrels before resuming her march, the pharaoh gave command that a division of his swiftest chariots should pursue them and cut them to pieces. But Israel had not stopped to become more and more disorganized. The march had been steady, and when the Egyptians sighted them they were en-camped along the sea waiting for the road to open before them.

The account of the escape of Israel from the pursuing Egyptians is not as clear as it seems upon first reading. Evidently there was great consternation in the camp at first, and perhaps for some time after Moses reassured them. But as night settled down, perhaps with a low-lying fog which concealed them from the Egyptians, and the road across the sea began to clear, hope returned. As soon as the path could be traveled the crossing began. The Egyptians could not see what was taking place until daylight.[33] When they saw the path leading through the sea and the last of the Israelites at some distance toward the opposite shore, they hurried by the same way to overtake them. But the soft sea-bed gave beneath the chariot wheels and impeded their progress. Difficulties increased as they went on; panic began to overtake them. Then suddenly the returning tide overwhelmed them in the midst of the sea and destroyed them.

Thus did Moses deliver his people out of the hand of pharaoh. There is a strong tendency in certain quarters to re-gard the whole story of the Exodus as highly legendary. To be sure, the centuries that followed may have added much to the story, but the whole atmosphere of the times, the strong accord of event and situation, the psychological verity of the account, the deity made to fit the social state, and even the avoidance of the strong border garrisons by crossing over the sea-bed, all ring so true to Egyptian affairs as we know them that there can be litle doubt that in the main the story is based

---

[33] Exodus xiv. 24, "Morning Watch."

upon fact. How far the Hebrews went below the border garrisons to make the crossing we do not know. Within the circumstances it was the only way an escape from Egypt could take place. Under cover of darkness and a fog, while the tide was out, the Israelites passed the dangerous border. That they took to the desert to conceal their movements in approaching this danger zone is naturally to be expected when guided by a leader who took every precaution against possible trouble. But if we had nothing but the persistence of the story of the crossing, we would still have a very strong reason for regarding it as possessing a high degree of historicity. Israel had nothing whatever to gain from manufacturing the Egyptian episode.

Let us pause here to sum up the facts regarding the beliefs and teachings of Moses to this point. He fled from Egypt, and the circumstances of his escape showed him that all Israel could be rescued if, by a ruse, he could get permission to make a three days' march toward the border. On Horeb he passed through an experience which convinced him that it was his duty to go to Egypt and bring Israel out of the country. He felt that God would be with him to aid him, that his efforts could not fail. But when he began to put his plan of deliverance into effect he met with such unforeseen results that he knew not what to do. He had fortunately two facts to which he could hold in his confusion: God had called him to this task, and God would see him through. There would be a way out. Thus when the plagues occurred they were to the alert and watchful leader a sign that God had begun the labor of deliverance. And as the plagues followed one another and the fears of the Egyptians increased, his courage grew. It was not that he was an opportunist with a few plagues on the credit side of the ledger; *he was in the midst of the plagues with a faith.* No man in the land was more convinced than Moses that these calamities came from God.

A further indication of the failure and confusion of Moses,

according to prearranged plan, may be found in the persistence of the opinion that man must fail that the salvation may be of God and not of man. Where did this item of Israelitish faith come from? Evidently it originated from the experiences of Moses in the days of the Exodus. When Moses was helpless, when he had completely exhausted every human means and had nothing more that he could do, God interposed between him and failure. Thus what others would have called the conspiracy of chance—the plagues, their continuation over a long period, the superstition of the Egyptians, the destruction of the pursuers in the Red Sea—was to him the direct help of the Almighty. Thus during this period the Almighty proved to be what He could be. All His power was used, and the God who formerly had brooded over his people and their enemies and who had prospered the Hebrews in their battles, became a God who fought with plagues and pestilence, with disease and death, and who used all the mysterious powers of earth and sky and sea to gain His ends. This is a marked expansion of the older conception of the Almighty. And when Israel has developed her ethical standards to conform to this idea of deity and has learned a fair amount of military discipline and strategy, she will be invincible upon the field of battle. We shall not be surprised that she could conquer Canaan, but that she delayed so long to undertake it.

There is, therefore, the highest probability that we shall find the true Mosaic contribution to Israel's religion, not in the covenant and sacerdotal details of Israelitish life, but in the belief that there must be signs and wonders and mighty acts wherever God is to be found. Israel on her part must trust, obey, keep the law, and follow; God will bring the downfall of strongholds and the salvation of His people. Thus Joshua, Gideon, Elijah, and David are in one sense the most characteristic representatives of the Mosaic tradition. The real difficulty in any attempt to discover all that Moses did is the many-sidedness of his activity. He was of the Joshua-Gideon-Elijah-David type, but he was ever so much more. He was also a law-giver, declaring the whole counsel of God. Thus he was also well represented by Isaiah, Jeremiah, Hosea, and Amos. And he was a great organizer of Israelitish life, and this side of him reappeared in Samuel, Hezekiah, and Ezra. In a nation which occupied the highroad of the march of empire for so many centuries and which suffered so many and varied fortunes, no one of these Mosaic functions could ever die out entirely. But in seeking for the God which Moses revealed, we shall do well to begin with the conception of the Almighty One. The rest follows, and is subordinated to this idea.

Israel turned southeastward after leaving the point of crossing the sea and entered the valleys and glens of the Sinaitic peninsula. This territory was the pasture land of the Amalekites who had their seat of government farther north, in the Negeb. When the Israelites entered this territory they were at once attacked by small bands of the Amalekites who hung upon their rear and sought to cut off their baggage and stampede their flocks. This hostility may be easily explained by the fact that the Israelites showed every sign of making a permanent occupancy of the country. With flocks and herds, with women and children, they might stop at any point in their march. The Amalekites sought to make them so uncomfortable that they would prefer to halt rather than face constant guerrilla warfare.[34] This also served to occupy the attention of the Hebrews until the Amalekites could collect their scattered shepherd forces for a pitched battle. Without knowing it, the Hebrews had been marching directly toward the main camp of the Amalekites.

At Rephidim the Israelites found the enemy in force. Battle could not be avoided. Moses selected from the tribe of Benjamin a young warrior by the name of Joshua and put him in

---

[34] Deuteronomy xxv. 18.

command of the troops. The two opposing forces met in the valley and the fortunes of the struggle went, now to one side, now to the other. Thus the battle continued until near nightfall when the Amalekites fled from the field, leaving their camp in the hands of the Hebrews.

A description of the plunder taken from the camp, together with the very fact that Israel was victorious over a warlike foe, [35] affords much information as to the character of the people delivered from Egypt. No doubt Israel possessed many fighting men who in this battle gave an excellent account of themselves. Since the battle was long drawn out, there must have been a considerable use of strategy and a need for the courage of trained soldiers. Such men in force could have come from no other source than the army of the pharaoh. How these troops would behave under Israelitish leadership, instead of Egyptian officers, was the real test. Victory therefore, meant much more to the Hebrews than freedom from the annoyance of an enemy. They were now full of confidence and the peoples round about conceived for them considerable respect.

News of the victory traveled far. The Kenites moved for a closer relation in an alliance with Israel, and the tribes in the peninsula and upon its borders were content to leave this new people to their own devices. In one way the battle was an evil, for it inspired overconfidence in the victors. At a later time they sought to push northward into Canaan. They encountered the Amalekites in their home territory and were defeated. Yet even this defeat must have been rather in the nature of a drawn battle, for the Amalekites did not press their advantage and none of the other peoples seemed eager to meet Israel.

One of the first requisites for national existence was therefore tested in this first battle with the Amalekites. No nation can maintain itself against warlike enemies unless it possesses

---

[35] Rawlinson, *Moses, His Life and Times*, p. 140.

both courage and military leaders. Joshua had proved his generalship and Israel her ability to face a powerful foe, for the Amalekites were regarded as one of the real military forces in Western Asia.[86] In thus meeting and defeating a considerable force of this strongest of the "nations" Israel had reason to feel that she had little to fear. She could maintain herself in the land.

Thus in one battle Israel had conquered a home-land. It was not exactly a land that flowed with milk and honey, but it was perhaps the best place for Israel, both because of her recent bondage and her previous tribal history. After an extended period of freedom and self-discipline she would be ready to try the experiment of creating a civilization like that she had encountered in Egypt. The fighting force of escaped slaves was excellent, but it by no means embraced every able-bodied man. Perhaps at first it consisted only of Benjamin and Ephraim. But a part of the activity of nomad peoples was to learn the art of war, and there can be little doubt that the intensive training of all Israel began immediately after this first trial of strength.

The march to Sinai was now continued without further interruption. The only hindrance to nationality resided in those customs which had been picked up during the days of slavery. This hindrance proved to be extremely slight and has therefore caused a number of writers to doubt that the Egyptian sojourn ever took place. But the reason for this freedom from Egyptian influence is easily explained. During the greater part of the sojourn Israel occupied the land of Goshen as a separate people. And throughout the days of slavery life was not materially changed in Goshen. The people continued to keep the flocks which the pharaoh had confiscated for his own use, or had assigned to the use of the Amonite priests. Even those who were engaged in forced labor upon the pharaoh's

---

[86] Numbers xxiv. 20.

building enterprises were not wholly disorganized and divorced from their native customs. They were still under their elders who no doubt labored to perpetuate the Israelitish traditions.[37] It would seem, therefore, that there was never any serious interruption of the ancient tribal practices. The Egyptians cared not how Israel lived so long as the will of the pharaoh was carried out.

At Sinai, therefore, we shall encounter no complete turnover of habits and customs. The Law will not be an introduction of new ethical ideas but an emphasis upon notions of morality and righteousness long held in some fashion by all the people. Not in ethical discovery, but in ethical enforcement, will lie the true advance achieved at the mount of God. Here the laws were collected into a simple code and the people obligated before God to keep them. Much is made of the resemblance between the Law of Sinai and the Law of Hammurabi, and sometimes it is implied that Moses copied his great predecessor. This conclusion is both true and not true. The code of Hammurabi is but the collection, and adaptation to Babylonian conditions, of laws long in practice among all Semitic peoples. Moses simply makes another codification of the same Semitic practice. There is an older mount from which both codes have come—the original home of the Semites, wherever that was.

That there was some way, some special act of worship, by which this Law of Sinai was consecrated no one ought to doubt. Moses, who knew the weather of this mountain region from actual experience, bade the people make preparation for the lofty impressions of divine revelation. The people were forbidden to come too near the mountain. "On the morning of the third day a heavy cloud covered the mountain-top; lightning flashed, and enveloped the mountain in a blaze of fire. Peals of thunder shook the surrounding mountains, and

---

[37] Exodus iii. 16; v. 15, 19; "elders," "officers." The Egyptians for convenience probably made the elders "officers."

awakened echoes. All nature was in uproar, and the world's end seemed to be at hand. With trembling and shaking, the old and the young beheld this terrifying spectacle. But its terror did not surpass the awfulness of the words heard by the affrighted people. The clouds of smoke, the lightning, the flames and the peals of thunder had only served as a prelude to these portentous words.

"Mightily impressed by the sight of the flaming mountain, the people clearly heard the commandments which, simple in their import, and intelligible to every human being, form the elements of all culture. Ten words rang forth from the mountain top. The people became firmly convinced that the words were revealed by God. Theft and bearing false witness were stigmatized as crimes. The voice of Sinai condemned evil thoughts no less than evil acts; hence the prohibition, 'Thou shalt not covet thy neighbor's wife . . . nor any possession of thy neighbor.' " [38]

All this, without remembering the Wonder-Worker of Egypt who used all Nature as a means to achieve His will, would sound like the veriest clap-trap. But the Ruler of the river, the storm, the wind, the fog, and the pestilence has previously revealed Himself in these fields of His jurisdiction. The mountain storm which envelops the peak of Sinai is thus naturally only another expression of the divine presence, and the thunders are but His voice speaking to His people. The lashing tumult of His presence, the echoings of His shouts among the mountains, cannot help but fill the people with awe. When Moses ascends into the region of the storm and brings back the tables of the Law, the act of consecration is fulfilled. Hereafter the ten words are more than ancient concepts of righteous conduct, for they have been spoken by the voice of God.

Graetz expands upon this event in his florid style: "This

---

[38] Graetz, *History of the Jews*, p. 21.

promulgation of the Law marked the natal hour of the 'distinct people,' like unto which none had ever existed. The sublime and eternal laws of Sinai—coming from Deity whom the senses cannot perceive, from the Redeemer who releases the enthralled and the oppressed—were revealed truths treating of filial duty, of spotless chastity, of social integrity, and of the purity of sentiment. The Israelites had been led to Sinai as trembling bondmen; now they came back to their tents as God's people of priests, as a righteous nation (Jeshurun). By practically showing that the Ten Commandments are applicable to all the concerns of life, the Israelites were constituted the teachers of the human race, and through them all the families of the earth were to be blessed. None of the others could then have surmised that even for its own wellbeing an isolated and insignificantly small nation had been charged with the arduous task of the perceptive office." [39]

The majority of men, upon second thought, will feel inclined to put the great work of Moses upon a broader aspect than that of the legal relation of Jehovah to His people. There were laws long before this, and they were very sacredly held among many peoples. In fact, the Sinaitic law must have grown out of the concepts of righteous conduct already in practice among the Hebrews themselves. Surely it was not the Law that was to make all the difference in the world of men, but the Law-Giver. It was not "a Law coming from Deity," but a Deity approving a law which was the foundation of a new people through whom the nations should be blessed. To conceive of all ethics as having its source in Deity is indeed a far-reaching force for civilization, but so is mercy, forgiveness, grace. The God who is Almighty, who gives a Law, who leads His people safely, who is willing to pardon their transgressions, and who practices infinite patience toward an often impatient and rebellious people—that is the great

---

[39] Graetz, *ibid.*, p. 22.

foundation-stone of Israelitish life. And the natal hour of
Israel dates from the time when this God stalked through
Egypt in self-revelation and awoke the hope of His despairing
people.

No one of course will want to detract from the glory of
Israel's law. He could not, if he should try it. It has become
the root law of all Western nations, or at least the norm by
which all notions of righteousness are examined; it embraces
that just control of human action without which organized
society cannot be set up. But please note that it is a *sanctified*
law. Its value resides in the character of Deity behind it, and
precisely in the particular Deity who is supposed to have
promulgated it. It is the varied and rich character of Jehovah
which gives this law its future, its force, and its deep hold
upon men's hearts. Without this God who continues to hold
the fear and adoration of mankind the Sinaitic Law would
be revered no more than the Code of Solon or the Code of
Hammurabi. The secret of the power of this law is to be
found in the fact that Jehovah hath spoken it.

The giving of the Law at Sinai ought, therefore, to be regarded as but another step in the Mosaic exposition of Deity.
The Almighty who can use all power to thwart the will of one
of the most powerful rulers is naturally, whether He is so
recognized or not, the real factor in determining human
destiny. The Law grows logically out of this conception of
His being. We should be surprised if He had no word to
guide His people, to keep them in that conduct which would
insure their future safety. That the word was spoken only
brings out the more clearly the general lineaments of the
God we have already seen at work in signs and wonders of
deliverance.

After Sinai, Israel marched to the region of Kadesh-Barnea
and established a permanent camp. Here was a spring of living
water sufficient for the flocks and herds. In the surrounding
country there must have been considerable pasturage, enough

to support all the cattle required for the immediate needs of
the population. But the real reason for the location of the
camp at this particular place must have been strategic. It was
the key to all the back-lying Peninsula. In this position with a
fast-growing armed force which had already distinguished
itself in battle, Israel could quickly intercept any army which
might seek to invade the peninsular region. To the north
was Amalek, to the west Philistia, to the north and east Moab,
Edom, and the Amorites. Israel was thus situated within easy
striking distance of the line of march of any of these peoples
on the way to Sinai.

This was a great blow to the supremacy of Amalek. Up to
this time she had held undisputed control of both the peninsula and the Negeb. Her dominions shut up Philistia and
Moab to a comparatively small region on the west and east.
She had rich agricultural lands and almost unlimited pasturage. Now she was deprived of her grazing lands and compelled to settle down to strictly agricultural pursuits. She must
have had a considerable population and these imposed restrictions could not help but reduce her wealth rapidly. Thus she
conceived a bitterness toward Israel which never disappeared.
All through the centuries she used every advantage afforded
her for taking revenge upon the nation which had humbled
her.

There was a limit to the population which the peninsula
could support, and when that point had been passed it would
be only natural for Israel to irrupt toward the north. But as
she strengthened her fighting force against this necessity
Amalek just as feverishly prepared to meet her. In the meantime Moses continued to teach and organize the people until
he had built up a strong bond of unity and an effective spirit
of coöperation among the several tribes. The loose confederacy
still remained a confederacy, but the idea gradually prevailed,
through common fortunes shared in the desert, that the destiny of all the tribes was one. The Liberator did not cause

tribal distinctions to disappear, but he brought about a community of thinking and a similarity of institutions which formed the essential first step in nationality. Under the all-embracing term of Israel, differences were suppressed and tribal ambitions held in abeyance. Israel had almost become a nation in our modern sense.

Forty years in the desert, a doubling and tripling of the population perhaps, and a corresponding increase in the number of flocks and herds required to support the increase, saw the end of the wilderness sojourn. It ended because it had to end, for more room had to be found for the people. Suddenly, like a threatening cloud, Israel appeared upon the border of Moab and asked for permission to pass through the land. This was refused her, and she marched eastward around Moab to invade the rich pasture lands to the north. Then she turned west to the Jordan and demolished the cities as she went. Moab had not taken the trouble to ally herself with these peoples and to lead them against Israel, and now, alone, cut off from all possible support from other nations, she was in great panic. What if Israel should turn south, now that Moab had been isolated! The conduct of Israel in respecting the refusal of Moab to let her pass through is the surest indication that Israel was led by a true general. To have invaded Moab would have stirred up the whole country east of the Jordan. Now Moab trembled apart, glad to do anything that might be asked of her; and Israel's losses in conquering "the beyond Jordan" had been negligible.

With scarcely diminished force Israel sat down beside the Jordan to await a favorable moment to cross over. This movement must have been accompanied by forays north and south to cloak her real intention. Moab was kept in terror; interference from the east and north could not be thought of; and Canaan had no idea that the various maneuvers meant anything more than a determination to hold the land already conquered. A shock of terror ran through the entire west

Jordanic country when it was learned that Israel had crossed over and was besieging the strong fortress of Jericho. And when it fell before the Canaanites had time to collect a strong army, the country was already as good as subjugated. There was no possibility of meeting successfully the courage and strategy and daring of Joshua who was sweeping everything before him.

One has perhaps already begun to understand how Israel has gradually seen less of Moses and more and more of Joshua during the past few years at Kadesh. This has not happened because Moses has nothing more to do, but because the problems before Israel require the labors of the military man. Moses has done his work in liberating the people, in revealing the being and power of God, in framing the law and organizing the government of the people, and in fostering the spirit of united action. Without him Joshua could not have gone forth to conquer Canaan, for he could not have had a common ground upon which the several tribes could unite. But with the work of Moses becoming more complete, it was possible to build a great army and to think in national terms. The young general had thus been busy through the years. At Rephidim he had won his spurs as a real warrior, and no doubt his genius determined the choice of Kadesh as the head-quarters of Israel during the sojourn. He could inspire men, he could employ them in battle, he could select strategic posi-tions; and his later maneuvers showed that he could call to his aid all the advantages of cloaked movements to disconcert his foes. Fortunate indeed is that people who has two such leaders as Moses and Joshua to supplement each other, especially when they come in the proper relation and sequence.

The encampment on the east of the Jordan saw the end of the personal labors of the great Liberator. We are told that he was not permitted to enter the promised land because of ill-considered action in leading the people; but no doubt the real reason is to be found in the decrees which affect all mortality.

He had lived long; he had toiled greatly; and he had given too much for Israel to be strong enough to view her triumph. Yet, he did see it. He knew by what Israel had already done that she would pass over Jordan to possess the good land. It had been written into the nerves and brain of this people, and his own hand had put it there. One cannot muster much sadness of regret over the lonely figure on Nebo's lofty height, for he saw too much as he looked to Canaan, felt too much satisfaction, knew far more to a certainty than is given to many another leader to know. He died there and was buried. His grave remains a mystery, probably because it was better that neither Moab nor Canaan should know that the great leader had gone to his rest.

Yet in a sense he could never die. The very God of his people would be seen through his eyes forever; his sense of duty and his vision of divine righteousness would seal and glorify his nation among all peoples; and his preparation for the liberty and development of the human spirit would mark out the road of the soul's quest through all generations. Such an immortal has little need for a grave.

CHAPTER VII

Isaiah of Babylon

The great spiritual leader of Israel in the days of the Babylonian exile is worthy to stand with the most exalted prophets
and teachers of mankind. It was he, more than any other man
among the prisoners, who reshaped the religious beliefs of his
people and gave to them a creed which lifted them above their
miseries and humiliation. No leader of a nation, with the single
exception of Moses, ever faced a more difficult task. He found
the prevailing doctrines of religion discredited, nationality
destroyed, the God of his people in disgrace and shame before
the gods of Babylon, the people dispirited and without hope.
He reinterpreted the being of God and set Him far above the
gods of the conquerors; restated the ancient beliefs in the
light of new revelations of truth; stirred the imagination of
the exiles, lifted their hearts, renewed their faith and courage,
and made them strong enough to recross the desert and to
endure the hardships which attended the reëstablishment of the
nation in the homeland.

His place in the religious history of humanity is the more
appreciated when we remember that without him there could
have been no reëstablished Israel and no national ground for
the flowering of both later Judaism and Christianity. A discredited Jehovah, forced to yield to the cruel and idolatrous
religious faith of Babylon and Nineveh, would have turned
religious development backward and have entailed such a
spiritual loss as could not have been recovered perhaps for
centuries. This great work of Isaiah of Babylon was accomplished by leading his people to break through the husk of

national religious limitations and to embrace a universal God who manipulated the events of history in the life of all nations. He made them realize that their God had not been over-powered by more resourceful deities than He. He showed them that their humiliations and disasters were due, not to the gods of Babylon but to Jehovah who punished them for their sins. And he caused them to see that their former leaders had taught this conception of God, and had done all in their power to avert the severe calamities that had come upon the nation.

It was inevitable that at some time a leader should arise who would press the logic of Israel's history and the conse-quences of the teachings of Moses, Isaiah, and Jeremiah. The power which Jehovah exercised upon Egyptian affairs, in the days preceding and during the Exodus, directly implies a God who controls the history of all men. The events of the con-quest of Palestine under Joshua proclaim the same truth. And both Isaiah and Jeremiah had, in foretelling the destruction of Jerusalem, made such a conception of deity their own principle. Isaiah of Babylon took these higher implications of the ancient faith and from them drew both the explanation of the divine purpose in the Exile and the hope of a restored Israel on Mount Zion.

The attention of the East was first drawn to Palestine through an appeal made by Ahaz of Judah to Tiglath-pileser III of Assyria for help against his enemies.[1] The king of Judah found himself confronted by the combined strength of Damascus (Syria), Philistia, and Pekah, king of Israel. Though he was counseled by Isaiah, the prophet, not to make the appeal, he did not obey; he believed no doubt that vassal-age to Assyria was preferable to the loss of his kingdom and his life. Tiglathpileser responded promptly, overran Philistia and Syria, and turned his attention to Israel. Pekah shut him-

---

[1] II Kings xvi. 5-10.

self up in Samaria and withstood the siege until a conspiracy brought about his death. Hoshea, who succeeded him, made terms with the enemy and thus became a vassal of Assyria. This event marks the beginning of the end of ancient Jewish nationality. Hereafter the two kingdoms of the Jews were forced to pay tribute to the succeeding monarchs of Assyria until that power was destroyed by Babylon. Israel revolted during the reign of Shalmaneser IV, upon being promised help from Egypt, and refused to pay tribute. In 724 B.C. Shalmanser IV came up against Samaria and besieged it. The desperate situation of Hoshea and his nobles made them hold out as long as possible. The siege continued through the following year. In 722 B.C. Shalmaneser IV died, but the siege was continued under his successor, Sargon, and came to an end in the closing months of the same year. The better classes of Israel to the number of 27,290 persons, were deported to Mesopotamia and Media.[2]

The later fate of these exiles is not known to us, but from the story of the Jews in Babylonia we may surmise that they quickly came to places of prominence in the dramatic scenes of the history that followed. Some of them, no doubt, made their way back to Palestine before and after the downfall of Assyria. The prophecy of Nahum [3] seems to have been written by an eye-witness of the conditions of Nineveh in the days of her siege and destruction. The prophet has stood in some doorway to watch the terrors and cruelties that occurred in the hour of the city's alarm. Perhaps he has dodged out of the way of the war-chariots which went racing through the crowded thoroughfares; he has seen the horsemen ride down and slay the crowds of citizens who were in their path; and he has watched the foot-soldiers go forward stumbling over the corpses that lie without number in the streets. Some of these dead were perhaps Jews, and the others may have been for-

---

[2] II Kings xvii. 1-10.
[3] Nahum iii. 1-3.

eign slaves who were suspected of being hostile to the nation. It was a bloody city, "filled with the noise of the whip, the noise of rattling wheels, of the prancing horses, and of the jumping chariots." But the Jews were not all slain. The city went down to destruction, but the people lived to play a part in the turmoil and change of the kingdoms that followed.

In the meantime Judah had continued with a relative measure of independence. She faithfully paid tribute under Sargon during the days of his struggle with Babylon, although she must have been sorely tempted to take advantage of the situation to throw off the galling yoke. Under Hezekiah, an ambitious and energetic ruler who succeeded Ahaz, the revolt was accomplished. Sennacherib came and overran the country, destroying forty-six cities of Judah and carrying away into captivity two hundred thousand people. [4] Jerusalem was spared only because a pestilence broke out among Sennacherib's troops, making retreat advisable. But Judah had already received a blow from which she would never recover.

During the days of Josiah, Necho, king of Egypt,[5] advanced into Palestine on his way to secure some of the spoil from the broken kingdom of Assyria. Josiah realized that it would be but a question of time until Judah would be required to pay tribute to Egypt. He hurried out to meet Necho and to do all he could to drive him back. The Egyptian monarch sought to evade battle, and sent ambassadors to confer with Josiah and to ask for free passage through the country. Josiah would not listen to them. He went into battle immediately and was killed. Necho, after this brief delay, hurried on to Carchemish where he was met and defeated by the armies of Nebuchadrezzar. He fled toward home and was pursued to the borders of Egypt by the Babylonians.[6] It is very probable that at this time Nebuchadrezzar took the opportunity to arrange that

---

[4] II Kings xviii 7; Goodspeed, *History, Babylonians and Assyrians*, p. 270.
[5] II Kings xxiii. 29.
[6] Goodspeed, *ibid.*, pp. 335, 336.

these western provinces of Assyria should send their tribute to Babylon.[7] He received news shortly thereafter that his father was dead and hurried home to claim the throne. His authority was, therefore, only imperfectly established in the west.

The haste with which he proceeded to Babylon has been interpreted by some writers as indicating that he expected trouble of some kind. Perhaps he may have feared that his brother would claim the throne. An inscription left by Nabu-palacur describes the ceremonial at the time of the rebuilding of the temple of Marduk, god of Babylon. Of the part his two sons took in the ceremonial he says, "Nebuchadrezzar, the first-born, the chief son, beloved of my heart, I caused to carry mortar mixed with wine, oil, and other products along with the workmen. Nabu-shum-lisher, his talimu, the offspring of my own flesh, the junior, my darling, I ordered to take the basket and spade; a dupshikku of gold and silver I placed (on him). Unto Marduk, my lord, as a gift, I dedicated him." [8] How much this second son was entitled to claim as revealed in this ceremonial, is not clear; neither can we guess how much he might dare if prompted by ambition and given the present opportunity.

We know that it was necessary for the king to take the hands of Bel each year as a public declaration that he received the office of king. Nebuchadrezzar could not become king until he had observed this ceremony. In the meantime the throne would remain unoccupied and the government more or less disorganized. In case of undue delay on the part of the legitimate heir in appearing to establish his claim, necessity or intrigue might fill the vacancy with some man strong enough to administer the government. The situation was such that anything might happen.

If, as has been suggested by some writers,[9] Nabupalacur in-

---

[7] *Ibid.*, p. 336.
[8] *Ibid.*, p. 337.
[9] See Winkler, *Altorientalische Forschungen*, II, ii, pp. 193 ff.

tended that his younger son should be king of Babylon and the eldest the ruler of the empire, we can see another reason for the haste. Nebuchadrezzar may have desired to disregard his father's wishes and to establish himself as both king and emperor. Fresh from his victory over Necho of Egypt, his army would support him in any ambition. If he could arrive before his younger brother had taken office, he could have what he wished. It is entirely possible that this is what really happened. At any rate it affords an explanation of the jealousy and treachery of the priestly party toward the descendants of Nebuchadrezzar. The line of priests derived from Nebuchadrezzar's brother would not soon forget that but for royal injustice they might be kings. And it is not unreasonable to suppose that when Nabonidus further threatened their prestige, by exalting other gods and priesthoods, they took revenge by opening the gates of Babylon to Cyrus.

We do not know as yet all the circumstances surrounding the coronation of Nebuchadrezzar; we know however that something kept him in Babylon for a number of years. Perhaps he felt that it would be unsafe to leave the capitol until he had firmly established his authority and had made revolt against him impossible. While he remained at home great changes were taking place in the far west. With the downfall of Nineveh the tributaries west of the Euphrates were naturally allocated to Babylon. But the Arabs who had been held in check by the untiring vigilance of the Assyrians now began to press northward, and their success emboldened the whole of Palestine to entertain revolutionary schemes. Jehoiakim continued to remit tribute regularly until 601 B.C. when, owing to the pressure of the revolutionists around him, he renounced his allegiance. He was left undisturbed for more than a year, and until Nebuchadrezzar found it convenient to send an army to reëstablish his authority. Jerusalem closed its gates and endured siege, hoping that it might receive help from Egypt or from the other conspirators. In the meantime

Jehoiakim died, and his son, Jehoiachin, succeeded him. When Nebuchadrezzar, who had followed his army westward, came to Jerusalem Jehoiachin gave himself up. The kingdom of Judah was punished by the deportation of its king and his court and about ten thousand of its best citizens.

Those who went into exile upon this occasion were probably settled in and about the city of Babylon. There was no studied attempt to break the spirit of the Jews at this time. The offense of revolt was more technical than malicious. It had to be subdued and the kingdom punished, but the prisoners who were carried away were no doubt treated kindly enough. The king and his courtiers were thrust into prison, but they were given all consideration as prisoners of rank. The artisans were employed in the extensive building operations about the city. The young princes were sent to school to be educated in all the wisdom of the Chaldeans. Those who remained steadfast in their faith hoped for pardon and freedom to return to Jerusalem at some time. This condition among the exiles lasted for ten years.

Then came an event which cast deep gloom over all the Jews and seemed at first to destroy the very foundations of Jewish life. In 588 B.C. Zedekiah, who had been appointed king over the remnant in Judah, allowed himself to be drawn into an alliance with Egypt. This was a fatal policy. Nubuchadrezzar once more marched westward and besieged Jerusalem. Zedekiah tried to hold out until help could be given him from his confederates, but none came. The city fell within a year and was destroyed by fire. Most of the people were carried to Babylon. The fate of the king was a sad one; after seeing his sons slain, his eyes were put out by the hand of Nebuchadrezzar and he was forced to end his days in a Babylonian prison. "Only the poorest and meanest of the people were left in the land."

Most of the blame for this calamity has been laid at the door of the kings who ruled Judah during her closing days. Josiah alone stands out as a man of strength and righteousness. He did much to reform Judah, but his work was necessarily incomplete because of the stolid indifference and natural conservatism of his people. Spiritual interests had been neglected too long for him to bring the people quickly up to the mark. Corruption and idolatry had done their work and the people had become calloused. Furthermore, there was a feeling that nothing like national destruction could possibly overtake them. The conquerors had come, they had besieged, and had carried some of the inhabitants away. But the walls of the city were still intact and the Temple remained upon the holy hill. A great body of worshipers lived in the city. All this was the clearest proof that God had vindicated His name and had preserved to him a people. Why be alarmed at the preachments of some ignorant prophet? God would continue to guard His holy city.

There is no saving a people which shuts its eyes to the forces that make history. The real reason for the downfall of Judah is to be found in the march of empire and in the geographical situation of the kingdom. There could be no great Egyptian empire without the control on her part of the trade routes of Western Asia, for they were necessary as a source of revenue. And there could be no great Babylonian world power without Babylonian control of the same territory. Judah was situated in the heart of this region and was therefore the natural battleground of the two rival world powers. To have saved Judah from destruction would have required the most far-seeing statesmen, men who could have known to the moment when to make and to break alliances. This could have been known only to men who possessed the most intimate knowledge of the actual situation in each of the rival empires. The aloofness and seclusion of Judah foredoomed her. In ignorance her leaders acted; therefore, her destruction was inevitable.

We here stand face to face with a new interpretation of the

processes which mold the life of the nations. One may read history in the light of divine purpose, but one goes far astray in the reading if he omits to take proper cognizance of the agents which strive and achieve. Up to the time of the exile the popular faith conceived of a miraculous emanation of divine force as the agent of deliverance. That force was not centered in human personality except as a means of moving the people here or there. The power was exercised by angels and heavenly powers which came down to hurl the thunderbolts and to direct the cataclysm. Now we come to the consideration of the implications of prophetic teaching—God works through men. The prophets who were themselves inspired agents of the Almighty read history as it flowed from divinely possessed personalities. Judah in thus overlooking the human part in the divine achievement missed the mark and was destroyed.

But a still more important modification of the popular creed had to be made. It was believed that God would punish his people when they were guilty. But only as individuals; the people as a whole would be spared short of annihilation. Amos, however, sought to point out the fallacy of such reasoning by proclaiming that God had no obligation to vindicate even the chosen people; [10] He would vindicate no one but Himself. If the vindication of divine integrity demanded the destruction of the chosen people, the destruction would come. It is apparent, of course, that popular piety never entertained for a moment the real implications of Amos' pronouncements. How could the nation be destroyed and leave a people to worship God? That Jehovah could select a Gentile people or work through Gentile personalities to the destruction of Judah was unthinkable. The prophets indeed had seemed at times to teach such things. There had been the destruction of individuals and armies by Gentiles, evidently by God's consent,

---

[10] Amos vi. 1 and ix. 10.

but the nation had persisted. Destruction of Jerusalem, of the Temple, and of the national life—that, of course, would never be. Then the nation fell and the people were carried away. The city and the Temple lay smouldering in ashes.

A glimpse of the popular despair which followed in the wake of the destruction of the holy place and the deportation of the people may be gained from the 137th Psalm: "By the canals of Babylon we sat down, yea, we wept when we remembered Zion. We hanged our harps upon the willows in the midst thereof. For there they that had carried us away captive required of us a song; and they that had wasted us demanded of us mirth, saying, 'Sing us one of the psalms of Zion.' How shall we sing the Lord's song in a strange land?" Consternation and bewilderment claimed the stoutest hearts and the most courageous minds. Even though the creed might be modified to explain the past, what of the future? Would there be a future? Or would God select another people for His praise? When such thoughts pierced the soul of the better minds of Judah we can begin to see how utter was the amazement of the simple, pious people among the exiles.

Some readjustment had to be made if the faith of Judah was to persist. Granted that God had used the Gentile power of Babylon to punish His people; how far was Babylonian customs and authority to operate? And how much of the truth did Babylon possess that was unknown to Judah? Wherein was Babylon right and Judah wrong? And wherein was Judah to maintain her theology against that of the Babylonians? To the majority of the Jews there was no real difficulty in arriving at a proper answer to these questions, once it was believed that God was in Babylon as surely as in Jerusalem. In the main the religious heritage of the Jew was sound. In personal piety the hymns of Babylon were lofty, but Babylonian theology was woefully deficient beside the sublime and elevated thought of Jewish monotheism. Those possessing the highest and purest system of thought will always take over the task of solving the great problems of the spiritual destiny of mankind. They do this because they already have the root of the answer in their previous thinking. To be sure, the spiritual problem created by the Babylonian captivity was a Jewish one; but we must remember that a theology advanced enough to have a problem can also struggle to the answer. When Marduk's temple sank in fire and ashes there was no problem. According to his theology, he was dead. And he has never since reared his head. The God of Judah sought right-eousness, not sacrifice solely; and he could not die as long as righteousness continued as a fact, no matter by what nation it was performed.

Such is the religious and educational advance which was necessary to the achievement of the religio-political system which is true Judaism. Through the labors of Isaiah of Baby-lon and others the advance was made. The exile became a measure carried out in the divine government of Jehovah who stretched His authority to all nations. As Fairweather observes, "It would be a mistake to regard the judgments meted out to Israel as merely punitive; they were educative as well, and intended to fit them for their unique divine calling and destiny." [11] Fairweather is speaking, of course, out of a post-exilic view of the exile; he gives it a divine purpose as a part of a still higher and more distant purpose. In other words, he is speaking out of the fully achieved system of Jewish thought. This interpretation of history was not possible in the days of the exile except to a few rare spirits, and they were the later saviors of Israel. Before such intellectual security could be gained much teaching had to be done. "In political servitude the people must regain spiritual freedom, and in a strange land and amid unwelcome surroundings they must revert to the love of truth and righteousness, and to the practice of faith and holiness." [12]

[11] Fairweather, *From the Exile to the Advent*, pp. 14sq.
[12] *Ibid.*, 15.

There are those who will declare that the Jew necessarily had to be saved, just because he was essential to the divine plan. There is a small element of truth in such a view; and yet, we must not forget that it was this identical philosophy which brought about the destruction of Jerusalem and the deportation of the Jews. That God could raise up a people from stones, or from the nations, was a truth which the Jew learned in great bitterness. The Jew was saved, not from divine necessity, but because of his intrinsic worth as the possessor of those elements of universal truth which made for spiritual elevation and human progress. The exile was the occasion which enabled him to be receptive to his greatest intellectual leaders. The Jew was saved by a theology which enabled him to read history in large terms and to discover the forces of national failure and success. A theory of divine government which had broken under the hand of Nebuchad-rezzar had been revised so that the Jew was able to see that Cyrus was on the way to world power. And best of all for Jewish salvation, he was now wise enough to make terms with the inevitable.

The home of the exiles was within and near one of the most remarkable cities that has ever been built. With the example of the magnificence of Nineveh before him, the ruins of which still existed, Nebuchadrezzar undertook to construct a far greater and more secure city. During the first years of his reign he organized his kingdom and established its government with a thoroughness typical of the forceful rulers of his day. Where kingdoms stubbornly opposed his sovereignty, he crushed them, deported their citizens to form new provinces or to become laborers, and forced those left in the land to pay heavy tribute. Thus he made war pay at both ends of the process. The constant flow of tribute filled his treasury and made possible the maintenance of a large standing army, and the thousands of prisoners carried on the vast work of public improvement as well as the wider cultivation of the reclaimed regions along the Euphrates. With peace quickly established, with immense revenues provided, and with an almost un-limited supply of artisans and slaves, he was able to undertake an unrivaled task in public building. And with forty years of sovereignty at his disposal he was able to achieve his plans. The Greeks were amazed at the immensity and grandeur of his operations, and Nebuchadrezzar, himself, in a burst of pride, exclaimed, "Is not this great Babylon that I have built!"

Herodotus,[18] the Greek, and Ctesias, the Persian, have de-scribed the ancient city. They do not agree with each other in speaking of details, but both agree in general with the Scrip-tural account of the magnitude of the city. It was a huge affair, and everything in connection with it was carried out upon an immense scale. It was built in the form of a square with the brick-lined bed of the Euphrates running through it. On each side there were twenty-five gates, enormous struc-tures of solid brass, and with specially devised machinery for opening and closing them. The walls of the city were three hundred feet high, and wide enough at the top for six war-chariots to drive abreast. From each gate was a street fifteen miles long connecting with a gate upon the opposite side of the city. This gave the city fifty streets crossing at right angles. There were also four streets which corresponded to each of the walls and which ran the length of the city. These were built up with houses upon only one side and permitted traffic to pass between the houses and the inner moat. This arrange-ment gave the city 676 squares, each two and one half miles in compass. The houses were three or four stories in height and were built on the outside of the squares, thus leaving in the rear a space for cultivation. There were open spaces be-tween the houses giving a view of the little fields and gardens in the rear. In case of siege, it was thus possible for the in-

---

[18] *History*, Book I. 179. 180. 181.

habitants to grow their own provisions within the walls. Behind these immense fortifications, and with these resources at hand to augment the food supply, the city was practically impregnable.

The capitol occupied a flat plain in which were no natural fortresses. But the energy of Nebuchadrezzar and his genius for engineering supplied all that was necessary for adequate defense. Huge trenches were excavated both inside and outside of the wall. The plan pursued in the building of these defenses has been described by Herodotus: "As fast as they dug the moat, the soil which they got from the cutting was made into bricks, and when a sufficient number were completed they baked the bricks in kilns. Then they proceeded to construct the wall itself, using throughout for their cement hot bitumen, and interposing a layer of wattled reeds at every course of bricks.[14] The bitumen was brought down the river from Assyria. All the remaining materials were at hand, and the dry season and great heat afforded a long period of constructive work each year. Thus Babylon's walls and the city itself became one of the seven wonders of the ancient world.

The architectural triumphs of Nebuchadrezzar are almost beyond description.[15] His most magnificent building was the Temple of Bel, Bab-bel, the Gate of God. It stood upon a base of two hundred square yards and rose in terraces to a height of six hundred feet. No temple or cathedral ever erected has equaled it in height. It was long the seat of Mesopotamian pagan worship and was described as "the terraced tower, the everlasting house, the temple of the seven lights of the earth." It was the depository of the sacred vessels taken from all plundered shrines. Here were placed the vessels which were taken by Nebuchadrezzar from the Temple at Jerusalem. The wealth stored here and the gorgeousness of the furnishings amazed all who beheld them. There were seven stages in the

---

[14] Book I, chap. 179.
[15] See Fairweather, *Exile to Advent*, pp. 16-19.

structure and each was dedicated to some one of the seven planets, and each bore in glazed brick work the color attributed to its planet. That dedicated to the sun was a gold color; that to the moon was silver; and that to Mercury was azure, and so on, employing each of the seven colors of the ray of light. Upon the summit of this high tower was the sanctuary of Nebo, containing a table of gold and an enormous couch of the same material. Many kings had left the tower unfinished, and the fear which deterred them may be the origin of the legend in the Old Testament regarding the attempt to build a tower to heaven. Nebuchadrezzar, however, records with pride that he completed it.

Another remarkable building was the royal palace, which is said to have been built in fifteen days. It had extensive grounds and was surrounded by a wall seven miles long. It was furnished with beautiful fabrics and paintings, and possessed everything necessary to the comfort and delight of the monarch. Within these grounds were the hanging gardens. They were erected in terraces which were supported by great arches and strengthened by stout walls. They were laid out with hills and dales covered with trees and flowers and were supplied with fountains and brooks, giving the effect of a well-kept park or pleasure ground. It is said that the Median princess, Nebuchadrezzar's queen, tired of the flat country of the Euphrates valley and longed for a sight of the mountains of her native land. To please her the king had this artificial mountain erected.

The genius and energy of Nebuchadrezzar manifested themselves in all manner of building, irrigational, and public improvement enterprises. Fairweather says that he constructed "ingenious systems of river banks, bridges, tunnels, canals, and artificial lakes by which this unique city was watered, connected, safeguarded, and adorned. 'Of the great waters'— so reads an inscription of Nebuchadrezzar—'like the waters of the ocean, I made use abundantly.' Under his magic hand the inland capitol became thus a sort of floating emporium to which traders from every quarter were attracted. Whatever could be done by an unlimited supply of bricks and bitumen, for these were furnished by the clay soil and the river springs; whatever could be achieved by an equally unlimited supply of labor, for that had been obtained from the wars; whatever an iron will and a great genius could accomplish, for both were united in Nebuchadrezzar,—all this combined to produce ancient Babylon." [16]

There has perhaps never been a more brilliant empire than that of Babylon in the closing years of the reign of Nebuchadrezzar. His policy of removing from the conquered territories the most gifted, skilled, and intellectual members of the society concentrated in Babylon the flower of human genius in his generation. His patronage of the sciences, arts, engineering, and education gave ample opportunity for self-cultivation and self-expression. His encouragement of study and research produced a vast literature which embraced the sum of human knowledge in that day. In the public libraries were books upon almost every subject,—natural history, agriculture, geography, mathematics, engineering, architecture, grammar, astronomy, religion, law, and government. [17] These books were written upon clay tablets in cuneiform and piled in well-catalogued libraries for the convenience of the public. A man might go into one of these libraries, give the librarian the number of a tablet from any work, and receive it in a few moments. There were also schools for both sexes, and large universities for higher education. There seems to have been no discrimination against the children and the young men of the captives. In the book of Daniel we read that the princes of Israel were sent to school and educated in all the wisdom of the Chaldeans at public expense. Every means was supplied and every care exercised that the student's health be preserved. Daniel's pro-

---

[16] *Ibid.*, p. 19.
[17] *Ibid.*, pp. 19-20.

posal to change the menu and the hesitancy of the student-governor show the strictness of the supervision and the zeal of the king in giving to his subjects the advantages of knowledge.[18] And when a captive had received his education the way was open to him to follow whatever course he was prepared to take. With such intellectual freedom progress was inevitable.

It would seem almost unnecessary therefore, to observe that the Jews with their history of politico-religious thought, with their minds trained from childhood to the consideration of national and folk problems, with their excellent gift for grasping the nature of the currents and drifts of spiritual forces, were able, under such freedom to supply one of the most astute elements to the political life of Babylon. Exiled because they were the most favored of a favored people, the captives quickly made the adjustments which a more advanced and complex civilization demanded. Accustomed to bring forth a good living from the barren soil of Palestine, they prospered and grew rich under the better conditions of soil and climate of the Babylonian plain. From of old they had learned to be good traders, and in the bustle of the larger commercial activity of Babylon they passed from huckstering to settled emporiums and modern business on a large scale. To the new commercial opportunity they brought their ancient frugality, their ability to bargain, their power to make their goods attractive, their skill in meeting competition, their keen understanding of business conditions, and their machine-like industry. They prospered, grew immensely wealthy, became a great influence in commercial circles, and wielded all the power that wealth affords in a materialistic civilization. The life of Babylon was rapidly becoming the story of the activity of the Jews behind the scenes.

The Old Testament mention of Daniel and Nehemiah is

---

[19] Daniel i.

enough to show the triumph of Jewish character. A goodly number of gifted Jews had entered every field of Babylonian life. They had been given every liberty and every encouragement from the first. They had not rebelled and languished, although they had the capacity for it. The Jew feels as keenly as any man. But he has a will to live, a wisdom which preserves him from the insanity and folly of his feeling. He can bank his fires, keep his counsel, work, and wait.

Here at last his accurate knowledge of social and political conditions kept him from any indiscreet opposition to the inevitable. He saw all the merits and all the faults of the Babylonian empire, saw the strength and the weakness clearly. And with a mind worthy of the race of the prophets he was able to look beyond Babylon and to behold the source from which her ruin would come. With a fortitude worthy of the breadth of his view, he set to work. He paid every price necessary to rise to power. Such a policy of caution, of industry, of practical wisdom, and of long-headed strategy in the conduct of Jewish life in Babylon argues well for the solidarity of Jewish life even there, and for the wisdom of Jewish leaders. Deliverance would come—they could see the signs of Babylon's fall. Walls of such proportions were not built against friends. But walls could always be passed. If the Jew were powerful enough to treat with the conqueror he could get anything he desired when the city fell. It has never been proved that the Jew contrived the downfall of Babylon, or that he helped; but that he had the wisdom to take advantage of the event cannot be questioned. Everything fell before the army of the Persians but the Jew. And there were heights from which he could have fallen, for he was represented by men of great power in government, industry, commerce, education, finance, and diplomacy. In fact, the Jew had become such a factor in the situation that when the city fell he supplied the cement which enabled the whole machinery of the structure to continue without apparent interruption. Trade went on even more briskly and nowhere was it evident that a conquering army was destroying the nation.

That such an achievement could be accomplished in the short space of fifty or sixty years seems almost incredible. The people had undoubtedly come empty-handed to Babylon. Without financial resources, without either national or religious hope, without anything but their minds and their hands, they were at as low ebb as it is possible for a people to sink. In bitterness, in humiliation, in poverty, in undying hate of the conqueror who had sacked their city, defiled their holy places, and murdered their brethren, they began their labor under a handicap that would have crushed almost every other people. And yet, fifty years later they formed the foundation upon which the Persian erected that powerful commercial and political structure which we know as Persian Babylon! What a story there must be between these two dates! A saga of immortal dimensions if we could hear it all, we do not doubt!

All this could never have been done without leaders. And what leaders they must have been! They put a new song upon the lips of the people; they put a new faith in every Jewish heart—faith in an apparently discredited national God, faith in the friendliness and good intentions of that God—something infinitely harder to establish than a belief in deity. They gave back beauty for ashes, the oil of joy of mourning. The Jew lifted his head, his eyes took on a new luster—the far-off, shining glance of hope. He regained his confidence, a loftier dignity than he had every known before, a supreme sanity of thought, a deep, calm trust that would outlast the clash of armies and the long, long toil of all the years. These leaders were indeed prophets: they had to be.

And chief among these leaders was Isaiah. We know nothing of his life except by inference from certain passages of Scripture bearing upon the nature of Jewish life in Babylon. No doubt he was one of many men who taught the people the ancient customs and hope of Israel. Perhaps he was another of those self-appointed leaders who invited the people to his home and there persuaded them of the glorious future which was still possible to the children of the covenant. There are scriptural statements that imply that the elders of the people exercised their accustomed authority. They formed in conjunction with the Babylonian authorities a convenient function in securing law and order, and did it in a way that prevented undue friction. The arrangement was such as to leave the Jew free to establish all of his native customs in the valley of the Euphrates. If his freedom was as great as these records would indicate, it is entirely possible that priests and Levites took up their accustomed ministrations. But the great leaders, Nehemiah, Ezekiel, and Isaiah, must have been somewhat independent of the priestly class, as were so many of the great prophets of the homeland. And it was these independent leaders, or prophets, who taught the people the new hope.

This work was begun by Jeremiah, who had done everything he could to avert the destruction of Jerusalem. His warnings went unheeded and the city fell. Scarcely had the Jews arrived in Babylon before they received a letter from him full of comfort and good cheer, of wise counsel, and of exhortation to trust God.[19] He warned them to beware in the future of the false prophets who had already deceived them and had helped to bring about their ruin. He advised them to live quietly in the city and land of their exile, to build them houses, to till the soil and plant gardens, and to settle down until the time of their deliverance should be accomplished. He also counseled them to seek the Lord constantly in prayer, for the thoughts of God toward them were thoughts of good will and not thoughts of evil. In seventy years their captivity would be accomplished and they would be returned to their own land.

More immediately following the work of Jeremiah in the

---

[19] Jeremiah xxxix. 1-23.

above counsel is the labor of Ezekiel. He began to prophesy in the fifth year of his captivity in Babylon, and, somewhere near the twenty-fifth year, he summed up his teaching and recorded it in full. He stresses the justice of Jehovah and declares that fidelity to Him and disobedience toward Him are quickly followed by His blessing or punishment. The loyalty of the pious man always reacts in good to him, and to him only, and just so long as he perseveres in his worthy conduct. In the same way the godless man, and he alone, is punished for his sins. He has no sympathy with the proverb, "The fathers have eaten sour grapes and the children's teeth are set on edge." It is the man's own sin which affects him, and that only. Applying this principle to himself he declares that the man who is warned and continues in sin can blame no one but himself if he die; but the man who dies unwarned may lay his death at the door of the prophet who has failed.

In applying the principle of Jehovah's justice it is worthy of note that Ezekiel makes no difference between Israel and the nations in this regard. The heathen nations are brought to destruction because of their sinful practices, and Israel can expect to fare no better. The only difference to be noticed in the description of the result for the two is the attitude of the prophet. He evidently dwells with some satisfaction upon the destruction of Tyre and the surrounding nations who have wronged Israel. For Israel he has sympathy, but he can find no mercy in the Highest until repentance and retribution have been perfected. In no case does Ezekiel allow his personal feeling to cast a shadow upon his notion of Jehovah's justice.

But if he is certain that justice will be visited upon Israel, he is no less certain that she will finally be restored. This is made clear by the copiousness of his details in his description of the restored nation. He might almost be regarded as setting forth a complete plan for the organization of the new Israel. "He describes the temple minutely; furnishes recommendations for the temple worship; and defines the rights of the

Prince and his obligations and finally gives regulations for the division of the land among the twelve tribes, the residences of the Levites and priests, and the arrangements of the temple-city."

This may seem at first to place Ezekiel in the position of having added nothing new to the religious history of Israel. He seems even more severe than Jeremiah in his application of the principle of divine justice; and he offers no great heartening explanation of the divine wisdom behind the justice. Even his extension of the power of Jehovah over the nations is ante-exilic in character, for these nations had wronged Israel and suffered the wrath of Jehovah in consequence. We cannot be sure that he has advanced to the conception of a God whose natural position is that of sovereign of the nations with Israel as his chosen people. We can be sure of only one thing, his profound interest in the temple worship. This of course he remembered and distance lent it such enchantment that he overlooked some of its corrupted features and regarded it as the highest expression of Israel's spiritual life. Others of his day must have felt as he did about it. Thus we find in Ezekiel the beginning of that priestly activity which served to perpetuate the ancient religious institutionalism of Israel. And while it may not have flowered to the degree assigned by Kuenen,[20] so that it rewrote the history of Israel and framed the whole of the priestly legislation, we may be sure that it claimed an influential place among those who pondered the return to Palestine and finally dominated the religious establishment when the return became a fact.

Ezekiel is thus more the prophet of the older type and has little to give to solve the puzzle into which the exile has plunged the nation. He has his place, however, in that he does not permit the nation to lose the outlines of the ancient faith. As to the great problems of the hour, he is too much a

---

[20] Kuenen, *Religion of Israel*, Vol. II, pp. 152-173.

part of the generation that is passing to create the great creed of spiritual and social deliverance. That is reserved to the younger men of God, those who have been reared in Babylon and who have spent their youth in this land of travail and humiliation. They have not been dismayed by memories of the great days of glory and defeat. They start from the ground —with their heritage and the sorrow of their people, with the forces at work in Babylon's destiny—and they see their surroundings clearly enough to reinterpret the nature of Jehovah and His deeds among the nations.

This ought not to surprise us. Age has the advantage of youth in wisdom and in the power to observe accurately the meaning of events; but age has its handicaps. It reasons from the events of the past and often dwells in the scenes of long ago. With its thought occupied with such matters, it often misses the vital thing in the present which can help to clear up many puzzles of past happenings. Age may see the immediate causes which led to an event; it is very likely to miss the causes which only later events can properly reveal. Thus Israel sinned and suffered punishment, according to the older generation; it was reserved for younger men who were well versed in Babylonian affairs to find the loftier purposes of God in permitting Israel to go into exile.

Yet in spite of his severe and conservative tone Ezekiel supplied a hopeful and constructive temper to the times. There were those who looked upon the fountains of Judaism as being dried up. Wise men of pessimistic turn of mind could see no future but bondage for Israel. This gloom is not to be regarded as unwarranted, for many things had happened since the receipt of Jeremiah's letter of good cheer. When the first deportation had taken place the Temple and the walls were still standing. Then came rebellion, the destruction of the Temple and the city walls, the burning of all the beautiful houses of the city, and a second and a third deportation. Calamity had followed upon calamity. It appeared that there

was not one thing left to serve in a revival of Israelitish life
and institutions. Many in Babylon began to say, "Our bones
are dried up, and our hope is lost: we are quite cut off." We
cannot begin to estimate the heartening value of Ezekiel's
simile of the valley of dry bones and the result which could
be achieved under the Spirit of God. Surely here is a beginning of that maxim, "God is able of the dust and the stones to
raise Him up a people." At least the same stirring, thrilling
idea is here in germ.

There were others who labored under the impression that
the consequence of sin is death. They now felt that the logic
of both Jeremiah and Ezekiel had left them no hope. Their
cup of iniquity was full to overflowing and they were being
utterly crushed by the wrath of God. There would be no
cessation of the afflictions until death brought relief. They
said, "If our transgressions and our sins be upon us, and we
pine away in them, how then shall we live?" To this question
Ezekiel replied in the tone of Jeremiah's letter. It was worth
while to pray and to repent. Had not God forgiven Israel
times without number in the past? Israel's history had dis-
proved the theory that sin must necessarily issue in the death
of the sinner. Thus by stating the efficacy of repentance, the
power of God's Spirit to revive the dry bones of Israel's hope,
and the certainty of national restoration, Ezekiel became a
steadying and constructive force among his despairing people.

And there were a number of encouraging events which contributed to the corroboration of Ezekiel's word. Graetz [21] tells
us that a part of the descendants of the Ten Tribes, scattered
for more than a century in Assyrian provinces and looked
upon as lost, had asserted their nationality: "Though long
separated by jealousy and artfully whetted hate, they approached their suffering brethren with cordial affection.
Those Israelites who had dwelt in the capital of Nineveh had,

---

[21] Graetz, *History of the Jews*, Vol. I, p. 335.

without doubt, left that doomed city at the destruction of the
Assyrian empire; and had fled to Babylonia, the neighboring
kingdom. Thus the prophet's words were again fulfilled,
'Israel and Judah shall dwell together in brotherly love.' "

Graetz's surmise is undoubtedly correct within certain limitations. We must not, however, regard all Israelites as fleeing
to Babylon. There is enough evidence to show that the chosen
race was scattered all over the East. They were in the north;
the book of Esther shows that they were in Persia; they were
in Egypt, in Palestine, in Babylon. But it is to be noted that
their sufferings had stripped them down to their fundamental
racial characteristics. Gone were the distinctions, the false
pride, the cliques, the Judean, the Israelite of the Northern
Kingdom. They had become once more the Hebrew, and
especially children of Jacob. It is noteworthy that Isaiah of
Babylon did not write for Judea alone, but for the children of
Jacob, the descendants of Israel. Israel and Judah had indeed
come to recognize that they were children of a common father
and followers of the same God.

The significance of this return to fundamental race-
consciousness cannot possibly be overemphasized. It brought
all the exiles to a realization of a glorious fact about their
race. They had not become degraded in their reversion to the
name of Israel; they had regained a glorious name and had
been reminded of their victorious capacities. Jacob had wrestled
with God and had prevailed. He had received a new name
and a blessing after his victory. And now the exiles of both the
Northern and Southern Kingdoms bore that God-conquering
name of Israel. What a name for a downtrodden people to
remember! Why should they languish in captivity? They
were a great race. They were the children of a man who had
risen above the consequences of his transgressions and had
claimed forgiveness and favor at the hands of God. That
capacity to claim the blessing was still present in his offspring.
They would have it! The memory of a great name, a great

family, a great accomplishment, and a great history has nerved
thousands of fainting hearts in all ages of the world. And, as
sons of Israel, the chosen people raised their drooping heads
when they recalled what manner of people they were.

This race-consciousness expressed itself in self-confidence
and race pride. Memory recalled all the great deeds and
thoughts of this great people. The priests of the sons of Zadok
brought out of their hearts the Torah (Pentateuch); the disciples of the prophets began to recite the eloquent words of
their masters; the Levites sang the psalms of Zion; the wise
men repeated the wise sayings they had been taught; and the
historical books were brought out of their hiding places to be
reread and pondered by reverent scribes. As Graetz correctly
observes, the people had brought with them a rich, brilliant,
and manifold literature, and it became a power that taught,
ennobled, and rejuvenated. Repentance followed, and four
days in the year were set apart as days of mourning. These
occasions were the anniversaries of Nebuchadrezzar's siege of
Jerusalem, of the conquest of Jerusalem, of the destruction of
Jerusalem, and of Gedeliah's assassination. This contrition
brought forth a new kind of psalm known as the Pentitential
Psalm. And the penitents became known as the "mourners
of Zion." Under this new spirit a great new literature began
to form. "The men of genius, disciples of Jeremiah and
Ezekiel, who had so thoroughly absorbed the spirit of their
literature that their own souls were brought into harmony
with it, now produced fruitful thoughts of their own, clothed
in elegant forms. An apparently inexhaustible fountain of
poetry flowed once more in a strange land, in the very midst
of the sufferings of captivity. New psalms, maxims of wisdom, and prophetical discourses followed each other in rapid
succession." Probably the books of Psalms, Proverbs, and Job
in their present form were the result of this new literary
activity. And it can scarcely be doubted that the whole history
of Israel was rewritten from the Exodus to the destruction of

Jerusalem and given a special treatment to support modern tendencies of priestly inclination and to reveal God's hand more clearly.

But not all the people were brought into the flow of this new national spirit. Graetz points out that "some of the most distinguished families among the Judeans adhered to their old abominations, and in addition adopted many of the errors of their heathen neighbors. The giant capital Babylon and the vast Chaldean empire exercised a magical charm over those "who stood highest" among the exiles, tempting them into imitating the Chaldean customs, opening a wide horizon before them, and giving them the opportunity of developing their talents. The products of the soil and the artistic fabrics of Babylonia, which were eagerly sought after and largely exported, formed the staples of a flourishing commerce. Thus the former merchants of Judah were able, not only to continue their calling, but to follow it more actively. They undertook frequent journeys for the purpose of buying and selling, and began to accumulate great riches. In a luxurious country wealth produces luxury. The rich Judeans imitated the effeminate life of the Babylonians, and even began to profess their idolatrous beliefs. So completely did the wealthy exiles identify themselves with the Babylonians that they entirely forgot Judah and Jerusalem, which until lately had been the goal of their desires. They could not bear to think of their return; they wished to become Babylonians, and looked with contempt upon the fanatical lovers of their own land." [22]

But fortunately the influence of these apostates was more than counterbalanced by the loyalty and courage of men equally rich and powerful. Men like Daniel and Nehemiah were a host in themselves in rallying the spirit of the nation. And they were not alone. Loyal men went everywhere, interested in trade, but far more interested in the preservation

---

[22] Graetz, *History of the Jews*, pp. 339sq.

of Israel. It was these traveling merchants which kept up the lines of communication between the far-flung outposts of this widely scattered nation. They carried with them news of the day, literary compositions, customs, and their own fervent hope. They were the missionaries to their own people and helped to cement the nation together. They may also have carried another commodity, so that it was not without some reason that the exile began to look upon Cyrus as the liberator of the Jew. The line which separates a traitor from a glorious patriot depends upon the point of view and the nature of the cause espoused. The Jew had at least the merit of a glorious cause; and if he trafficked with Cyrus to help turn the wheels of divine intervention, his crime is surely not much greater than that of the pious man who seeks by prayer and good works to change the complexion of a corrupt government. And after all, success in an undertaking has a way of justifying itself under the pretentious phrase de facto. Whether any overt act against Babylon can be traced to these travelers matters little. They brought to Cyrus the story of the hope of the Jew. The conqueror knew that some of the resources of that great city would not be used against him. And the traveler conveyed to the men of Israel in Babylon and elsewhere, the story of the conqueror's preparations, his policy, ambition, and chances of success. The unusual interest which the Jews showed in the career of Cyrus before he assaulted the gates of Babylon is enough to prove that they had long known that he was on the way.

At any rate the lines of prophecy and history began to converge to establish the reasonableness of Israel's expectation. It began to appear as if the words of Jeremiah would be fulfilled to the letter. Nebuchadrezzar died in 561 B.C., and his son, Evil-Merodach, succeeded him to the throne. Better times seemed in prospect for the Jew, for the new monarch treated the prisoners kindly and even admitted Jehoiachin to court. The hope of a return to Jerusalem, however, was not to be realized, probably because Evil-Merodach was killed after a short rule of only two years. The opportunities just opening to the eager Jewish leaders came thus to an end. Neriglissar, brother-in-law of the late king, ruled for four years and was succeeded by his young son, Laborosarchod. But the malady of Eastern despotisms had begun to afflict Babylon, and after nine months the boy king was put to death by the nobles. Nabonidus seized the power and made himself king. Once more the hope of the Jews rose to fever heat. Nabonidus permitted Merbal, a noble Phoenician, an exile of the royal house, to return to his own country and rule over his people. Graetz thinks it likely that Shealtiel, the son of Jehoiachin, made a similar request and was refused.[28] This act on the part of the usurper enkindled a burning hatred for Babylon among the patriotic Jews. Their feeling, for once, overcame all caution and expressed itself in word and deed. Imprisonments and persecutions followed. It was during this period of Israel's distress and outrage that Isaiah of Babylon came forward with his great prophecies.

His first great task, and his chief one, was to rationalize the sufferings of Israel. The author of the book of Job had struggled with the question and had succeeded in doing little except to heighten the tragedy by his vivid style. He had, of course, rather successfully combated the prevalent belief that suffering came as the result of sin, but he had not given any final solution to the problem. Indeed there could be no solution except national deliverance—the people must be saved out of their distresses. As that seemed somewhat remote, too remote for many who would die in exile, there was nothing left but endurance: "Though he slay me, yet will I trust him." That this unfaltering faith was worth something was not questioned; but the degree of benefit, as well as the real object of God in permitting the affliction, was left with a God

---

[28] Graetz, *ibid.*, p. 342.

whose ways were known to no one but Himself. The author of the book of Job concludes with a mystery too great for him and leaves the future to God. Isaiah of Babylon gives an answer—at least an answer that revives the discouraged and persecuted Israel.

To Isaiah the sufferings of Israel were the natural result of the great rôle which God had assigned to her among the nations. She had sinned—Isaiah is consistent with his predecessors thus far; and she must pay. After she has suffered awhile in exile she is forgiven, not for her own sake nor because she has ceased to sin, but for the sake of Jehovah's name:

> Thou hast brought me no sweet cane with money,
> Nor filled me with the fat of thy sacrifices:
> But thou hast vexed me with thy sins,
> And wearied me with thy transgressions.
> I, even I am he that blotteth out thy transgressions
> For mine own sake
> And remembereth thy sins no more.[24]

Isaiah reverts to this thought many times. Sometimes it is the faithfulness of God to His promises that restores Israel; at other times it is His love for her which moves Him. But though she may be forgiven, she is not yet set free of her afflictions. God has a work for her to do for Him. She is his servant called to witness to His glory in the heathen world.

That the prophet so presents Israel as the servant is clear from his own words:

> And thou, Israel, my servant,
> Jacob, whom I have chosen,
> Seed of Abraham, my friend.[25]

> And now hear, O Jacob, my servant,
> And Israel, whom I have chosen.
> Thus saith Jahve, that made thee and formed thee,

---

[24] Isaiah xliii. 23-25.
[25] Isaiah xli. 8.

That helpeth thee from the mother's womb:
Fear not, my servant Jacob,
And Jeshurun, whom I have chosen.[26]

Ye are my witnesses, saith the Lord,
And my servant whom I have chosen:
That ye may know and believe me,
And understand that I am he;
Before me there was no God formed,
Neither shall there be after me.[27]

Remember these, O Israel and O Jacob;
For thou art my servant;
O Israel, thou shalt not be forgotten of me.[28]

The character of the Servant and the Servant's task are
made clear when the prophet has Israel speak his views to the
nations:

Hearken, O inhabitants of the coast, unto me,
And listen ye people from afar.
Jahve hath called me from my mother's womb;
Even before I was born, he made mention of my name.
And he made my mouth like a sharp sword,
In the shadow of his hand he hid me;
He made me a sharp arrow,
And put me away in his quiver.
Then said he unto me, "Thou art my servant,
Israel, in whom I will glorify myself."
And I said, "I have labored in vain,
Without fruit and for naught have I spent my strength:
Yet—my right is with Jahve,
And my reward with my God."
But now saith Jehovah,
Who formed me from my mother's womb to be his servant,
That he should bring back to himself Jacob,
And gather to himself Israel,
While I am honored in Jahve's eyes,
And my God is my strength;

---

[26] Isaiah xliv. 1, 2.
[27] Isaiah xliii. 10.
[28] Isaiah xliv. 21.

Thus he said, "It is too little that thou shouldst be my servant,
To raise up the tribes of Jacob,
And bring back the liberated Israel:
Therefore have I appointed thee for a light to the nations,
That my salvation may reach to the end of the earth." [29]

There are other passages, however, which indicate that the messengers, or prophets of Jehovah, are also his servants.[30] This shifting of the meaning from Israel to the prophet makes it sometimes difficult to determine which is meant by a reference to "His servant." Kuenen observes that there existed two kinds of Israelites—Israelites in name and in reality.[31] Those who were faithful were Israelites in reality and composed that ideal Israel which was to be regarded as the Servant of Jahve. Of this ideal portion came the prophets, the patriots, and the heroes of faith. They are as individuals regarded by Isaiah as belonging to the Israel that shall redeem the apostate Jacob and the nations of mankind.

It is just here that we come to an advance upon the position of Ezekiel. He had taught that the guilty suffered for his own sins, and that the righteous received only good, a position controverted by the author of the book of Job. It was a matter of daily experience in Israel that the just suffered along with the ungodly. The righteous man had also been carried away into captivity and had been as deeply humiliated as the most ungodly man among the people. Why was this? These servants of Jehovah composed that ideal portion of Israel which should bear the sins of the nation and suffer to bring the glory of Jehovah to the knowledge of the whole earth. This gave dignity to the sufferer instead of confusion; the consciousness that he was thereby benefiting his nation instead of paying a penalty for his own misdeeds, especially when he had no consciousness of having sinned. Thus Isaiah gives an an-

---

[29] Isaiah xlix.: 1-6
[30] Cf. Isaiah xliv.: 26.
[31] Kuenen, *Religion of Israel*, Vol. II, p. 134.

swer to all those men of faith who asked why they were compelled to suffer along with the ungodly who had brought
about the nation's calamities. God had sent them to be an example and a means of saving their brethren. They were a
sort of sacrifice offered for the redemption of their own people.

This idea is clearly stated in the passage describing the
sufferings of the Servant:

> But he was wounded for our transgressions,
> Bruised for our iniquities:
> The chastisement which would give us peace was upon him,
> And with his stripes we were healed.
> All we like sheep had gone astray
> And had turned every one to his own way,
> But Jehovah laid upon him the iniquity of us all![32]

Thus does this prophet achieve two important forward steps
in religious advance. First, he presents the facts of actual experience in a more rational manner. Innocent and godly men
suffered. But they suffered, not for the nation's past evils, but
for the future of Jehovah's cause among mankind. Second,
he extended the power and the dominion of Jehovah, thus
freeing Him from the limitations of space and the territorial
boundaries of Israel in Palestine. By the prophet's vision Israel
entered upon the far-reaching and endless spectacle of Jehovah's sovereignty as His chosen servant to declare his glory
and truth to all humanity.

It is to be noted, of course, that while Isaiah takes it for
granted that Jerusalem shall be rebuilt, he has advocated a
world-view which makes the return only an incident in the
larger destiny of his nation. So long as Jehovah had the least
limitation to locality the return to Zion was vitally necessary
to the continuance of Hebrew religion. Isaiah of Babylon
seems to advocate a view that would make Jerusalem only a
point of emanation for that world-leavening spiritual force

---

[32] Isaiah liii. 5-6.

which was to be the new Israel. Indeed, his position is such that we may well wonder whether he shaped the later Jewish policy or permitted his teachings to be molded by the policy. When the day of return came, many of the Jews remained in Babylon. Not all of these expatriates were also apostates. In fact, large numbers of those who remained behind were among the most devout Jews and heartily favored the return of their brethren. They contributed vast sums for the rehabilitation of Palestine. No actual settlement of the homeland could have proceeded without the financial support of these expatriates. By remaining behind in Babylon they served as witnesses to the honor of Jehovah as they could not have done if they had joined the pilgrims who returned. Surrounded by a pagan population that could not be ignorant of the piety and benevolence of these Jews who carried the financial burden of the settlement in Palestine, every such expatriate was a constant witness to the excellency of his God. The new conception of the function of Israel as set forth by Isaiah provided a noble justification of the conduct of the pious who did not return.

Furthermore, this view provided a means of easily winning the Jew who had yielded to the temptation to remain for the sake of the worldly advantages of Babylon. He could continue where he was and make restitution for his past infidelity. The Jew did not go to his mount, for his mount had been brought to him in Babylon. This concession could not help but produce a wholesome effect upon a people so race-conscious as the Jew. Thousands that might have fallen away under a more austere policy now turned gratefully to the support of the rehabilitation enterprise. Thus Isaiah proves himself to be not only one of the greatest of religious leaders and reformers but also one of the shrewdest statesmen of all time. Whether his vision precedes the beginning of the return, or is contemporary with it, is beside the point. It observes both the exigencies and the expedients involved in the return. We shall look in vain for a man who has conceived a more successful basis of political and religious unity.

The prophet's interpretation of Jehovah's character was made to appear the more reasonable by placing the God of Israel in contrast with the Babylonian divinities. The fact that there is but one God is set forth in words attributed to Jehovah himself:

> Thus saith the Lord the King of Israel,
> And Israel's redeemer the Lord of Hosts:
> "I am the first, and I am the last;
> And beside me there is no God.
> And who, as I, shall speak and shall declare it,
> And set it in order for me,
> Since I appointed the ancient people?
> And the things that are coming,
> And shall come, let them show them to the people.
> Fear ye not, neither be afraid:
> Have not I told thee of these times,
> And have declared them? Ye are my witnesses.
> Is there a god beside me? No! I know none."[33]

Then follows a description of the character of the men who made the gods of Babylon:

> Who hath designed a god,
> Or molten a graven image that is profitable for anything?
> Behold all his fellows shall be ashamed:
> And the workmen—they are men:
> Let them all be gathered together,
> Let them stand up; yet they shall fear,
> And they shall all be ashamed together.
> The smith with his tongs worketh in the coals,
> And fashioneth it with hammers,
> And worketh it with the strength of his arms:
> But when he is hungry his strength faileth;
> When he drinketh no water, he is faint."[34]

---

[33] Isaiah xliv. 6-8.
[34] Isaiah xliv. 10-12.

The actual origin of the Babylonian gods is presented by the prophet in such detail and such realism that no idol can escape the scorn of the worshiper of Jehovah. He says:

The carpenter stretcheth out his rule;
He marketh it out with a line;
He fitteth it with planes,
And marketh it out with a compass,
Making it after the figure of a man,
According to the beauty of a man;
That it may remain in the house.
He heweth him down cedars,
And taketh the cypress and the oak,
Which he has grown in the forest:
He planteth an ash and the rain has nourished it.
Then shall it be for a man to burn:
He can take thereof and warm himself;
He can kindle it and bake bread;
Yea, he can make of it a god and worship it;
He can make a graven image and fall down thereto.
He burneth part thereof in the fire;
With part thereof he eateth flesh;
He roasteth roast and is satisfied:
Yea, he warmeth himself, and saith,
"Aha, I am warm, I have seen the fire."
And the residue thereof he maketh a god, a graven image:
He falleth down unto it, and worshipeth it,
And prayeth unto it and saith,
"Deliver me; for thou art my god."[35]

The prophet accounts for this blindness of the Babylonian to the true character of his god on the ground that his very practices have blinded his understanding and closed his eyes and heart so that his folly is unperceivable. Thus there is no knowledge to say: "I have burned part of the tree in the fire; I have baked bread upon the coals; I have roasted flesh, and have eaten it; is it possible that I can worship the part that remains,—fall down on my face and revere a stump?" [36] Those

---

[35] Isaiah xliv. 13-17.
[36] Isaiah xliv. 19.

of the Israelites who may have made terms with the "stumps"
of Babylon will be hard put to it to keep their bargain after
such ridicule. They will find themselves the laughing stock
of their fellow Israelites. And ridicule of this nature is a
powerful force for national solidarity. There may not be any
great show of repentance on the part of the apostates; but
they will be sure to stay away from the shrines and temples of
the Babylonian divinities, and they will silently steal back to
the congregations of their own people.

And the way is made easy for all such as have turned to
the idols of the conquerors. The lofty and favored position of
Israel is stressed in a great appeal:

> Remember these things, O Jacob and Israel;
> For thou art my servant: I have formed thee;
> Thou art my servant:
> O Israel, thou shalt not be forgotten of me.
> I have blotted out, as with a thick cloud,
> Thy transgressions, and, as with a cloud,
> Thy sins; return unto me;
> For I have redeemed thee.[37]

The theological argument closes with a description of the
faithfulness and power of Jehovah—a fitting passage, and
one that stresses all the more the futility and worthlessness of
the gods of the heathen. Jehovah is presented as one who
"maketh diviners mad," who confounds the wisdom of the
wise, and maketh knowledge to be foolishness. He saith to
Jerusalem, "Thou shalt be built, and I shall raise up the
waste places." The prophet is seeking to recall all Israel to a
renewed trust in their God and in His power to save them.

The Israelite by the time Isaiah appeared was in no mood
to be persuaded with mere phrases. He had been through too
much humiliation and pain. Doubt and cynicism must have
been a very prevalent religious attitude with large masses of
the people. They were no doubt ready to give the prophet a

---

[37] Isaiah xliv. 21-22.

hearing, for they had learnt in bitterness of soul, that the predictions of Jeremiah had been all too completely fulfilled. But we may be very sure that they required that the prophet prove his way, at least that he appear reasonable. It was not enough to tell the average Israelite that he would be delivered. He had been told that many times, and always his hopes had been dashed in the shuffle of political forces in Babylon. Evil-Merodach had seemed ready to grant their desire, but his career had suddenly been cut short. Later, Nabonidus had raised their hope and had destroyed it almost at once. Then Cyrus [38] appeared over the eastern mountains to make his way northward and westward, sweeping all before him. News of his conquests made it a time of speculation and prophecy. And when success followed success, and the Persian power began to encircle and isolate Babylon, it must have been clear to almost any intelligent man that the Chaldean empire was doomed.

The average Israelite, however, could scarcely understand the meaning of this spectacle of successful warfare, even if he knew of it. To him the scene was remote, and the walls of Babylon were impregnable. But the survivors of the days of the fall of Jerusalem would be ready to entertain the possibility of Babylon's fall without any urging from the voice of their desires. They had seen an impregnable city fall, a city defended by the Lord of Hosts. If it were a part of God's plan to destroy Jerusalem, it might also be a part of His plan to destroy Babylon. The more intellectual Israelites, those gifted with the power to penetrate into political motives, would see at once what Cyrus was about. When the conqueror had cut off all possibility of a coalition of nations against him he would reduce Babylon at his leisure. He was now attempting to complete the first stage of his plan and was sweeping up the nations as the wind scatters the dust.

---

[38] See Appendix to this chapter.

One may with some reason ask, How could the prophet feel so sure that Cyrus would liberate the Jew and send him back to his homeland? Those who declare that God revealed it to him, and who mean by their statement that God told him outright by word of mouth, dispose of everything but the historical situation. In fact, they come precious near to destroying the necessity to live by the light of any revelation. If God be forever telling a man what is to happen, and tells him by word, rather than by implication from His nature and events, there is little place for reason in the godly life. One can then go blissfully on until God speaks the word. We may feel reasonably sure that the prophet was not told in this fashion. The predictions concerning the restored Israel and the actual Israel after the restoration do not coincide enough to approximate our notion of advice derived from omniscience. The prophet is reading the signs of his time with the aid of his conception of God, and he sees enough truth to inspire confidence and to predict the trend which history will take.

There were a few accessory facts which made the prediction seem all the more certain of fulfillment—facts which the prophet knew would weigh heavily in the actual shaping of history. First of all, there was a marked similarity between the religion of Cyrus and the religion of the Israelite. There was nothing to produce a conflict between the Jew and the Persian at this point. Furthermore, the final settlement of Cyrus with each of the nations he had conquered had been humane and tolerant. He would not be likely to reverse this policy upon conquering Babylon. And toward the conquered peoples exiled within the territory of Babylon, he would be all the more kindly disposed. He would be all the more likely to send them home that they might found a friendly power. Even when all possibility of a previous understanding between the Israelites and Cyrus is given up, there is enough to support the prophet in reading the future as he did. Cyrus will be friendly. He will liberate the Jew and send him home to found a buffer state in the far west, a barrier against the possible ambition of the Egyptians.

All this must have been quite clear to Isaiah as he watched Cyrus making his way westward, overturning empires and striking fear into the heart of any who might be likely to come to the aid of Babylon. And when he saw that Cyrus had not touched Palestine, he was all the more sure that the conqueror would welcome the opportunity to establish a friendly power in that region. As all this conspiracy of event and common religious interest and ambition became clear to the prophet, he saw his faith confirmed and his hope made sure. Surely God's hand was clearly visible. The long-looked-for deliverance was at hand. Then came the conviction that such good news should be told to the people. A new prophet arose to declare the deep things of God, a God who wrought among the nations by the hand of Cyrus:

> Jehovah saith of Cyrus, "my shepherd,"
> And "he shall perform all my pleasure,
> By saying to Jerusalem, Be rebuilt!
> And to the temple, Be founded!"[39]

> Thus saith Jehovah to his anointed, to Cyrus,
> Whom I hold by his right hand,
> To cast down nations before his face
> And to loose the girdle of kings,
> To open doors before his face
> And to keep gates not shut.
> "I will go before thy face
> And make hills level;
> Gates of brass will I break in pieces
> And cut in sunder bars of iron.
> And I will give thee treasures that lie in darkness
> And hidden riches,
> That thou mayest know that I am Jehovah,
> Which call thee by thy name, the God of Israel.
> For the sake of Jacob my servant

[39] Isaiah xliv. 28.

And Israel mine elect,
I called thee by thy name,
I spake unto thee, while thou didst not know me."[40]

The words of Isaiah reveal the real religious significance of
Cyrus to the Israelite. Cyrus is not a worshiper of a pagan god.
He worships a god whose character reveals that he is actually
Jehovah, the God of the Israelite. Isaiah in another place
(41:25) describes Cyrus as calling "upon Jehovah's name,"
but the closing sentence of the reference cited above shows
that Cyrus did not know that the true name of his God was
Jehovah. There is more than a religious reformer in Isaiah,
more than a discoverer of the universal dominion of his own
God. He is one of the great religious leaders of mankind. He
discovered in the days of the Babylonian captivity a truth which
so many devout men are not even yet willing to grant: he saw
that Jehovah had revealed Himself to other peoples and had
taught them through a period of history quite comparable to
the history of His revelation to Israel. And this vision comes
from a race supposed to be the most clannish and bigoted of
mankind! Compare Isaiah's wisdom with the theologian who
argues that every nation but his own is without God and
without hope in the world. Has religion gone forward or
backward since the days of Isaiah of Babylon?

With such liberality in religious thought we need not
wonder that many Persian elements were drawn into the
popular creed of Israel. The accretions, of course, made no
modification of the God of Israel. He has remained the same
in all ages of the world, but he was now better understood by
his followers. The Persian assistance may have constituted
a contribution outright, and it may have done no more than
state in somewhat better terms what Israel already possessed
in germ. As we review the creed of Israel before and after the
exile we discover not only expansion but a marked corre-

---

[40] Isaiah xlv. 1-5.

spondence here and there with ideas which existed previously in Persia. Naturally, after hearing the language of Isaiah in describing both Cyrus and his religion there would be friendly interchange of ideas. Curiosity alone would bring it about.

On the whole it was a great religious age, one that pushed creative religious thinking about as far as it has yet gone. And what people other than Israel could have so anticipated the loftiest positions of the creeds of the modern world? Truly that nation was the elect, the favored of God. And the words of God have been correctly recorded by the prophet:

Behold my servant, whom I uphold,
Mine elect, in whom my soul delighteth:
I lay my spirit upon him,
He shall proclaim right to the nations.[41]

I, Jehovah, have called thee in righteousness,
And will hold thine hand,
And will keep thee and place thee for a covenant of the
    people,
For a light to the Gentiles.[42]

Such was the great contribution of this unknown Babylonian Israelite to the religious thought of mankind. He dwelt in the flesh in the days of ignorance and confusion and sorrow. His eyes looked upon cruelties and wounds and death. But he looked on other things also. He saw the white peaks of the centuries before him and all the far-stretched pathos and questing of men. It is small wonder that many of his own people did not understand all he said, for there are all too many of the supposedly modern peoples who have not yet reached the spiritual lands he saw. Perhaps in breadth of view and in liberality of spirit Isaiah of Babylon has touched the highest point to which religion can rise. At any rate, his spirit belongs to the ages, for he will be found to be as progressive in

[41] Isaiah xlii. 1.
[42] Isaiah xlii. 6.

all ages as the youngest member of any group of rebels. What became of Isaiah, what he did later on, what his real name was, and where he died—all this would be interesting could we know it. But such facts of his life matter little. He discharged his duty according to one of the loftiest visions it has ever been given a prophet to behold. He was the savior of his people and the light for all future ages. Having performed a work of this magnitude, he can well afford to remain anonymous.

APPENDIX TO CHAPTER VII

Professor Charles Cutler Torrey of Yale, in his recent book, *The Second Isaiah*, has moved the author of Isaiah, chaps. xl-lxvi, to the supposedly brilliant creative age near the close of the Persian period. In taking this position he seems to us to have disregarded a number of very potent arguments against his conclusions.

Not the least of these is the fact that great prophets the world over have risen out of the throes of great social distress. It is conceivable, of course, that genius might have produced these chapters of Isaiah at any time; but a study of the origin of the religious classics will show that genius, like lesser grades of ability, is subject to adequate stimulation— that thinking is always a reaction. At least there is always enough social data to lead one to infer that this rule has applied all along the path of history. A proper regard for the social coefficient will, therefore, compel the student of Isaiah to look for the social upheaval which could have reacted to produce these closing chapters of the book of Isaiah. The quiet time Professor Torrey describes seems favorable to creative work of high order until we reflect that no great social program has ever been conceived apart from a situation which presses for solution. In looking about for a social condition

which could have provoked the profound intellectual and religious reaction which appears in Second Isaiah, we are forced
to decide upon the days of the Babylonian captivity.

Dr. Torrey supports his view by declaring that all references to Cyrus are interpolations from a later date, later even
than the Persian period. In other words, the poet himself made
in his prophecies no mention of Cyrus. These additions to
the text, we are told, disturb the rhythm of the poem and
could not have been included by the prophet. Dr. Torrey concludes that the author never had any thought of discussing
affairs in Babylon but confined himself to the new mission
of Israel, a conception which grew out of the international
outlook achieved under Persian supremacy.

But even if we grant that all mention of Cyrus and Babylon
is a later corruption of the text, it seems to us that it in no
way invalidates the view that the poems were originally written in Babylon for the comfort of the Jewish exiles. It appears
to us to be just as reasonable to suppose that the author may
have had very good reasons for omitting names that would
endanger the safety of himself and his fellow countrymen.
His own age would understand him. Later the Jews of a restored Palestine might require interpolations, or side notes,
which finally were incorporated into the text. The presence
of interpolations would therefore seem to us to support the
traditional view rather than that of Dr. Torrey.

A further looseness in Torrey's thinking has led him to
discover a "recent historical event" which he uses to support
the late date of Second Isaiah. The Jews had seen an opportunity to restore the independence of their nation and had
sent envoys with gifts to some king to secure his aid against
Persia. Dr. Torrey concludes that the overtures were made
to Egypt. "The one time," he says, "of all others when the
Jewish province seemed to have an opportunity of advancement was when Egypt threw off the Persian yoke in 407 B.C."
If Dr. Torrey had not decided upon this late period for the

authorship of Second Isaiah he would have had a well-known historical episode to explain the words of the prophet (Isaiah lvii. 9f). We know that the king of Israel closed his gates against the armies of Nebuchadrezzar and waited anxiously for aid from Egypt. The expected relief did not come and Israel "went down to the pit." The prophet in this poem tells his people that it was unreasonable to suppose that any power but the God of Nations could have delivered Israel. And if she is to come out of the pit it must be by the power of Jehovah working through the nations. Even then Israel must be righteous and worthy of deliverance.

But Dr. Torrey passes over this possible explanation and infers that the prophet looks to a deliverance from Persian supremacy. But according to the traditional view Second Isaiah is the most ardent supporter of Persia. And if we accept Dr. Torrey's view we must admit that the favor is very popular and long drawn out—the interpolations were added long after the book was composed by the prophet. Torrey himself tells us that this book was widely circulated and that it became the inspiration for almost all the other prophecies. Why should such a pro-Persian book be devised, and become so highly acceptable to all classes of people, when its "king" has but recently sent ambassadors to secure aid from Egypt in throwing off the Persian yoke? Dr. Torrey is in great need of a situation which will account for the appearance of Second Isaiah.

The real weakness of his position lies in the fact that he seems to feel that culture in Western Asia was a late development, perhaps coexistent with the rise of Greece which achieved its golden age at about this time. But the results of archeological discovery indicate that Western Asia had reached such a level of refinement that Second Isaiah might have been written there at a time long before the appearance of Moses. The possibility of its being written by a Jew would depend only upon his being brought up in proper surroundings. A

Jew born and educated in highly civilized Babylon is enough to account for the literary achievement.

Torrey makes much of the fact that many Aramaic, late Hebrew, and Persian words appear in Second Isaiah. But in a cosmopolitan center like Babylon we have just the atmosphere to produce a new Jewish language. The very fact that the Jews became such an important factor in the life of Babylon would indicate that in both commercial and intellectual interests they became increasingly international. Without a nation of their own to hold them in its provincial groove they moved about rather freely and drank in the lore and language of the whole East. And the strange circumstances of the fall of Babylon would indicate that Persia had her friends in this teeming city.

We owe to Dr. Torrey, however, a considerable debt because he has so ably defended the literary worth and single authorship of Second Isaiah. Modern criticism by means of the composite theory of authorship had almost destroyed the value of this portion of the Scriptures, and it was high time that some scholar capable of true literary appreciation came to its defense. We feel nevertheless that Dr. Torrey's historical sense is far behind his literary understanding. His whole thesis seems to us to be greatly weakened by his late date for Israel's golden age of literature. It is being demonstrated more fully every year that it is very unsafe to presume upon the intellectual incapacity of man in any age of the world.

CHAPTER VIII

SOCRATES

Search as one will it is very difficult to find sufficient materials to afford an adequate reconstruction of the life of Socrates. Those writers who have given him mention in their pages have usually been controlled by their own theses and have been content with but a few facts about him. Even the philosophers treat him as only a philosopher, often with but brief mention of his predecessors and contemporaries and with a tendency to hasten on to the place where men and materials have fared better at the hands of Chance. The Sophists are accorded a few paragraphs, enough to state briefly that impasse of skepticism and atheism which overtook these thinkers, leaving them but clever jugglers of logic or teachers of rhetoric. The social conditions are barely mentioned: we are informed that the Persian wars awoke the genius of the Greek mind; but we are not told often that almost the whole of the mature years of Socrates coincided with the most terrific struggle in which the Greek states ever participated. We are not given the least view of the power and wealth of Athens which excited the jealousy of her neighbors and brought on this long-drawn-out war in which Athens fought for an overseas empire and lost it. Thus presented without background, this greatest teacher of Athens appears to have sprung suddenly from nothing and to have aimed at nothing except the scientific pursuit of knowledge.

But meager as our information is, there is enough, when we take the age into consideration, to do more by Socrates than has usually been done. The brief biographical note, so often encountered, when put into the tense drama of Athenian life, will reveal Socrates in interesting and greatly varied scenes. We find him a man of his time, a citizen of Athens, a dweller in a long-threatening danger. He is revealed as a devoted patriot, subject to all the laws and customs of his city, and engaged in the pursuits which the city's emergencies demanded of him. A review of the life of Athens in his day, a study of its laws, its statesmanship, its activities during the Peloponnesian War, and its requirements of every male citizen able to bear arms, give not only background but a point and purpose to the labors of Socrates. He appears no longer as a mere intellectual engaged in academic theorizings. His city is engaged in its death-struggle; to lose it through lack of either courage or of wise leaders is to lose all. It is, therefore, no mere chance that he so frequently speaks of the nature of virtue, courage, the duties of statesmanship and preparation therefor, the duties of a general, a cavalry officer, and the proper government of a state. These are all matters of tremendous concern at the moment.

Such an approach to the study of Socrates will enable one to behold a living man, one intensely alert to all that will preserve the state and its power. And as we read of him and watch him move through these volcanic scenes of peril, we shall be able to judge of the truth of such statements as the following: ". . . we can yet see his ungainly figure, clad always in the same rumpled tunic, walking leisurely through the agora, undisturbed by the bedlam of politics, buttonholing his prey, gathering the young and the learned about him, luring them into some shady nook of the temple porticoes, and asking them to define their terms."[1] Socrates was, as we know, rather indifferent as to his manner of dress, and he may have been "ungainly." But we know that he was a man of great strength, able to meet the best-trained troops of his

---

[1] Durant, *Story of Philosophy*, p. 11.

time and to hold his own against them. Once he defended the wounded Alcibiades single-handed and saved him from losing both his weapons and his life. At another time he carried the wounded Zenophon out of the mêlée to a place of safety. And on another field Alcibiades found him alone, greatly outnumbered, fighting like a lion, and making a safe retreat before the enemy. It was only his plebeian origin, and the fact that he himself voted for Alcibiades, that prevented him from receiving the laurel wreath and public citation for valor in the face of the enemy. We must remember that the man we seek to know was a seasoned soldier who more than once was clad in armor and faced the foe sword in hand far from the shaded porticoes and from the bedlam of politics.

Zenophon [2] tells us that Socrates talked publicly and always where men were accustomed to assemble. And what is more natural to such a man? Whatever interests the citizens of Athens is of interest to him. Has he not fought for Athens, not once, but in two great battles? Has he not endured hardship and the gravest dangers a soldier can face? But for timely help in each battle in which he fought, there might have been no glorious story of Greek philosophy to tell. He is then no stay-at-home, uninformed talker, but a man who has come back from the mouth of Hades to tell out of his thought and experience his opinion of vital public matters. And we do not encounter the listless eye of a speculative dreamer when we look into his face; his eyes are clear, penetrating, keen, and intensely practical. Any one acquainted with him must see at once that he has a right to be heard not only for his apparent understanding but also for his valorous and unselfish services to the state.

How much he loved his native city, how much it was a part of him, can be judged more from his later manner of life than from his bravery in warfare. Men often fight courageous-

---

[2] *Memorabilia* I. 10.

ly because of the peril of their situation or from personal honor. Socrates very probably faced men who had been taught to bring their shields back in honor or be carried home upon them. His own people were not inferior to the Spartans and others of the Peloponnesian League in courage. They had won the battle of Marathon; they had compelled Xerxes to return home by their victory at Salamis. Thus almost alone they had twice by their courage stemmed the Persian tide. Athenian honor would have made Socrates give a good account of himself in battle, and we know also that his situation in each case was perilous. But he devoted all his spare time to teaching men to be good citizens, and for this he would take no pay. He was misunderstood and ridiculed by Aristophanes; he was blamed for the vice and treason of some of his disciples; and was charged with denying the gods of his people. When warned not to appear in court lest he be sentenced to death, he promptly appeared; the laws of Athens must be obeyed. And when he had been condemned to death, he neither elected exile nor accepted a sure means of escape; the laws of Athens must be honored and obeyed. Such conduct reveals the chief object of his affection. Athens, his home, the city he loved and had fought for, was his abiding concern. We cannot understand him or behold his purpose until we know something of the beauty, the rich achievements, and the perils of Athens.

The Greek was an unusually gifted man and belonged to a race which embraced the most widely divergent capacities. The form of government, the polis, which prevailed throughout the Greek world, was well suited to bring out and develop this many-sidedness. In each city there was exhibited in the manner of life and point of view a distinct quality of the Greek spirit. Men of Athens, Thebes, Sparta, Corinth, Ephesus, and Syracuse were all unmistakably Greeks, exhibiting the common characteristics of their race; and yet all were easily distinguishable the one from the other because of the selection each had made from the rich racial patrimony. The Spartans have been described as "a valiant, gifted, ancient-lineaged race whose intense Greek characteristics of toughness, obstinacy, and one-sidedness comes out with luminous disinctness all along the lines of Greek story." The Athenians were brave, crafty, endued with all pliancy and grace, adaptable, possessed of great capacity for commerce and statesmanship, artistic, and intellectually clever and profound. Together with the Ionians they seem to have received a full measure of the many-sidedness and artistic richness of the Greek nature. The Corinthians were essentially a commercial people, but en-dued with much of the Athenian love of luxuriousness. On the other hand they were not crafty in either war or statesman-ship, and having experienced this weakness in their natures they were not so courageous in battle as either the Spartans or the Athenians. The Thebans were an inland people, more like the Spartans in temper than any other of the Greeks, but possessed of a large share of the versatility of the Athenians. If they had lived upon the sea, as did the Athenians, there seems little reason to doubt that they would have built up a great overseas empire and have added an untold chapter to the already glorious history of this amazing people.

It was the Persian Wars that revealed to the Athenians their superior capacity for warfare. Up to this time they had been brave, proud, and given to commercial and artistic pur-suits. In time of war they contributed a not inglorious part in preserving the independence of Greece, but a lack of con-fidence in their ability to face the enemy alone made them lean upon the reckless and irresistible courage of the Spartans. When the Persians landed for the first invasion of the coun-try, the Athenians were compelled to face them without the assistance of Sparta, who was then observing one of her fes-tivals and did not believe it expedient to take the field until the festival had been concluded. The Athenians, know-ing that they must fight immediately to save Athens and all northern Greece, fought the battle of Marathon practically unaided. Their spirited and desperate onset amazed the Persians. They could not believe that such a small army would be so indiscreet as to attack. Then as the Athenians swept all before them and heaped the field with slaughter, amazement turned to panic and the Persians fled to their ships, thinking to reach Athens and burn it before the Athenian army could defend it. They arrived to find that the Athenians had double-quicked to Athens and stood ready for its defense. In chagrin the Persians withdrew. The Spartans came shortly afterward, went on to view the battle field, and returned to pay the highest tribute to the courage and prowess of the Athenians.

The result of this first trial of arms convinced the Athenians that they had both the courage and skill for great warfare. Their generals had beaten the Persians in strategy at every turn, and the common soldier had demonstrated that he could face and conquer a foe superior to him in numbers. Thus when Xerxes came with his millions, they were not wholly dismayed. Leonidas with a small army added an inextinguishable fame to the glory of Sparta and all Greece, but the real strength of Sparta was again late in making its appearance and came to find Athens in the hands of Xerxes. The Athenians had fled to the islands and to their ships. The Spartans were for falling back to the Peloponnesus; but the Athenians, utterly reckless because they had been taunted with being a people without a city, hurled themselves upon the Persian fleet and destroyed it. Xerxes, seeing the result of the sea fight and realizing that the Greeks could destroy the bridges over the Hellespont and cut him off from home, hurried at once to get back to Asia. The perils of his march home, exposure, hunger, and disease left him but a feeble remnant of the vast horde with which he had set out. One of his generals was left at Thebes in command of a very large body of troops, but these were soon cut to pieces by the combined Grecian arms. The chief glory of this second war, however, went again to the Athenians.

The subsequent triumphs of the Athenian fleet, which swept the sea of all remaining Persian ships and liberated the cities of Ionia and Asia Minor, made possible the undisturbed flowering of Greek civilization. Men everywhere in Greater Greece entered upon a new era of life as a result of the stimulation of new ideas and of the uncircumscribed outlook. But as may reasonably be expected, it was to the Athenians that the greatest measure of benefit accrued. They had discovered themselves, had found unsuspected abilities, and were not slow to see the significance of their new-found powers. They augmented their fleet rapidly to such enormous proportions that they became the undisputed masters of the seas; they re-fortified Athens and connected it by an impregnable wall with the sea port four miles away, thus making it impossible for enemies to successfully besiege it by land; and they contrived through the formation of a league with overseas cities to make Athens the most powerful city in all Greece, so much so that the jealousy of Sparta and Corinth was aroused.

Gradually now Athens, by being quick to take advantage of any revolt by a member of the league, reduced the allies to tributaries. Immense sums went to keep up her enormous sea power and to enrich her public treasury. All this was not accomplished, however, without much resentment among the Ionian and Asiatic cities. Thus the policy which made possible the empire of Athens also paved the way for its downfall.

The battle of Platea in 478 B.C. freed Greece forever from the threat of Persian despotism and made the Greeks a free and happy people. Except for occasional battles between Athens and certain members of her league, there was peace for the next forty-eight years. During that time the city which was to be the home of such men as Anaxagoras, Pericles,

Socrates, Plato, Aristotle, Demosthenes, Euripides, Aeschylus, Sophocles, Zenophon, and Thucydides, consolidated her power and developed, slowly at first, then by leaps and bounds, until her citizens were the richest, the wisest, and the most cultivated in the whole world.

Two men, Pericles and Anaxagoras, stand out during this period of development as contributing most to the greatness of Athens. To Anaxagoras, in spite of the highly metaphysical character of his philosophy, must go the honor of emancipating the best minds of Athens from the narrowness and superstitution of the prevailing religion. He explained to his pupils that many phenomena which the common people ascribed to gods and supernatural beings were due to natural causes. By the character of his philosophy he was able to minimize the possibility of the existence of the popular gods and to assign all causes to the harmonious workings of Nature, or Reason. All fears, errors, and even treasons came from non-being, or the lack of Reason. Thus the intellectuals of Athens, her teachers, statesmen, and soldiers, were enabled to make the last great step to freedom and to enter upon their duties with clear minds and without fear. The average Athenian citizen continued to be subject to popular superstitions, but the great men, no less pious and far more wise, kept their counsel and took for their guide the dictations of human and divine Reason.

Pericles, a pupil of Anaxagoras, advanced rapidly to the chief place in the government. The state was a democracy, but the wisdom and achievements of Pericles gained for him such power that under his administration the government became practically an aristocracy. He had his critics and his enemies, but he triumphed over these by his merit and personal force. He belonged to one of the most aristocratic families of Athens; was thoroughly taught in music and elegant accomplishments, in philosophy, rhetoric, and argumentation. He was an unusually far-seeing and efficient statesman and brought easily to the advantage of his city the best fortunes of peace and war. He kept away from the crowd, avoided banquets and drinking bouts, and was careful to appear in the assembly only when he had something vitally important to say. When he spoke there he made a profound impression; his thundering voice and flashing eyes, his lightning strokes of logic, wit, and sarcasm earned for him the title, "The Olympian."

In his public labors he silently carried out the logical consequences of the freedom implied in the teachings of Anaxagoras. Those who stood nearest to him must have been less discreet than he, for we learn that he was vaguely accused of advocating new-fangled gods. Whether the accusation refers to the religious advances introduced by the cult of Orpheus or to a modification of the nature and power of the ancient gods to conform to the metaphysics of Anaxagoras, we perhaps cannot determine. In public he was conservative enough, and fostered the arts which magnified the gods of the common people. He filled the city with temples, statues, and monuments—every bright and lovely object which art could provide.

He has been described as "the greatest of all Athenian statesmen, a noble orator and democrat who yet belonged to the bluest of blue Athenian blood. The period of his lifetime embraces the loftiest and noblest period of Grecian story, the period in which Athens became supremely ascendant in arts, politics, and letters, and wrought such poems and marbles, such temples and trophies of intellectual greatness, as have rendered her name forever memorable. The "Olympian" Pericles was indeed the Zeus of Athenian culture, oratory, and accomplishment: a luminous intelligence, quiet, profound, far-reaching, well balanced, neither too piercing nor too obtuse, the fine flower of antique Greek civilization and its highest justification." [3]

---

[3] J. A. Harrison, *The Story of Greece* (Famous Nations), p. 394.

His detractors described him otherwise. Because he had such serenity and poise, such composure and dignity, that no interruption during his public speaking could disturb him, they ridiculed his gravity, declaring that it was a pose. They were answered, however, by Zeno, who counseled them to adopt the same manner that through an attempt to counterfeit it they might learn to appreciate the noble qualities that sustained it. Socrates is presented by Plato [4] as questioning with some reason both the fundamental sincerity and the value to the state of the services of Pericles. Socrates did not mean, of course, that Pericles had accomplished no good, for his achievements and his wise statesmanship were too apparent. He felt, however, that if Pericles had abandoned the art of persuasion and all personal interest he might have taught the people such virtue and intelligence that they would not have crowned his labors by accusation and a suspension from office. This is a penetrating criticism, and one that would have claimed the respectful attention of Pericles himself. Aristophanes casts a slur upon him by assigning as the real cause of the Peloponnesian War a low quarrel over three women of tarnished reputation, two of whom were owned by Aspasia, the consort of Pericles. But neither criticism, open hostility, nor calumny could finally obscure his value to the state. After a brief suspension from office, the "Olympian" was returned with more power than ever and died soon after of the plague, a leader highly honored and deeply appreciated by the city.

Athens was already a rich and prosperous city when Pericles came to power. It was the most joyous, gay, and progressive city of the Greeks. But Pericles saw in the unmistakable jealousy of Corinth and Sparta that war was inevitable between them and Athens. In that struggle the loyalty, virtue, and intelligence of the whole citizenship of Athens would

---

[4] *Gorgias,* sec. 152.

constitute her safety. He, therefore, distrusted the view of the aristocracy, his own party, that with their few numbers they could impress the people with a love of these essential qualities. He early set to work to break down the influence of Cimon, a strongly entrenched politician and aristocrat who was then the real power in Athens. The struggle between the two was long drawn out and shrewdly conducted on both sides, but at last Pericles succeeded in having Cimon banished. Meeting now with no considerable interference, he turned himself to a restoration of the democracy. The citizens were induced to attend the Assembly and to listen to the oratory; education was fostered; plebeians were assigned to jury duty that they might have a part in deciding great issues and thus become acquainted with the conduct of government; restrictions which discriminated against the lower orders were removed; and all who complied with the spirit of his undertaking were paid for their services at public expense. Even attendance at public functions was rewarded. It was the belief of Pericles that the state had most to gain from such publicly attended functions and that she should be willing to pay for the benefit.

He was such a patron of the arts that "temples, porticoes, and colonnades sprang up and soon swarmed with the exquisite and tranquil creations of Greek chisels. Pictures in public places revealed what great things the gods had done for Athens in days of yore, and what memorable triumphs her general and admirals had won by land and sea. A group of divinely gifted poets, beginning with Aeschylus, who had fought at Marathon, and Pindar, who was crowned poet-laureate of the Olympic and Pythian Games, awoke as if by enchantment and made the air of Greece tuneful with sweet and mighty song. The play-writers wrote series after series of unrivalled plays, which were performed, at the expense of the state, in the open-air theater of Dionysus, under the acropolis, before throngs upon throngs of eager listeners." [5]

---

[5] J. A. Harrison, *The Story of Greece* (Famous Nations), p. 406.

All this required immense sums of money. The theater, the temples, the upkeep of the mighty fleet, the doles given to citizens who attended public functions and served on juries, or attended the meetings of the Assembly, and the training of every male citizen in the art of war required an almost inexhaustible exchequer and an unusually resourceful public treasurer. Pericles attended to the expenditures very largely in person. And there were times when all his influence with the people and his financial ingenuity were taxed to the limit. But perhaps he was not compelled to take the step which Plutarch and Cornelius Nepos have said we was forced to take. They declare that Alcibiades saw him one day in a pensive mood and asked the reason. Pericles replied, "Great sums of public money have passed through my hands, and I know not how to make up my accounts." "Contrive then," said Alcibiades, "to give no account at all." In pursuance of this advice Pericles involved the state in the Peloponnesian War. It is highly probable that Alcibiades may have told this story to lessen his own villainy in the eyes of the Spartans and other Greeks. Thucydides gives evidence that the war was long overdue and that only accident had prevented the Spartans from committing the act which would have constituted actual war. According to Thucydides the acts which made Athens the aggressor were only the part of wise statesmanship in the face of a well-known situation. As to the public accounting and the alleged dishonesty, it may be dismissed; for when the Athenians complained of the amount of expense incurred in public building Pericles offered to pay the bill out of his own pocket, stipulating only that he be allowed to put his name upon each structure. The Athenians shouted as one man, "Take what money you want, and spend it as you please!"

Even with such liberty it may be altogether probable that he cracked the constitution and found it necessary to manipulate his accounts. But he was too wise to be caught. When his chief architect and sculptor was accused of keeping back some of the gold allowed for a certain statue, the people found to their surprise that the gold had been so arranged that it could be taken off and weighed. And it was found to be full weight! Thucydides declares that Pericles never increased his private fortune by one mina during his administration. The detractions from the good name of Pericles have all to prove their way while the achievements he wrought are known to all. In spite of all that may be said against him, he gave Athens her greatest glory, a glory that endured long after her military power was only a memory. But great leaders of democracy have always fared thus at the hands of their enemies.

That there was some ground for gossip and slanderous criticism must be admitted. His evident hatred for Magara had to be explained in some way, and since he remained silent his enemies were afforded an opportunity of explaining it for him. They did not, naturally, urge his wisdom in standing firm against the meddling demands of Sparta; they made mention of the theft by the Magarans of a brace of harlots from Aspasia, the mistress of Pericles. After all, there *was* Aspasia. Domestic difficulties made it necessary for Pericles to give up his wife to another. He installed Aspasia in her place, paying no heed to gossip. But there had been, or there were later, other women. When the plague carried off his last legitimate son, he went to the Assembly and requested that the law against bastardy, a law he had himself been instrumental in passing many years before, should be repealed that he might have an heir. An illegitimate son was at once inducted into the tribe of Pericles and was thus qualified for the inheritance. The incident, however, gave a semblance of truth to all that the enemies of the statesman had alleged against him.

Inasmuch as Aspasia has been assigned the abilities which framed the public policies, composed the speeches, and supplied the grace of manner of Pericles and others, among them Socrates, it may be well to speak of her more at length. One cannot understand Athens without considering her, for she was but the most distinguished member of a class permitted by the laws and customs of this powerful and pleasure-loving city. She reveals by her manner of life and the position she held a drift of Athenian life which presented a hindrance to the fundamental purpose of Socrates. Whether Socrates tracked the difficulty to its source and condemned it, is beside the point. It is illuminating to reflect that the Athens of Socrates was such that there could be an Aspasia.

She is said to have been of Milesian origin. She settled in Athens where she at once attracted much attention by her great beauty and accomplishments. Her house was frequented by the most learned Athenians, who often brought their wives to hear her discourses, and this in spite of the fact that her profession was neither honorable nor decent. Plutarch says that she kept courtesans in her house.[6] Aristophanes makes Pericles a partner with her in her profession when he declares that Aspasia's loss of two harlots made Pericles so angry at Magara that he plunged all Greece into war.[7] This is but the poet's irony to be sure—he knows that his audience will know what the truth is—but that such things could be said tells us much about the woman who was associated with the greatest man in Athens. Another poet has been more direct in his description of her:

> To him Vice bore a Juno new,
> Aspasia, shameless harlot.[8]

Perhaps the best that can be said for her is that she showed a shrewd discrimination, reserving her favors for the most powerful persons in Athens.

On the other hand, the sharp conscience of the poets and of the critics of Pericles may be suspected of being rather insincere. At any rate, their implied horror of Aspasia was not

---

[6] Plutarch *Lives*, "Pericles," xxiv.
[7] Aristophanes *Acharnians*.
[8] Plutarch "Pericles," xxiv.

generally felt among the aristocracy. We know that some of the most cultivated and high-born women of Athens visited her, for Pericles was accused of meeting them clandestinely at her home.[9] After Pericles was separated from his wife he became as closely associated with this "shameless" woman as the law against marriage with foreigners or non-Athenians would allow. And the fact that he could thus install her in his house without stirring up powerful public indignation reveals much concerning the conditions which prevailed in aristocratic circles.

Aspasia was no doubt a woman of great ability. Pericles is said to have received from her most of his wisdom and his oratorical finish. Socrates and his circle visited her often, and the philosopher is said to have taken instruction in rhetoric from her.[10] The opposition against Pericles, which arose later, also included Aspasia, for she was thought to be the author of many of his policies as well as the chief force which kept him in power. Some said that Pericles prized her only for her wisdom and political sagacity. Plutarch believes, however, that he was more enamored of her person than of her intellect, and says that it is reported that he never went in or out of his house during the day without kissing her.[11] His affection for her is further revealed by his conduct in court when she was being tried for impiety and other crimes. He entreated the judges with tears and so moved them that they did not condemn her.[12] Thus her ability seems well established, for no ordinary member of the 'hetoera' would have been accused, nor could she have commanded such great services. After the plague had taken off the last legitimate son of the statesman, it was, according to some writers, the son of Aspasia who became his heir.[13]

---

[9] Plutarch "Pericles," xxxii.
[10] Ibid., xxiv.
[11] Plutarch "Pericles," xxiv.
[12] Ibid., xxxii.
[13] Ibid., xxiv and xxxvii.

Pericles died of the plague in the third year of the Peloponnesian War. At that time Socrates was a soldier in the heavy-armed division of the Athenian army and had served with distinction in the successful campaign against Potidea. The future philosopher was then somewhere near forty years of age, in the prime of his strength, seasoned by years of exercise with arms in training and in actual warfare, a hero in spite of the fact that he had voted the honors to Alcibiades, his young comrade and tent-mate, and a wise, fearless, generous man who had already begun to see the needs and perils of the city which Pericles had made the most glorious in all Greece. It is very improbable that this soldier who had met the foe and had done his part to heap the fields with the dead, who had endured the fatigues of the march and siege and the rigors of lying in the trenches during a severe winter, was a peddler of academic abstractions. He was a philosopher, no doubt, for he was already fairly well known in that capacity, and there is sure to be an epidemic of philosophizing during and after every great war; but, being a soldier, he probably talked to the situation of the moment while the war was in progress. The Peloponnesian War ended only five years before the death of Socrates; and five years is not enough time to clear the air of war-memories, especially among a defeated people. This fact, together with another—the accusations lodged against Socrates because of post-war bitterness—shows clearly enough what interests were uppermost in Athens during the philosopher's teaching years.

Previous to this the active, acquisitive mind of Socrates had been ranging the length and breadth, the height and the depth, of the rich spectacle of Athenian life. And what a spectacle it was! In no other time in all the world were such treasures of art created. Never, perhaps, was there a greater statesman at the head of a nation. Clever, capable, and extraordinarily gifted men and women swarmed the city and turned their genius to practically every human interest. Poets, architects, philosophers admirals, generals, merchants, orators, and skilled artisans in every craft, never before or afterward excelled, contributed to the opulence, the entertainment, the beauty, and the glory of the city. It was a period in which almost the whole range of human capacity was pushed to the last degree of development. Now all this achievement and the manner of life which had made it possible were in danger of being destroyed. The situation was one well worthy of the analytic and constructive powers of a Socrates. Others since his day have speculated often as to the causes which led up to the destruction of Athens, but no one has seen more clearly than Socrates. And sure of his analysis and solution, he set about with all his genius to circumvent destruction by seeking to make such leaders as would keep the city safe.

It is worth while to note that Socrates did not seek to revamp the old polytheism. The work of Anaxagoras had been a powerful leaven within the intellectual circle. His view of Nature, and the logic with which he had supported it, made impossible any attempt to reinstate the naïveté and credulity which are the first requisites for polytheistic faith. The new teaching had also brought forth its own credential of worth. There was less confusion in thought: the view of Nature coincided with the systematic nature of the mental process; the notion of deity made the divine person too great for petty human passions and thus met that criticism which had already destroyed man's faith in the ancient gods; and superstition had been forced to depart—to leave the human spirit free to pursue its purposes unhindered and unamazed. Eclipses of the sun might now fall at the moment the fleet was setting sail without causing the admiral to steal tremblingly back into the city, cowering before the apparent displeasure of the deity. The fleet could sail forth without delay; and whether any actual value came from its naval operations or did not, a great moral victory was gained through its returning safe to port. It would take all the genius of a thinker like Socrates to discountenance such a spirit, and he was too wise to attempt it.

We must observe also that, in spite of the spirit of his time, he never sought either by word or act to destroy any man's faith in the ancient gods of the people. He maintained toward each divinity a becoming reverence and was often to be seen at the several shrines taking part in the prescribed worship. We cannot know his inner thoughts upon such occasions, or discover how he reconciled his conduct with the teachings of Anaxagoras, which he certainly knew and which in part he undoubtedly accepted. It may be that he found at each place the one God partially revealed, and that he, through each approach, came to a more complete knowledge of the deity. But more significant for us is the fact that he left the religious question where he found it and gave his attention to matters which he deemed of more practical value to the state. Religious liberty he granted without giving it the peril of being discussed.

His silence about the gods and his apparent piety and religious tolerance, are evidence enough that he did not believe that the religious character of the city would greatly affect its future. He probably felt that if silence were preserved in this direction there would be freedom to develop those qualities of character which would be of greatest value to the state. He therefore set about an attempt to deliver thought from the agnosticism into which the Sophists had brought it, and to develop a belief that incisive thinking could discover a ground for both moral and intellectual pursuits.

As matters stood, the Sophist held that thinking could not find the truth, for there was nothing universally true. Each man found his own truth, that which was true for him but true for no one else. The only way out for the Sophist was to persuade men to his way of thinking, to make them look through his eyes, to induce them to accept his views. Thus the Sophist abandoned the pursuit of knowledge and sought to prepare men for the duties of public life by teaching them the art of persuasion.

Socrates realized that such reasoning would deliver Athens into the hands of the demagogue. Thus a relatively incompetent man, one who knew little about generalship and the art of government, could play upon the prejudices and ignorance of the people until they were willing to do his bidding. The peril of this course was to be found in the limitations of the orator. When he had no faith in the power of thought to find the truth, and did not believe in the universal character of truth, how could he turn his oratorical victory into a leadership based on justice and looking toward public virtue and safety? How could there be such a thing as justice and virtue? How could the reasoning process discover them? Each orator would therefore make his own selfish desires and ambitions the only end to be sought. The state could not exist if internal rivalries divided the people and displaced united action under a wise and well-trained statesman. This peril must be averted if Athens were to triumph against a nation of men so well trained and so competently led as that of Sparta.

Socrates thought of government as being the administration of affairs in such manner as to promote the highest and noblest human relations among the citizens and to conduct war and foreign affairs to the advantage and safety of the state. This called for an investigation of human relations and the discovery of the true nature of the good. The virtues must be defined and their relative importance determined. The whole science of war must be developed by men who were trained not only by competent generals and admirals but by practice in command during actual conflicts. And the vocation of statesmanship must be approached only by those who were fully acquainted with the art of government. Only by these varied preparations could the state be saved from the perils attending the triumph of the demagogue.

This process of reasoning will explain why Socrates took every opportunity to engage the Sophists and the rhetoricians in debate, and why he sought constantly to discomfit them. They were, according to his way of thinking, the most dangerous persons in the city. They were casting doubt upon the value of the only means of providing the city with true leadership. And we begin to see why it is that he deplored the oratorical prowess of even a Pericles,[14] and believed that he was a failure as a leader just in proportion as the people were swayed by his eloquence. Truth, not uninformed and primitive emotions, must be the ground of all right action. Therefore, the leader who gains his ends by anything less than a declaration of the truth is sure to leave an uninstructed and emotional mob behind him. Pericles had done great things for Athens, but by his appeal to popular feeling he had ignored the highest duty of the statesman—the obligation to instruct his people in virtue, to increase their capacity for self-government, and to make them wise and self-contained. It is the worst that can be said against Pericles, and perhaps it is not wholly undeserved. After his death, others no less ambitious and certainly less competent were inspired by the memory of his power to emulate his example. And the people were not wise enough in matters of government either to provide a sufficient check to such selfishness or to govern themselves from their own ranks.

It is not possible that Socrates, who was always observant of the administration of public affairs, could be mistaken in his estimate. One less penetrating or more ambitious might reach an erroneous conclusion, but not he. Whenever possible he avoided taking public office. He was content to observe, to point out to his followers the merits and faults of men in public life. To this task he brought a thorough knowledge of the artifices of the orator, for he had been trained by Aspasia

---

[14] Thucydides' *Peloponnesian War*, by Wm. Smith, p. 76.

who at that moment groomed the greatest man in the state for all his public speeches. Surely Socrates would know well the effect of the orator upon the people and how little they were benefited by the oration. And he saw what even Thucydides seems to have missed, that Pericles [15] loved power and kept it at the expense of the best statesmanship. The Olympian, loving his thunders, kept his hearers too uninformed to do more than admire them. What would Socrates think of that tearful appeal for Aspasia before the Assembly? And what would be his private thoughts when Pericles asked that the law concerning bastardy be repealed? Of all this not one word, although we know that it sounds a key far below Socrates' notion of the conduct of a true statesman. Perhaps it is because the philosopher realizes that even a statesman must be permitted a few private interests and feelings upon occasion. And thus, on the whole, the great critic of life and morals is very fair in speaking of Pericles.

The form of the government, no less than its administration, presented many possibilities of disaster, and Socrates saw them clearly. What sort of wisdom was it which could put the destiny of this great city in the hands of artisans, farmers, sculptors, tradesmen, and even aristocrats, chosen by lot and without regard to training and fitness? The best minds of all time had labored to create the power, the wealth, and the beauty of the city. When it had been made into the most lovely and glorious habitation which human genius could construct, it was put into the hands of men who knew neither its value, its intimate structure, or its dangers. It was like putting the most priceless and delicately constructed piece of statuary into the hands of a child with a hammer. Chicanery on the part of a demagogue who was himself untrained to government could inflame the emotions of thoughtless multitudes and make them vote their own destruction and that of

---

[15] *Gorgias*, secs. 151, 152.

their city. Socrates was not slow to speak his mind of a government by lot. And he ridiculed the manner of selecting the rulers by saying that if it were a temple to be built, a statue to be sculptured, a disease to be healed, men would be employed who were expert in these matters. One can put the bitter sarcasm of his thought into words: "But we, who have the noblest city in the world to govern and preserve, select men who know nothing about the affairs entrusted to them."

It was not possible for Socrates to write a new constitution or to change the existing form of government. Neither could he instruct the whole citizenship, although few have tried harder to do so. Always he haunted the crowd when he had a mind to speak, and he was to be heard in the market-place discussing the loftiest questions of human conduct and government. Whoever had an ear might hear him. But there was no power to compel the people to attend to his words and no way of creating minds able to understand him. He gathered about him, therefore, only those who were able to appreciate his worth and who came to him voluntarily. Thus he became the center of a young aristocratic group whose native intelligence responded to his own genius. Under the existing form of government no wiser policy could have been devised to provide the city quickly with great leaders. With such trained men—orators, statesmen, generals—the people could not lack for counsel and competent defenders. The plan had a fatal weakness, as we shall see later, but it was the best that even a Socrates could do under the circumstances.

As we have already observed, Athens was engaged during all the teaching period of the life of Socrates in a struggle with the Lacedaemonians to preserve her empire. Her foes invaded her territory and encamped often before the city, thus adding to the excitement, the fear, and the impatience of the citizens who demanded of their leaders immediate deliverance. But wisdom dictated an avoidance of battle with the heavy-armed troops of Sparta and her allies. Even if the Athenian army should have the good fortune to destroy the invaders, the losses would be heavy and irreparable. Pericles explained this in defending his policy of sitting safely behind the city's walls while the Lacedaemonians ravaged the land. He said, "A tree will sprout up when it has been cut down; but we cannot grow men once they are destroyed." Athens must conserve her army to put down the rebellions of her allies and to man her ships to sweep the sea of all foes and to bring her food. The common people could not always see the wisdom of the leaders nor understand why they did not work miracles of deliverance. And the constant menace of the invader, the tension due to confinement within the walls and ignorance of how matters were going overseas, made the government of Athens little better than rule by an inflamed and fearful mob —surely the most unsafe form she could have had.

Another factor which contributed to the mob spirit within the city was the idle and pleasure-loving character of the citizens. Instead of a vigorous, busy, valiant people, willing to listen to their leaders and to do their part in defending the city, they were debauched, rebellious, fault-finding, and unwilling to risk their lives in the conflict. The ancient Greek spirit had greatly degenerated since the days of Marathon and Salamis. The fleet was manned by means of the amount of compensation paid to the marines and the soldiers who fought overseas. And the people were influenced to favor a leader and his policies by means of public feasts, entertainments, and the sums paid for attendance at public spectacles and for jury duty. Patriotism had perished and the amount of the dole was everything. Pericles is blamed for this condition, for it was he who first began to pay the citizens for attendance at the sessions of the Assembly, at spectacles, and at all public functions. It was just this condition of the citizenship which more than anything else contributed to the fall of the Athenian empire. If they had been loyal, less prominent in the government, and less inflammable, they could not have been persuaded by jealous and unprincipled leaders to depose their great men in the hour when they had most need of them. On the other hand, if all the leaders had been virtuous, honorable, and wise, the people would not have been led astray. Socrates seems, the more we look into the situation, to have acted with a full knowledge of his time and with the highest wisdom. There was nothing that Athens had greater need of than competent and honorable leaders.

It was this situation, so full of danger, so highly explosive, so riven through with jealousies and intrigues, so susceptible to the skill of the unprincipled orator, and so degenerate, that Socrates sought to remedy. If he could have reached all of the aristocracy, and if all his pupils had been true to their instruction, he would have succeeded in his undertaking. As it was, he became such a force in the city that he served to keep up the morale for many years, and but for the utter stupidity of the Athenians one of his less virtuous pupils might have preserved the power and glory of Athens until another no less competent could have taken over her defense.

II

Socrates was born in 469 or 470 B.C. He was the son of a sculptor and in his youth worked at his father's trade. He is said to have executed a group of marble Graces which was preserved on the Acropolis for a number of generations. He was a man of great strength and of abundant health. It is recorded of him that he was utterly indifferent to heat and cold and fatigue. At all times, summer and winter alike, he wore the same plain clothes and went barefoot about the streets of Athens. In personal appearance he was somewhat unattractive, especially to the Athenians who admired the physical perfection of man scarcely less than the beauty of women. Socrates had thick lips, bleared eyes, or protruding eyes, and an upturned nose. His frame was thick and massive, making impossible the graceful, rhythmic movement which was regarded so highly among the lovers of beauty. Add to all this a tendency to stand about for hours in abstraction, utterly oblivious of those who passed, and it is not difficult to understand why he should have been the object of much ridicule.

From his earliest childhood he felt that his actions were subject to the direct influence of the deity. This influence made itself felt by means of a kind of voice which warned him when he was about to undertake something unwise, yet never urged him on. Whether this voice was subjective and spoke wholly from within, or was for him external, an audition, he does not tell us. We may surmise, however, that its warnings operated to control his whole life, and that it approved his action when he entered upon the career of the Sophist. It would not permit him to abandon his special work, once he had taken it up. At his trial he declared that if they would free him on condition that he cease to teach, he would not dare to accept the terms.[16] Neither would his "voice" allow him to receive pay from those who heard him. Thus divinely compelled to his labors he avoided public office as much as possible and gave all his time to the task the deity had assigned to him.

He was not a rich man, and a number of references have been made to his great poverty. Compared with the aristocratic young Athenians who attended his lectures or conferences, he was without doubt very poor indeed. Alcibiades [17] could command millions, and later, by means of his wealth, which he used lavishly in chariot-racing and public entertainment, he secured rapid advancement in public life. He would come into the presence of Socrates, clad in a trailing tunic of rich materials, swollen with pride from much flattery and imagining himself to be some very great personage. But the barefoot, plainly clad teacher never failed to reduce him to a sane and

[16] Apology.
[17] Plutarch Lives, "Alcibiades," vi.

proper appraisal of his real worth. The tact, the kindliness and the brilliance of Socrates commanded respect from all who heard him, and even Alcibiades, who was himself one of the most gifted Athenians of his time, stood in awe of him. The master never ceased to be a source of wonder to these well-fed and pleasure-loving youths, for though he was poor he lived within his scanty income and found it ample for his needs.

In all things he set them an example to follow. His exercises with arms and in wrestling, his custom of eating only as he had need and then most sparingly, his strict temperance, his continency, and his complete avoidance of all injurious habits kept him strong, in good health, and clear-headed. Thus unaffected by the fashions and vices which came in with the growing wealth and splendor of the city, he was in the midst of the profligacy and evil of his day perhaps the only remaining example of the manhood and spirit of earlier Greece. And he revealed by his virtues and his elevated cast of thought the kind of man who could build and preserve a city.

The first great task of Socrates was to restore a belief in universal truth and to demonstrate the power of the human mind to find it. The Sophists, as we have already noted, denied that there was a truth which was common to all men. The whole function of thinking was but an expression of the individual, a reflection of individual idiosyncrasies, individual desires, and individual possibilities. Other men might be persuaded to accept the opinions of any person who had the power to play upon their feelings and to make his views plausible; but such views were after all only the views of the man who had at first advocated them. For all other men they were only second-hand materials. There is a truth in this, to be sure. The majority of men are not able to do profound, investigative thinking. They must live by the results of other men's labors. But Socrates held that even this fact did not disprove his view that there was an order of truth which was true for all men. In fact, the acceptance of another's views constitutes a proof that there is such an order. Acceptance would be impossible unless the views accepted conformed in some measure to the universal order and was a part of it.

The danger of the Sophist's doctrine does not lie in the fact that a truth once discovered is viewed as individual property. Such a truth would be valuable to society no matter how its acceptance came about. But the peril of such a conception of the nature of truth resides in the fact that critical thought is excluded. There is no room for the correction of error in the logical process. Your truth is true for you, but there is no necessity which compels me to accept it. You may take me unawares, trick me through my emotions or desires into accepting it, but I have only surrendered my soul into your hands. Thus no man is compelled to criticize his own thinking, to seek virtue, honor, righteousness; these do not exist apart from the individual's wishes in regard to his behavior. It is quite easy to see the breakdown of all law and justice as a result of such intellectual confusion. The demagogue is free to seek whatever end he pleases and by whatever means comes to hand. He can do no wrong, for the only fault with which he can reproach himself is his failure to dominate and exploit his fellow citizens.

Socrates met this position, not through arguments to disprove it, but by conducting such investigations as actually discovered the truth which was accepted by all men. His method of procedure was that of chiseling away at the crude lump of idea and opinion until he had liberated the conception which all men could accept. This he contrived by means of asking questions and securing definitions of terms, by subjecting the definitions to criticism through further questioning, and by proceeding in this manner until he had chipped away all error to leave the form of the universal clearly revealed. Concept after concept was brought forth by this method until there could be no longer any doubt among his pupils that there was a common order of truth to be found and that it was within the power of thought to find it.

The value of this method cannot be measured solely by its discovery of the truth and its encouragement to the thinker. It provided a ground for virtue as well. One could not proceed to urge his own uncriticized views upon the people without incurring the blame of having advocated an untruth and of thus bringing upon himself and others the penalty of error. It became, therefore, the obligation of the citizen to find the truth and to live by it, and the chief purpose of the statesman to see that he conformed to the truth in all his official acts.

The process followed by Socrates in his questioning was inductive. He would take an idea and examine it in a number of cases and in various relations until he had come to the core of the truth which operated in each case and relation. But he did not believe that truth could be found by the individual alone—in isolation from his fellow-men—but only by means of a number of investigators who would bear witness one with the other that the truth had been found. Of oneself, therefore, he could know nothing, for his witness might be modified by investigation and by a comparison with the thoughts of other men. Truth was universal, not individual. Socrates was consistent with his theory when he declared in the Assembly that he knew nothing, and equally consistent when he chided a fellow investigator who refused to answer his questions, saying, "How can you expect me to find the truth if you will not help me?"

When the discovery of the truth is thus a matter of public investigation among thoughtful people, a matter of universal assent, there is no place for stultified individualism or for those selfish and dishonorable motives which so frequently determine the policies and actions of public officials. State problems must be solved openly and among men competent to investigate them on their merits. There can be no solution which rests upon individual opinion and the art of persuasion.

Conclusions must be reached coolly, by logical processes, by an investigation of ideas, and by a comparison of concept-relation with concept-relation. They must *inevitably* arrive. No unbiased investigation is possible where one party is over-awed, or so influenced by another that its ideas are not its own. Each member must contribute of its own experience to the truth which all are seeking.

The truth is therefore not a thing to be made by thinking. It is found, set free from the envelope of individual experience in which it is concealed. Socrates would take someone who was proud of his culture and knowledge and lead him to dis-cover his great ignorance. Those who could endure to have their shallowness exposed and maintain a desire to know the truth were taken at once into partnership in the serious task of common thinking. Thus by thinking together the truth was born. Socrates in describing the part he performed in the arrival of the truth spoke of it as a "kind of midwifery."

The nature of the truth he sought was the truth about man in his relations to other men. In substance it was such as may be generalized under the term Ethics. It was the common element in all the particular ideas which had forced them-selves upon individuals in individual relations. All ideas con-cerning Nature were strictly excluded from his investigations. In his eyes it was a waste of time to inquire into them, for they were matters about which man could know very little. Why should one seek to know the truth of things so remote until he had learned all about man? With this question he brushed aside the whole field of natural science.

His apparent impatience with those who were interested in an investigation of Nature is very easily accounted for. Surely in his day, when the safety of Athens depended upon the proper conduct of her whole people, a knowledge of human relations was of paramount importance. Virtue, courage, self-control, obedience to the law, justice to oneself and toward all men—these were vital national questions and such as caused the rulers much anxiety. It is related by Zenophon that Pericles the Younger in a conversation with Socrates exclaimed, "I wonder, Socrates, how our city ever degenerated!" To this Socrates replied, "I imagine that as some other nations have grown indolent through excessive exaltation and power, so likewise the Athenians, after attaining great preëminence, grew neglectful of themselves, and consequently became degenerate." [18] How could a great patriot who had fought so well for his country engage in searching out the secrets of the moon and stars when life in his city had become so degenerate as to be a source of anxiety to all thoughtful men?

The wisdom of the self-imposed limitations of Socrates is implied by the further conversation:

"By what means then," said Pericles, "could they now recover their pristine dignity?"

"It appears to me," replied Socrates, "not at all difficult to discover; for I think that if they learn what were the practices of their ancestors, and observe them not less diligently than they, they will become not at all inferior to them; but if they do not take that course, yet, if they imitate those who are now at the head of Greece (the Lacedaemonians), adhere to their institutions, and attend to the same duties with diligence equal to theirs, they will stand not at all below them, and, if they use greater exertions, even above them."

"You intimate," returned Pericles, "that honor and virtue are far away from our city; for when will the Athenians reverence their elders as the Spartans do, when they begin, even by their own fathers, to show disrespect for older men? Or when will they exercise themselves like them, when they not only are regardless of bodily vigor, but deride those who cultivate it? Or when will they obey the magistrates like them, when they make it their pride to set them at naught? Or when will they be of one mind like them, when, instead of acting in concert for their mutual interests, they inflict injuries on one another, and envy one another more than they envy the rest of mankind? More than any other people, too, do they dispute in their private and public meetings; they institute more law-suits against one another, and

---

[18] *Memorabilia*, Book III. 5.13.

prefer thus to prey upon one another than to unite for their mutual benefit. They conduct their public affairs as if they were those of a foreign state; they contend about the management of them, and rejoice, above all things, in having power to engage in such contests. From such conduct much ignorance and baseness prevail in the republic, and much envy and mutual hatred engendered in the breasts of the citizens; on which accounts I am constantly in the greatest fear lest some evil should happen to the state too great for it to bear."[19]

Such a confession on the part of the chief man in the state is enough to indicate a situation that would claim the services of one who is as public-spirited as Socrates. And when we compare his heartening reply to these forebodings with the general character of his teachings, we see that he is doing all he can to avoid disaster. The degeneracy of Athens and the primitive vigor of Sparta are facts which fill all discerning minds with premonitions of doom.

But let us hear what Socrates has to recommend:

"Do not by any means suppose, Pericles, that the Athenians are thus disordered with an incurable malady. Do you not see how orderly they are in naval proceedings, how precisely they obey the presidents in the gymnastic games, and how, in the arrangement of the choruses, they submit to the directions of their teachers in a way inferior to none?"

"This is indeed surprising," said Pericles, "that men of that class should obey those who are set over them, and that the infantry and cavalry, who are thought to excel the ordinary citizens in worth and valor, should be the least obedient of all people."

"The council of the Areopagus, too," said Socrates, "is it not composed of men of approved character?"

"Undoubtedly," replied Pericles.

"And do you know of any judges who decide causes, and conduct all their business with more exact conformity to the laws, or with more honor and justice?"

"I find no fault with them."

[19] *Ibid.*, III. 5.14-24.

"We must not, therefore, despair," said Socrates, "as if we thought that all the Athenians are not inclined to be lovers of order."

"Yet in military matters," observed Pericles, "in which it is most requisite to act with prudence, and order, and obedience, they pay no regard to such duties."

"It may be so," returned Socrates, "for perhaps in military affairs men who are greatly deficient in knowledge have the command of them. Do you not observe that of harp-players, choristers, dancers, wrestlers, pancratiasts no one ventures to assume direction who has not the requisite knowledge for it, but that all who take the lead in such matters are able to show from whom they learned the arts in which they are masters; whereas the most of our generals undertake to command without previous study? I do not, however, imagine you to be one of that sort; for I am sensible that you can tell when you began to learn generalship not less certainly than when you began to learn wrestling. I am sure, too, that you have learned, and keep in mind, many of your father's principles of warfare, and that you have collected many others from every quarter whence it was possible to acquire any thing that would add to your skill as a commander. I have no doubt that you take great care that you may not unawares be ignorant of any thing conducive to generalship, and that, if you have ever found yourself deficient in any such matters, you have applied to persons experienced in them, sparing neither presents nor civilities, that you might learn from them what you did not know, and might render them efficient helpers to you."

"You make me well aware, Socrates, that you do not say this from a belief that I have diligently attended to these matters, but from a wish to convince me that he who would be a general must attend to such studies; and I indeed agree with you in that opinion."[20]

Such is the situation. Athens is degenerate, indolent, and without true leadership. In a number of activities the people reveal that they have the capacity to become again the great, vigorous nation of antiquity. When properly led they respond with enthusiastic obedience and are capable of perfecting the

---

[20] *Memorabilia* III. 5.18-24.

highest discipline. But the most powerful man in the state is incompetent, according to his own confession, willing to rest upon the great name and achievement of his father rather than make himself efficient by applying to every source to gain the skill of a commander. Once again we understand why Socrates has adopted a method which makes the aristocratic youths gravitate to him. He is in the business of creating a great leadership for his city.

Thus we begin to see more clearly what Socrates is attempting to do. An age that has listened to the Sophists has come to question both the existence of truth and the power of the mind to discover a rule that can be applied to all men. Men have come to public office, especially to statesmanship and military pursuits, unprepared for their tasks. There is no truth which can be learned. Each situation must be met as it arises and in entire isolation from all previous experience. Defeat and perilous blunders attend the activities of such men, and the people are extremely reluctant to obey them. In every other field those who accept direction of the people have been trained in the principles of their art, never questioning that such principles exist and never doubting for a moment that they can be learned. The statesmen and generals, however, have learned but one thing—the art of persuasion—and count it sufficient if they succeed in influencing the people to accept their uncriticized views. Athens is woefully degenerate, but the reason for her plight lies in the fact that she has begun to decay at the top. The fact that Socrates is so evidently concerned with applying a remedy to the upper classes makes him appear, not as the mere exponent of scientific knowledge, but primarily as a teacher of the philosophy of government and statesmanship. His deliverances on the nature of knowledge are thus made but the preliminary steps in this far more vital undertaking.

For over twenty years Socrates toiled to reach the most favored and intelligent young men of Athens, and to prepare them to approach the responsibilities of public life with seriousness and with a desire to be competent in the discharge of their duties. That his lectures must have been generally regarded as a preparation for political life is implied in the statement of Zenophon, who says of Critias and Alcibiades: "They knew that Socrates lived with the utmost contentment on very small means, that he was most abstinent from every kind of pleasure, and that he swayed those with whom he conversed just as he pleased by his arguments; and seeing such to be the case, and being such characters as they have just been stated to be, whether will any one say that they sought his society from a desire to lead such a life as Socrates led, and to practice such temperance as he practiced, or from an expectation, that if they associated with him, they would become eminently able to speak and act? I myself, indeed, am of opinion, that if a god had given them their choice, whether they would live their whole lives as they saw Socrates living, or die, they would have chosen rather to die; and they showed this disposition by what they did; for as soon as they considered themselves superior to their associates, they at once started away from Socrates, and engaged in political life, to qualify themselves for which they had sought the society of Socrates." [21]

The results attending the labors of Socrates were such as to attract much attention. Many of the leading men of the city were quite willing to send their sons to him for instruction. Those who understood his point of view realized that his chief task was to make useful, virtuous citizens who would give strength to the city and prove an ornament to the state when called to public life. Zenophon reveals the social aspect of the teaching of Socrates when he says: "Crito was also an attendant on Socrates, as well as Chaerephon, Chaerecrates, Hermocrates, Simmias, Cebes, and Phaedondes, who, with

---

[21] *Memorabilia*, Book I. 2. 14-16.

others that attended him, did not seek his society that they might be fitted for popular orators or forensic pleaders, but that, becoming honorable and good men, they might conduct themselves irreproachably toward their families, connections, dependents, and friends, as well as toward their country and their fellow-citizens." [22] Such, therefore, was the purpose of Socrates; and he carried it out with an unusual measure of success. There were two men, however, Critias and Alcibiades, who by their later actions brought disrepute upon their master. They had not remained with him long, and had not really been in sympathy with his teaching and manner of life; but the fact that they had some time attended his lectures afforded their enemies an opportunity to proceed against Socrates.

III

We must connect the downfall of Socrates with the events which attended the destruction of Athenian power. Since the leading figure in these last scenes of tragedy and bitterness was at one time a pupil of Socrates, we must expect the faults of the pupil to reflect upon the master. Alcibiades, a man of brilliant parts and a very great general, was to Athens by turns a withering flame of vengeance and her restorer and greatest hope. When disaster came there was at first a period of repentance as the people realized that it was their treatment of Alcibiades which had brought them all their woes, if they had continued to trust him they would have remained ruler of the seas. Then rage and poisonous hate superseded repentance as the heavy hand of the conqueror wrought its ruthless will. The Athenians could not forget that the hated Spartan had, through the help of Alcibiades, administered the first staggering blow to Athenian supremacy. They forgot their own injustice toward him, their utter stupidity in de-

---

[22] *Memorabilia* Book I. 2. 48.

posing him when they needed every man of genius in the nation to preserve them, and blamed him for all the calamities that were being visited upon them. And since Alcibiades, through their own and Spartan treachery, was now out of reach of all enemies they turned against his friends. It was not possible that the guide and teacher of such a man could escape their wrath.

Alcibiades was no doubt a very ambitious man and naturally a very selfish one. He was proud, conceited, a libertine, a poseur, a technical traitor, a boaster, and a man interested only in the adulation and the promotions which the Athenians could give him. But there is much to be said for him. He was brave, a very great general, a popular leader not to be excelled, and when given confidence and loyal support the savior of his nation. Socrates saw his genius, worth, and many good qualities beneath the pose and the color of his shocking deeds. When he would be led away by flatterers who enticed him to some pleasure, Socrates would go after him as if he were a runaway slave and would bring him back. He is not admirable throughout, but he is not altogether to blame for seeking a refuge in Sparta when the Athenians denied him the right to defend himself in an immediate trial and sent him away until they were sure that they could convict him and put him to death. A nation which practices such injustice can scarcely cry treason when its victim turns the tables upon it.

Since the circumstances of the death of Socrates are actually connected with the history of Alcibiades, it will be well for us to give some attention to the events in the life of the so-called traitor which have a bearing upon the fate of his teacher. It is not necessary here to note the military career, the public benefactions, and the political maneuvers by which Alcibiades became one of the leading men of Athens. All this reveals his character but contributes nothing toward an understanding of Socrates. We shall begin when Alcibiades has come to power, when he has become a dreamer of great imperial dreams—the conquest of Syracuse, then Italy, Carthage, Egypt, Phoenicia, and finally, the Peloponnesus. He has made many powerful enemies, some through his triumphs over them and others through their dislike of his haughtiness and his debauched life. He has revealed to the younger men his dreams, and they are eager to follow him to any length. The expedition against Syracuse is finally assured. His enemies, seeing that he may become far more powerful than he is already, prefer charges of impiety against him. Some vandals have broken a statue to one of the gods, and Alcibiades is accused. Furthermore, it is charged that he and some of his drunken companions have parodied the initiations of the Eleusinian Mysteries. He is to be brought to trial; but when it is clear that he will be acquitted, he is hurried away to Syracuse. Then when all is ready to secure conviction, he is summoned home to stand trial. Knowing what his fate will be, he leaves the ship which is taking him to Athens and enters into negotiations for a refuge in Sparta.

At the court of the king of Sparta he encouraged the Lacedaemonians to raise the siege of Syracuse. Through his suggestions it thus became possible for Sparta to destroy two Athenian fleets and the army encamped before Syracuse. Great was the consternation in Athens, for the city was in danger of losing her allies and perhaps her own independence. Alcibiades was tried in his absence and condemned to death. Not being able to proceed against his person, the priest was ordered to curse him. Everything possible was done to brand him as an outlaw and a person hateful to all pious Greeks. Alcibiades, with a shrug of indifference, merely remarked, "Nevertheless, I am still alive, and they shall have cause to know it," and went on with his plotting against Athens.

But his sojourn in Sparta soon came to an end. Nothing was done without consulting him, and this aroused the jealousy of the leading Spartans. In addition to this he debauched the queen while the king was away at war, and boasted openly that his son would sit upon the throne of Sparta. Shortly after the king's return the nobles decided that justice should be meted out to the offender. Alcibiades, being warned of his peril, fled to the protection of Tissaphernes, the Persian. Here he encouraged his host to deny aid to Sparta that, when both Athens and Sparta were exhausted in their struggle, it would be easy to conquer both. This move undoubtedly saved Athens from immediate destruction.

But after a time Alcibiades began to long for the life of his native city. He therefore sent word to the Athenian fleet at Samos that he would undertake to bring Tissaphernes over to the assistance of Athens. He would not do this for the people of Athens because he could not trust them; but he would do it if the nobility would put an end to the insolent behavior of the lower orders, and would themselves undertake to save the city and the empire of Athens.[23] Necessity helped the leaders of the fleet to a favorable decision. The government of Athens was seized and the rule of the Five Thousand (in reality the Four Hundred) was instituted. This company of oligarchs, now firmly established, and thinking the form of government would be approved by Sparta, paid no further attention to Alcibiades. But they put to death a number of Athenians who opposed their rule, and this so enraged the officers of the fleet that they sent for Alcibiades, elected him their general, and bade him lead them against the despots. He refused to lead Athenians against Athenians, and succeeded in convincing them that such a course would cause such losses that the city would be at the mercy of her enemies. Shortly thereafter his friends espoused the popular cause and succeeded in overthrowing the oligarchs and in reëstablishing the democracy.

Alcibiades now set sail with the fleet to destroy the enemy and to chastise the rebellious allies of Athens. He swept the

---

[23] Cf. Plutarch, *Lives*, "Alcibiades," xxv.

seas clean. Having thus made Athens once more the undisputed mistress of the seas, he returned to his native city to be received with open arms by the people. His restoration was quickly voted, his property was returned to him, the priests were ordered to retract the curses which they had invoked against him, he was honored with golden crowns and elected sole general with absolute power by land and sea.

He was practically invited to take over the government, and the leading citizens, fearing that he would become despot of Athens, hurried him away with the fleet to meet the enemy. Success attended him, but those who feared him sought to minimize his achievement and to thus cause him to lose influence with the people. The people did not realize that he was hampered by the lack of funds and that he was therefore unable to compete with the Lacedaemonians, who had Persian gold with which to procure marines and sailors. However, he was more than a match for the enemy in battle. Then came an event which was the beginning of the end. Alcibiades went to Caria to levy contributions and left the fleet in charge of Antiochus with orders to avoid a battle with the Lacedaemonians at all costs. Antiochus disregarded his instructions and foolishly challenged the enemy to do battle. Lysander, the Lacedaemonian commander, came out and engaged him. Antiochus was killed and many of his ships were captured. Alcibiades returned and challenged Lysander to a second conflict, but the Lacedaemonian was well satisfied with what he had already accomplished and would not come out.

Thrasybulus, an enemy of Alcibiades, sailed for Athens and represented that Alcibiades had ruined their affairs by putting the fleet, in his absence, under the command of incompetent men. The Athenians in anger sent out new generals to supersede Alcibiades. These went each day to challenge Lysander to do battle and, when he refused to comply, returned to their rendezvous. Alcibiades warned them that their position was dangerous, but they insulted him and declared that they, and not he, now commanded the fleet. They fell into the hands of Lysander soon afterward, and the entire fleet was destroyed. Athens was now without means of defense and was quickly forced to yield. Her long walls were demolished and a government known as the Thirty Tyrants was forced upon her. Alcibiades remained at large for some time thereafter to inspire his city with the hope that perhaps even yet all was not lost. But Critias, one of the Thirty, told Lysander that the Lacedaemonian empire could never be safe while Alcibiades lived. This warning was probably communicated to the government at Sparta, for shortly afterward by order of King Agis Alcibiades was hunted down and put to death. Thus ended the last possibility of the restoration of Athenian supremacy.

The city learned nothing, however, from her defeat. Her momentary repentance changed to snarling and unreasoning hate. Alcibiades became once more the symbol of treason, the evil genis which had compassed her ruin. Only the coöperation of the ablest minds could have met the exigencies of the time and prevented the many crimes that followed against justice and humanity. This, however, was prevented by demagogues who exploited the antagonism of the people toward the aristocracy. Unprincipled and incompetent men thus came to power, and these, for the sake of their positions of leadership, posed as the advocates of democracy and at the same time worked with their conquerors. Previous to the city's downfall Socrates had played his part in the struggle. He had fought as a soldier and had been a senator. At one time, when a number of men had been abandoned to their fate during a sea fight, the people demanded that the ten generals who had taken part in the engagement be put to death. At great risk to his own life Socrates stood out alone against both the senate and the people and thus saved the lives of the generals.[24]

---

[24] *Apology*, 10.

And when the Thirty Tyrants commanded him to go to
Salamis to bring Leon to Athens to be put to death, he went
to his home and omitted to obey the order. For this contempt
of the ruling power he probably would have been put to death
if the people had not soon afterward driven out the Tyrants.[25]
Both of these incidents must have thoroughly disgusted the
wise and virtuous Socrates. And when the city fell because of
the jealousies, disloyalties, and stupidities of both people and
rulers, he was, very probably, not slow to fix the blame. His
outspokenness would be endured for a time, but when Alcibiades had become the scapegoat malice would be kindled by
his condemnations.

Those who hated Socrates because of his criticism of public
affairs waited patiently for him to antagonize a sufficient number of prominent people to warrant his prosecution. Five years
passed. They were turbulent and bitter years. An oligarchy had
been established and overthrown; the last great general had
been murdered, and with him had perished the last hope of
the city; despicable politicians had wrought their will during
the prevailing confusion; and the loss of commerce and tribute
had brought poverty to thousands. The lavish sums formerly
spent by the state in stimulating and supporting industry and
in buying the favor of the populace could no longer be obtained. The city indeed realized that her glory had departed
and that it would never return. Socrates continued to teach
and to be a scourge to rhetoricians, orators, and self-seeking
politicians.

Then suddenly his enemies found their chance. Anytus, the
leader of the democracy, had a son who was attending the
lectures of Socrates. This son turned against the popular belief
in the gods and laughed at his father's old-fashioned views
concerning them. It was no time to question anything which
the people believed, much less the existence of the ancient

---

[25] *Ibid.*, 20.

gods. When mankind is in confusion and distress there is always a turning to the long-neglected objects of devotion. And in this hour of poverty, defeat, and hopelessness the citizens of Athens returned to their precious superstitions and their former sanctities. The gods, the laws, the shrines, the statues, the temples, the writings of the poets, and the democracy itself became the rallying point of a lost nation. Woe to the man who was then, or had ever been, the least amiss in his reverence toward them. Thus the son of Anytus unwittingly brought his teacher into very grave peril.

There were many others who had a grievance against Socrates, and among them were Miletus and Lycon. Miletus had not relished the philosopher's biting criticism of his political activity; and Lycon had deeply resented the many caustic remarks which Socrates had made publicly concerning the orators and the rhetoricians. Miletus and Lycon therefore united with Anytus in the prosecution, and preferred against Socrates the charge that he denied the gods and corrupted the youth of the city. The ground of the prosecution was cleverly conceived, for to both counts the circumstances of history were favorable. Alcibiades, who was now hated again as a traitor and the cause of the city's downfall, had been a pupil of Socrates and had once been charged with defacing and breaking the statues of Mercury and with having parodied the initiations of the Eleusinian mysteries. Critias, another pupil of Socrates, had been one of the most arrogant and cruel of the Thirty Tyrants. Thus it appeared that Socrates had for many years been guilty of corrupting the youth of Athens—the case of the son of Anytus was but one among the many. Still further, Aristophanes had represented Socrates in "The Clouds" some twenty years before as swearing by the gods, if there be gods. All the facts of history were well known to the people who would vote the punishment Socrates should receive. With such facts in their favor the prosecution could scarcely fail to secure a verdict of guilty.

Anytus, seeing how the trial would terminate, and no doubt moved by contrition, urged Socrates to exercise his right in the case and to prevent trial by remaining at home.[26] But Socrates as a matter of principle could not take advantage of the privilege. The law and the courts could not be treated with contempt. On the day appointed he appeared and stood trial.

From the circumstances just recited, it would appear that the prosecutors never really intended to put Socrates to death. They were perhaps overweary of his much talking in public and his unpleasant criticisms. They would give him a real fright. With a charge which could be established and with conviction certain, they would have a club to use against him. He would, of course, stay at home. That would leave a bit of unfinished business to hang over his head which would make him walk more circumspectly in future. Thus he would be silenced. To add to whatever misgivings he might naturally have about the trial, they informed him that if he appeared his conviction would be certain. And they further revealed their real intent by warning him to stay at home.

It is extremely improbable that Socrates entertained the least hope that he would be acquitted. The manner in which he conducted his defense shows what he thought. He knew the mind of his prosecutors: they were determined to silence him, but shrank inwardly from exacting the death penalty. That was why they had warned him not to appear. He would compel these scoundrels to go through with it, and he would show them that law was not to be used for private purposes but for public ones. He would be convicted. In the present temper of the public mind there was not a chance that he would be set free. With the full consciousness that he was going to be the victim of the worst crime the state had ever committed, he set out for the court-room. But he had won his case before leaving

---

[26] *Apology* 17 and *Crito* 5.

his home—a case against those who imagined that Socrates, the soldier, could feel such a thing as fear.

To the arguments made by the prosecution he answered in his own way. He did not attempt to reply to either of the charges directly, for he knew that it would be useless. He therefore, probably from scorn of both prosecutors and people, adopted a superior manner, declaring that he was divinely called to his work and that if the people would release him on condition that he cease to teach he would not comply. He went out of his way to anger the people, saying, "It is impossible that any man should be safe, who sincerely opposes either you, or any other multitude, and who prevents many unjust and illegal actions from being committed in a city. It is necessary that he who in earnest contends for justice, if he would be safe for but a short time, should live privately, and take no part in public affairs." [27] His contempt for democracy could scarcely be put more directly, nor could he have revealed more clearly what he thought of the long list of crimes of which democracy was guilty. Here the philosopher and teacher of the aristocratic party tells the people the truth. There were cries against him, but he kept on and asked, "Do you think, then, that I should have survived so many years, if I had engaged in public affairs, and, acting as becomes a good man, had aided in the cause of justice? Far from it, O Athenians; nor would any other man have done so. " [28]

He declined to beg for his life out of regard for his own character and theirs. If there is sarcasm here, it is obscured. We know, however, what he thought of their character; it is not such as would inspire an upright man with awe. It is evident, therefore, that Socrates anticipated conviction, that he despised the character of his prosecutors and the people, and

[27] *Apology* 19.
[28] *Ibid.*, 21.

that he went through the motion of pleading his case only that he might speak his opinions of such government.

When the verdict of guilty was voted he tells the people that he had expected it, and by an even larger majority than was cast against him. He then had the privilege of awarding to himself the form of punishment he hoped to receive and of making a plea for it—for a fine, for imprisonment, or for exile. He declined to award himself any punishment, declaring that he was guilty of no crime against the state. Since he must make the award according to his just deserts, he awarded himself full maintenance by the state in the Prytaneum.[29] He is not trying by audacity to create a demonstration in his favor, for he has been looking into the faces of the people, missing nothing, and making no mistake in estimating what he sees; he knows that they will award him death.

When his judges vote the death penalty, he declares that he does not fear it and looks upon death as gain. The voice of deity which has guided him through all his life has now brought him to his death; under such circumstances, why should he fear the end? He addresses his judges personally and says: "You, therefore, O my judges, ought to entertain good hopes with respect to death, and to meditate on this one truth, that to the good man nothing is evil,—neither while living nor when dead, nor are his concerns neglected by the gods. What has befallen me is, therefore, not the effect of chance. It is now clear to me that to die, and to be freed from my cares, is better for me." [30]

Surely from first to last his daemon has done nothing by chance. But it is a strange daemon, one that has kept its eye upon the political fortunes of Greece and has prompted the leading mind of the age to seek the public good. All has been

---

[29] *Ibid.*, 26.
[30] *Ibid.*, 33.

done that could be done by human agency. Against the approaching peril Socrates had prepared, though somewhat imperfectly, a man who was once able to save the city and who would have done so again if he had been left to his own devices. Stupidity, jealousy, and political dishonesty have done their worst. The disaster which Socrates has labored so long to avoid has come, and the empire of Athens is no more. Worse still, the citizenship has degenerated, or changed in character, and there is nothing to save but the monuments and memories of a spirit that has passed away forever. What need is there which would demand that the savior tarry when the thing he has come to save is irretrievably lost? Socrates, with his daemon standing by, sweeps the whole past with an appraising eye; he sees all that might have been and knows surely that now it can never be. Then his eyes revert to the mob which has been left in the wake of the departed glory.

It is all a little bewildering at the last—that look at the might-have-been, the hope which he has served and lost, and this turmoil and inchoateness of a present which has found him hateful to it. Angus says, "The Sophists are credited with having first inoculated Greek life with the germs of individualism; in reality the germs were only nurtured by them. By questioning the authority of the polis, inquiring into the validity of law, pointing out that what was law at Magara might be unlawful at Athens, by rejecting tradition, by asserting the subjectivity and relativity of all truth in the words of Protagoras, "man is the measure of all things," they threatened to reduce society to atoms. Socrates saw the menace and stepped forward to save and reform the city-state, but indirectly undermined its authority by calling attention to the eternal value of the individual, and by finding the ultimate basis of moral action neither in the laws nor the religion of the state, nor in tradition, but in man's reason and consciousness. In the Athenian law-court he advocated the right of private judgment against the State by reminding his judges

that he must obey God rather than man." [31] Society is composed of individuals, and when the state is called upon to meet
any great strain its units must be made stronger. But there is
a penalty attached to any overemphasis of the individual, one
that almost every democracy has suffered sooner or later.
Socrates could see clearly what Pericles had begun with his
payment of juror's fees and his expenditure of vast sums to
encourage attendance at the Assembly and at spectacles. He
had made authority subservient to the individual—to the
meanest man of the disorganized multitudes who learned thus
to feed his own desires and to put the state in fee. That policy
had been the beginning of the end for the city-state. And now
the end had come.

What did the future hold in store? The great champion of
the polis cannot tell. The end of the old order has come, at
any rate. Humanity has made a change of front, and will not
go back to the ancient customs. What a picture he makes
standing there, barefoot, plainly clad, the last living pulse of
the spirit of old Greece! Imperceptibly for twenty years the
new age has stolen in to take captive and change everything
but this one man. He has waged a long and glorious battle.
Perhaps as he looks about him his daemon may be whispering,
"Do not grieve for Athens and Alcibiades; what has happened
was from the first inevitable." Sadly he turns away, saying:
"It is now time to depart,—for me to die, for you to live. But
which of us is going to a better state is unknown to every
one but God." [32] He was the prophet of yesterday. It is time
indeed to go.

Everything possible was done to save him. His disciples had
arranged to carry him to a place of safety.[33] Perhaps the authorities had agreed to look the other way—worse things had
been done before. But Socrates would not leave and thus

---

[31] *The Mystery Religions and Christianity*, p. 182.
[32] *Apology* 33.
[33] Cf. *Crito*, sec. 4

brand himself with an appearance of guilt. He would keep his good name to the end. They might have his body, and bury *him* too, "if they could catch him."

On the day appointed for his death many of his friends went to the prison to be with him until the end. They found Xantippe there, holding his little boy and wailing loudly. Socrates took his leave of her and of his son and had them taken home. Then he turned to spend the day in conversation with his friends. In these last hours Athens was relegated to the region of all lost dreams, to the forgetfulness which overtakes the noblest example the great man leaves behind. He spent the day in reviewing the possibilities of immortality and in contemplating that unseen land of mystery and shade. When the fatal hour had come the gaoler performed his duty with profound apologies and many tears. Socrates was deeply touched by this show of sympathy and stood with the fatal cup in his hand watching the strange pageantry of earth's many contradictions—the all too fickle heart of man that will continue to wash its stains away in the tears of repentance forever. Then he drank the hemlock readily and calmly, walked about a little until he felt a heaviness in his legs, and lay down to be borne away by the boatman who spans the river Styx. As the wind from the farther shore embraced him with its healing breath he roused himself to speak, "Crito, we owe a cock to Aesculapius: pay it, therefore, and do not neglect it." Thus passed this infidel of the ancient world, his last words containing a command that the divine Physician be properly rewarded.

CHAPTER IX

Jesus of Nazareth

Jesus was born in Bethlehem of Judea about 4 B.C. and lived until somewhere near the close of 30 A.D. Whatever may be the fate of the story of his miraculous origin, the doubt that there was ever such a person as Jesus cannot be seriously entertained. The rise of the Christian church and the facts which necessarily preface the rise of such movements force us to assume an actual person. The worst, therefore, that the opponents of the belief in the historical Jesus can urge is the statement that the facts of his life are no better accredited than those concerning the life of Confucius, or Buddha, or Socrates.

And when we turn to an examination of the motives behind any denial of the historicity of Jesus we discover that they spring from two principal sources: first, a scientific frame of mind which refuses to entertain the story of his supernatural character; and second, a theory of origins for both faith and institutions which makes myth and legend the first cause. The first objection is easily found to affect only the origin of Jesus and not to involve the question of his historical appearance. The second is based upon an hypothesis of origins which has received many staggering blows as a result of archeological investigations. Many of the supposed myths are now found to be based upon facts of history. Thus the historical problem in connection with the birth of Jesus has changed so that it may be put in the form of the question, What are the actual facts in the case?

This is a very important question for all concerned and

affects the modernist's view of Jesus even more than that of the traditionalist. Of what value is it to insist upon an abandonment of orthodoxy in favor of "the spirit of Jesus" when we know too little about history to know what spirit we are of? And an historical church must, of course, be founded upon actual historical fact.

In seeking an answer to our question it will be well to assume that the background and experience of Jesus were Jewish. Never during the days when his character and opinions were being formed was he outside of the land of Israel. Furthermore, he lived in the small village until he was about thirty and knew only that simple piety which is to be met with in sequestered village life in every land. In his daily contacts he probably encountered no ferment of new ideas, no great temporary currents of strange opinion, no influence from the Gentile nations of Greece and Rome. And if any such drifts of culture and opinion had penetrated to Nazareth, they would have been stoutly opposed and would have made him and his neighbors all the more loyal to the teachings and customs of Israel. If patriotism and religion had lagged before, they would now have taken on new zeal because they had been challenged. Thoughtfulness, reverence, and loyalty would therefore have remained the prevailing attitude of the people of Nazareth toward their national heritage. Thus in both doctrine and practice there would have been no departure from the best traditions of Judaism.

The importance of this background cannot possibly be too greatly stressed in any worthy attempt to understand Jesus. The fundamental habits of his whole nature were fixed in this atmosphere. New ideas were viewed by him from the Jewish angle; the national issues, policies, and decrees passed over him like the clouds of heaven and his feet were in Nazareth no matter where he went. Upon the cross the sights and sounds of his village were with him, coloring his thought, shaping themselves with his voice, and remaining with him

as long as life remained. Not until his last breath did he escape
the spell of Nazareth. Thus during all the days of his ministry he reasoned from Nazareth outward.

It is therefore no accident that when he began his ministry
he sought to establish a theocratic condition rather than a
pagan empire, that he stressed just the politico-religious interests of the Jew rather than the politico-philosophical
interests of the Gentile world. He was inspired and compelled
to do this, to be sure, but inspired and compelled in no small
measure by his Jewish nature and training. He never thought
of approaching the salvation of his nation with any other
plan than the one he adopted, just because he was a Jew born
and reared in the bosom of his people. In his teaching he
may have advocated new departures; but they were only departures, a progress from the best traditions of Judaism and
designed wholly to meet the perils of the Jewish nation. His
problems, temptations, aims, and views were Jewish to the
core.

And the education which he received was identical in nature
with that which was given to every Jewish boy of that time.
Simeon Ben Sheta is said to have established in every town
a system of compulsory education for all children over six
years of age. Whether or not this system had extended to
Nazareth we do not know; but Jesus' familiarity with a wide
range of current Jewish literature would indicate that he attended such a school, and that his unusual ability admitted
him to the more advanced studies provided by the system.
Edersheim thinks that in spite of the poverty in Jesus' home
his family possessed a copy of the Sacred Book, and Klausner
believes that such is entirely possible. At any rate, Jesus was
as expert in the Scriptures as the best Pharisees of the day, and
could use the Pharisees' expository devices as well as any
teacher in Israel. He was perfectly familiar with all the great
ideas of the Prophets and the Psalms, and could make every
legitimate use of them. He was versed in the "traditions of

the elders," the decisions of the Pharisees, and the words of the Wise. In his public teaching he excited the envy and the respect of the Pharisees who heard him. He could enter into controversy with them and confute them by his use of both Scripture and later tradition. There can scarcely be any doubt that all this information was gathered through long study and that his skill in debate came from actual practice. National piety was undoubtedly of a high order in Nazareth and such devotion had secured worthy teachers.

Nor was the education of Jesus only so much precept and religious information. It came vitally into contact with Jewish life; indeed, it could not have been otherwise, for Jewish religion *is* Jewish life. Rather the education of Jesus came to grips with the national hope, as it was conceived at the moment, and as it was related to Israel's actual political situation. Galilee was the home of the Zealots, that group of patriots which had determined that nothing short of death would end their opposition to Rome. The land of Galilee was full of bitterness, whisperings, intrigue, revolt, and intense hatred of the conqueror. Had there been no studied attempt on the part of the teachers of the youth of Nazareth to emphasize the Messianic hope of Israel, the very spirit of the times would have made it a topic of continued discussion. Every leader of a band of rebels would have been the object of endless speculation; "Is he the one who will deliver Israel? Is it possible that he can be the Holy One?" Thus every item of that hope would have been thoroughly familiar to every group at the corner of a street and its main features the subject of investigation by those more familiar with the whole body of Jewish literature. Jesus would, therefore, have had reason to ponder this highest point of national interest and to brood over the character of that mighty One who would save his people.

The Messianic hope of Israel grew out of the belief that the nation itself had a soul and that it would be rewarded and punished according to its prevailing spirit. The soul being indestructible, the nation would persist through the days of its judgment. Jeremiah taught that Israel would fall before the power of Babylon but that after the days of her punishment the people would return to Zion. This prophecy was fulfilled, thus strengthening the popular belief in the immortality of the nation.

The fall of Judea, the exile in Babylon, the return of the captives to Jerusalem, came finally to serve as a vehicle for the interpretation of history. Gentile nations might oppress Judea but she would triumph, and there would be a Day of the Lord in which the oppressors would be punished. A very ancient account of this time of judgment held that the punishment would be universal, and that on that day the whole world would be judged. There would be drought, famine, war, great moral corruption among the peoples, and great and dire punishments visited upon the nations. These calamities began to be regarded as the "pangs of the Messiah," the birth-throes of the coming age. But before this terrible season Elijah would appear to give announcement of the nearness of that age and to make all preparation possible for its coming. Elijah would blow his trumpet and the scattered Jews would be assembled together from the four corners of the earth. He would preach regeneration, the healing of feuds among kinsmen and brothers, and would turn the hearts of the fathers to the children.

Then the Messiah would appear to overwhelm the heathen and to restore the kingdom of Israel. He would rebuild Jerusalem and the Temple and make Mount Zion the spiritual metropolis of the whole earth. The nations which survived the judgment, because they had not oppressed Israel, would become proselytes to Judaism, and thus God would become the Lord of all the earth. The Messiah would be a son of David and would sit upon the throne of his father to rule the nations. His rule would be marked by joy and righteousness and peace. The nations would come unto Mount Zion with songs of everlasting joy upon their lips and the most happy brotherliness and good-fellowship would prevail among all peoples.

This is in outline the generally accepted view of the coming of the Messianic age. Some did not hold that the Messiah should be the son of David, but most of the Pharisees did. It is to be noted that they rejected the Maccabeans from Messianic consideration because they were not of the line of David but of the house of Aaron. It was because they were known to regard the origin of the Messiah as Davidic that Jesus opposes them with the quotation from the Psalms, "The Lord said unto my lord, sit thou upon my right hand until I make thine enemies the foot-stool of thy feet." Jesus evidently did not share the belief that the Messiah need necessarily be a son of David. The genealogies of Jesus which appear in the canonical Gospels, tracing the lineage of Jesus through Joseph to David, lose their point if we accept the dogma of the Virgin Birth. To put the matter in other words, Jesus is a son of David *only* if he be the son of Joseph. But what is the point in confuting the Pharisees if Jesus be a son of David? It begins to look as if the genealogies might be very similar to the illustrious one with which Confucius was supplied.

Lacking in detail as the Messianic hope appears—the mere skeleton of the age to come—it was sufficient to stir the imagination of Israel in the days of her oppression under the conquerors. By the time of Jesus the people were ready to listen seriously to the claims of almost any wonder-worker and teacher. So almost insupportable was the lot of the people that it was generally believed that the Messiah would not long delay his appearing. He would be a political and spiritual savior, a king-Messiah, a liberator of the enslaved Israel. Consequently, any revolutionist who gained the least success sent a thrill throughout the land. And any worker of miracles who collected about him a following was regarded with both hope and suspicion. Hope defeated many times is still hope; but it is wiser, and more careful to prove its way.

It is apparent that the Messianic hope will remain in the background when the nation is independent and in no danger from enemies. It began as a very brief creed, resting upon the belief that God was king of Israel, that He would punish but save His people. To work complete justice toward all, God would be compelled, necessarily, to punish the oppressors also. From this slight statement, which was made before the fall of Jerusalem and the return from Babylon, the Messianic hope grew through the centuries of Israel's subjection to Assyria, Persia, Alexander the Great, the Ptolemies, and the Seleucid dynasty of Antioch. Practically all of the doctrine of deliverance which is of value toward an understanding of Jesus was developed during this long period under the control of the nations. After a brief epoch of independence under the Maccabees, the nation came under Roman control during which time the old hope of deliverance became prominent again. Any true understanding of the purpose of the teaching of Jesus must come as a result of a review of his faith and of the historical conditions in which he lived.

What was the faith of Jesus? Did he accept the religous beliefs of his nation? From the nature of his education, the environment of his childhood and young manhood, and from a comparison of his utterances with those of the Pharisees, we can discern beyond the shadow of a doubt that in substance the faith of Jesus was the faith of the Jewish nation of his time. A leper whom he cleansed was ordered to show himself to the priest and to take to the temple the offerings which Moses had ordained. Jesus was careful to adhere to all the religious observances which had been approved by the most sacred customs of the Jews. Klausner says: "He keeps the ceremonial laws like an observing Jew; he wears 'fringes'; he goes up to Jerusalem to keep the Feast of Unleavened Bread, he celebrates the 'Seder,' blesses the bread and the unleavened cakes and breaks them and says the blessing over the wine; he dips the various herbs into the 'harosheth,' drinks the 'four cups' of wine and concludes with the Hallel." In the Sermon on the Mount Jesus says, "Think not that I am come to destroy the Law or the Prophets: I am not come to destroy, but to fulfill; for verily I say unto you, Till heaven and earth pass away, one jot or one tittle shall in no wise pass from the law till all things be accomplished. Whosoever, therefore, shall break one of these least commandments and shall teach men to do so, shall be called least in the kingdom of heaven: but whosoever shall do and teach them, he shall be called great in the kingdom of heaven." This was Jesus' way of being more true to the law than were the Pharisees. In order that the law might be brought up to date and be made to apply to current situations, the Pharisees were accustomed to "interpret" the law, giving to it meanings that were never originally intended. On the other hand, the Pharisees were not as strict as they should have been in observing the moral law. Jesus says, "Except your righteousness shall exceed the righteousness of the Scribes and the Pharisees, ye shall in no wise enter into the kingdom of heaven." But Jesus felt the importance of the ceremonial law also, for he exclaims, "Woe unto you Pharisees! for ye tithe mint and rue and every herb and pass over judgment and the love of God: but these ye ought to have done, and not have left the other undone." The faith of Jesus is the ancient and lofty faith of Israel. He recognizes the law, both moral and ceremonial, and recognizes its value in preparing the nation for the advent of the kingdom of God.

The faith of Jesus is, on the whole, closer to that of the Pharisees than that of any other sect in Israel. It is true that Jesus condemns the Pharisees in no uncertain terms, but his condemnation is aimed at their moral life and not at their religious faith. He made his position clear when he said to his disciples, "The Scribes and the Pharisees sit in Moses' seat; all things therefore, whatsoever they bid you, these do and observe: but do not ye after their works; for they say and do not." That Jesus was a firm believer in performing the faith appears from many other utterances. When at Jericho he was asked by a Scribe, "Teacher, what shall I do to inherit Eternal Life?" he answered, "What stands written in the Law? How readest thou?" The Scribe replied, "Thou shalt love the Lord thy God from thy whole heart and with thy whole soul and with thy whole strength and with thy whole mind, and thy neighbor as thyself." Jesus said to him, "This *do*, and thou shalt live." But the Scribe evidently felt that Jesus did not hold the Pharisaic position that one's neighbor meant a fellow Jew. He asked, "And who is my neighbor?" In reply Jesus related the story of the Good Samaritan and asked, "Now which of these three seemeth to you to be neighbor to him that fell in with the thieves?" The Scribe was compelled to say, "The one that took pity on him." "Go thy way," said Jesus; "and *do* thou also likewise."

Other incidents show the faith of Jesus and indicate his peculiar social angle. When the Rich Young Man came and declared that he had kept the commandments from his youth up, we are told that Jesus loved him. It was the keeping—the doing—which won the heart of Jesus. The reply to the Scribe in Jerusalem brings out the same position. The Scribe said, "Of a truth, Master, thou sayest well, for God is one and there is none else save he; and to love him with all thy heart and with all thy soul . . . and to love thy neighbor as thyself is greater than all burnt offerings and sacrifices." Here was the proper relation of the moral and the ceremonial laws—a position which Jesus believed to be the essential spirit of Judaism and he answered, "Thou art not far from the kingdom of heaven."

The kingdom of heaven, or the kingdom come from heaven, was unquestionably the Messianic Jewish kingdom which had been foretold by the prophets. There was no little liberty exercised in viewing the details, the time, the occasion, and the various steps by which the kingdom would be established. Each teacher no doubt had his own personal view of these matters, and Jesus was no exception. But for him, as for all other Jewish teachers, the kingdom of heaven was the Messianic kingdom to come. Whether it was or was not to be ruled by a descendant of David, it was to be a great kingdom like that of David and Solomon; and it was to rule from Mount Zion, the actual mountain then situated within the city of Jerusalem. It was also to be a Jewish kingdom, triumphant over the Gentile world. However much Jesus may have modified, in his own mind, the lineaments of this kingdom, its general features were not changed; he was the King of the Jews.

That Jesus held essentially to the Messianism of the prophets, and to the popular hope of Israel as the only true means of saving the world, may be seen from certain of his statements to people who were outside the provisions made by the Covenant. To the woman of Samaria he said, "Ye worship what ye know not, we worship what we know, because salvation is of the Jews." And to the Canaanitish woman he said, "It is wrong to take the children's bread and throw it to the little dogs." According to Matthew, Jesus added to these words the statement, "I was not sent except to the lost sheep of the house of Israel." When he sent out his disciples to declare that the kingdom of heaven was at hand, he directed them, "Go not the way of the Gentiles, neither enter into any city of the Samaritans; but go unto the lost sheep of the house of Israel." Evidently the business relating to the kingdom of heaven was first of all an exclusively Jewish matter. It might later reach out to the Gentile world, but that time had not yet come. It must be established in Israel because God had made Israel the chosen vessel of light to all the world. Nothing, therefore, could be gained at present by laboring among people who were not Jews.

Just how it happened that the Messianic hope of Israel

became during the lifetime of Jesus a subject of consuming national interest can be learned only from a study of the political fortunes of the nation. During the days of independence under the Maccabees Jewish nationalism received its greatest stimulus. There were denationalizing forces at work at the same time, for Hellenistic culture had made great headway against the solidarity of Judaism. In fact, the ruling classes had already been won by the supposedly superior features of Greek wisdom and the Greek mode of life. A certain Jason who occupied the high-priesthood is said to have built a Greek gymnasium under the castle of Jerusalem, and to have encouraged the noblest of the young men to assume the Greek dress. So completely was the government in the hands of the Hellenistic party that almost no one except the common people remained true to Judaism. The rulers of Israel conspired with Antiochus Epiphanes to hasten the Hellenization of Israel. Accordingly, Antiochus prohibited the worship of God and the observation of those rites and ceremonies which made the Jew a Jew. By force, and on pain of death, he compelled the priests to offer sacrifices to the gods of the Greek world. It was this measure which precipitated the Maccabean revolt with its almost miraculous consequences. But the Hellenizers were never completely wiped out. And when the Hasmonean dynasty had established itself, it entered that sphere of world outlook where political expediency, the ambition for power, and the possession of great wealth dictated the policy of a working understanding with the rich and influential Hellenizers.

Thus, even in the Maccabean period when independence had been won on purely nationalist grounds, political expediency caused a shift of policy on the part of the Hasmonean kings which resulted in the formation of two mutually antagonistic parties—the Hellenists, or nationalists, and the patriots, or orthodox religious party. The presence of these widely opposed factions within the same nation deepened, through strife and arguments, the convictions which drove them apart. And thus originated that long period of political struggle between the nationalists and the patriots of Israel and those Gentile forces within and without which finally brought about the destruction of the nation. While this struggle was in progress Jesus appeared and taught. His teachings, because of the political conditions—the loss of independence and the degradation and humiliation of subjection to Rome—could not help but have the most profound nationalist significance. History had conspired thus to make the Messianic hope the most vital of all popular interests. And the words and method of Jesus indicate that he regarded himself as the answer of the Most High to the situation which the political struggle had produced.

Klausner says of the political situation, previous to and during the time of Christ, "The Maccabeans built up a Jewish Palestine; the Herodian kings destroyed it." The Jews who returned to Palestine after the fall of Nebuchadrezzar's line, i.e. those who returned during the reigns of Cyrus, Darius, and Artaxerxes, built up a tiny Judea surrounded on every side by strong independent Gentile cities. "So insignificant a state was Judea that it was indistinguishable within the great Perian Empire, and even within the satrapy of Transpotamia (Syria). Those Greek writers who were contemporary with the Maccabees scarcely knew of the existence of Judea: Syria they knew and Philistia they knew, but not Judea. Herodotus, painstaking though he was, never mentions it and only refers to 'the Syrians of Palestine.' " But tiny and unknown as Judea was from the days of Zerubabel to the time of Jonathan Maccabeus, the great majority of her people observed religious rites and lived a manner of life which could not help but impart a strong sense of nationality. Perhaps there has never been before or since a technique of living which could so completely and effectively mold and set apart a group of men as could the Judaism of this period. When the worship of

Judea was endangered and the rites were forbidden by Antiochus, it was not merely patriotism which was aroused; it was the whole man and the whole people which arose in revolt. Opposition to the tyrant was most profoundly a measure of self-preservation, for it sought to secure the only life which could be life to the Jew.

No one would have dreamed that in such a tiny Judea, and in an obscure family, there resided the courage, mystical faith, military genius, and unquenchable hope that would Judaize all Palestine and win the respect of such world conquerors as the Romans. Not even the Maccabees, who achieved all this, had the least suspicion that they possessed these powers. Outraged, indignant, determined to defend the truth and die, they acted. They found themselves surrounded by thousands of their fellow countrymen; they discovered in actual battle that they had the gift to lead armies to victory; they hammered their enemies into the dust and set up an independent Jewish kingdom. Then they began to extend the borders of their kingdom. "Jonathan annexed Ekron and the three Samaritan districts, Ephraim, Lydd, and Ramathaim, while his brother Simon annexed Jaffa, Gezer, and Beth-Zur; but those who were mainly responsible for extending Judea into a Jewish Palestine were the three Maccabeans, John Hyrcanus, Judas Aristobulus, Alexander Jannaeus. . . . John Hyrcanus conquered Samaria, Edom and part of Moab, and also, perhaps, Lower Galilee; he converted the Edomites to Judaism and settled Jews in Samaria and Moab. Judas Aristobulus, who assumed the crown but reigned only one year, succeeded during his brief reign in conquering and Judaizing a part of Galilee—apparently Upper Galilee, while Alexander Jannaeus completed what his father John Hyrcanus, and his brother Judas Aristobulus, had begun. He conquered Gadara, Amathus, Pella, Dium, Hippos, Gerasa, Gaulana, Seleucia, the fortified city of Gamala across the Jordan, and the towns of Philistia which had been completely Hellenized: Rafia, An-

thedon, and Gaza—He subdued such parts of Moab as had
not been conquered by his father, Gilead, and, before he died,
laid siege to the town of Ragaba across the Jordan, which
place was captured immediately after his death. He thus en-
larged the insignificant Judea until its boundaries were vir-
tually identical with those of David and Solomon." [1]

There was about this conquest of Palestine, however, certain
spiritual and religious forces which helped to secure victory
and which immediately afterward began to contribute to
national destruction. There was, first, the great confidence in
the invincible power of the Jewish army in battle. Small numbers had cut off and routed well-trained and superior armies
sent against Judea. This fostered a tendency to disregard the
power of the enemy and to depend upon the miraculous
element which was supposed to reside within the nature of the
Jewish cause. There was no proper consideration of Maccabean
genius for military leadership, and no proper appreciation of
the inherent weaknesses of the generals sent against them by
Antiochus. This led them to hasty revolt against powers that
could not be defeated and brought about the destruction of
great numbers of the bravest men in the nation. Second, the
victory had been secured by means of alliances with Rome,
and, later, conserved by actual military assistance from the
Romans. This friendliness to Rome became a matter of expediency in the struggle with Syria. It constituted a debt; it
led to dependency; then to the loss of even an appearance of
independence. The Roman wolf, called in as a friend, had
devoured Judea. Third, the unity of all life, religious, political,
and cultural, admitted of no compromise with the policies of
the Gentile overlord. Political measures were regarded as
fundamentally opposed to Judaism when those measures originated outside of Judea—a Roman tax was looked upon as
constituting the actual loss of spiritual and religious indepen-

---

[1] Klausner, *Jesus of Nazareth*, pp. 135, 136.

dence. Since religion covered all life, the yielding of a single point to Gentile control was sacrilege. Fourth, a misunderstanding of the Jewish temper and religion led the conquerors to take numerous steps which irritated the sensitive Jewish soul and multiplied the grievances which led to rebellion.

And yet, even these forces might not have had an opportunity to operate to the final destruction of the Maccabean kingdom had not Hyrcanus II and Aristobulus II, sons of Alexander Jannaeus and his queen Shelom-Zion, become rivals for the throne. The eldest son, Hyrcanus, seemed at first to be quite willing to permit his younger brother to be king and to take for himself the position of the high-priesthood. But Antipater, the Edomite, the father of Herod, persuaded him to press his claim to the throne. Civil war followed between the two brothers. Aretas of Arabia championed the cause of Hyrcanus and defeated Aristobulus. Pompey appeared and forced Aristobulus to accompany him in a campaign against the Arabs and, when these had been defeated, turned his victorious army against Jerusalem. The party of Hyrcanus opened the gates of the city to the troops of Pompey, but the party of Aristobulus fortified the Temple Mount and resisted bravely. When Pompey finally subdued the city he put twelve thousand Jews to death and partitioned Judea, reducing it to the tiny state it was before the Maccabean conquests. Hyrcanus was made ruler of the people, but he was deprived of the title of "king" and was in reality only the high-priest. Aristobulus and his son, Alexander, continued to fight, but were captured at last, carried to Rome, and eventually put to death. When civil war broke out in Italy, Hyrcanus, acting upon the advice of Antipater, espoused the cause of Julius Caesar and sent Jewish soldiers to his assistance. The real power in Judea, however, was in the hands of Antipater, and Caesar acted accordingly. He made Antipater viceregent and Hyrcanus ethnarch, or Chief of the People—an empty title.

Antipater, who was the real head of the new government,

appointed his sons, Phasael and Herod, governors of Jerusalem and Galilee. The Galileans opposed Herod bitterly and drove him to the most bloody cruelties to hold them in check. Revolts continued, and Herod, with the assistance of the Romans, subdued Samaria, attacked Jerusalem, then in revolt against the Edomite and Roman rule, and slaughtered so many of the Jews that even Herod exclaimed, "Would the Romans deprive the city of all its inhabitants and leave me king of the wilderness?"

Then, after the death of Antipater, Herod, with the aid of the Romans, succeeded in making himself king of Judea. It is said of him that "he stole along to his throne like a fox, he ruled like a tiger and died like a dog." From the death of the queen Shelom-Zion until Herod became all-powerful (67-37 B.C.), more than one hundred thousand Jews, the pick of the nation, fell in battle. During the reign of Herod (37-4 B.C.) very few Jews died in warfare, but the fact that nothing, not even torture, could compel the Jews to recognize him as their king brought about the Herodian policy of seeking out and of putting to death unfriendly citizens, and this procedure was more disastrous than all the wars that Judea had fought up to this time. When, after his death, a Jewish delegation went to Rome to seek to prevent his son, Archelaus, from gaining the succession, it was charged that "He (Herod) committed acts of tyranny which might have made an end of the Jews, and also devised new things according to his own mind which were contrary to the spirit of the Jews; and he killed many men with a cruelty unparalleled in history.

"He reduced the people to abject poverty though he had found it, apart from exceptional cases, in a condition of wealth. The property of the higher families—whom he had condemned to death on the slightest pretext—he confiscated, and those whom he suffered to remain alive he deprived of their wealth. Not only were the taxes levied on all the inhabitants year by year exacted mercilessly and by force, but it was impossible to live without bribes to himself, and to his domestics, and his friends and officers who were entrusted with the gathering of the taxes—Herod behaved to the Jews with a cruelty as great as though a wild beast had been given rule over mankind. Though the Jews had before suffered many hardships and oppressions, their history had never known so great an affliction as they had suffered at the hands of Herod." [2]

The real objection to Herod, however, was his interference with Jewish customs. He reduced the Sanhedrin to a body which dealt only with unimportant religious questions and which was forced to submit all civil matters to his dictation. The office of high-priest he made an appointive position and the appointees and the deposed formed a long procession of Edomites, Babylonians, Egyptians, and Jews who were permitted to remain in office only so long as they pleased him. To secure himself against assassination and to enforce his tyrannies, he surrounded himself with an army of mercenaries —Thracians, Germans, and Gauls. His civil offices, the treasury and high state positions, were filled with Greeks and foreign eunuchs.

Archelaus, in spite of the protest of the Jewish delegation against him, succeeded to a part of his father's kingdom, and ruled in Jerusalem for ten years (4 B.C.-6 A.D.). He put down a rebellion in Jerusalem with great slaughter and thus proved that he was a true son of Herod. In other matters also he walked in the way of his father. He made constant changes in the office of the high-priest and exacted large sums for building enterprises from the already greatly impoverished people. His cruelties against both Jews and Samaritans caused them to forget their animosities and to unite to complain to Augustus against him. The emperor was so enraged by the charges that he summoned Archelaus to Rome, confiscated his possessions, and exiled him to Gaul. Judea was then attached

---

[2] Josephus, *Antiquities* XVII, 11:2.

to the province of Syria and put in charge of a procurator. This enabled the Jews to be governed by a Sanhedrin and to enjoy a large measure of autonomy—a privilege for which the delegation to Rome had asked when it went to protest against Archelaus' succession ten years before.

The advantages which the Jews had hoped to gain under a procurator were, however, only apparent. The Sanhedrin held jurisdiction in religious matters but could conduct only a preliminary trial, or investigation, in capital cases. They could not conduct war or police the cities. During the Great Feasts the governor left Caesarea and went up to Jerusalem with a Roman army to insure the peace. At such times Roman sentinels held the galleries surrounding the Temple. Even the robes of the high-priest were in the keeping of the governor, who gave them into the priest's charge only for the duration of the Feast. Taxes were collected by tax-farmers or publicans, who extorted all they could from the people. When such regulations were exercised by the procurator, what was there left of Jewish autonomy?

One act of government under the new arrangement must be especially noted, for it marks the beginning of that hostility to Rome which culminated in the final destruction of Jerusalem in 70 A.D. Quirinius, the governor of the province to which Judea had been attached (Syria), ordered the taking of a census to form the basis of taxation. This order was regarded by the Jews as being contrary to the will of God. When David numbered the people a plague broke out, thus manifesting the divine displeasure. But the chief objection to the census may be found in the fact that it would enable the Romans to exact the tax with an even greater oppression. There could be no surer mark of the complete servitude of the people to the will of the foreigner.

Judas the Galilean from Gamala, sometimes called Judas the Gaulonite, together with Zadok the Pharisee (probably also of Galilee), organized a revolt against Rome and opposed the taking of the census. Their followers were men who were determined to uphold the Jewish Law and the honor of the nation. They demanded, in spite of the condition of the country and the apparent suicide in any rebellious move, that the nation rise as one man against those who sought to carry out the census. We are told in Acts, "After this man rose up Judas of Galilee in the days of the taxing (enrollment) and drew away much people after him: he also perished and all, even as many as obeyed him, were dispersed." Luke tells us that the census under Quirinius took place at the time of the birth of Christ, which would put the rebellion of Judas the Galilean at a date near the death of Herod. Klausner tells us that immediately after the death of Herod "Judas of Galilee collected a large body of desperate nationalists, attacked the king's armory, seized the weapons and with these armed his followers. The warrior-zealot then fought against all those, Gentiles and Jews, who opposed the idea of freedom; and as is usual in such campaigns, he made little distinction between actual traitors, and those who were merely peace-loving Jews. He put the fear of himself on the whole of Galilee." Klausner admits that the man who opposed the census may be the same man who led the rioting in the days after the death of Herod. We may not be able to clear up all questions about Judas of Galilee or to account for Luke's chronology (he omits the whole reign of Archelaus after Herod and puts the census of Quirinius at least ten years before it could have been taken); but that the opposition to the census was the beginning of the last step in the tragedy of Jewish nationalism we cannot doubt. The battle cry of Judas, "No tribute to Rome," was heard in the land almost constantly for the next sixty years. Scarcely a year went by without wars, rebellions, outbreaks—all carried on by bands of guerrillas who made their place of refuge the broken country of Galilee.

Such was the volcanic political atmosphere into which Jesus was born and in which he lived the whole of his life. There were almost daily popular demonstrations which were misunderstood by the Romans, who imagined that these outbursts were the beginnings of revolt. Such popular protests were always put down without mercy. Men were imprisoned, slain, driven from their homes in flight. Such cruelties led to further protest and to increased oppression. Greater and greater became the strain as the Jewish antagonism against the Roman became more bitter. The leaders—Herodians, Sadducees, and the priestly class—knew the full peril of conflict with Rome; but the common people, given to the conviction that God would deliver His people, and ignorant of the actual power of Rome, would recognize no master but the God of their fathers. Before the danger they could see, they were outwardly peaceful and obedient; but within, the feeling was so intense that the least promise of relief was embraced and trusted. The wars, the many revolts, the increasing impoverishment of the country, and the heavy taxation of the Caesars, all contributed toward a condition which was fast becoming insupportable. The thought of deliverance through the promised Messiah became therefore the abiding wish of the nation.

Jesus could not help being deeply influenced by this terrific national drama. Only a few hours' journey from his home Judas the Galilean had raised the standard of revolt against the taking of the census. Thousands and tens of thousands of Galileans and other Jews had fought under his command. Judas and many of his followers had been slain, but thousands had dispersed and had gone to their homes. These were alive during the whole of the life of Jesus and were to be met in every village of Galilee. The cause was for the moment lost, but there was never a time when these Zealots would not have sprung to arms if the nation as a whole had called them. This attitude of readiness to fight, this atmosphere of tension, the deep bitterness in the heart of these patriots, would all be matters of much concern to Jesus. He would examine every angle of their convictions. And because he was wise enough to see clearly the national calamity that would result from any trial of strength against the Roman, he would be sure to seek a way of action that would save his nation.

Thus surrounded in his early years by the most zealous and pious section of Judaism he would be intimately informed concerning the two most vital forces in the nation. He would be steeped in the lore and spirit of prophecy, and he would understand the psychology of these later heroes of the faith. A teacher who comes out of such a religious and political situation will address himself to the situation as it exists, and will seek to indicate the possible future of his people. The message will not, therefore, be a dissociated and remote philosophy of consolation, but a social policy adapted to the needs of the moment, one calculated to avert the perils of the hour. That the words of Jesus may be forced into the mold of a world-religion is already a matter of history; that they contain this possibility in outline may be gathered from both the substance of the teachings and from the implied social purpose of Jesus. But not enough emphasis has been given to the actual Judean situation to which Jesus addressed his every word. His message was calculated to heal the ills of the world, but only after he had saved the land of Israel.

Too much, therefore, has been made of the supposed simplicity of Jesus and the lowliness of his peasant origin. The result of this error is such that many regard him as being a naive, uninformed, rather ill-balanced, but well-intentioned person on the one hand, and a harmless poet and mystic of impractical and other-world tendencies on the other. An analysis of his teaching, however, shows him to be intensely practical, always saying, "This *do* and thou shalt live," always speaking out of a closely knit and well-digested system of religious thought, and declaring at every turn the loftiest morality the world has ever known. There is nothing simple about Jesus except the language he uses to express his teaching. Only a very little reflection upon the main principle set forth in any one of his parables will carry one immediately into the regions of universal truth. One comes face to face with those ideas which must ever be met in any worthy attempt to solve the spiritual and social problems of a people. And one realizes that he is following in the steps of one who knows this region so well that out of his great certainty he is able to translate its life and color into the most beautiful and simple human speech. It is only our own conceit and stupidity which makes us adopt a patronizing manner toward the "sweet-natured" and "simple" Nazarene.

Nor is there anything to be gained by seeking to classify the beliefs of the people of Galilee—Pharisees, Zealots, Essenes— and by comparison attempt to show that the gospel of Jesus is the resultant of all these beliefs. Jesus shows himself to be both profound enough and original enough to formulate a teaching entirely his own. There is nothing wooden about either the mentality or the procedure of Jesus. He sees clearly enough to preserve just the relation to Judaism that will make his words understood, and to utter, when it is necessary, that caution which will prevent them from becoming entangled with the errors of the several sects which flourish in his day. He superimposes his teaching upon the current Judaism with a sureness which reveals at once that he knows what he is about. He is no Pharisee or wandering Rab, feeling his way along, the slave of a method and the retailer of tradition; he has made everything his own, has thought his way through to unimpeachable conclusions, and is therefore able to proceed with confidence and authority. It is true that an immense amount of his teaching may be found scattered about in the welter and voluminousness of Judaic writings, but it also true that Jesus brought them together with point and sense and system, with a coördination and organic relation not met with before. And the more we explore the Judaic background, and the peculiar turn these teachings take in the mind of Jesus, the more we become convinced that here is an absolutely new voice in Israel.

Essential, therefore, as a knowledge of the historical background and the political situation may be to the understanding of Jesus, this knowledge is important only because it helps us to see the situation as it is and to know how it came about. It enables us to see what Jesus was trying to correct and to avert. In like manner a study of historical and current Judaism, as Jesus knew it, helps us to understand what he was trying to fulfill and to reform, what he was seeking to direct to the only development which would permit the nation to live. The faith of Jesus is the historic faith of Israel—more historic than current, perhaps—but his recommendations for those who hold this faith are original, practical for all their Messianism, calculated to save Israel from that militancy and antagonism toward the conqueror which, if allowed to go on unchecked, will leave not one stone upon another.

A word of caution may not be out of place at this point. One must not assume too easily that the Messianism of Jesus clouded his vision of national redemption and made him make impossible recommendations. Jesus is no fanatic, bewildered by extravagant sights of a glory that exists nowhere except in his deluded mind. He sees the actual situation too clearly for that. The Sadducee is already out of the picture of the future that is indigenous to Israel, and there are very few patriots who do not know it. But there are not so many who realize that Pharisaism, for all its liberal and progressive spirit, has also come to the end of its constructive work. There are of course many exceptions, as the words of Jesus plainly show—there are Pharisees and Pharisees—but Pharisaism as a factor in the nation's future has lost its virtue through its "play-acting." The Pharisee who questioned Jesus in Jerusalem was not far from the kingdom of heaven, but his class, nevertheless, deserves the scathing denunciation Jesus poured upon it, just because it had within it the possibility of proper leadership and had become but a whited sepulcher full of dead men's bones. The few upright, devout, and noble-minded men within the class would not be able to breathe into the sepulcher and to vitalize the bones, to make out of the teachings and the traditions of departed leaders the gospel that would save the nation from death. Fanatics do not see into social conditions with such penetrating analysis as Jesus revealed.

And we shall go equally astray if we regard Jesus as retreating from the bitter facts of the world and as turning to that realm which is the refuge of all despairing visionaries—a kingdom not of this world. The whole ministry of Jesus and almost every word of his Gospel refute such a view. Others of his time did seek the shelter of a deep faith, a humble and lowly spirit, and good works, "hoping and quietly waiting for the salvation of the Lord," but Jesus did not. He was essentially a man of action. He got out among the people—the method which every successful social and political leader has pursued. It is true that his kingdom came not by observation, nor by the display of force, as worldly kingdoms come; his kingdom came as a grain of mustard seed—a seed-thought, a vision, which would grow into a great tree. He did not need to gather an army and fight for it. It would come as all understanding comes, little by little, but it would become great enough at last to fill the earth. As a propagandist, a creator of public opinion, the founder of a new epoch in human affairs, he was most vitally concerned with the people and their life. And he knew that he was no futile quiescent entertaining a harmless dream: "Think not that I am come to bring peace upon the earth; I come not to bring peace but a sword." But his sword was not made of steel; it was made of truth, a truth that would save a nation, and its flashes would be like light. Though it should be grounded a thousand times in history, some one would wield it again until it should prevail. Whoever seeks by actual contact with people, and by their instruction, to set up a saving wisdom among them is no monastic fleeing from reality. A man who goes to his death with a bit of steel in his hands is no more in the thick of this world's affairs than he who goes with a vision in his brain. It was the claim of Jesus that his vision would save the nation and that, if Israel took the sword, she would perish by it. At last, when his teaching had been rejected, he wept over the capital of his nation, for he saw that her doom was sealed. Mystics and visionaries do not weep over nations; they rejoice in the paradise they have found, the peace to which they have attained.

Just when Jesus became persuaded that he had the way and the truth and the life for Israel, we do not know; but we may be very sure that he began to see that way as soon as he realized fully the exact nature of the peril of the Jewish people. Having been reared in Galilee, he would no doubt share with his patriotic neighbors their intense hatred against Rome. But he would soon see the futility of such feeling. His unusual intelligence and his power of analysis would show him the stern and naked facts, the utter folly of local or even of national resistance to Rome. He would see in the head-long courage of the Zealots a constant threat against the life of the nation. The caution of the Pharisees, a caution which merely held resistance in check, constituted a no less danger. A moment would come when the strain would snap the power of self-control and the pent-up feeling would break forth like a storm. Then the Roman would come with all his thunder-bolts and would level everything even with the ground. The very feeling against Rome constituted Israel's greatest danger. The only way to guarantee national life would be to eradicate this hatred. Israel must adopt a new attitude toward the conqueror; she must repent, experience a change of mind (metanoia) or she would perish. She must adopt toward her oppressor the attitude God maintains toward friend and foe!

"He maketh his rain to fall upon the just and the unjust, and his sun to shine upon the evil and the good." Israel must achieve this perfect love if she would live.

The utter rightness of this attitude, the saving power of this policy, was to Jesus no mere theory. He saw that it would save Israel, that it was the only thing that could save her. It came to him in the course of his thinking, but it came as a flash of prophetic insight. It was an imitation of the magnanimity of God on the part of His people. To adopt it would be to follow the ways of God; and those who did the works of God, and followed Him, would be most truly the children of God. Again the supposedly impractical dreamer is found to be a preacher of action; if Israel would thus *do the will of God* she would not perish but have everlasting life.

This great vision of the Way of national redemption must have come to him long before his baptism by John. At some time while he was toiling at his trade and brooding over the certainty of national destruction, if the present attitude continued, it flashed over him. Then as he continued his daily tasks he set it alongside the great body of Jewish teaching. Just here perhaps began that toil of collecting, of systematizing, of garnering the word and spirit of Judaism from its isolation in various writings and in oral tradition—a work which Jesus undoubtedly performed at some time. He traced the principles of Judaism to their logical conclusions, related them to his vision of the Way, and saw clearly that he had thus reached the goal to which all revelation led. And because his vision did constitute the highest truth of Judaism and the only way of national salvation, he became the more assured that this knowledge had come down from heaven. His new insight cast a great illumination upon the teachings of the prophets and the traditions of the fathers. How his heart burned within him as the light of this Way opened to him the Scriptures!

Thus long before he felt the urge of the Spirit of God to

redeem the lost sheep of the house of Israel, he was very sure that he had found the path of life. In his carpenter-shop at Nazareth his brain beat out, in unison with the stroke of hammer and mallet, the whole wonder of this Way. Here he answered all objections; saw the play-acting of the Pharisees and scourged them with his indignation; avoided the swift retribution of a too zealous course; met the learned Scribes and the Sadducees, considered their wiles, framed his notable replies, and refuted them; looked the dangers squarely in the face; and perhaps—who knows?—saw the shadow of the cross as the inevitable consequence of such teaching. If one wishes to build a shrine of pilgrimage anywhere to Jesus, let him search out the location of this carpenter-shop where the gospel came throbbing into being.

One thing is certain, despite any charge that may be preferred against this view as having yielded unduly to imagination: Jesus was ready when his call came. He went about his work with a caution, a certainty, a precision, and an effectiveness not possible to one who trusts to the inspiration of the moment. He had though this way through and knew just how one ought to proceed. And his conviction—that this Way would save the nation and that he knew how to declare it—constitutes one of the chief elements, on the human side, in his Messianic consciousness. The very fact that he had received the vision is but a step away from that sense of obligation which compels him to seek and to save that which was lost. We do not know just how a God of history works in engineering the conjunction of the man and the divine purpose, but we do know something of the history of a conviction in its development in the human mind. Surely there is no one who will deny that the brain of Jesus was a part of his humanity. And this brain, for all its unusual power and sensitivity, served in human fashion to search out the Way of Israel's future.

And because we know something of the history of human convictions, we can approach with less bewilderment that strange experience of Jesus when he went to hear John beyond the Jordan. What went Jesus out into the wilderness to see? A reed shaken by the wind? He saw a man of great strength and stature, whose voice was like the sound of many waters and whose brow was wreathed with the thunder of a wrath to come. Was he a prophet? His clothing of camel's hair proclaimed that he had accepted the rôle of the prophet, and his leathern girdle and his mantle were so pointedly reminiscent of Elijah that Jesus knew at once the character John was seeking to portray. Furthermore, the teaching of the Baptist was in substance just what Elijah would declare: the kingdom of heaven was at hand; the Messiah was already present in the world, ready to appear; the ax of destruction was already at the root of the tree of Israel; the Messiah would thoroughly purge the nation; the people must therefore be baptized unto repentance and remission of sins in preparation for the Messiah's manifestation. Yes, John was a prophet, and more than a prophet; he was the spiritual Elijah, the forerunner of the Messiah.

Some have sought to point out the dissimilarity between the teachings of John and the teachings of Jesus, forgetting that any fundamental conflict of opinion between Jesus and John would have made it impossible for the Baptist to crystallize the convictions of Jesus as he undoubtedly did. The experience of Jesus at the time of his baptism is without doubt the greatest event in determining his career. And when he was asked in Jerusalem by what authority he taught, and who gave him that authority, he replied, "The baptism of John, was it of God or of men?" The step which Jesus took after his baptism came from this experience, and we may be sure that it could not come from a dissimilarity of views.

Indeed, the basic likeness of the social understanding of the two men is so apparent as to make any attempt to point it out almost superfluous. The Pharisees and Sadducees appear and John said to them: "O generation of vipers, who warned you to flee the wrath to come? Bring forth therefore fruits meet for repentance. And think not to say within yourselves, We have Abraham for our father; for I say unto you that God is able of these stones to raise up children to Abraham. And now also the ax is laid unto the root of the trees . . ." Jesus, who had already seen the impossibility of averting national disaster through the guidance of either the Pharisees or Sadducees, would experience a shock of surprise upon hearing these words. Did he not know that the general hatred of Rome was an ax that was already poised to cut down the nation? "His fan is in his hand, and he will thoroughly purge his floor." Had not Jesus seen how thoroughly Israel must be purged of her dangerous frame of mind? "Repent therefore and be baptized unto the remission of sins." Only by such a spiritual awakening would it be possible for Israel to accept the high moral and spiritual standard which the Way implied. Jesus had seen it all, just as John saw it. Here certainly is no conflict of ideas. Jesus was startled and electrified to find his own opinions echoed from the lips of another man. Surely this preacher *was* a prophet! Surely he *was* the Elijah to come! And the Messiah? He must be now in the world! Who was he? Then he heard John saying, "I am not the Christ, but there standeth one among you whom ye know not, who shall come after me, the latchet of whose shoes I am not worthy to unloose." The Messiah was here in this group to whom John was preaching!

It requires a type of mind which takes itself very seriously to feel the call of God to some special work in the world. It may be described as imaginative, but its chief and ruling factor is its sense of the reality of its philosophy of the world and life—the world and human affairs are directed by God, and man finds his true place only through divine intervention and direction. Thus inner urges to exalted things, flashes of understanding, and even the flow of outward events are assigned the importance of being subject to the direct agency of the

Almighty. Such a mind easily accepts the force of the accidental and merely contiguous circumstance. It can think as
Klausner has pictured the thoughts of Jesus: "Was there any
reason why *he* should not be the imminent Messiah? Perhaps
his very name 'Jesus'—'he shall save,' may have moved this
simple villager to believe that he was the redeemer, just as
Shabbethai Zvi was influenced by the fact that he was born on
the 9th of Ab, the day when, according to a legend, the Messiah was to be born. Dazzled by the blinding light of the
Judean sun, it seemed to him as though the heavens were
opened and that the Shekinah shed its light upon him." But
there are a number of facts which make the last item of such
an experience utterly impossible to Jesus. First of all, he was
not a "simple villager"; he possessed a penetrating intelligence
of very high order, one which was perhaps equaled by that of
but one other man in the nation. And he was not 'a great
imaginative dreamer' who manufactured out of sunlight the
bath qol, or Shekinah. Jesus saw the cold, bitter facts as they
were, and his conviction that he was the Messiah was a part
of that same cool-headed seeing. His feeling that he was the
Messiah originated in the fact that the testimony of John confirmed his opinion that he had the vision that would save
Israel. Jesus took himself seriously, to be sure—the philosophy
had its influence—otherwise he could not have felt the personal obligation to declare the saving Way to Israel. But the
experience of Jesus is too close to actual human events—too
intellectually practical, too surely a matter of having his political views corroborated—for such other-worldly imaginings as
Klausner attributes to him. The fact that Jesus deplores the
point of view of the Zealots and regards them as the chief
national danger is enough to show the temper of his mind.

The account of the voice from heaven and the Spirit flutter-
ing as a dove bears perhaps too many marks of the conventional theology of the day to be accepted literally. One must
never forget that it has always been a Semitic tendency to

dramatize an inner experience. There is a voice here, and it has something startling to say; but the whole drama takes place in the mind of Jesus. For us the important thing is the sudden realization on the part of Jesus that he is the Messiah. There is therefore a profound truth in the pronouncement, "Thou art my beloved son; this day have I begotten thee" (some versions of Luke iii. 22). Jesus himself regards this experience as revolutionary, recreative, a new birth, an experience so vitally essential that he realizes that no one can obtain a sure and certain grasp of the Way of life without passing through a similar experience. Hence his word to Nicodemus who declared that Jesus is a teacher come from God, "Verily, verily I say unto you, Except you be born again you cannot see the kingdom of God."

In like manner must we view the temptation which took place shortly after the baptism. It is but another dramatic presentation of an inner experience, the story which reveals the process by which the Messianic procedure was determined. The general outline of Jesus' meditation is clearly discoverable behind the various movements of the pageant. "Man shall not live by bread alone" tells us that Jesus had considered and rejected the view that material prosperity improves the tone of a nation. Yet again, "the dreamer" reveals his practical mind. His nation had been greatly impoverished by the Edomite kings, and the rule of the Romans had not greatly improved its general condition. Much of the bitterness against the conqueror grew out of the nation's poverty. And yet, a nation may be prosperous and escape none of her enemies. "Thou shalt worship the Lord thy God and Him only shalt thou serve" reveals the loss to the nation through any acceptance of Gentile religion and civilization. The Jewish people might thus gain the world but they would lose their own souls. There could be no averting the threatened destruction by this method; the damage to Jewish life would be beyond repair. "Thou shalt not make trial of the Lord thy God" indicates that Jesus rejected any thought of leading the people in one headlong attempt at independence, trusting that the miraculous intervention of God would save the nation from that which seemed to be certain destruction. Again the truth derived from his much brooding over the nation's peril is confirmed: Israel must be saved by a change within, by an attitude which will allow the conqueror to find no fault in her. The method of Messianic deliverance may now be expressed; "Ye have heard it said, Thou shalt love thy neighbor, and hate thine enemy. But I say unto you, love your enemies, bless them that curse you, do good to them that hate you, and pray for them that despitefully use you; That ye may be the children of your Father which is in heaven: for he maketh his sun to rise upon the evil and the good, and sendeth his rain on the just and the unjust. If thine enemy hunger, feed him; if he thirst, give him drink; for in so doing thou shalt heap coals of fire upon his head. Be not overcome of evil, but overcome evil with good."

Such a spiritual transformation of the nation could not possibly be accomplished if he should announce his Messiahship at once. Contemporary Messianic legend and doctrine would make any such announcement on his part but a signal for national turmoil. Some would brand him as an imposter; he would need to prove that he was a son of David. He would be called upon to give a sign of his Messiahship and to perform miracles at the request of the people—"If thou be the Messiah, show us a sign that we may believe." But the Zealots would flock to him by thousands and tens of thousands, demanding that he lead them to battle against their oppressors. He would be forced into a variety of functions—Judge, Refiner of the Nations, Conqueror of the Gentiles, National Deliverer, and Founder and Ruler of an Everlasting Kingdom. He saw clearly that this militant rôle would destroy the nation he had come to save. Once more it must be admitted that Jesus could weigh faith and fact against each other in a way no religious dreamer could do. Not even his own consciousness that he was the Messiah could betray him into underestimating the strength of his nation's foes.

He therefore, began his labors cautiously and quietly, being careful to conceal for the moment his true character that he might be able to bring about in the life of a few the transformation he sought for his nation. He announced, "The time is fulfilled, and the kingdom of heaven is at hand." [3] In the synagogues he selected those scriptures which testified of him and expounded them, proclaiming at the same time the nearness of the kingdom of heaven: "The spirit of the Lord is upon me, because he hath anointed me to preach deliverance to the captives, and recovering of sight to the blind, to set at liberty them that are bruised." [4] And he began to say unto them, "This day is this scripture fulfilled in your ears." [5] And he healed the sick, for it was through his healing quite as much as by his teaching that he was able to reveal the unspiritual and the false in current religious practice. Thus publicly he presented the necessity for reform. He gave them the truth that the truth might make them see all their perils.

He looked upon his time as the season of the beginning of sorrows, the time which, in the scheme of Messianic history, is known as "the pangs of the Messiah." The afflictions of Israel under the Edomites and their continued oppression under the Romans had greatly extended the duration of this period. It could not last a great while now. The kingdom of heaven was at hand, even at the door. The exact place of his time in the coming kingdom was so clear to him that he had no patience with those who could not see it: "The Pharisees also with the Sadducees came, and tempting him, desired that he would show them a sign. He answered and said unto them, When it is evening, ye say, It will be fair weather: for the sky is red

---

[3] Mark i. 15.
[4] Isaiah xlii. 1.
[5] Luke iv. 18-21.

And in the morning, It will be foul weather today: for the sky is red and lowering. O ye play-actors, ye can discern the face of the sky; but can ye not discern the signs of this time." [6] The time had the sign of heaven's will stamped upon it clearly, but the leaders of Israel could not see it. Could these blind lead the blind? Would they not both fall into the ditch?

And yet in spite of the apparent hopelessness of Israel's condition, Jesus knew that she contained within her the light and wisdom that would save the world. Salvation was of the Jew, for Israel was the chosen race—the nation that would carry to all peoples a redeeming spiritual message. "Ye are the light of the world. A city that is set upon a hill cannot be hid. Neither do men light a candle, and put it under a bushel, but on a candlestick; and it giveth light unto all that are in the house. Let your light so shine before men, that they may see your good works, and glorify your Father which is in heaven." These words have in them a profound grasp of historical fact. The time had come when Israel could not hide from the world in that seclusion which had been her condition before the Roman came, and which had made her unknown to Herodotus. She had become a part of a world-wide empire and her people had carried her religion to practically every important city in the Graeco-Roman world, a world that was more religious perhaps than any that has succeeded it. It was distinctly an age that sought everywhere for a saving knowledge of God. Israel was like a city set upon a hill. And God had set her there that she might be seen. He had not lit her light that she should put it under a bushel. She must let it shine that it give light to all nations.

But this lamp must be trimmed and made bright against the coming of the Messiah. There were ten virgins. Five of them were wise and five were foolish. Those that had oil in their

---

[6] Matt. xvi. 1-3.

vessels with their lamps went in with the bridegroom to the feast when he came. Those who had none arrived to find that the door was shut. They had no part in the Messiah's glory. Jesus presents the same warning in a different way: "Ye are the salt of the earth. But if the salt have lost its savor, wherewith shall it (the earth) be salted? It (the salt) is thenceforth good for nothing but to be cast out and to be trodden under foot of men." These words contain a mighty challenge to the nation. She is being oppressed, the kingdom of God is at hand, those who lose the virtue that shall redeem humanity do not deserve to live. They shall be cast out and trampled by the hungering multitudes that will press on to find their salvation. A remnant, the wise, shall live and shall bless the world.

It is at this point in the thought of Jesus that the necessity to repent and to do the works of God appear as an immediate national necessity. Nothing could save Israel but a spirituality that would cast out all malice and hatred and rebellion. Nothing could give Israel her rightful place as the light of the world except this same exalted spiritual victory. To bring this experience about before the door should be shut against the whole nation, was now the consuming passion of Jesus. And it was necessarily slow work. He must awaken the people to a sense of their blindness; he must arouse the enfeebled moral conscience; he must inculcate that spirit of love and kindness that would not be overcome of evil, but would overcome evil with good; and he must implant that courage and will to sacrifice that would be willing to endure even to the losing of life that life might be gained. Nothing but a regeneration of the inner life of the nation, as individuals, could accomplish this end.

And as he labored he was not to be deceived by the flattery of Nicodemus and his ilk, or by the enthusiasm of the multitudes. "He knew what was in man," says John. He knew those who followed him for loaves and fishes and those who watched to see the wonders he might perform. How few were truly sincere, he knew. As he reviewed the results he said, "Wide is the gate, and broad is the way that leadeth to destruction, and many there be which go in thereat. And strait is the gate, and narrow is the way, which leadeth unto life, and few there be that find it." [7] Such acute understanding of men makes it highly improbable that he could have been taken unawares by his fate.

On the other hand, he was so certain of his place in the history of Israel that he was not hindered by any undue modesty. So clearly did he realize that his vision was the way, the truth, and the life, that he denied himself in the very declaration of his nature. "I am the door: by me if any man enter in, he shall be saved, and shall go in and out and find pasture." [8] "I am the light of the world: he that followeth me shall not walk in darkness, but shall have the light of life." [9] "The men of Nineveh shall rise up in judgment with this generation and shall condemn it: because they repented at the preaching of Jonas; and behold a greater than Jonas is here. The queen of the south shall rise up in judgment with this generation, and shall condemn it: for she came from the uttermost part of the earth to hear the wisdom of Solomon; and, behold, a greater than Solomon is here." [10] "Blessed are the eyes that see the things which ye see: for I tell you that many prophets and kings have desired to see those things which ye see, and have not seen them; and to hear those things which ye hear, and have not heard them. [11] "Woe unto you, Chorazin! Woe unto you, Beth-saida! For if the mighty works had been done in Tyre and Sidon, which have been done in you, they would have repented a great while ago, sitting in sackcloth and ashes. But it shall be more tolerable for Tyre and Sidon

---

[7] Matt. vii. 13-14.
[8] John x. 9.
[9] John viii. 12.
[10] Matt. xii. 41-43.
[11] Luke x. 23-24.

at the judgment than for you. And thou, Capernaum, which art exalted unto heaven shalt be cast down to hell." [12]

We find many facets of light in these utterances. First, there is a sense of his worth to Israel that overcomes all hesitancy and what would be in others a becoming modesty. Second, there is the profound knowledge that a saving truth comes not through revelation by flesh and blood, but by the leading of the Spirit. Knowledge which reaches the roots of conscience must come as a personal discovery, as a religious experience. We can tell too much, yet reveal nothing. Jesus gave a clue, but he left his true nature shadowed that an awakening soul might discover that he was the Messiah. Third, there is revealed a sure penetration into the spiritual state of the nations, both past and present. Luke's narrative precedes the "Woes" with these words, "It shall be more tolerable for Sodom in the day of judgment than for that city." Sodom had not the witness of the cities of Israel—a solemn commentary on the life Lot lived within her walls. When Nineveh received a warning she repented. And the extreme religiosity of the Gentile world in the days of our Lord was not unknown to him. A study of historical materials reveals that the one consuming passion of the nations from the time of Alexander the Great to the third century of our era was a desire to escape sin and to secure eternal life. It is not possible that Jesus was ignorant of the proselytizing zeal of Israel among the nations, or that he was unaware of the results: "Ye compass sea and land to make one proselyte; and when ye have gained him, ye have made him two-fold more the child of hell than yourselves." [13] "The centurion answered and said, Lord, I am not worthy that thou shouldst come under my roof: but speak the word only, and my servant shall be healed. For I am a man under authority having soldiers under me; and I say to this man, Go and he goeth; and to another, Come, and he cometh; and to

---

[12] Luke x. 13-15.
[13] Matt. xxiii. 15.

my servant, Do this, and he doeth it. Jesus marvelled, and said to them that followed, Verily I say unto you, I have not found so great faith, no, not in Israel." [14] And his encounter with the Syro-Phoenician woman, a Greek, revealed to him the spiritual condition among the common people in the regions of Tyre and Sidon.[15] Daily contact with the many Gentiles which made up large portions of the population in Galilee must have supplied him with an understanding of the Gentile world. Is it not an added tribute to the understanding and analytic powers of Jesus that he was able to see the spiritual hunger of the Gentiles and to realize that the remedy for it was a revived spiritual Israel? Perhaps the true explanation of his delay in granting the request of the Syro-Phoenician woman was his desire to teach her that Israel, in spite of its faults, possessed the hope of the world. Having made his point, he exclaimed, "O woman, great is thy faith!"

It is this breadth of view, this keen appraisal of the relative spirituality of Israel and the Gentiles, and his straightforwardness in declaring it, which explains the hostility of his hearers to his message. As Simkhovitch correctly observes: "One does not need to look very far to find the reason for the antagonism to Jesus. Was it not he who in the midst of brewing rebellion was teaching: 'That ye resist not evil: but whosoever shall smite thee on thy right cheek, turn to him the other also'? It was Jesus who was teaching, 'But I say unto you, Love your enemies, bless them that curse you, do good to them that hate you, and pray for them that despitefully use you, and persecute you.' Under the circumstances, therefore, those who understood and followed Jesus were certain of meeting violent antagonism from a people that was on the eve of rebellion and disaster." [16] But his statements which compare the condition in Israel with that of the Gentile world

---

[14] Matt. viii. 8-10.
[15] Cf. Matt. xv. 22-28.
[16] V. G. Simkhovitch, *Toward the Understanding of Jesus*, pp. 53, 54.

were the chief cause of the antagonism: "I have not found so great faith, no, not in Israel. And I say unto you, That many shall come from the east and west, and shall sit down with Abraham, and Isaac, and Jacob, in the kingdom of heaven. But the children of the kingdom shall be cast out into outer darkness: there shall be weeping and gnashing of teeth." [17] It was not possible for those who heard this statement to interpret it eschatologically; it meant the Messianic kingdom to them. And there appears to be little ground for believing that Jesus meant anything beyond a spiritually elevated earthly kingdom of Israel. He did mean the Messianic kingdom, and was not that kingdom, however spiritual, to be ruled from Jerusalem? It was the condemnation of Israel and the importance assigned to the Gentiles, which made all the trouble. Was not Israel the chosen people? Was not the Messianic kingdom a kingdom of and for the Jews?

There are moments when Jesus seems to throw all tact and good judgment to the winds by his utter frankness. John's narrative records that in a conflict with the Pharisees Jesus baited them to madness: "They answered and said, Abraham is our father. Jesus said unto them, If ye were Abraham's children, ye would do the works of Abraham. Ye are of your father the devil, and the lusts of your father ye will do. He was a murderer from the beginning, and abode not in the truth, because there is no truth in him. When he speaketh a lie, he speaketh of his own: for he is a liar, and the father of it." [18] One must expect antagonism after using such language. Scarcely less mild is Jesus' dealing with the people of Nazareth: "Ye will surely say unto me . . . whatsoever we have heard done in Capernaum, do also here in thy country. Verily I say unto you, No prophet is accepted in his own country. Many widows were in Israel in the days of Elias, when the heavens were shut six months, when great famine was

---

[17] Matt. viii. 10-12.
[18] John viii. 39, 44.

throughout all the land; But unto none of them was Elias sent, save unto Sarepta, a city of Sidon, unto a woman that was a widow. And many lepers were in Israel in the time of Eliseus the prophet; and none of them was cleansed, saving Naaman the Syrian."[19] His failure to perform miracles in Nazareth proclaimed that even his home town had less faith than the widow of Sidon and Naaman the Syrian. To utter such things in the home of the Zealots who, more than any other sect, held to the belief that Israel was the chosen people, was to court death. Why did Jesus say such things? Perhaps because he knew that the words that had angered would not soon be forgotten; afterward they would be pondered thoughtfully when reason had taken the place of passion.

It is thus clear with what zeal and courage and steadfastness Jesus sought the regeneration of Israel. Nothing can explain this action except a belief on his part that such a spiritual awakening was vitally necessary to the establishment of the kingdom of heaven. Klausner says: "The real necessity was to stir up a great popular movement of penitents and well-doers; thus the kingdom of heaven would be brought still nearer and with it the occasion of Jesus' manifestation as Messiah. If only the people of Galilee and Judea and beyond Jordan would wholly repent and reach the highest level of moral conduct humanly possible, so that a man would love his enemies, forgive transgressors, associate with publicans and sinners, and extend the cheek to the smiter—then would God perform a miracle and the kingdom would be restored to Israel." [20] Klausner of course forgets that repentance, forgiveness, association with publicans and sinners, and extending the cheek to the smiter are precisely the miracle to be expected. Thinkers the world over have always ridiculed this idea, pointing out that such humility would lead to further persecution. Jesus himself said that it would be followed by a season of

---

[19] Luke iv. 23-27.
[20] Joseph Klausner, *Jesus of Nazareth,* p. 403.

tribulation and that, unless the reformation were genuine enough to overcome evil with good, great calamity would afflict the land. But the merit of this way would at last assert itself. Then would come judgment—then the establishment of the kingdom.

Simkhovitch quotes Isaiah's statement of the conditions accompanying the establishment of the Messianic kingdom, and remarks: "Of course, Isaiah's Zion was judging, Jesus' Zion was saving. Still in Isaiah is an indication of Christ's consolation for the children of Israel." [21] It is necessary to ask but one question to dispose of this observation; Who has pictured the Judgment of Israel the more vividly—Jesus or Isaiah? Even if we rule out of consideration Mark ix 43-48 as being a description of the final state of the wicked rather than of the Messianic judgment in Zion, we still have some very grave utterances upon the occasion in question. Matthew [22] uses the phrase five times, "There shall be weeping and gnashing of teeth," and each use undoubtedly refers to the fate of the unfaithful in Israel when Messiah sets up his kingdom. Luke [23] uses the expression once, with the same connotation. The words of Jesus are not always clear as to the time of the judgment referred to—he admits that he does not know just when it will come—but he has no doubt of its coming. In that day repentance and good works will have their weight.

It is precisely the fact that Jesus represents a return to the solemn sense of national sin and its penalties—something the great prophets felt profoundly—which makes him not a destroyer of the law and the prophets but their fulfiller. The religious life of the majority of Israel's leaders had become formal, a matter of observing traditions—a condition which received its warrant from an exegesis which was but a poor attempt toward an adjustment to more modern conditions.

---

[21] V. G. Simkhovitch, *Toward the Understanding of Jesus*, p. 50.
[22] See Matt. viii. 12; xiii. 42, 50; xxii. 13; xxv. 30.
[23] See Luke xiii. 28.

The situation was described by Jesus as being "a saying without doing," "a washing of the outside of the cup and platter while within was all manner of uncleanness," a meticulous observation of small things to the "neglect of the weightier matters of the law," "a making of the law of God of none effect through tradition." It was his hope to put Israel back upon the right road again. In no other way could she gain the faith and the spirit that would save her.

It is quite evident, also, that Jesus represented the most advanced prophetic position. He is not an enemy of the traditions and theological accretions which are true to the loftiest prophetic ideals and which are the logical and legitimate development of the best prophetic opinion. He held that God was both forgiving and judging. He believed in personal immortality, and realized that Israel was made up of individuals. Whatever future was to be secured to the nation was to be wrought out through those who composed the generation then alive. And he did not lose sight of the fact that each individual becomes a factor in creating that moral and spiritual condition which would prevent disaster. His modification, or interpretation, of the moral code was such as to demand the highest personal purity and personal social righteousness. Thus his teachings are personal and practical, rather than general and theoretical. There is no way by which the citizen may shirk his obligation toward the citizenship. The broadsides of his fire were therefore directed, not at an abstraction, the nation, but at classes, persons, sects, and opinions. His method, consequently, represents the prophetic technique of the great prophets, but modernized, sharpened, and tempered into a new and gleaming sword.

Thus the "simple villager," the "meek and lowly Nazarene," the "great dreamer of dreams," and the "wistful, pathetic figure" becomes upon occasion a firebrand, a divider of homes, a creator of turmoil, and a great, courageous fighter who asks no quarter and gives none. To some he may seem to be the most contradictory person who has ever lived, but he presented in his manner the two sides of the divine medal—mercy and judgment. How far the mercy extended may be glimpsed in the forgiveness of the harlot brought into his presence, the healing of the helpless man at Siloam, in the teaching "until seventy times seven," "the good shepherd giveth his life for the sheep," and "God is love." But those who had filled the cup of wrath and remained impenitent found him indignant and unsparing.

Too much weight, therefore, is assigned to the view of a panic-stricken Jesus after the arrest of John the Baptist: he hastened beyond the reach of Herod and spoke in parables to the people that he might continue to teach and at the same time conceal his true character. No doubt Jesus did exercise the proper measures of prudence under the circumstances; but the nature of the end he hoped to accomplish, and the results among a volatile Galilean population that any outright claim of Messiahship would have precipitated, seem to have had the most weight in determining his procedure. As we have already seen, wisdom would have dictated, in any event, the course Jesus pursued. When occasion arose he could make his claims and defy Herod also.

How well Jesus succeeded in concealing his Messiahship from the people may be judged from that report of his ministry which came to the ears of John the Baptist in prison. What John heard did not fully convince him that Jesus was the Messiah; but the healings, the miracles, and certain sayings of the reported teaching made him wonder. Could this man be the Messiah he had foretold? He decided to send his disciples to ask Jesus who he was. The disciples came, witnessed the healings, and heard the preaching. Then Jesus told them to report what they had seen and heard. It may seem to some that Jesus evaded the question. It was the best he could do under the circumstances. Any direct answer would have had hindering consequences. He was compelled to trust to the faithfulness of the messengers in reporting what they had seen and heard, and to the penetration of the Baptist to find the right answer.

Much devout imagination has shocked itself by holding that John "had lost his faith" through "the reaction of confinement upon his vigorous nature." There is no ground for this view. The account given by Luke which presents the Baptist protesting against the need of Jesus to be baptized is greatly weakened by an obvious contradiction in the corresponding account in the gospel of John. John's gospel describes the Baptist as greeting Jesus with the exclamation, "Behold the Lamb of God which taketh away the sins of the world." Four verses later in the same account it is evident that the Baptist could not have known that Jesus was the Messiah until after the baptism, for the sign he was to receive was the descent of the dove. John could not, therefore, have known that Jesus was the Messiah previous to the baptism. The exclamation, as well as the protest recorded by Luke, are thus rendered improbable. And they appear all the more so when it is noted that Mark, an older gospel, omits all reference to any conversation between Jesus and John at the time. The more probable view presents Jesus as coming for baptism like any other candidate and with no suspicion of what awaited him; he was baptized, experienced his call, and went into the wilderness to think it through.

Jesus told the disciples of the Baptist to report to their master that the poor had the gospel preached to them. Since the Messianic nature was not declared, it is apparent that the preaching concerned that manner of life that would save Israel. What did he preach? Much that was already a part of the great body of Jewish belief, as we have already noted. Also the prophetic morality at its highest and best, and freedom from that blind subservience to the ceremonial law which excluded the warmth and reality of the living religious act. It was his chief hope to so revive the life of Israel's religion that it would be in every act a true religious experience. Then by a lofty imitation of God's love and forbearance, the individual would gain that self-mastery which would make him blameless, harmless, and a force for national and Gentile regeneration. The nation thus revived would be free of its prejudices, its hatreds, its desire for victory in battle over Rome, which were so sure to bring about its destruction. By thus gaining the victory over itself it would be strong enough not to be overcome of evil but to overcome evil with good.

This Way, contrary to the opinion of some who have criticised the teachings of Jesus, is not an abandonment of Jewish nationality.[24] A nation does not lose its life when it continues to develop its historical spirit and to pursue the destiny which such a spirit logically implies; when it continues to occupy its homeland and to perpetuate its legitimate institutions, and when it becomes a force which conquers its conquerors and which exalts the life and tone of every nation which it encounters. There is a vast difference between losing the scepter and losing the soul. Is it not the boast of the Jew that his nationality has endured through the centuries though the Jewish citizenship has been scattered throughout the whole world? There are two wonders here: the longevity of Jewish ideals and the world-conquering power of the teachings of Jesus. Who can say that Israel would not have held her homeland and have brought the world in spiritual fee had she wholly accepted that policy of national expediency and that everlasting future which Jesus taught? The two fragments of the divine revelation have persisted, memorializing the observation of the Almighty One: "My word shall not return unto me void; it shall accomplish that whereto I sent it."

Nor should we look upon Judaism, past or present, as gross error condemned and supplanted by Jesus. "The Law and the Prophets continued until John; since then the kingdom of

---

[24] Klausner, *Jesus of Nazareth*, pp. 369-376.

heaven is preached," said Jesus. But please observe that this is only a change in method and only an advance upon the past dispensation; the Law and the Prophets were not revoked. Not "one jot or one tittle of the Law shall pass until all things be fulfilled." "I am not come to destroy the Law and the Prophets. I am not come to destroy, but to fulfill." How thoroughly Jesus drew upon the rich spirit of Judaism to compile his teachings is apparent to any unprejudiced student of Israel's faith. And any comparative study of the Gospel and Judaism will reveal that Jesus gave the right estimate of his position. A religion which makes such notable contributions of its spiritual wealth is not condemned nor supplanted. It is all there in the new position—its spirit, its genius, its visions, its hopes—and more. And if we accept the word of Jesus, "the more" is not something different; it is more of the same thing. And because Israel has possessed such large measure of the truth her faith has not passed. Every man gains for himself only a limited amount of revelation, and can make only a little of that truly his own—truly a part of his religious experience. As a pilgrim and a sojourner in the earth, he takes the little light he has, be he Jew or Christian, and seeks through righteousness that divine approval which will save him to the uttermost. And whoever has gained enough light to seek the Source of Truth reverently and obediently shall not perish in the dark.

But what awful ironies have overtaken us because we have followed in our blindness our blind guides! The Sadducees, the Pharisees, and the Zealots, though as sects they contained many great and noble men of God, failed to supply Israel with that religious force and political sagacity which could have saved her life in the homeland. Jesus, whatever may be said against him as the logical exponent of Israel's religious spirit, was the one man who could have bridged the chasm toward which the nation moved. He was rejected, and the full fruit of a rebellious heart brought destruction. The Gospel of Jesus,

because it had the technique of securing to the individual a
lofty spiritual life, went out and took captive the Gentile
world. But there was no Mount Zion to which the nations
might bring their honor and their glory! All had become
crumbled stone and dust! Then the Gentile world, forgetful
of the fact that Jesus forgave those who crucified him and
controlled by base superstitions and devilish hatred, regarded
the Jew as being under a curse and afflicted him with such
cruelties as to negate the true spirit of the words of Jesus.
Can a sensible man believe for one moment that there was
ever a Jew or a Roman who should have suffered persecution
for the crucifixion of Jesus after the words, "Father, forgive
them, for they know not what they do"? When room was
given to hatred there was incorporated into Christianity that
element of contradiction which has cursed us throughout all
the centuries. And what of the Jew in the meantime? Judaism
possessed such a volume of the truth which Jesus taught that
she has been able to go on adjusting, modernizing, advancing,
until within herself, in both spirituality and ethics, she is
nearer the spirit of Jesus than many Christian bodies and
Christian leaders. According to the standards of Jesus there is
not the least doubt that in the sight of a righteous God some
Christians are more accursed than some of the Jews.

The ministry of Jesus was also an attempt to bring men
closer to God through a better understanding of His nature.
God was a God of judgment, but he was also a God who was
slow to anger. The sinner was not too quickly hailed into
judgment; he was given an opportunity to repent. And meanwhile God continued to bestow upon him His blessing. God's
sun rose upon him just as it did upon the just; and rain came
upon him just as it did upon the good. Therefore the individual must imitate God and not be too hasty with his foe;
time must be given for repentance. And meanwhile the foe
must be loved, though he resort to further persecutions.

Such teaching has always been a puzzle to many Christians

and Jews alike. It seems to advocate that which is divinely and humanly impossible. Klausner says: "Jesus tells his disciples that they must love their enemies as well as their friends, since their 'Father in heaven makes his sun to rise upon the evil and the good, and sends his rain upon the righteous and the ungodly.' Here is no case of Jesus justifying himself against the Pharisees who blamed him for eating with publicans and sinners—'they that are whole need not a physician but they that are sick'; the 'sick' are no longer under consideration; both publicans and sinners are 'whole' in the sight of God: sinners and non-sinners, evil and good, ungodly and righteous, all alike are of the same worth in God's sight. It follows, therefore, that God is not *absolute righteousness*, but *the good* before whom is no evil ('There is none *good* save one, and he —is God'). He is not the God of justice, in spite of his Day of Judgment: in other words, *he is not the God of History*." [25]

We imagine that Jesus, who "was the most Jewish of all Jews" kept very close to the historical Jewish conception of God. He had read that God was "merciful and gracious, slow to anger, and plenteous in mercy." [26] And even if he checked this statement by a comparison with Psalm lxxxvi ("plenteous in mercy unto all them that call upon him"), he knew there were many who sinned without knowing it. And he was wise enough to see that somewhere an absolute justice and a great mercy must come face to face. Is it possible that even he did not see that it is the very nature of mercy to give relief against the recognized rights of justice? Did he suppose that mercy was only that which one may lawfully claim—that mercy was after all nothing but justice? Did he then try to replace Israel's God with One who *would be merciful*, One "which Israel could not accept"? Surely not! Klausner has only momentarily descended from the usual excellency

---

[25] Klausner, *Jesus of Nazareth*, p. 379.
[26] Psalms ciii. 8.

of his thinking. Jesus is presenting the God of History, trying
to reconcile the nation to Him before it comes to disaster.

To reconcile a nation to a righteous God involves on the
part of the individuals of that nation such repentance and
such personal righteousness that God may forgive them and
preserve them. To bring this condition about is the object of
Jesus in all his labors and teachings. He believed—in his consciousness of himself as the Messiah, he knew—that his vision
of personal and national redemption was the only way of
safety. If the citizenship, and therefore the nation, would live,
they must "take his yoke upon them, and learn of him." The
heavy laden and the wearied, made so by oppression, would
be able to find in his Way a rest for their souls.

But the first step was to come to him. For the benefit of the
slow of understanding he dramatized his position in the
scheme of life in true Semitic fashion: "I am the door of the
sheep. I am the way, the truth, and the life. I am the light of
the world." There was no coming into the approval of God
but by him. "By me if any man enter in," the blessing of salvation was conditioned. To continue to follow after Pharisee,
Sadducee, and Zealot leaders was to lose everything. "All that
ever came before me," said Jesus, "are thieves and robbers.
. . . The thief cometh not, but for to steal, and to kill, and to
destroy." This may be the overemphasis of the Oriental manner, but it is true in a sense—such leadership would end in
death and destruction. Then there were hirelings, those high-
priests appointed by Rome, who cared not for the sheep and
who were anxious but for one thing—their own lives. When
they saw the wolf coming, they would flee, leaving the sheep
to the wolf who would kill and scatter the sheep. A little
stretching of this figure to embrace the nations and the fate of
Israel will reveal a surprising correspondence with historic
fact; some will say too much so to have been spoken by Jesus.
But there is too much minimizing of the genius of Jesus; if

let alone, such critics would make him too small to have framed any sort of gospel whatever. We must realize that the Nazarene saw the various factors that were making the history of his time—that he saw them with a clearness that made him a man "who never smiled."

The next step was to do the works of righteousness, to bring forth the fruits of the kingdom into which one had been initiated. "By their fruits shall ye know them," said Jesus. When the day of sifting comes, "the tares shall be separated from the wheat," the worthless taken in the net "shall be cast away," and the tree that has continued to fail to bear figs shall be dug up, root and branch, and be thrown out of the vineyard. What was the fruit of this kingdom? The fruit of spirituality? Yes. But a spirituality which gets down to earth and which deals with every human need. "I was an hungered, and ye gave me meat: I was thirsty, and ye gave me drink: I was a stranger, and ye took me in: Naked, and ye clothed me: I was sick, and ye visited me: I was in prison, and ye came unto me." [27] Jesus is a Jew. His new spiritual state touches the whole of life. Whether we interpret the above passage eschatologically or after the Messianism current in the time of Jesus, the faith will show its presence in the life a man lives. This represents the great difference between Jesus and the majority of the Pharisees. They said, but they did not perform. His followers must perform; they must bear fruit.

It is at this point that we discover an explanation of Jesus' attitude to the ceremonial law. We find him both condemning it and faithfully observing it. Why this seeming contradiction? He has seen how easy it is to make ceremonial righteousness the whole of religion—to substitute ceremonial performance for social doing. He has seen the moral unrighteousness of the ceremonially perfect. The ceremonial law is fulfilled to the letter, but the heart is still evil and the welfare of the

---

[27] Matt. xxv. 35-36.

poor and the unfortunate is neglected. He is not, however, antagonistic to the ceremonial law as such, and continues to observe it to the last day of his life. But he will not permit it to make him a slave or to delude him into a neglect of moral and social obligations. When he is reproached for any failure to observe it strictly, he seems to be defiant. Again we behold how surely Jesus grasps the range of the principles of Judaic thought. The ceremonial law is important and must be observed, but the moral law must not be neglected. To do so will thwart the whole purpose of Israel's religion by removing it from actual contact with life. Israel's religion is Israel's life, and nothing, not even the most sacred laws and traditions, can be allowed to interfere. When two principles of law stand face to face, it is the life of Israel's people which must be served. Therefore he heals on the Sabbath, permits his disciples to eat with unwashed hands, allows them to rub the wheat in their hands on the Sabbath. Israel must live, and the ceremonial law was made only to help her live. To demonstrate his attitude Jesus asserts the liberty he would recommend. It is the only way to escape from the bondage to ceremony and to secure again a religion that is life and a life that is true religion.

There must, then, be such a social performance as will put the life of the individual in accord with the nature and will of God. Jesus invited those who heard him to come to him that they might learn what that manner of life was. His consciousness of himself as the Messiah made him also conscious that his was an approved life. He said, "I seek not mine own will, but the will of my Father which sent me." [28] "And he that sent me is with me: the Father hath not left me alone; for I do always those things which please him." [29] Therefore, Jesus reasoned that between him and God there was such perfect agreement in interest, will, and works that they two

[28] John v. 30.
[29] John viii. 29.

were as one at all these points. When he was asked, "How long wilt thou keep us in doubt? If thou be the Christ, tell us plainly," he answered, "The works that I do in my Father's name, they bear witness of me. . . . I and my Father are one." [30] Still further upon the same point, he is reported to have said in prayer: "That they all may be one; as thou, Father, art in me, and I in thee, that they also may be in us: that the world may believe that thou hast sent me. And the glory which thou gavest me I have given them; that they may be one, even as we are one: I in them, and thou in me, that they may be made perfect in one." [31] It was this community of interest, will, and works between man and God which constituted the great ideal of Jesus. It was to be expressed in man's dealings with men, and from man to man, until the spirit of such a life should overcome the world.

When Jesus began to preach the Gospel which we have thus briefly outlined, he gathered about him twelve disciples, or learners, to whom he could expound his doctrine more intimately and in greater detail. He selected them from the trades that they might not be so thoroughly grounded in the current interpretations of Israel's religion as to view all he said in the light of their former learning. He could not go to the Scribes, for the Scribe would inevitably bring out his treasure of things old as well as new. There would be an admixture of new and old ideas and a division of loyalty which would be fatal to the future of the Gospel. This new wine could not be poured into old bottles, else the bottles would be broken and the wine spilled. Nor could Israel be saved by putting new patches upon the present garment of Judaism. He must begin with men unspoiled by past teaching that his ideas might be received in their purity. Twelve Nicodemuses would have been a woeful mistake.

The plan had its discouraging features. Often it appeared

[30] John x. 24, 25, 30.
[31] John xvii. 21-23.

that the men selected were both too unimaginative and too stupid to grasp any of the teaching. Nor were they altogether untaught; they had heard and had accepted the outstanding articles of Jewish faith—had accepted them with a literalness that was appalling. And how they held on to their notion of Judaism! Jesus would describe the kingdom of heaven as leaven, and then warn them to beware of the leaven of the Scribes and Pharisees. They would respond by saying among themselves, "It is because we have brought no bread on this journey." All during his ministry he struggled with their obtuseness and lack of faith. And on the last night of his life, after he had presented over and over the fact that he was revealing God by his teaching and manner of life, Philip said, perhaps challengingly, "Show us the Father, and it sufficeth us." There is the sorrow of infinite and long-taxed patience in the reply of Jesus, "Have I been so long time with you, and yet thou hast not known me, Philip?" One wonders how the Gospel could with reason be entrusted to such men; and yet, they were able to receive it and to communicate it, in spirit at least, to others.

To add to the difficulties of Jesus there was the constant heckling of Scribes and Pharisees. The questions asked may often have been honest ones, but Jesus knew that the majority of men of the two classes were too bigoted and self-important to receive his message with any degree of real intelligence. It was rare for him to find one who would actually think with him. The lawyer who asked, "Who is my neighbor?" thought with him, though rather unwillingly. It was the learned Scribe in Jerusalem who was great and sincere enough to be fair. The majority of questioners sought to discomfit him, to cause him to lose influence with the multitudes, and to entangle him to his hurt. They came near enough to the accomplishment of their purpose to prove both annoying and dangerous to him.

As the preaching continued and opposition grew, Jesus began to warn those who heard him of the peril of rejecting his teaching. He was seeking to bring to them the privilege of having a place in the Messianic kingdom, and they were losing their chance of life either through paltry excuse or through a desire not to lose caste. Regarding the first cause of his rejection he spoke the parable of The Supper and described the fate of those who refused to come: "Then the master of the house being angry said to his servant, Go out quickly into the streets and lanes of the city, and bring in hither the poor, and the maimed, and the halt, and the blind. The servant said, Lord, it is done as thou hast commanded, and yet there is room. And the lord said unto the servant, Go out into the highways and hedges, and compel them to come in, that my house may be filled. For I say unto you, That none of those men which were bidden shall taste my supper." [32] David Smith observes, "The denizens of street and alley were Israel's outcasts, the tax-gatherers and sinners who made so ready a response to Jesus; and those outside the city, who wandered on the highways and sheltered beneath the hedges—who were they but the Gentiles?" [33] Thus those who made excuse were never to enter Messiah's kingdom. Even the Gentiles would be better off. Regarding the second reason for rejecting him, Jesus said, "He who putteth his hand to the plough and looketh back is unfit for the kingdom of heaven." [34] "Whosoever he be of you that forsaketh not all that he hath, he cannot be my disciple." [35]

The opposition continued to increase, and Jesus did nothing to still the storm that was rising against him. Indeed nothing could be done, except give up his ministry or change the nature of his teaching. Both possibilities were out of the question for him. God had called him to be Messiah, and the king-

[32] Luke xiv. 21-24.
[33] David Smith, *In the Days of His Flesh*, p. 308.
[34] Luke ix. 62.
[35] Luke xiv. 33; cf. also Luke xiv. 25-32.

dom of heaven could not be established without a gospel that
would regenerate Israel. He watched the growing animosity
animosity and knew its mind perfectly.

Whether or not Jesus knew of the fate that awaited him before his journey to Golgotha is now a matter about which
writers differ. Some say that he knew of it from the first, and
gathered about him his disciples and trained them to carry on
his work after him. Others say that it was gradually borne
in upon him that he must die. At first he had believed that
he would become the Messianic King of popular faith and
would sit upon the throne in Jerusalem. Then he realized that
he must die; he foretold his death frequently, and realizing
that, since his word was rejected, Israel would be destroyed, he
accepted the cross, believing that God would send him to
earth again when the time had been fulfilled. And there are
yet others who declare that he never believed that he would
be crucified. He permitted himself to be arrested, believing
that he could call twelve legions of angels to set him free at
any moment he chose. To Pilate, who intimidated him, saying,
"Speakest thou not unto me? Knowest thou not that I have
power to crucify thee, and have power to release thee?" he
answered, "Thou couldst have no power against me, except
it were given thee from above." [36] Not until he knew that he
was at the door of death did he lose hope that God would
save him. Then he cried out, "My God, my God, why hast
thou forsaken me!"

We shall not undertake to say which of the above views will
appeal to the majority of people. One thing seems certain,
no matter which view we accept: Jesus knew what his enemies
were about. He knew the law in Israel against blasphemy;
and he knew quite well the manner in which both justice
and injustice were administered. Prophets had been slain in
Israel before his day. In penitence the later generations had

---

[36] John xix. 10, 11.

erected costly tombs to these ill-fated leaders, but the stonings continued for all that. Whether or not he knew that he would die, he did know that, if the occasion ever arose, he would not flinch from the worst. He declared that he was the good shepherd, and he added, "The good shepherd giveth his life for the sheep." That was his answer to the threat he saw in the increasing hostility toward him.

The more we study the mind and the method of Jesus the more we are forced to admit that, at the last at least, he knew no illusions about either the actual results of his ministry or the attitude of the rulers toward him. A mind which reveals such power of penetration into the nature of its time, such unerring judgment upon the worth and the weakness of current Judaism, such grasp of the nuances of Hebrew thought, such appreciation of the nation's peril, and such wisdom in recommending a saving policy, cannot long be deceived in such matters. Such political understanding could not possibly reside in the same mind with the folly and stupidity which is often attributed to Him. He knew! We are thus shut up to two possible conclusions: either Jesus believed that the Father would deliver him from his enemies, or he planned his fate, well knowing what it would be. A question may help us to choose the right view: Is it reasonable to suppose that Jesus believed that he could not die? There is much evidence which contributes toward a negative answer. He took care to avoid unnecessary danger—until his time should be accomplished. He walked the streets of Jerusalem on the way to Golgotha knowing that he was on the way to his death. And there are a number of his statements which indicate that he went to Jerusalem with the full knowledge that death awaited him. Such considerations go far toward disposing of the question, Did Jesus believe that the Father would save him and reveal him as the Messiah? The very nature of the Gospel is also against such a possibility. Israel must be regenerated, and Jesus by actual experience knew that no immediate revelation

of his true character could contribute to that end. Furthermore, he saw clearly that no intervention from heaven would
help: "If they hear not Moses and the prophets, neither will
they be persuaded, though one rose from the dead." [37] There
is perhaps but one point to be decided: When did Jesus know
that he must die?

From his own statements, after he knew what his fate was
to be, it seems somewhat unlikely that he knew from the
first. Of the times and the seasons no man knew, not even
the angels of heaven; only God knew. The question arises
as to whether he felt more sure of the times and the seasons
in the early days of his ministry than he did after actual experience with the Gospel. Apparently he did. We hear that he
said, "The time is fulfilled—the kingdom of heaven is at
hand." It was only later that he saw with utter clarity that
Israel could not be saved from destruction: "O Jerusalem,
Jerusalem, . . . how oft would I have gathered you together
as a hen gathereth her chicks under her wings and ye would
not! O that thou hadst known in this thy day the things that
belong to thy peace, but now they are hid from thine eyes!
And they shall dig a ditch about thee—and lay thee even
with the ground." The whole story of the changing purposes
of Jesus is in these exclamations. At first, and often, he would
have saved Israel from destruction by Roman arms; now he
knew that she could not be saved. A regenerated and saved
Israel would have modified the situation somewhat—the
Messianic kingdom would have been an accomplished fact.
Now that it had not been realized, other measures must be
taken.

As we have already seen, Jesus was well aware that death
might overtake him—the most ardent doubter must admit as
much. And we may be sure that as Jesus reviewed this possibility it would suggest two alternative views of Messianic

---

[37] Luke xvi. 31.

consummation—one, if he succeeded; another, if he failed. In the event that he failed to regenerate Israel and save her, how would the Gospel be affected? Not at all. There could be no Messianic kingdom without the regeneration of a part of Israel. The kingdom was already here, in germ, of course; Jesus said, "The kingdom of heaven is among you." But it had yet to grow, like the leaven, like the grain of mustard seed, until it embraced a considerable portion of the peoples of the Mediterranean world. How would his methods be modified by the admitted possibility of his death? He must leave the Gospel as a witness of the way to regeneration and life. Whatever his fate might be, he must continue to preach the Way; and if such preaching brought him to death—he could die. And he must prepare his disciples to carry on the work effectively after his death.

There is much to indicate that Jesus had been working, for some time before he entered Jerusalem, on the presumption that he might be put to death—far more than there is to support the view that death came to him as a surprise. And always, no matter what view of Messianic consummation he may have held, it is clear that he was conscious of himself as being the Messiah. There is no more sure fact about him than this.

It is entirely possible that his conviction that he must die grew out of the circumstances attending his labors. The slow progress he made, the knowledge of an utter lack of any clear understanding of his message on the part of the people, the opposition to him which began early and continued to increase, the growing dangers resulting from his conflict with Scribe and Pharisee, the sure knowledge that he could not trim his truth to suit any person or faction—all this could not help but bring him face to face with the possibility of his being put to death. And such a mind as Jesus possessed—one with unusual powers of political vision—would be able to read the meaning of such facts in the day of their first appearing; in other words, amazingly early.

But how would he be able to reconcile his possible fate with his consciousness of himself as the Messiah? There is a possible clue to the line of thought Jesus followed in solving this problem. In the synagogue at Nazareth he read from the Deutero-Isaiah a passage of Scripture which he said he was fulfilling at that moment. This passage undoubtedly refers to the Suffering Servant of Jehovah who is to become the light of the world. To follow this assumption which he made at Nazareth through all that is recorded of the Suffering Servant is to find enough materials to sketch the whole career of Jesus. In the fifty-third chapter of Isaiah we will find, first, a very accurate description of the opposition the Servant must endure—something Jesus had already experienced and which he knew would very probably end in but one way; second, a description of the ultimate failure and death of the Servant. In thus taking the prophecy of the Deutero-Isaiah to be Messianic, Jesus could not help but conclude that his death was in some manner a part of the procedure leading toward Messianic consummation.

But one must be very careful not to misconstrue the mind of Jesus at this point. His faith is Jewish, and so is his nature —his mind, his habits of thought, his whole view of life. There is not the least doubt that he knows what the prophet in Babylon meant by such language—knew it as well as any one else of that day, or of any day to come. If he attached only a predictive intent to the prophet's words, he was the dreamer some have declared him to be. But Jesus' mind is a new and free mind in Israel, for all its racial and national characteristics—so new that very few Jews of any time have been willing to follow him to his conclusions. The clarity with which he sees a situation will prevent him from lapsing into literalness and into that sense of fatalism and mystery with which so many approach the interpretation of prophecy. The manner in which Jesus toys with the predicament of such minds in their perplexity over the Scripture, "The Lord said unto my lord sit thou on my right hand until I make thine enemies the foot-stool of thy feet" is enough to show how superior he is to such intellectual slavery.

His use, therefore, of the Suffering Servant is the employ-ment of a device which he finds ready to hand, and which, because of its parallelism with the function he is to perform, will help the people to see what he is about. The fifty-third chapter is but a continuation of the parallelism. It is not that the prophet has seen Jesus Christ, or that he is describing the career of a man in history; he is describing Israel, as Jesus well knew. But the Nazarene sees that there is a principle of life concealed in the Deutero-Isaiah's words: Social regenera-tion and world salvation, whether undertaken by a nation or a man, are not accomplished without suffering and sacrifice of some kind. And from his intimate knowledge of his time Jesus knows the road over which he must travel if he would bring about a true state of righteousness in Israel and the Gentile world. He is the fulfiller only because, as the teacher of that which he knows will save Judaism, he must repeat the history, in some measure, of all true servants of God. It was, therefore, his experience with the actual historical sit-uation, and his supreme accuracy in seeing how it would eventually react toward him, which revealed to him how com-pletely the principle of regeneration through sacrifice would repeat its eternal story in his career. It is the usual thing to conclude from such evidence of his deep understanding that he was divine. We must, at the very least, admit, once again, that he was not the person to be pitied because of any lack of discernment.

Theologians have built up an elaborate magic of regenera-tion about his words which refer to this vision of his fate. At times it would seem that they regard his very blood as being contained somewhere in a spiritual reservoir that sinners plunged into its crimson flood may lose their guilty stains. That such legalism and bad poetry could be imposed upon Jesus, whose every word approaches poetry at its best, and who was the most pronounced foe of legalism, is one of the most ironical facts of human history. Jesus did die in line of duty. No doubt, he realized that he was dying because of and for the sins of men. But only as the Suffering Servant died—as the witness to testify to the glory of God. Not by blood nor by wounds, primarily, but by his witness, his people and the nations were to be healed. It was a healing come from more accurate knowledge of God. It was the truth which was to make men free—truth about God.

And that truth could be put in a word: God is love. Such a God does not need to be placated by some one's death. It is man who exacts it of his fellow man. In Israel the hatred of Rome, the desire to be revenged, in fact the whole spirit of bitterness, submerged and destroyed the true mission of Israel. How could the people witness of God when their actions proclaimed them to be a revengeful and irrational people? How could they even endure? God, who is love, can be given a proper witness only by those who understand and who imitate His nature. The true Israel, therefore, the Suffering Servant, is as a sheep led to the slaughter. By its very meekness and inoffensiveness in the midst of its afflictions, it shall redeem the reputation of its race and thus secure the nation's life. The teacher with such ideas in his head cannot very well avoid death if his enemies seek to exact it. And Jesus saw from the very turbulence and bitterness of his nation that sooner or later misunderstanding of his words would bring the charge of blasphemy; for Messianism, in his thought, was inseparable from the future of the true Israel (the Suffering Servant). He was the spokesman for that true Israel, an Israel which, by its gentleness under affliction, would be the true revealer of its God. He was called to found the Israel that Isaiah of Babylon saw.

Some such interpretation of the actual Jesus must be accepted. Gospels of redemption do not fall upon a time like meteorites from the skies. They are the logical outcome of past wisdom—the needs of the time met by the nation's genius, the old creed made triumphant over the times by some constructive and politically penetrative soul. And the man who sees the vision of redemption is, in some sense, always the product of his age and generation, not its slave, else there will be no true gospel; but of the time, else his word will be only impractical and unrelated speculation. Such a man is splendidly alive to his time. He drinks at its best fountains. He has a mind to which neither man nor the events of the day are opaque; he has moral perception, of a grade which may be styled genius; and he has a constructive imagination which puts together the capacities of his people in the possible wonder of to-morrow. He seldom produces the full spiritual revolution he has visioned. Life is too short; social inertia is too unyielding; and the vision he declares contrasts too greatly with the actual to seem either logical or engrossingly desirable. But the redeemer's vision is, for all that, the best fruit of a generation made into a picture of the epoch to come. Jesus took the genius, the spirituality, the skeleton of prophetic insight, and the accumulated knowledge of God, which were the heart of true Judaism, to construct both a nation and a people. And in the sense that he drew the tangents which mapped the future correctly, he defined the way of humanity for all ages and made his gospel timeless.

The sayings attributed to him, and which have the authentic ring of his personality, prove over and over that he possessed the intelligence and the sanity of outlook which would compel him to find the right answer to the trend of national feeling. And when he had once seen the Pharisaic reaction to his teaching, he would see also the valley of the shadow. View him as we will, make him divine or leave him entirely human, he is capable of seeing the possibility of death long enough in advance of the actual event itself for it to cast its spell over nearly his entire ministry. And there need be no supernatural prearrangement in the case; the quality of his mind is enough to account for any prediction of his death he may have made.

Later developments served more and more to confirm his earlier surmisings. The constant spyings of the Pharisees, the nature and manner of their questionings, would reveal to him all their heart as clearly as if they had told him outright. And after the events attending his teaching in Solomon's porch during Passion Week there would not be the slightest question in his mind as to what would happen if he came into their hands. Of what avail was it for them to affect surprise and make denial when he told them frankly what was in their mind? "Thou hast a devil," they said; "who is seeking to put you to death?" But they knew that he was not deceived, and they were the more enraged against him.

Thus under the shadow of this menace he went from place to place preaching his gospel of redemption. When idle multitudes incapable of quickly appreciating his message thronged him, he moved on; when immediate danger threatened to terminate his labors, he departed. And when his work was done he went up to Jerusalem, knowing that it would probably be his last attendance at the Feast. From his understanding of men we may be sure that he was aware of the source of his greatest danger. He may not have known previous to his entry into Jerusalem that Judas was a dangerous man, but before the week was over he knew that the thief was also planning treason. We are not told what specific thing Judas did to indicate what he contemplated doing, but he did or said something to reveal his thoughts.

Just how much of the impending death was introduced during the Last Supper we very probably do not know. We know that it was a very sad occasion for Jesus, for, after the departure of Judas, he knew that he was in grave danger. It is not without reason that some writers declare that Jesus did not invite his disciples to "eat of his flesh and drink of his blood." If the disciples had not been revolted, they would have been too overcome with sorrow to have complied. But the conduct of Judas would be a fresh grief to Jesus and would serve to remind him of how much he had suffered for "this cause." Therefore, when he came to break the Bread of Affliction he would no doubt say something by way of personal application to himself. And in like manner he would give to the cup a symbolic meaning—probably just what we have. It was the cup of the new witness, the new word of life. The solemnity of this meal, the symbolic reference to the bread and wine, and the injunction to remember him upon all future observances of the Passover would insure its perpetuation as a memorial in the early church. Those who are accustomed to assign everything to a later age must admit that enough was said to serve as a foundation for all that a later time may have added.

When Judas did not return to the upper room, and was not found to be waiting in the garden, Jesus knew that his premonitions of danger were well founded. In the agony of the sudden certainty of his situation he left the disciples and went forward a little distance to pray. What infinite anguish was in his heart! What a conflict of flaming thought deluged his mind! It may well have caused the perspiration to run in great beads from his brow, as blood runs from a wound. And would he not pray at first, in the sudden realization that all that he had so long anticipated had at last come to pass, "Father, if it be thy will let this cup pass from me"? But during the second prayer he arrived at resignation, "Nevertheless, not my will but thine be done."

The gospel record of the words of Jesus at the time of his arrest are just what we should expect of men who sleep and wake in turn. Jesus came back from his season of prayer each time to speak to them; after the first, to rebuke them gently; after the second, to say, "Sleep on now and take your rest."

Later,—we cannot know how much time passed while he kept his lonely vigil,—he heard the soldiers coming. He hurried to his disciples and awoke them, saying, "Behold, the hour is at hand! The son of man is betrayed! Rise! Let us be going! Behold he is at hand that doth betray me!" There is panic here,—stamped upon every sentence. Was it the case that even as he spoke Judas came forward to salute him? Can that explain the arrested flight which appears imminent? That Jesus was speaking when Judas approached him there is no reason to doubt, but much had happened between that first moment of panic and that moment in which he responded to Judas and his companions with such perfect poise. What was it? There is one saying of Jesus, doubtless authentic, which fits well this terrific interval, "Now is my soul troubled, and what shall I say, 'Father deliver me from this hour'? But for this cause came I unto this hour. Father glorify thy name!" At any rate, he regained his composure between the time he awakened the disciples and the arrival of the traitor.

The trial of Jesus took place almost immediately and was in accord with the legal procedure of the time. The Sanhedrin had not its ancient power. In fact, it could not really try capital cases. Where the penalty of death was involved only a preliminary hearing could be conducted by the Jews. The findings of the Sanhedrin were reported to the procurator together with recommendations for punishment, but the procurator could ignore the findings and the recommendations and proceed to try the case as if nothing had happened previously. It is true that according to Roman law Jesus was not "worthy of death," but it is equally true that his language in the Sanhedrin, as understood by the court, merited the death sentence according to Jewish law. Pilate simply chose in this case to carry out the recommendations of the Sanhedrin—something he had a right to do according to the arrangement between Rome and Judea. Those who dwell upon the gross illegality of the procedure are either ignorant of the actual historical situation or are controlled by a feeling of anti-Semitism—often, perhaps, by both.

Another argument against intentional illegality is Jesus' evident expectation that he would be put to death. The charges against him were not substantiated by the witnesses called, and it was not until he uttered his own condemnation that anything worthy of death was found in him. Jesus knew the law, and knew well enough in what light his words would be construed even before he uttered them. How could their interpretation by the court be either a surprise to him or a ground for complaint? His statement to the women in the street who stood weeping while he passed to his death, "If they do such things in the green tree, what will they do in the dry?" is but a protest against the spiritual blindness of his generation. As to the trial, he knew that it had been all too legal.

Jesus paid the supreme price for "the cause." And even in death he was still in his own mind the Messiah, still the soul of the Suffering Servant of God. As he observed the several acts attending his execution another parallelism with Scripture came to mind. Like the Psalmist who suffered to declare the truth that "all the ends of the world should remember and turn unto the Lord," he also was suffering. Here on the cross he was a reproach; he was despised by the people; and his hands and his feet had been pierced. In the very words of the man who had preceded him in travail for "the cause" Jesus cried out, "My God, my God, why hast thou forsaken me?"

There are many writers who regard this utterance as an evidence of the spiritual anguish Jesus suffered when he realized that God had deserted him. A few, Klausner [38] among them, seem to think it the expression of the bitterness Jesus felt when he knew that all was lost. Others think that it came out of the darkness and despair which God permitted him to feel

---

[38] Klausner, *Jesus of Nazareth*, pp. 353-354.

that he might be the savior of the ungodly.[39] Both views
probably arise from the long-prevailing custom which takes
Scripture without reference to its setting. It was precisely the
setting that recalled the quotation to Jesus. While the parallel
between the Psalmist's words and the actual events attending
the crucifixion was perhaps not as complete as the Synoptics
have made it, there was enough correspondence to provide the
association. Would Jesus miss the high point in the Psalm,
the purpose of the suffering? It would seem extremely unlikely.

As we know, he regarded himself as doing the work of a
Suffering Servant, not the Suffering Servant of the Deutero-
Isaiah; he knew that that Servant was Israel. He has seen
both the principle which underlies the regeneration of a nation and the hand of God as the ground of the principle. Thus
his mind, always swift as light, and now racing under the
quickening of death, would scarcely fail to see that God "hath
not despised the afflictions of the afflicted." Neither would it
miss the whole implication of the Psalm: when the afflicted
cry, God hears; and, Suffering achieves lasting good toward
both the sufferer and the cause for which he suffers. It is easier
to prove a triumphant spirit from this cry of Jesus than a
despairing and embittered one. The work God gave him to
do has been done: "A seed shall serve him; it shall be accounted to the Lord for a generation. They shall come and
declare his righteousness unto a people that shall be born."
And the price has been paid to the full. Indeed, "It is finished!"

It was contrary to the Jewish law to permit the body of one
who had been crucified to remain all night upon the cross.
Great haste was therefore necessary in disposing of the dead
in this case, for at sundown the Sabbath would begin. An
order was given that the legs of the sufferers should be
broken that death might be hastened. Just before sundown

---

[39] David Smith, *In the Days of His Flesh*, pp. 501-502.

the lifeless bodies would be taken down and cast into a pit. But when those who came to carry out the order approached Jesus, they found that he was already apparently dead. They made sure by thrusting a spear into his side. In the meantime, Joseph of Arimathea had asked Pilate for the body of Jesus. As soon as the procurator was assured by the centurion that Jesus was dead, the request was granted. The body was then taken down from the cross, wrapped in grave-clothes, and placed in a tomb in a nearby garden.

Three days later there was great rejoicing among the disciples, for they had passed through an experience that convinced them that Jesus was alive, that he had risen from the dead. What did they see? We must admit that they saw him in some manner—in a form that was for them positive evidence that he was alive. They knew that he had been crucified and that every precaution had been taken by the authorities to make sure that he was dead. They did not expect him to rise from the dead. They were in despair, for he whom they hoped would establish the kingdom was dead. Then suddenly the feeling of defeat gave way to triumph and a joyful declaration of the good news. Nothing short of seeing Jesus could have produced this change in them. We are told that the disciples saw him, but did not know him until he gave them a token to indicate his identity. Then he disappeared from their sight. All this is puzzling until we read Paul's account of his own meeting with Jesus. He tells us that he saw Jesus in the same manner that Peter saw him. Thus we have a fairly correct idea of the character of the resurrection experience. The "appearances" were described as visions.[40]

In that age the "appearances" were the center of Christianity. Without them there could have been no church. To those who are dominated by a concreteness of thought which brands as "unreal" everything which does not express itself in material

---

[40] See Smith, *In the Days of His Flesh*, pp. 508-518; also Introduction, pp. xxxviii-xlii.

form, the resurrection experience will be either a stumbling-block or a rock of offense. But back of all Oriental thought there is an idealistic realm no less real than the material one which we behold with the actual senses. Our logic implies the existence of this unseen land and our intuitions now and then seize upon its substance and fact. But in our superficial sense-interests we have burrowed so deeply into the actual earth that we are inclined to question the existence of anything which will not yield itself readily to chemical analysis and mathematical formulae. A careful reading of Paul's words will give us a clue to the nature of the facts which compose the evidence in this case: "We look not at the things which are seen . . . for the things which are seen are temporal; but the things which are unseen are eternal." In this realm beyond the material and visible, which may be reached in the prophetic state and by quickened intuitions, one arrives at the door of the eternal country and upon occasion beholds the risen Lord. This is not a region of unreality, but the highest reality we can know—it is the goal of all faith and philosophy—the being that becomes for a brief moment the visible world and reverts quickly to its original and invisible state. The "vision" of such things is a glimpse of the wisdom of God, the chief substance of that certainty which has supported all our very greatest Christians.

Finally, no theory of the resurrection "appearances" can ignore the fact that the whole trend of events in the life of Jesus represents a procedure carried out with the consciousness that death was to be the end of the road. If the cause was not to end in defeat and pass to oblivion, some provision must be made for this event and its consequences. The reported words of our Lord bearing upon his fate look beyond death and fit well into the resurrection experiences of the disciples. He was going away, but he would come again; he would not leave them comfortless. And when he had returned their joy would be full. Thus, whatever view we take of the nature and source of the resurrection "visions," there is the highest probability that Jesus made beforehand every possible preparation for them. They are the logical consummation of his whole conduct, his gospel in its complete form, and his words of comfort previous to his arrest and trial. At the same time, they are the only adequate explanation of the profound triumph which made the Christian church—the feeling that Jesus had opened a door to the life above Time and Sense and that those who followed his Way possessed the highest meaning life can know. In other words, the believer took on the image of the heavenly state which he beheld, and passed beyond the power of death.

All this is in complete accord with the highly spiritual nature of the Messianic kingdom. It was in the world, but not of this world. It was just beyond the physical senses, yet all around the company of believers and even among them. It was a kingdom of heaven, a kingdom come down from heaven, and a kingdom having the substance and aspect of spiritual or heavenly things. Israel had the faith and religious method which could most quickly apprehend it in its true character; but to achieve it, Israel must be regenerated. Then by the few redeemed or spiritually regenerated ones, the world could be approached and brought into subjection. This is not something to be gained by the rational processes of the Greek or the legalism of the Jew. It is a mystic experience achieved by a new nature to which the kingdom may be revealed. In that kingdom, be it on earth or in the skies, or in that new region where earth and heaven meet, the company of the believers find their Lord and receive the knowledge of God.

The problem of the resurrection is therefore, not a problem to be solved on the ground of materialism but on spiritual grounds and by an investigation of the whole realm of mysticism and idealism. In this house are many mansions and they are prepared for those who are worthy to enter them.

This is that lofty impractical dream of the Nazarene, but impractical only because we have not the faith to practice it—a dream which has furnished the driving power of that faith which has achieved every great epoch in Christian history. Herein consists that miracle of wisdom which has confounded the wise of all ages and put to naught the greatest powers of the material and visible world. To bring this life and immortality to light Jesus taught and suffered death on Calvary. Without him this door of hope would not have been opened to a fearful and hungering world.

"But what of the mystics who before Jesus found this religion?" asks some one. We may give in reply the answer of Jesus, "I am the way, the truth, and the life." After all, there is a divine law controlling all human experience, a proper and an improper way of reacting to every item of the universe. Jesus marked out the true meaning and function of all our knowledge and experience—love toward God and toward man. The most exalted and heavenly moment in the life of any person must find its earthly meaning in that immortal company, the Suffering Servant of God. This is that way and truth and life which overcomes and saves the world. Come and see for yourself the worth of this answer.

CHAPTER X

SAUL OF TARSUS

Saul the first great Christian missionary was a Jew born in the city of Tarsus in Asia Minor. After having completed his education at home he followed the prevailing custom of the students of the University of Tarsus and went abroad for further study. He arrived in Jerusalem, completed his studies under Gamaliel, and later identified himself with the Pharisees who were seeking to stamp out the rising sect of the Nazarenes. In an official capacity he one day heard the preaching of Stephen, and when the preacher was condemned he was in charge of the execution.

Something in the manner of Stephen, perhaps his exaltation and certainty of faith, touched a deep chord in Saul's nature and disturbed him profoundly. And although he secured letters and hurried off to Damascus to apprehend other Christians, his mind grew more and more troubled. Stephen had let fall a great revolutionary idea in the address he had made before the Sanhedrin, and in spite of every effort to do so Saul could not put it out of mind. On the way this idea continued to clarify itself until suddenly it burst forth in all its majesty, in a light above the brightness of the sun, in a voice that sent him bound by the Spirit to save the Gentile world.

Behind this simple story is the profound meaning of two lives. In the Sanhedrin all that was Jesus and all that was Saul stood face to face in the message of Stephen. On the Damascus road these two found reconciliation in a new man, Saul the Christian evangelist.

What was this gospel that Stephen preached? Evidently the actual words of a man, however specifically they may deal with some local situation, are always interpreted in the light of their age, in their bearing upon the problems which confront all mankind in the day in which they are spoken. This message, therefore, meant one thing in Judea, but a far larger thing when placed upon the background of world interests. That the words of Stephen found in Saul a world-background is clear from the fact that they immediately began to make an apostle to the Gentiles. Therefore, to learn this larger meaning we must discover just who and what was Saul of Tarsus.

The account we have of the preaching of Stephen occurs in the Acts of the Apostles, a treatise ostensibly from the hand of Luke who was associated with Saul. The account for our purpose, therefore, has the highest value, since Luke must have received his information from Saul, who would have remembered just the items which particularly impressed themselves upon his mind at the time. When we turn to this address we find that it is a recital of Israel's historical failure in spirituality. All along the way God has revealed Himself to His people, but they have turned against His counsel and provisions for their noblest life. At last the tabernacle of witness has given place to a house, and true religion has perished in the devotion to the temple and all its accompanying ceremonial. Through this devotion Israel has lost her way and has become the murderer of her prophets. Thus when her Just One, the Messiah, came, she betrayed and murdered him.

The people were "cut to the heart and gnashed upon Stephen with their teeth." But instead of being affrighted he looked up to heaven and said, "I see the heavens opened, and the Son of Man standing on the right hand of God." Such blasphemy caused the people to stop their ears and to cry out with a loud voice as they rushed upon him with one accord. He was turned over to Saul, who took him outside of the city and had him stoned. Here the record as it came from Saul to Luke continues, "And they stoned Stephen, calling upon God and saying, 'Lord Jesus, receive my spirit.' And he kneeled down, and cried with a loud voice, 'Lord, lay not this sin to their charge.' And when he had said this he fell asleep."

The boldness of Stephen's words is clear to all, and at least one man is struck by their truth. On the experimental side of his own religion Saul has found that works of the law can never be the whole of religion. When it is made so God recedes from the heart and communion with Him is impossible. Furthermore Stephen's words reveal how intimately he enjoys the presence of God, for he is permitted to look into heaven and to see the face of God. And as the prisoner steps forward to meet his death he calls, "Lord Jesus, receive my spirit." Then as the executioners take up the stones he kneels and cries out, "Lord, lay not this sin to their charge." The address of Stephen, his trust in Jesus, and his great forgiveness in death, touched Saul of Tarsus to the heart. Here in his presence a man was dying who had gained through Christ all the religious triumph which he had sought and had never been able to secure.

Saul had had, of course, abundant opportunity to know of the claims of the followers of the Nazarene before this; but we may reasonably doubt if he had ever seen their religious value against the background of Jewish history. Nor had he seen before how this faith could support one as he went forth to pay the extreme price of his belief. In furious despair Saul set out at once for Damascus. The city with its bitterness and debate suffocated him. He made all haste to get upon the road where he could be alone with his thoughts—where he could look at all he had seen with eyes uninfluenced by the narrow provincialism of the petty officials of Jerusalem—for he had caught a glimpse of a profound truth and power in the conduct of the man who had just died.

We need no better evidence that Saul was something more than a Jew than the simple recital of his conversion. His reactions were different, deeper, and more nearly those of a man of the outside world. The intensity of his Jewish feeling against Stephen's words cannot drown his sense of their justice, cannot keep his rational processes from admitting that Stephen has found the substance of true religion. Inevitably he is driven to take account of the claims made for the Nazarene, and just as inevitably be discovers a correspondence between them and that which he knows the whole Gentile world is seeking. Presently there comes to him a staggering, blinding light of thought in which he sees the purposes of God for all mankind and the true place of Israel among the nations.

It would be the height of foolishness to spend time in trying to explain the nature of that light or in trying to fathom the mental make-up of the man who experienced it. For us the matter of chief interest is the fact that he has seen the claims of Stephen upon the screen of world history and conditions. A sense of their tremendous meaning for mankind, and for every man of the Gentile world, has struck him down. And he has been lifting his hand against God's plan!

No doubt those who are skillful in such matters will discover a means of accounting for all that took place, or seemed to take place; and in the future, as in the past, they will leave little to respect in either the man or his vision. But fortunately the vision has borne its fruit and the man has achieved his place among the earth's immortals. We shall therefore spend our time dealing with the world-fact which he saw and which made him both a Christian and an apostle.

What a man sees is always very much determined by his native place, his family life, his education, and his social position. How varied were the forces that determined the outlook of Saul of Tarsus becomes clear to us when we remember that he was reared in no mean Greek city; that he was a Jew surrounded by the best traditions of Judaism, a Pharisee of the Pharisees, and of the tribe of Benjamin; that he was educated in Tarsus and Jerusalem; and that he enjoyed by birth the distinction of being a Roman citizen. Perhaps few men of his day were so well qualified to know the actual pulse of both the East and the West. There were rulers of this period who could boast of their Jewish origin, their Roman citizenship, their Hellenistic culture, and their wide education. But, after all, they were rulers, and because of their seclusion and apartness could not know the lower orders of society in both the East and West quite so well as Saul knew them. As a tent-maker, he was of the people, enjoyed their confidence, and shared both their wisdom and their desires.

That these factors had their influence upon Saul cannot be doubted, for there are a number of elements in his thinking which no Palestinian Jew would have advocated. For instance, there is a strange correspondence between the emperor cult of the Roman empire and the Jesus cult. Jesus is King of a kingdom also until he turns it over to the Father. The emperor and Jesus are objects of worship, they are deified. The Messianic king would very probably never have been the object of worship among the Jews, for they could have had no other gods before Jehovah. And while the Jewish Christian would never have worshiped the Roman emperor, we must admit that this correspondence is very significant—its origin is the empire, not Jewry. There is also the unmistakable influence of Greek civilization upon the thought of Saul. The Roman empire was very anxious to further the feeling of brotherhood and solidarity. This we know, was a borrowed policy. It was the Greek civilization that first attempted to establish these social factors, and Alexander in particular. Greek tolerance and patronage extended to every religion and philosophical system from the Indus to Sicily. And it was a Greek poet who wrote, "In the Divine we live and move and have our being," thus bringing all men together as brothers in the divine nature. This idea, adopted by Saul as the apostle to the Gentiles, was a further proof of Gentile influence.

These features, and others, which distinguished the think-

ing of Saul from that of the Palestinian Jew, must have come
directly from the fact that he was born and reared in the
Greek city of Tarsus. In no city of Palestine would he have
been encouraged to such independent thinking. Indeed he
would have had there no opportunity to know these views of
man and society which were so directly opposed to the current
teachings of Judaism. Thus to understand the mentality of
Saul, the Tarsian Jew, we must understand Greek life and
Greek thought in Tarsus.

And in beginning this undertaking we must recognize
the very large measure of success which attended the efforts of
the Greek rulers to Hellenize the East subsequent to the conquests of Alexander the Great. How subtle and powerful was
the impact of the Greeks may be seen in the fact that, when
the Greek world was taken over by the Romans, Greek civilization Hellenized even Rome. How did it happen that a
spirit so individual, so vigorous, so clear-cut in its thought, and
so essentially different from the rest of the world in its aims
and interests, should make such a lasting impression upon
Jews, Phrygians, Persians, Babylonians, Romans, and Egyptians? It must have come about through the method employed.
Greece, even when deprived of her nationality, continued to
be perhaps the most successful colonizer the world has ever
seen.

Ramsay tells us that from the time of Aristotle Hellenism
had been attempting a new and stupendous task—it had gone
forth to conquer the East: "The attempt was successful in a
remarkable degree, because Hellenism adapted itself to the
new problems which it had to solve: it did not seek to impose
itself in rigid purity on its Asiatic subjects, but profoundly
modified itself in the school of practical life. With the armies
of Alexander, Seleucus, and Ptolemy marched also the philosophy and the literature and the art of Hellenism. It was
merely one symptom of the wider impulse that Alexander
carried everywhere with him the poems of Homer. Perhaps it

was also a pseudo-historic fancy of later time which invented the story that a bronze statuette of Hercules by Lysippus accompanied all his marches, adorned his dinner-table, and was affected with emotion at his death; but the tale embodies the historic truth that those marches made Greek art a factor in the development of human life as far East as the Indus and the city of Bactria." [1]

We see the method. Greek civil authority was forced upon the East by the strength of Greek arms. But there was no attempt to interfere with the more intimate liberties of the conquered peoples. A Persian could continue his national religion and customs and remain in everything except in his loyalty to the Greek ruler, the Persian he was before. And it was the chief strength of that sovereignty that he was granted this liberty and protected in it. Greek art was there for him to behold; Greek philosophy was taught where he might hear; and Greek literature was open to him to read. If he had any criticism to make, his opinion was respectfully heard. If he had a philosophy of his own, he was actually encouraged to teach it—not to his own people only, but to all the Greeks. Thus there came about a happy stimulation of the genius of the subject peoples. The encouragement to individual expression and opinion, the courtesy and respect shown to every true thinker and workman, the actual understanding and appreciation shown by the Greek, and the Greek organization of the government to support the interests of the individual, won the heart of the whole East with the exception of a few selfish and ambitious princes. And strangely enough most of these belonged to the Greek aristocracy.

Out of this willingness of the Greeks to learn from their conquered subjects and to permit their own offerings to be refused or modified by the conquered, arose a new spirit and a new civilization. The deepest chords of the Oriental and

---

[1] *The Cities of St. Paul*, pp. 31, 32.

Greek soul were set vibrating, yet left absolutely free. Comradeship, mutual respect, and appreciative understanding inevitably produced a new empire, an empire that seemed as Oriental as before but which actually was Greek. But it was not the Greek civilization of former days. The old abstractness of thought was left behind. A practical bent replaced the theoretical through actual experiment and an exchange of ideas. Thus that which had made the Republic of Plato fail was eliminated and the ideal State began to be a fact. Perhaps the Greeks had learned from their own experiments in democracy, in oligarchy, in dictatorships, and in the Athenian empire to regard their governmental theories with a wholesome doubt. At any rate, they were willing to listen to suggestions from every quarter. And this very attitude produced loyal coöperation from all peoples.

The enthusiasm with which all men threw themselves into the task of producing this ideal State set free the intellectual powers of both the East and West. There could be no *pure* Greek nor Persian ideas. Dogmatic opinions from any person were so out of place and so inharmonious to the great enterprise that they gained no great influence. Art, philosophy, literature, and even religion made use of all available materials from both East and West. The influence of the East began to be felt in the West; the West began to modify the East. Then the artists, the philosophers, the writers, and the priests began to strike out boldly to create a new order. There was neither East nor West, neither border nor breed nor birth. The East and the West had not been amalgamated; they had grown together into a new organization. Art was not a hybrid but a new species. And of primary importance for this study, a new type of religion emerged.

A generation of effort in this direction made a certain attitude toward the future habitual. The ideal had not been achieved, but the actual successes gained and the progress made warranted enthusiastic hope. The best was yet to be, and it would be. Growth and development became the dominant feature in both thought and ideals. Society in the East was actually wedded to the Socratic method of investigation. Every person and every generation chipped away a little of the native rock to set the statue of the ideal State free. Many minds made the ideal figure sharper, bolder, more graceful, more practical. Thus the prevailing thought of the Alexandrian world was growth and development.

Without having breathed this spirit from birth and without having witnessed the results of it upon both government and religion, no Jew would have dared attempt that modification of Judaism which Saul of Tarsus advocated. In fact the venture of necessity had been begun by his father, and perhaps by his grandfather, before him. Saul grew up in a home where the lines of sanctity were necessarily already somewhat loosened. No one generation would have dared go the whole length of the Pauline gospel. There is too much tolerance toward Greek, Roman, and Oriental modes of thought in the mind of Saul, and too much willingness to modify his own religion, for him to have been the product of a home of strict Palestinian Judaism. Hellenism had taken hold upon the Jews of the Diaspora with the same subtle charm with which it had captivated the other Orientals. And the Romans had been wise enough to continue the regime which had been so successful in meeting the East.

And just at this point it may be well to observe that Saul, by his preaching, was perfectly in line with the ideals and purposes of every teacher in the Alexandrian world. He was trying, as were they, to make his contribution to the great task of the ideal state. His preconceptions and fundamental theories were somewhat different from those of the other teachers, but his ideal, his object, was truly of the Alexandrian world. And, as we shall observe hereafter, there was a striking correspondence between the religion of Saul and the standardized religion of the Gentile world of that age.

Ramsey [2] points out that the service which Hellenism performed for the development of mankind was taken up as an element of the Pauline proposal for the reorganization of society. It was, he declares, the aim of the Greeks to make the freedom of the individual consistent with an ordered and articulate government, and to set up a system of State education. Perhaps, however, the aim of the Greeks can be better stated as an attempt to develop the highest individual and to set up an ordered and articulate government which would best serve the interests of this new individual. Ramsay means that, but he has come to his democracy by way of the English constitutional development. His phraseology, therefore, still smacks of the divine right of government. To be sure, it is only a manner of speaking, but it is misleading. The Greeks were not so much concerned with making the individual fit the government; they had already grasped the fact that when the government fits the individual the cause of government is safe. Their whole care, therefore, was to bring the individual to his maximum of possibility and to devise a government which would further this aim.

Note again the correspondence between the Pauline motive and the Alexandrian enterprise. Can it be purely accidental that a gospel which comes from a soil that has been from time immemorial nationalistic—the individual existing solely for Israel—is now wholly individual in both aim and method? To be sure, there has been also for some time a new spirit in Israel. A doctrine of personal judgment and personal immortality has been developed, or more properly borrowed. Israel's benefactions are many, and there is no desire to minimize them. But the interests of truth compel us to take note of the fact that, after foreign contacts, her theology has always become the center of debate. The conflict between Pharisee and Sadducee over these very items—the resurrection of the dead

---

[2] *The Cities of St. Paul*, pp. 34sq.

and all it involves—proves beyond doubt that the modifications are resisted on the ground that they have a "foreign" look. Is Saul as a Pharisee only going the Pharisees one better in his gospel of the individual? In any event the history of the Pharisees, and the fact that Saul was one of them, is not without significance for the Pauline position.

The lines in Israel were strangely drawn during this period of the nation's life. The Sadducees were the ultra-conservatives in theology, but the ultra-liberals in national policy. They steadfastly refused to accept the developments of theology which took place subsequent to the Babylonian conquest and which were most heartily adopted by the Pharisees. On the other hand, they did all in their power to Hellenize Judea! The Pharisees, who were liberals in theology, were conservatives in national policy. They stood for theological development but opposed Hellenism with all their might. And what a strange contradiction is Saul of Tarsus among them! He is so liberal in theology as to be much more than a Pharisee; and he is as kindly disposed to Hellenism as any Sadducee could possibly be. And, just at first, he seems to be the only consistent man among them.

But all this apparent contradiction on the part of Pharisee and Sadducee is cleared up somewhat if we remember the chief principle which guided the policy of each school. The Sadducees were theologically conservative. With them the individual found his value in the nation. The nation had their first thought. The preservation of the nation dominated all their actions, even in those strange motions of Hellenizing Judea. They made the overtures to Rome and enjoyed the fruit of their submission. These were only measures of political expediency, to be sure—the inevitable course to be taken in view of the power of military Rome. The Pharisees on the other hand had begun to see the importance of the individual. They took note of the miseries of the people; they were interested in personal righteousness, in personal consolations, in personal immortality. Through the individual the nation must be saved or lost, for the many individuals made the national tone and the national life. The Pharisees therefore admitted those theological innovations which stressed the importance of the individual. And they were quick to see that Rome cared nothing for the individual, for Roman policy increased the burdens of the common man and neglected all measures that would increase either his effectiveness or his personal happiness. The Pharisees formed the popular party; the Sadducees the group of Roman bureaucrats. The Pharisees became the nationalists; the Sadducees the apparently disloyal party.

It is therefore comparatively easy to see how Saul could claim to be a Pharisee and be proud of his race, and yet urge further advances in both theology and Hellenism. His liberal theological outlook comes from the Pharisaic lineage, and his Hellenistic leaning comes from the liberal tone of his home and the atmosphere of his native city. These factors, which were harmonized in him as a member of the Diaspora, had rent his nation in twain. Small wonder that he was acceptable to neither party and seemed to both "the most unJewish of all the Jews!" He was not national enough in theory for the Sadducees—he went too far in the direction of Rome; he was too liberal for the Pharisees—his religion followed the prevalent Gentile type. And he was liberal in both respects because he came out of the Greek city.

He avoids, however, the worst features of both Sadducee and Pharisee. He has not allowed his patriotism to sink to the level of hypocrisy and mere motions of empty expediency as have the Sadducees. He knows the power of Rome as well as they. But he has thought things through, and his recommendations are the result of sincere conviction. His liberal attitude toward the Gentile as a man saves him from that fanaticism which led the common man of Israel into that conflict with Roman authority which could end in but one way. The Pharisee, of course, never meant to lead his people into the ditch of destruction. And we may be fairly sure that all the dangers of the Pharisaic position were well known to the Pharisees themselves. They dogged the steps of Jesus, stoned the prophets of revolution, and did all in their power to prevent a premature popular uprising. But the very antagonism to the Sadducees increased the hatred of Rome. To urge the Pharisaic position was to increase the growing force of the national volcano. And yet, almost every one knew that the Sadducee would give up everything that was truly national. We have seen how Jesus attempted to step into the breach and rouse the Jew to his great sacrificial and servant rôle as the only way to national security. And we see Saul of Tarsus hurrying to apply its vision to Jews and Gentiles. Is his silence on the national danger due to the fact that he is unfamiliar with it, or because he sees that it is inevitable? I think it is because he has seen a far more consuming fact: the highest point of Judaism is for him the recognition that there is neither Jew nor Greek, neither circumcision nor uncircumcision; the Servant perishes for the sake of the Kingdom of God.

But the religious liberalism of Saul was not due to his Pharisaic background alone. The correspondence between the faith he declared and the religions of the Gentile world is too close to be purely accidental. Not that Saul, being a Jew, consciously took these religions for his model and forced Christ's words into their mold. What he knew of the teachings of Jesus and his own experience enabled him to see the correspondence. No forcing was necessary. It was just this correspondence which flashed over him as a divine preparation of the world for the Gospel and which prepared him for that blinding vision before Damascus. He had found in Christ just the thing the whole Gentile world had been seeking; he had found in Christ also the fulfillment of the vision of the prophets and the contemporary Messianic hope of his own nation. In Christ the world could be reconciled to God!

Some writers have minimized the influence of the Mystery religions of the Gentiles upon the religion of Saul. And in a way, they are right. Nothing that Saul could have put together with his own intellect could have enlisted the unfailing enthusiasm and lordship over his soul as did the truth he saw in Christ. All that his religion was or became was primarily grounded upon his conviction that it was revealed to him from God. He was then, and always afterwards, too much the Jew to formulate without divine aid, consciously and with express intent, the faith of his soul. No Jew would, in Tarsus or anywhere else, have made his religion as the Greeks made their philosophies. But a man sees the vision he is prepared to see, even a divine one. And Saul of Tarsus was eminently prepared by his knowledge of the religions of the Gentile world to see that Jesus was the Lord these nations were seeking. Yes, the very Lord he himself had been seeking also. The correspondence is a discovery on the part of Saul, not something he made.

Just what were the Mystery religions? Any complete answer to such a question is impossible. The Mystery religions were secret cults and were kept among the members of the cult by oaths to secrecy. "In the very nature of the case the secrecy to which initiates were pledged rendered it impossible for outsiders to become acquainted with the inner history of religious societies: such history could be written only by those whose vows forbade them to divulge the *mysteria*." [3] But there is much to be learned from the symbols used, for the initiate was permitted to portray the mysteries publicly by means of symbols. There are also fragments of hymns and prayers in existence, inscriptions, cult emblems, frescoes, painted vases, and the ruins of temples and chapels. From these we may gain a general idea of the character of a Mystery religion.

Each of these religions no doubt regarded the initiation as

---

[3] Angus, *The Mystery Religions and Christianity*, p. 39.

in itself the making of a new creature. The initiate was taught the two orders, the carnal and the spiritual. By initiation he gained, through the sight of the symbols, through the ceremony, the lights and darkness, and the sacramental acts, together with the instruction given at the time, the impression that he had escaped from the evils of the flesh and all past sins. Furthermore, the initiate was made to feel that he had been given access to God. Thus each religion had its means of mediation between the candidate and the deity and provided him with a sense of safety and protection. In other words, each religion was redemptive in character. The worshiper was also supplied with a knowledge of the secret ways of God, thus satisfying the desire for fundamental truth. The highest point in each religion was a sacramental drama in which was portrayed the travail and sufferings of the deity and his final triumph over pain and death. Each religion was democratic in spirit, open to to all who might apply and who had the price of initiation. Finally, each of the Mystery religions brought hope of life and immortality to confront the darkness and dissolution of the grave.

In their earlier stages of development the several Mystery religions must have been quite distinct from one another in both truth and ritual. But as time passed and each cult began to fill up with people who belonged to other cults, there was both conscious and unconscious modification to include the superior features of each religion. Thus in time all the Mystery religions became so similar from first to last as to be essentially the same in teaching and purpose. The spiritual poverty of the indigenous Greek and Roman religions and their incompetence before the growing intelligence and culture of the Mediterranean peoples of this period caused great spiritual unrest. The West in its hunger for divine fellowship and for a gnosis of certainty turned eagerly to these religions of the Orient. The extravagant public claims made by the priests and the prevailing proselytizing eagerness of the time drew all classes of the empire. And so strong was the thirst for the knowledge of God that it became the rule to join as many Mystery cults as one could afford. Competition for the better classes and for the patronage of the rulers further contributed toward syncretism and produced at last that standardized form of religion which Christianity was forced to meet in its struggle for the conquest of the Gentile world.

Once more we behold the effect of the tolerance of the Greek spirit and witness a proof of the organic nature of the Alexandrian empire. The artists, sculptors, philosophers, and rhetoricians of Greece made their way to all parts of the East, and the priests, merchants, artisans, and teachers of the Orient found an eager welcome for their wares in the West. When Rome fell heir to the major portion of the Alexandrian conquests she took a page from the book of Greek success and continued the tolerance and welcome toward all the Orient had to give.

Angus says: "All the pre-conditions for an all-around syncretism obtained in the Graeco-Roman world—the decline of constructive originality and the advent of criticism, the fall of the city-state and the correlative rise of universalism, the international policy of Alexander, the breaking up of national faiths and philosophies, the spread of the *Koiné*, the intermingling of diverse populations at a high state of culture, the success of Stoicism with its *cosmopolis* and unifying allegorical interpretation, the rise of the Roman Empire, Roman law, roads which joined together the ends of the earth, the passion for novelty in religious matters, the tolerance of paganism, the rise of proselytism, and the continuous convergence of East and West." [4]

The policies of the Alexandrian empire and the subsequent Roman conquests produced another social result strongly favoring the vogue of the Mystery religion in its ultimate

---

[4] *The Mystery Religions and Christianity*, p. 187.

form. As we have already seen, it was the chief aim of the Greeks to develop the individual. No policy could have been conceived which would have been more in keeping with the spirit of the age and which, therefore, would have had a better chance of success. Alexander swept away the existing nations. Individualism rose from the ruins, just because the individual always survives the catastrophes of history, reorders his life amid the wreckage, and develops the power to preserve himself when all his former sources of safety have been destroyed. The Greeks in their government of the East were by instinct just the people to encourage the individual in this necessary task of rehabilitation. The break-up of the ancient kingdoms and priestly colleges of the East, and the dissemination of the long-hoarded and fabulous treasures of court and sanctuary, stimulated commerce and caused an unparalleled period of speculation and individual enterprise. The shrewd merchants and tradesmen rose to the top and became individuals exerting unusual power and influence. In the general fever and excitement aroused by these successes the Greeks pushed eastward to every city and court in search of gain, and large companies of Orientals emigrated to the West. Men learned to depend upon themselves and to feel at home in any part of the Alexandrian world.

The conquest of the East by Rome merely widened the scope of activity of this individual which had been developed by Greek policy. There was a further breakdown of ancient institutions, an added impetus to the fever for gain, and the eager pressing of Oriental teachers into the new field which the Roman empire offered. But there was little to comfort the man of only average ability. He could not compete with his more gifted rivals. Furthermore, the frequent changes in the government which followed, the internal strife, the heavy Roman taxation, and the general decay of ancient faiths produced in the masses a great despair and a deep longing for security, both social and spiritual. In the insecurity of these unstable times there was a recurrence of that almost universal pagan philosophy—the view that decay and degeneration is the law of all things; that the Golden Age is behind us; and that every change that comes is a step downward from the primitive goodness and happiness of men. Ramsay says: "We are apt to pooh-pooh this ancient doctrine as merely an old fashion, springing from the natural tendency of mankind to praise the former times and ways. But it was much more than this. It was the reasoned view of the philosophers. It colored almost all Greek and Roman literature. It lay deep in the heart of the pagan world. It produced the tone of sadness which is hardly ever absent from the poetry of Greece and Rome, heard as an occasional note even in its poems of pleasure. A feeling like this cannot safely be set aside as false." [5] This feeling is old because war with all its evils was known to every generation of the Mediterranean world. All that is important for us to know is the fact that this philosophy was very old and that it recurred to the common man in every period marked by unsettled conditions. Rome had given great hope to all her subjects, at first; but about the time of the Christian era hope had almost wholly disappeared. The highly developed individual fostered by the Alexandrian world tasted despair all the more in the unstable times which Rome had brought.

Angus states that the cry for salvation was loud, persistent, and universal: "In a bewilderingly new age, when venerable systems had collapsed, when the customs and conventions that had regulated human intercourse were rudely cast aside, when property was rapidly changing ownership, when life was unsafe because of conspiracies and jealousies, there arose in all hearts a longing for a more settled state of affairs, for social stability and political permanency. During such epochs of transition, when men are driven out of their old ruts and

---

[5] *The Cities of St. Paul*, p. 30.

compelled to fresh thinking, the evil of the world and the ills that infest human life become more intolerable; the pain and sorrows of the individual become more intense through the consciousness of his isolation. When the *nouveaux riches* rise to lord it over families which for centuries had been cradled in the lap of ease, when the man who was the ornament of society to-day might to-morrow be on the way to the scaffold or to an island place of banishment, when the 'slings and arrows of outrageous fortune' baffled the best, when parting with friends added bitterness to death, when the heretofore available and orthodox means of consolation failed, a cry arose for deliverance from the present order of things, for a Savior. Men sought deliverance from the uncertainties of social life, the upheavals of political life, from the burden of grief and sorrow, from the reign of death, the universal power of demons and the malefic astral deities, from the oppressive tyranny of fate, the caprice of *Sors*, of *Fortuna*, the pollution of matter, the consciousness of guilt, the wasting of disease, from the *taedium vitae*, and from the ills that 'made human life a hell.' 'The fulness of the times' was marked about the beginning of our era by a universal demand for salvation, by an *Erlösungs-sehnsucht*, such as has perhaps never been equalled except in the pre-Buddhistic India." [6]

It was to this situation, social and spiritual, that the Mystery religions addressed themselves. They were not primarily reasoned faiths, but religions of authority. They were supported by their great antiquity, their texts, forms, and scriptures. They asserted man's immortality and through sacraments of initiation and worship provided a means by which man might become godlike and share the imperishable nature of the gods. By symbols rather than by logical proof, by assuming certainty rather than by reasoning about possibilities, they created faith. It is, therefore highly important for our study to note that this

---

[6] *The Mystery Religions and Christianity*, pp. 226, 227.

social and spiritual condition of the empire existed, and that some of the Mystery religions in their final form were on the ground and prosecuting their work with great success before "another Oriental religion came out of Galilee to strive with them for the souls of men."

Some have maintained that Saul could have had no knowledge of the Mystery religions. In that case he could not, of course, have been struck by the parallel between the teachings about Jesus and the doctrines of the standard Mystery faith. But there is enough evidence to show that it is highly probable that he knew all too well the nature of the Mystery cults. For instance, he knew them well enough to declare in the beginning against all syncretism, and for an exclusiveness which permitted no Christian to become a member of any one of these cults. Christ could have no fellowship with Isis or Osiris. How he could gain this knowledge without being a member of some one of these cults will be clear if we remember that the Jews of the Diaspora were industrious proselytizers. Their synagogues were open to all peoples and became perhaps the chief medium for the intercommunication of ideas. "In the synagogues of the Diaspora, Greeks, Romans, Syrians, Persians, and islanders of the archipelago were attracted; there they learned to know each other and the people who were the intermediaries between the East and West. . . . The God-fearers conveyed to the synagogues the best ideals of Paganism and to the non-Jewish world the ideals of righteousness." [7] There have always been men who could contain no secret, especially when they renounced their former ties, as did the proselyte. From these it would not be difficult to learn all there was to know about the Mysteries. And besides, there must have been a free exchange of ideas and ideals which were perfectly legitimate and allowable. With new pledges to silence, secrets have been passed on since the world began.

---

[7] *The Mystery Religions and Christianity*, p. 193.

And the very fact that in spite of all Saul's care and strictness some of his own followers went over to the enemy is evidence enough to show that he knew the object and main features of the teaching of these cults.

Just how widespread was the doctrine of Messianism in the Gentile world we do not know, but there is a surprising amount of proof that the idea was current from the city of Rome to Bactria. Ramsey [8] points out that the Fourth Eclogue of Virgil which deals with this idea, while apparently only a reply to Horace, is far more. First, the association of the Better Age with the birth of a child is Hebraic, not Greek or Roman. Second, the poem is a metrical experiment and exhibits characteristics that are distinctly those of Hebrew poetry. Ramsey feels that this poem cannot be explained without recognizing that it is an imitation of some Hebrew poem which contained this idea of the Better Age. It came to him from the Diasporai—the Jews in Rome. But in our study of Zoroaster we encountered the Messianic idea; and while it is without doubt a later addition to the Zoroastrian teaching, it was not too late to be felt in Judea in the Babylonian and Persian periods. And if Mithraism, which is of Persian origin and which became the religion of the soldiers of the empire, made this idea prominent, we have an added reason for its prevalence, for the soldiers of the empire were levied from all the subject peoples. There is no way of knowing whether or not Virgil was a member of the cult of Mithra, but there was nothing to exclude him. Even slaves were permitted to join. The very fact that Horace was a soldier under Brutus and came back to Rome to enter the service of the existing government may indicate that he was a member. It is possible that one member of the cult of Mithra is answering another out of a ritual they both revere?

In any event, the idea must have been somewhat familiar to

---

[8] *The Cities of St. Paul*, pp. 59-69.

every worshiper of Mithra. At the services of this cult "the tried 'soldiers' of Mithra joined in the sacrament of bread and water mixed with wine, which to the Christians appeared a travesty of the Last Supper. In such a communion service the Mithraist believers were strengthened in their faith that Mithra would assure them of victory here, and would come again from heaven to bring forth the dead from their graves for a judgment at which the Mediator would be the Advocate of the initiated soul, which, purified through his rite, would ascend through the seven planetary spheres to Paradise." [9] Such correspondence of theological doctrine with that of the Christian eschatology is enough to make us wonder if any religious idea in the Roman empire could have been the exclusive possession of any city or province. Since Bactria, Rome, and Jerusalem were acquainted with the Messianic idea, it is more than probable that a man of Tarsus would know the outstanding doctrines of the Mystery cults.

The rapidity with which the Mystery religions spread in the West, and their persistence even after the religion of Jesus began to be preached, is an index to both the times and its religions. In an age that was aggressively religious and serious, an age in which practically the whole world was seeking for spiritual consolation and the knowledge of God, they made their greatest strides. One could scarcely find a better proof that these faiths were able to satisfy the religious needs of the people. It is true that not all these religions were on the same level of exaltation and refinement—some were crude and often revolting in their symbolism—but the aim of all, and the general truth taught, was practically identical. "The majority of them had the same aims as Christianity itself—the aim of worshiping a pure God, the aim of living a pure life, the aim of cultivating the spirit of brotherhood. They were part of a great religious revival which distinguished the age." [10]

---

[9] *The Mystery Religions and Christianity*, p. 123.
[10] Hatch, *The Influence of Greek Ideas*, pp. 291sq.

But their chief aim, whether consciously or unconsciously arrived at, was to meet the disaster which had overtaken the individualism fostered by Greek civilization. In the disaster attending the frequent political changes of the Roman empire the individual witnessed the destruction of everything precious to him—his city, his home, his friends, and all too often the gods to whom he prayed. And the entire known world was in the clutches of a system which he could not escape by any earthly power. In Tarsus, Antioch, Jerusalem, Corinth, Ephesus, or Athens, the same forces were around him and likely at any moment to snatch from him all his possessions. No human power could help him, and government was not stable enough to give security. All feeling of solidarity and racial and national sufficiency had disappeared. The individual was alone and helpless unless some new god intervened. The Mystery religions sought to supply the divine help required, to respond to the loneliness of the individual by bringing him into fellowship with God, and to lift him above his disasters by teaching him to aspire above earth and matter to a place with God. In other words they attempted to save the individual from the stern fact that individual striving had become as futile and meaningless as the venture of nationality.

It is frequently asserted that the Mystery religions really came into their own only after Saul had preached to the cities of the Gentile world.[11] This in a way is undoubtedly true. A number of the great Mystery cults made their bid for the Roman world subsequent to the appearance of Christianity. But we err in imagining that either Christianity or the later Mysteries could have made any considerable progress without a proper religious foreground of both thought and organized faith. And while it is true that no one can tell whence the wind of the Spirit cometh and whither it goeth, it is not difficult to determine the general direction in which it is moving.

---

[11] Machen, *The Origin of Paul's Religion*, pp. 8f., pp. 255-290; see also Glover, *Paul of Tarsus*, pp. 131-135.

There were sounds and movements enough in the Gentile
world to show what this wind was about. Saul was able to
read these signs and to see what they meant—to find the shape
of the *Zeitgeist* in the welter and flow of philosophical and
religious opinions.[12]

And this was not difficult in view of the fact that the imperfect and fragmentary always precede the perfected system
of thought in any forming age of the world. From his Jewish
and Oriental background Saul possessed already the full fruit
of all this inchoate but striving religious spirit. In so far as
the movement achieved articulateness it took on the general
contour of that profound religious construction which was to
be found everywhere in the East and which had in Judaism
reached its highest significance in the Apostolic faith. If the
proselytizers of the later great Mystery faiths could see the
signs of the time and take advantage of them for their purposes, we need not wonder that Saul, who had thought
through one great religion, would be able to read the meaning
of all he saw in the Gentile world. He did not require the
spectacle of a world in the grasp of a highly developed Mystery
cult to show him the age that was on the way.

We know also that there were Mystery religions already
upon the ground and securing disciples long before Alexander
turned his armies toward Asia. These had flowed westward
silently and irresistibly and had adjusted themselves to the
older pagan institutions of religion. The Alexandrian conquests had greatly accelerated the flow. This religious situation was ready to receive the preaching of Saul without a
break in the general line of its development.

That the time was ripe for a world-religion seems to have
been recognized on all sides. The rapid spread of the Mysteries
proves that the former religions of the empire had ceased to
commend themselves and that the people had not lost their

---

[12] Cf. Glover, *Paul of Tarsus*, p. 142.

capacity for religion. How well known to the priests of the Mysteries was the true significance of this success, we can only surmise. The majority were no doubt only stupid and emotionally guided evangels of their cult—devoted but ignorant men who had not the capacity to see the why and the wherefore of their successes. On the other hand, there must have been men of unusual ability in almost every priesthood who at least glimpsed the possibilities the situation afforded—the not remote probability that by proper guidance and diplomacy their cult could become the State religion. At any rate, either Augustus or his counselors were not slow to see what it all meant, and to take the bold measures the state of the empire demanded: they established an imperial religion—the cult of the Emperor.

This was an attempt to meet logically the results of all former religious training. The gods had heretofore been the true rulers of every land. Laws and governments might exist as the instruments of men's hands, but the voice of the gods had sealed these documents with divine approval. Government was not a human institution erected in accordance with divine will; it was the divine will expressed manward. With the establishment of the Roman empire there was, by theory, a conquest of the gods of other nations by the gods of Rome. But the gods of Rome were in no sense able to appeal any longer to the religious needs of even the Romans. The god who had erected this vast power must therefore be some god as yet unknown. Who was he? Mithra? He was the god of the soldiers; and they had had much to do with making the empire. Perhaps in the Fourth Eclogue of Virgil, or as a result of it, we gain an insight into the spirit that is abroad in the land. The emperor is the head of all. In him the policies that have produced this Augustan Age frankly originated. The undercurrent of Oriental Messianism affords a clue which explains how he can thus create this Age. In him the divine power comprehends itself; he is the divine agent, the divine force which rules the world.

The force of this teaching with regard to the actual power behind all government is surprisingly deep-seated and persistent. Perhaps only one sect has ever been able to successfully distinguish between God and the existing government and to maintain toward that human instrument of law and order the highest respect, namely the Quakers. They can be trusted to affirm the truth. The rest of us, unless we are cautioned to answer as we expect to answer on the last great Day, seem to regard the administrators of law as too vulgarly inquisitive to be worthy of a share in our secrets. But, of course, it is altogether possible that we have so degenerated that we never speak or think seriously until we look on Death, hence the view of the Great Assize when we are asked for solemn actualities. Is it not because we have still the feeling that all true government must be divinely spoken? At any rate, no politician who expects to secure office ever even intimates that he is sufficient for all emergencies and can safely leave God free for other business. No, there is always a long, long recital of glorious history achieved under the hand of Providence and the express intimation that the candidate is the vicegerent of God.

Octavius and his counselors, for the sake of the empire's unity and safety, went beyond inference and frankly admitted that the emperor was the representative of God. Yea, more; he was God. Octavius (Augustus) did not dare make this statement in Rome where he was well known, and he was always a little ashamed that he had made it in the provinces; but government had to have some god commensurate with its far-flung authority. That it was only a political expedient must have been clear to every thinking man, for the Mysteries seem not to have lost any of their popularity as a result of it.

The claim came to nothing finally just because the emperor could not find subordinates with sufficient probity and wisdom to see that justice was done the subject peoples. And besides, there were some to whom the idea was utterly repulsive and who had the moral courage to say so.[13] The Jews for instance, positively would not have the image of this "god" in their city. The Greeks, no doubt, were less serious in their reactions—either smiling at the image with amused contempt or remarking courteously, "We will hear you again on this matter." The value for us in this incident lies in the fact that it indicates the religious need of the empire, the need for religious unity and brotherhood. The rulers sought to meet the need in the interests of government, but the "god" they set up failed to claim the devotion of the people of the provinces because he had feet of clay and wielded the sword of injustice.

We may conclude, then, that the religious situation demanded a God of universal dimensions and that the type of Mystery religion and the success of its appeal indicate what the future religion must be. Ramsey asks: "How far did Paul understand and foresee the issues that were nascent in the Empire during the first century? Who can say exactly how far a great statesman can foresee in detail the distant consequences of rejecting the salutary measures that he advocates? It is enough to say that he sees the cure for existing evils, and advocates with all his might the only possible remedy, and warns the State that ruin is the only alternative. So much we can say that Paul saw and did."[14] "To understand and foresee the nascent issues" of one's time—that is precisely what every savior of mankind has been able to do. Angus has truly observed: "Every living religion must take into account the spirit of the age; it must interpret the Zeitgeist. But a living religion must not conform to, but transform, the spirit of the age."[15] Saul did observe the spirit of his age. The only proper question for us to ask is, Did he make a religion to fit the spirit

---

[13] Josephus, *Antiquities* XVIII, 3.1.
[14] *The Cities of St. Paul*, p. 75.
[15] *The Mystery Religions and Christianity*, p. 253.

of the age? And to this question we have already answered in the negative. He found suddenly, and in a blinding light, that the religion of Jesus was at once the logical meaning of Jewish Messianism and the goal of all Gentile seeking. Out of that vision came also his own individual responsibility in a voice he could not choose but obey.

A further proof that Paul was intimately acquainted with the spirit of the times appears in his knowledge of the Greek tongue. His epistles were written or dictated in the *Koiné*, the *lingua franca* of the provinces. His command of this language must have served for all his ordinary needs of communication with the people of all classes. In this tongue the thoughts of the common people would be expressed, and they compose the age. That which is upon the tongue of the common man—the news of the day, the home-made philosophies, the private judgments and opinions, the beliefs and doubts, the expressions of hope or distrust—these reveal the heart of an age. And if we wish to go higher, there was the Septuagint from which Paul quoted in all his letters. The literature of Greece cannot have been a closed book to him, for at Athens he quoted from the Greek poets. Nor was he ignorant of the substance of Greek philosophy. He knew its weakness—its abstract character and its lack of vital relation to everyday life. He was at all times the Jew, and was not to be deceived by preachments which did not make gospel and daily life one and indivisible. His religio-ethical heritage, the Jewish habit of making religion embrace the whole life, kept him from being amazed by the great philosophers; and it supplied him with just the habit of mind which could appraise the social forces of his age. He was not only equipped to communicate with the Greek world, but he was trained as a Jew to see what these communications signified in social terms.

And he used his ability. From his epistles we discover that he was present in the theater, at the games; that he watched the soldiers, observed their arms and equipment; that he knew the ships, the markets, the temples, the feasts, the courts, the houses, and the traits of various peoples. Intuitively alert and unerring, he knew the motives of men, the hidden meaning behind their words and their conduct of public affairs. For instance, he saw that not moral aspiration but covetousness dictated the many visits with which Felix honored him in prison, and that behind the non-committal pose of Agrippa there was perfect knowledge of all that had been said in his presence. There can be little room to doubt that Saul knew the Greek provinces.

But did he know Rome? Did he know his Greek world from the Roman point of view—know it as a Roman problem and a Roman responsibility? Could he see it as a Roman would look at it? It is evident as we approach the Gentile world from this standpoint that not enough has been made by Christian writers of the Roman citizenship of Saul of Tarsus. A subject people presents an entirely different aspect when viewed from the top, from the position of the conquerors and rulers. There is always about such a people an air of mystery, an unfathomable something, that the rulers cannot penetrate. Impatience, suspicion, and harshness inevitably creep into the ruling policy. Saul of Tarsus would be well acquainted with this attitude, and he would also know why it existed and wherein it was unjust. As a Christian missionary he would not be blind to Rome's faults, nor to her merits.

This knowledge did not come from the ordinary observation which any man could make. His father was a Roman citizen before him, perhaps his grandfather also. That this rank carried with it great and unusual privileges is shown by what happened when Lysias ordered him to be scourged in Jerusalem. Saul said to the centurion who was binding him, "Is it lawful for you to scourge a man who is a Roman, and uncondemned?" The centurion fell back in amazement and hastened to tell Lysias, saying, "Take heed what thou doest: for this man is a Roman!" Then the chief captain put by his other business and hurried to interview Saul. "Tell me, is it true that you are a Roman?" "Yes," said Saul. A little doubtful, the chief captain replied, "With a great sum obtained I this freedom." His words implied, "How could you obtain it?" With evident pride Saul answered, "But I was Roman born!" That was enough. Those who had been sent to scourge him fell back in grave alarm. Even Lysias was uneasy, simply because he had put the prisoner in bonds. The bonds were loosed and Saul was given every courtesy and protection. Men who are born to such privileges acquire the mind that goes with them. The Roman outlook upon the Gentile world, the Roman sense of superiority, the Roman aims, in fact the whole Roman administrative attitude, would be certain to be a distinguishing mark of the mentality of Saul. Even if his father were not actually employed in the colonial service he would have access to this social group composed of the overseas officials of the empire. Thus Saul would mingle with them in an intimate way from his earliest youth. And we have already seen that he knew the official mind, that he discerned the thought behind the official mask. This was possible because he knew the colonials and their point of view.

When the report from the provinces caused Augustus to take the step of self-deification it represented the actual consensus of official opinion based upon the observation and best thought of this official class. The report very probably made no recommendation, least likely of all that the emperor become a god, for the Roman official was not altogether lacking in a sense of humor. It did, however, report the actual religious situation. There was a lack of unity. The various peoples could not be made into Romans. They were loyal enough outwardly, but within they were still barbarians and Greeks; they could not achieve the Roman spirit. Nothing short of a common religion could ever make them think together. And the ancient religion of Rome had not the slightest appeal, as actual trial and study of results had shown. Something had to be done; a remedy must be found, else the empire would crumble before the first considerable threat to Rome.

The class of officials able to make such penetrating observations of the people over whom they exercise authority is intellectually worthy to represent its home government. But it has also found a cause for worry, a ground for suspicion and fear, a reason for watchfulness, and an excuse for harshness. When the remedy actually proved to be no remedy, it would be this same class that would be first to see it. And with this group Saul associated. He heard their opinions, their gossip about Roman interests, aims, failures of policy, and governmental problems. This class in Tarsus would represent a little island of Rome, but more alert, practical-minded, and informed on matters affecting the provinces than any group in Rome could be. And as officials came and went by way of the Cilician Gates to places of service in the East and West, this circle in Tarsus would gain a fairly correct knowledge of the truth which never got to Rome.

The information which Saul gained in this way could not help having its effect upon his attitude toward all peoples of the Gentile world. It gave him the comprehensive outlook of the world-citizen and delivered him from the provincialism of the mere resident of Tarsus. It is the Roman citizen who travels by land and sea; who talks of Ephesus, the cities of Asia, and Greece; who takes the whole world for his nativity and dreams of bringing all nations under subjection to Christ. This world-consciousness must have preceded his call to give to it its strong compulsion and undying lure.

And yet, he was a Jew. In spite of the composite nature of his personality—the many Gentile elements in him which made him speak and think as no Palestinian Jew would ever have done—he was a well-accredited member of his race and entitled to all the sacred privileges of the national religion. He, therefore, had not lost his close connection with the center of the Jewish religion, the Temple at Jerusalem. Each year he paid the annual temple tax of two drachmae. His command of Hebrew (Aramaic) which enabled him to address the Jerusalem mob in its native tongue, his official mission to Damascus with letters granted by the Jerusalem authorities, and his evident technical knowledge of the Jewish Law and spirit show that he was no mongrel Jew or outcast. He was a Hebrew of the Hebrews, of the stock of Israel, of the tribe of Benjamin, circumcised the eighth day. There had been no lack of viligance in keeping the genealogy or in obeying the strictest Jewish customs. And to complete his Jewish character and training he had come to study at the feet of Gamaliel. Here he so distinguished himself that he won the confidence of the Jerusalem authorities and was received among them in an official capacity.

He could scarcely have been under such circumstances a man who turned against the religion of his fathers because he did not understand its true character. If he had been as en-amored of Hellenistic culture and Roman ways as some have asserted, he would very probably have gone to Athens to study, or to Alexandria, instead of to the school of Gamaliel. It was precisely his Jewish blood and family training which turned his steps to Zion. And there he secured from one of the most celebrated of Jewish teachers the deeper meaning and loftier intent of that faith in which he had been reared.

"And there in the city of the temple," says Deissmann," the Jew felt himself, in spite of the foreign rule of Rome, proud as one specially favored with great privileges. Warnings in Greek and other languages inscribed in stone (one of these preserved to this day) forbade on pain of death any non-Jew from entering the holy enclosure of the temple. At this abode of grace, where the sacred fire of the burnt-offerings was never extinguished, the longing of the pilgrims was satisfied. Here they heard the choirs of the singers and the sound of the harps; here sat the far-famed teachers of the law and gave of their best; here it was possible, if one was present in the sanctuary on the great day of Atonement, to participate, if it were but faintly, in the most solemn ritual service of the whole year. And here every one breathed the sultry atmosphere of the most fervently nationalistic Messianic expectation." [16]

"In spite of the foreign rule of Rome," and in spite of foreign residence, perhaps, Jerusalem and its Temple would make a profound impression upon any man brought up in the home of strict Jewish piety. But the impression would not be identical in the case of every individual, we may be sure of that. Even blood brothers of the same household do not gain identical emotions and thoughts from the same experience. And Saul of Tarsus? What would he think and feel? Whatever his reaction it was no pale and sickly experience, for it was not his nature to be dull and phlegmatic. This Temple service overwhelmed in utter majesty the pagan counterpart in the shrines and temples of Greece and Rome. Here was no repulsive symbolism, no idols and images to seize and fetter the reverent imaginations of men, no trivial word or phrase in the ritual, no hymning of low morals and divine whimsies unworthy of a self-respecting man. The lofty idealism of a dreaming race had found its God above the stars and beyond the sense, an invisible being whose invisible power controlled the round world and ruled the nations for righteousness and peace. The Jew of Tarsus was enslaved by it, and became at once one of its most devoted defenders.

But in his devotion he was like all the rest of us, loyal to just what it meant to him individually. Here, as at Damascus, he could not be disobedient to the thing revealed to him. And just here we come to the heart of Saul's whole view of religion: Living religion was a vital, immediate contact with God. It was not a contact induced by any exercise. It came as a divine visitation, in dreams, in visions, in meditation. But it precisely was not a human affair. "The strings within vi-

---

[16] *Paul, A Study in Social and Religious History,* p. 88.

brate at the touch of God's fingers; the trembling soul reacts
to revelation." [17] The Spirit of God comes to the worshiper
and endows him with power to behold. Not of himself can he
fathom the mysteries of God. "But God reveals them unto us
by His Spirit, for the Spirit searcheth all things, yea the deep
things of God." Revelation, then, the vision, was the means
of discovering the mind of God. Authority in religion, therefore, rested on the revelation to the individual. For Paul, it
was in the voice that spoke to him out of the vision, and in
that same voice speaking at other times in his troubled but
victorious life.

And this we cannot doubt was the direct result of his Jewish religious background. He was following in the footsteps
of the great prophets of Israel, and was receiving his directions from the Lord as they had received theirs before him.
We could not ask for a stronger proof that he was a Hebrew
of the Hebrews; and if not of the tribe of Benjamin, then
certainly of the tribe of Elijah and of Jeremiah. How mightily
did the vision take hold of the mind of the men of this great
succession! Elijah and Jeremiah faced untold dangers that
they might not be disobedient unto the heavenly vision; and
Saul says, "I bear about in my body the marks of the Lord
Jesus."

> Of the Jews five times received I forty stripes save one.
> Thrice was I beaten with rods, once was I stoned,
> Thrice I suffered ship-wreck,
> A night and a day I have been in the deep;
> In journeyings often, in perils of waters, perils of robbers,
> In perils of my own countrymen, perils of the heathen,
> Perils in the city, perils in the wilderness,
> Perils in the sea, perils among false brethren.
> In weariness and painfulness, in watchings often,
> In hunger and thirst, in fastenings often,
> In cold and nakedness.

---

[17] Deissmann, *Paul*, pp. 105-106.

A further proof of the succession may be gained by comparing the utterances of Jeremiah and Saul in regard to their duty. Jeremiah says:

> If I said, I'll not mind Him
> Nor speak in His name,
> Then in my heart 'tis a burning fire,
> Shut up in my bones.[18]

And Saul exclaims, "Woe is me if I preach not the gospel." Out of the same consciousness the two men speak; the same Voice has given birth to the great task of each. There is no denying the mold of Saul's spirit. He is unquestionably the Jew.

But that which is so distinctly Jewish in him, the individuality which originates in the special call of the Voice, was augmented by the atmosphere of the Greek city. There individualism was the prevailing spirit of civilization, but individualism in Judea came always with another quality—not self-consciousness only, but God-consciousness also. A man's self was most truly realized in God, in association with Him, in an identification with His will and purpose. Saul was already bent by this atmosphere of individualism about him in Tarsus, but it took the Jewish form. It took him to Jerusalem to study under Gamaliel, to seek a career in the Lord's service. It made him a zealot, a champion of Judaism, and it prepared him to see the vision and hear the voice before Damascus. It is not the Greek individualism we encounter in Saul, but the kind that made the patriarchs, the prophets, and the heroes of Israel.

And we come to a similar result when we examine the effect of his Roman citizenship. Rome has not changed the corpuscles in his blood nor the cells in his brain. He does not talk like a Jew, but only because he has seen beyond Palestine

---

[18] Jeremiah xx. 9, George Adam Smith's translation.

and has begun to talk like Isaiah of Babylon. Once more the Jewish power of adaptability proves itself, for Saul is able to put on the mind of Greece and Rome without putting off the mind of his people. He can be as cosmopolitan in his outlook as any one and yet remain a member of the chosen people.

This is just what we should expect from one of Saul's mental make-up. He is not a man of speculative, even temper, a man of plodding mold. He is of many moods, with a mind that darts like the sweep of an eagle in its intuitions. He sees the problems of the world, but they are precisely agonizing religious problems to him; he does not miss the strength of the wave in his sight of the foam. And perhaps the chief reason he never pursues any course of reasoning to its end lies in the fact that he has not the patience to do more than indicate the direction his mind intends to leap. We get from his reasoned passages the impression that we are looking at the tumultuous movements of a soul on fire with conviction, that we are looking into the seething cauldron of a volcano that is sure to erupt at any moment. And then it does erupt, leaving the Greeks to cry "hiatus" in condemnation of his style and us to be amazed at the swiftness and vitality of his thought. Here is a man who actually can be all things to all men, who is just the person to become the apostle to the heterogeneous population of the Roman empire.

Deissmann makes much of the fact that he was of the lower orders of society, that he attracted no particular notice in his day, and that he was more at home among the common people. And yet even he confesses that Saul's place was determined for him by the fortunes of the Gospel. In contrasting Saul with Philo he says: "Philo belongs to the upper classes, Paul to the middle and lower classes; Philo represents high literary culture, Paul the strength that wells up from the common people. Philo is a Pharos, Paul a volcano. Philo is a student and theologian, Paul a prophet and herald. Philo worked at his desk for the great literary public, Paul hurried from the workshop to the market-place and the synagogue, to see his hearers face to face. The nephew of Philo, Tiberius Julius Alexander, was procurator of Palestine and Praefect of Egypt and his name is not only immortalized by Josephus, Tacitus and Suetonius, but has also a monument in stone on the wall of the propylon of a temple in the Great Oasis—one of the most famous inscriptions of the early imperial period. Paul's nephew, trembling for the safety of his uncle, as he was questioned by Roman officers in Jerusalem, appeared an unknown man out of the great crowd of the nameless and then at once disappeared. Philo traveled as an ambassador to Rome and was received by the emperor, Paul only had connections with the imperial slaves and was transported to Rome as a prisoner.

"The whole mass of contrasts between the man of Alexandria and the man of Tarsus may be summed up thus: Philo is a Platonist, Paul will be what he will be in another; Philo, the Jew, stands at the end of ancient civilization, Paul, the Jew, stands at the beginning of the new world-religion." [19]

But for the choice Saul made—"What things to me were gain those I counted loss for the excellency of the knowledge of Christ Jesus my Lord"—there might not have been this disparity between the social standing of Saul and Philo. There is, to be sure, the inevitable difference in temperament between the two. Philo had the patience to be as plodding as his age; Paul was impatient because he saw two ages of the world at once. Philo felt and tried to demonstrate the harmony of Biblical and Greek thought. Paul saw the spiritual goal of the Gentile and the Jew—the logical outcome of the aspirations of each—and began to bring in the new age. Philo received his good things during his lifetime; Paul was content with wounds and chains that he might fight his fight, and

---

[19] *Paul, A Study in Social and Religious History.* pp. 109, 110.

finish his course, and keep his faith. For him to live was Christ, and to die was gain. Both were working at the same task—the salvation of the Gentile world by bringing it to a knowledge of Israel's God; which one had the better method history has already declared.

Not from the top could this enormous dream be accomplished. The world was a volcano which blew away emperors, philosophers, temples, and religions too often for one to put his faith in the power and pride of man. But when the volcano subsided the common people always remained. An abiding work of redemption could not be housed in a temple made with hands, but only in the hearts of the lowly. One has the feeling that it was another of those sublime intuitions which caused Saul to court the slaves of Caesar's household rather than Caesar himself. Down close to the ground the winds of destruction were less violent. When political tornadoes swept away the great trees of the world, the smaller ones would be spared. And when some upheaval came to carry away some world-ruler and all his policies, good or bad, the lowly would take up their burdens again in the strength of the living God. If the people could be won the cause of the Christian movement was safe.

We might with profit go even further in this matter of contrast which Deissmann has begun, and put Saul in opposition to the most celebrated priests of the Mysteries or to the best of the Roman emperors. He will not suffer by the comparison. Indeed, it will become increasingly clear that this strange genius of Tarsus could have been almost anything he cared to be—great Platonist, great Hebrew expositor and exegete, or great Roman administrator. But he saw his world too clearly to make the mistake of selecting that which was sure to pass away. Administrative post of great prominence— of what value was it to be even the Caesar? There was Brutus and his dagger, and the practice of poisoning. Greek philosophy—of what value was it finally to salvage Platonism, an

intellectual construction whose sole value lay in the fact that
it indicated the road the Greek spirit was traveling and how
far it had gone along that road? When the world had progressed only a little farther this house of thought would be a
tomb filled with dust and bones from which the spirit had
forever departed. And as to the learned and glorious documents of his nation's religious experience—he saw what God
was about; and, looking down the ages to come, took)his stand
at the goal. He could have felt only pity for Philo, if he had
ever come to know him, for Saul's expressed scorn for the
philosophers of his day shows that he knew how incomplete
was a finished task like Philo's. A new age was at the door;
why try to patch up the old one? Saul would have only the
new.

It appears, then, that Saul knows exactly what he is about,
so much so that we begin to see that there is a profound truth
in his words, "So fight I, not as one that beateth the air." No,
this man's blows are amazingly well calculated and delivered
with an accuracy that produces a staggering effect. From his
standpoint it is a good fight. He knows all the vulnerable
spots and knows just how to use the strength of his opponent
to bring about the desired result. When Death, that finisher of
all men's tasks, was drawing near, he made a quick and sure
appraisal of his results: "I have finished my course; there is a
crown laid up for me." He had won the battle, and knew it
as no one else could possibly know. Any man who can read
the social and religious future of the world with such certainty
is entitled to more than panegyrics; he merits study and
understanding.

To sum up this phase of the discussion: Saul knows his
world—all its subtle forces and hidden vitality. He knows
Greek thought—what it has done and what it cannot do hereafter. He knows the spirit of the Alexandrian civilization—
its merits, its faults, its present great social tragedy. And he
knows Rome, the borrower, the fumbling adapter, the social

octopus. But he is too great to feel only scorn for her; she has her possibilities, and in the divine economy is spared for that very reason. This power, after all, is ordained of God. She is missing the mark and is doomed if she continues upon the present path, but she is worth winning. Furthermore, he knows his own people—their genius, their destiny as the light of the world and the Servant of God among the nations, their social blindness and the danger involved for those who are directing affairs, their recent great Prophet who has expressed the true technique of achieving vital unity with the living God. And after a world-view that blinds him with the dazzling light of its possibilities, he goes forth to preach the truth which is the goal of all human seeking and the way to that world-redemption which Philo and the Prophets have felt must come to pass. Such was Saul of Tarsus.

How did he set about the task which was designed to give to the Gentiles the religion of truth and certainty they needed and were seeking? He began to teach. But we shall miss our way and wholly misunderstand him if we look for a systematic body of truth, cogent and sufficient within itself. The perfect logical demonstration is after all not an end in itself, but only a guidepost on the road of the Spirit. That was just where the Greek philosopher went astray. He ended with his logical mouse-trap. Saul and all living, toiling men wished to know, "What does it mean? Where do we go from this point?" The philosophers did not know except in the vaguest way, but Saul knew. It must lead to God, to conscious unity with God. We find in the teaching of Saul excellent reasoning which philosophically seems to get nowhere, or at best only so far. We encounter definitions of a kind, evidently only sketchy outlines, bald strokes to guide the thinking, or to speak more accurately, the intuitions. Of what need is there for a completely reasoned system when system is not the object of the enterprise and will be sure to call attention to itself? A few strokes are far better, provided one does not begin at once to try to make a theology out of them. In Christ, in God, is the goal; not the appreciation of the logical consistency and efficiency of the Universe. Any man with average wit can see that things hang together; but can one be conscious of his own relation to Him in whom he lives and moves and has his being? Can he extend that consciousness to victorious life, to an unamazed calmness and sense of safety no earthly disaster can disturb? It is a triumph in *being* that Saul is trying to achieve, a new person; not knowledge per se.

Here again we are forced to distinguish between the Greek individualism and that of Saul. The Greeks labored for an individual who was strong through his possessions—through his knowledge, his properties, his skill, his virtues, his art, his utter freedom within and without. Saul seeks to immerse his individual in the Deity, to bind him with the divine will and nature, to make him strong and free by making him a new creature. The Greek individual must use tools, the means to power. The new man Saul hopes to raise up *is* all power, because of the deity that works in him. Of what value is it to reason about ethics? The new man must *be* ethical. And of what value is it to demonstrate the logical and metaphysical unity of all things? The new man must *be consciously unified* with the Source of all things. The Greek stands outside the door of his house, admiring, tinkering, explaining; the new man Saul seeks *is* his house, a living temple made for the indwelling of the living God. We miss everything if we fail to use this clue and proceed to become this new creature.

How misguided and futile, therefore, is that exercise which ends in a discussion of Paulinism—Pauline theology, Pauline eschatology, Pauline ecclesiasticism, Pauline Christology, or anything else that is Pauline. Saul did not preach in order to furnish his hearers with a lingo, a few big words to roll on their tongues. That was just what the Greek philosophers had done. Blind guides who led the blind—the whole Greek world had fallen into the ditch of rationalism. And Saul who sees exactly what has happened is certainly trying to avoid their predicament. The Christian world has not made enough of this distinction. Hence we have had our revolt from sacramentarianism only to fall into the theological pit. This is not the Slough of Despond from which Help extracted Pilgrim, but it is just as bad. In exasperation we now and then do a great deal of mud-slinging, but our zeal only tramps us deeper into the mire. Woe to those gifted gentlemen who left us floundering here!

But we need no one to help us out. If we remember that it has been the tendency of all religions to pass from actual religious experience to a reasoning about the experience, we may turn to an attempt to be like Christ rather than to a reasoning about Christ. Every true reform in the Christian church has been an attempt to restore actual religion. From Gregory the Great to Wesleyism the attempts have succeeded and failed in turn. Deissmann says: "The means by which it was sought to keep Christianity free from the danger of disfigurement from this source are amongst the greatest achievements of both Catholic and Protestant theology. The Catholic method (coarser, plainer and more adapted to the mass of men) was the idea of the Church. The Protestant method (simpler, and more profound) was the idea of Scripture and even more the idea of revelation, especially when revelation was not supposed to be contained within certain chronological boundaries. Within this precinct, however it were named, it was possible to tend the holy flame ignited from God's own volcano, and there over and over again as the lava became cool to re-melt it in the fiery flood of the original heat. But alas when Church and Scripture themselves became chilled to black stone!" [20] We need only to remember the spiritual object of both Church and Scripture and to act upon their clues to make religion a living fact again. As a clue, the Church, or

---

[20] *Paul, A Study in Social and Religious History*, p. 119.

Scripture, is efficacious; but unless we by intuition arrive at the fact beyond the clue, we can be nothing but blind zealots storming our shibboleths at one another.

It is a further evidence of the genius of Saul that he saw the significance of Gentile religious aspiration and the deepest fact of Israel's religion, and sought in the new man, to which both were tending, to put an end to all shibboleths but one— to achieve a spiritual goal in which there would be no further conflicts among theologians, no further debates among philosophers, neither Jew nor Greek, neither bond nor free, but only brothers sharing a common religious experience. It is just this unity, this at-oneness with God, which is the one and sole fundamental of Christianity, and at the same time the one credential of true religion no matter by what method it may be gained. That having been secured, we may use logic, philosophies, and theology without becoming possessed with an exaggerated sense of their importance. We may differ with one another without resorting to blows and to such conduct as proves to all the world that we are not one whit nearer the Christian life than the most stupid heathen. This fact about true religion the theologian, above all men, must not fail to observe. It is far better to be like Saul than to fall into the error of losing our religion. Know nothing save Jesus Christ and him crucified.

What was the unity with the divine nature through Christ which Saul thought of as accomplishing this new man? We shall perhaps secure our most valuable information on this point by turning to the facts attending and constituting his own new nature in Christ, his experience before Damascus. Deissmann thinks "we shall never reach the point of completely unraveling this experience psychologically, not even by the help of the numerous analogous accounts of conversion in the history of religion." [21] But Deissmann goes on to do some

---

[21] *Paul, A Study in Social and Religious History*, p. 129.

unraveling, and concludes, "The Christ-mystery has been made known to him by revelation." [22] . . . "What happened at Damascus ought not to be isolated, but it should be regarded as the basal mystical experience of the religious genius to whom also in later life extraordinary and even ecstatic experiences were vouchsafed. All that can be called Paul's Christ-mysticism is the reaction to this initial experience." [23] "The conversion of the persecutor into a follower and of the Pharisee Apostle into the Apostle of Christ was a sudden one. Yet it was no magic transformation, but had its psychological preparation both negative and positive." [24] Deissmann goes on to state that the negative preparation consisted of those experiences through which the soul of the young Pharisee had gone in its passionate hunger for righteousness under the yoke of the law. The positive preparation came through the prophetic inwardness of the Old Revelation which had influenced him even as a Jew, and through a relatively close touch with the genuine tradition of Jesus and with the effects wrought by Him in the characters of the confessors whom he persecuted. "So the lightning of Damascus strikes no empty space but finds deep in the soul of the persecutor plenty of inflammable material." [25] No doubt the most positive thing of all was the ecstatic utterance of Stephen; "Behold, I see the heavens opened, and the Son of man standing on the right hand of God." The sight of Stephen's face never disappeared from Saul's mind until it faded in that light above the brightness of the sun.

And that light, it was both within and without. "He appeared to me also," [26] in the same way that He appeared to the other disciples after the resurrection. But the word he uses for "appear" means "appear in a vision"! Again he says, "It

---

[22] *Ibid.*, p. 129.
[23] *Ibid.*, pp. 130, 131.
[24] *Ibid.*, p. 131.
[25] *Ibid.*, p. 132.
[26] I Corinthians xiii. 8, ὤφθη

pleased God . . . to reveal his son in me, that I might preach him among the heathen." [27] The subjective character of the vision is thus fairly clear. Finally, he speaks of being "apprehended" [28] of Christ Jesus. Here his word refers to the "mystical seizure." But this light was also, to Saul, objective as well as subjective, affecting his organs of sight so that he was compelled to depend upon the help of his companions to find his way into the city. In one of the accounts these companions are represented as hearing the voice but seeing no man, [29] in another they saw the light but did not hear the voice. [30] How much they shared in Saul's experience is after all beside the point. The theophany was in full accord with the then current Hebrew theory of revelation, or was so regarded by Saul. It had no meaning whatever for Saul's companions. As to the value of their witness for purposes of verification, Saul himself had no need of it; and the more we study the composite nature of Saul's previous education and experience the more we are inclined to favor his account of that moment when all things became clear in a blinding light.

The place of the theophany in the early church is well established. On the day of Pentecost it affected the whole assembly of the apostles—the Holy Spirit descended upon them and was visible as light and fire. Peter preached in the house of Cornelius and even the Gentiles present received the Holy Ghost. Stephen in a moment of ecstasy saw the opened heavens and Jesus standing on the right hand of God. Peter on the house-top saw a vision of God's will for the Gentiles. The only way in which we can penetrate this psychological puzzle is by a study of the ecstatic state of all the Prophets and of the accompaniments of all vision and appearance which attend Old Testament revelation. And this is so because the accep-

[27] Galatians i. 6.
[28] Philemon iii. 12.
[29] Acts ix. 7.
[30] Acts xxii. 9.

table theophanies of the Apostolic Age were but a continuance of the Hebrew prophetic experience. We have not given enough attention to this feature of the early church. The experience of a risen Lord, the descent of the Holy Spirit, the calls to preach, the deliverances from prison, the prosecution of the Christian ministry as affected by any change of plan or new decision—all these are profoundly colored by the prophetic ecstasy, so much so that we may regard the whole drive and certainty of this period as springing from the prophetic experience. The Apostolic Church was a prophetic church.

And yet the ecstasy was not sufficient in itself. The Apostles applied a merciless criticism to the claims and manifestations of divine visitation. Not every voice was accepted. Ecstatic counsel was forced to submit to the sovereignty of reason— there could be no calling Jesus accursed, no conflict with the claims of Jesus or his actual utterances, no violation of his spirit and attitude, and no conflict with the substance of formerly accredited revelations. God precisely did not speak foolishness. In other words, there was an application of a norm of judgment to these states, one that must have been far older than Christianity and one that was applied by the Hebrews in all the history of Prophecy.

All this affords much illumination upon two items of early Christian thought—the new man, and the manner of his making. Receiving the Holy Ghost was undoubtedly an essential factor in the making of a Christian. In one place Saul seems to regard it as the final sealing fact in making the new creature, "in whom (Christ) also after that ye believed, ye were sealed with that Holy Spirit of promise" [81] When in one of his journeys Saul came to Ephesus and met there certain brethren, he asked them if they had received the Holy Ghost since they had become believers. They answered in the negative, declaring that they had not so much as heard that there

---

[81] Ephesians i. 13.

was a Holy Ghost. It was then learned that they were followers of John the Baptist and had not received the Baptism into the name of Christ. After proper instruction Saul baptized them, "And when Paul had laid his hands upon them, the Holy Ghost came upon them; and they spake with tongues and prophecied." [32] That inquiry concerning the Holy Ghost is significant, for it seems to have been the final proof that the believer had become a new creature. That it was very early regarded in some such way is further established by the controversy that arose over Peter's going to the Gentiles. Of the event in question Peter said: "And as I began to speak, the Holy Ghost fell on them, as on us at the beginning. Then remembered I the word of the Lord, how that he said, 'John indeed baptized with water; but ye shall be baptized with the Holy Ghost.' Forasmuch then as God gave them the like gift as unto us, who believed on the Lord Jesus Christ; what was I, that I could withstand God?" [33] The very fact that the Holy Ghost came upon these Gentiles is a proof that they are as well-accredited Christians as any in the early church. The order of experience leading to full membership seems to have been hearing, believing, accepting, baptism into the Name, and finally the receiving of the Holy Ghost.

This indicates that the type of certainty sought, in the Gentile world at least, was an actual experience of contact with God. It was to be found in a state of exaltation, of ecstasy. In the new religion of Jesus it occurred subsequent to baptism and through the medium of the laying on of hands. A number of unwholesome specters rise to greet us as we ponder this method of the reception of the Holy Ghost, but the results of the human and divine contacts were edifying. We have seen how this mystical experience grows out of the notion of the prophetic state. We can therefore understand how it would not be antagonistic to the previous beliefs of certain

---

[32] Acts xix. 6
[33] Acts ii. 15-17.

of the Jews. But the Mystery religions of the Gentile world were also urging a mystical contact with the deity in the initiation and "new birth" of their novitiates. Along this single path of mysticism, this contact with the Deity and its ecstatic results, the Christian movement won its way in all lands. On this road no cleavage into nationalities and races was encountered—no Jew nor Greek—but the common nature of all humanity.

The mysticism of Saul was, however, very different from the mysticism of India in both method and result. Buddha submerged his individual in the bosom of deity and thus caused the individual to blend and be lost in God. Saul thought of the man as entering into fellowship with God; the individual was an even more pronounced and effective individual than before. Buddha produced this mystic state through "mystical exercises"; Saul was endued with power from on high. Saul was apprehended by God; Buddha seized upon deity. Thus in the Christian church God must move toward man and bestow upon him the grace that would enable him to commune immediately with Deity.

Deissmann in describing mysticism in general says: "The aim of mysticism is either unio or communio; either oneness with God, or fellowship with God; either loss of the human personality in God or sanctification of the personality through the presence of God; either transformation into the deity, or conformation of the human towards the divine; either participation in the deity or prostration before the deity. In fact ego-centric mysticism or Theo-centric mysticism! Mysticism of aesthetic intoxication or mysticism of ethical enthusiasm! Mysticism that denies personality, or mysticism that affirms personality." [34] Deissmann goes on to say that Saul was conscious of the difference between the two types: "His conflict with the 'spirituals' at Corinth is the protest of reacting mys-

---

[34] *Paul, A Study, etc.*, pp. 150-151.

ticism against the ecstatic chaos caused by the mysticism of intoxicated enjoyment developing into unrestrained action. But he had also conquered in the same battle within his own breast, when the old mystical activism had whispered to him in words of temptation, eritis sicut Deus—'ye shall be as God.' No doubt it was out of such a struggle that that wonderful paradox was born: 'I—yet not I,' which repeatedly flashes out of the lines of his letters." [35]

Here it must be confessed that the attempt to erase all lines of nationality and races is actually by means of a very pronounced racial instrument. The mysticism of the Alexandrian world is precisely the mysticism of the rest of the Orient. Mithraism is from Persia, perhaps a Zoroastrianism which has been touched by Buddhist influence. At any rate, the mysticism is just this mysticism of central Asia and India. But Jewish mysticism is, at its highest point, a vision of God and His will. The individual is subject to a God of history—the man receives his treasure in earthen vessels that the exceeding greatness of the power may be seen to be of God and not of man. Angus has already pointed out that the spiritual condition of the Gentile world is almost identical with that of pre-Buddhistic India. [36] And the Orient is meeting it just as Buddha would have tried to meet it! The result? Greek individualism overflows the induced divine consciousness, asserts itself at the expense of deity; instead of becoming suppressed, in true Buddhist fashion, it becomes intoxicated with the joy of having become as God. Here, then, we encounter in the instructions of Saul to the Corinthians the substance of the essential difference between Christian and Eastern mysticism. Saul has therefore seen the best and the worst of the mysticism of the Mysteries—its promise and possibility as well as its weakness and unwholesomeness. He urges the only way which can combat it and yet make the most of it. Salvation becomes

---

[35] *Ibid.*, pp. 153-154.
[36] *The Mystery Religions and Christianity*, pp. 226, 227.

therefore the triumph of the genius of one people over that of all peoples. Salvation is of the Jew.

It was the Gentile longing, however, and its predisposition toward this very Eastern mysticism which constituted Saul's great guarantee that he would win the Alexandrian world. He had only to substitute communion for union with the Deity, to replace intoxication as the end of divine contact with ethos as the goal of all aspiration, and to replace human exaltation by a participation in divine essence with fellowship which expressed itself in "co-workers together with God." What seems to us at first, therefore, a very complex and highly differentiated system of thought, and one not easily wrought into form by the most gifted of our theologians, is after all a comparatively simple gospel. Deissmann says: "The message of Christ which the tent-maker of Tarsus preached to the simple people of the great Hellenistic cities in the age of the Caesars, must have been simple—or at any rate understandable by the simple—transporting and inspiring to the common people. There is a way by which we can recognize even today the popular simplicity of the Pauline gospel. We must take seriously the observation, which is also to be made in the case of Luther, Paul Gerhardt, Herder and most other classical and religious writers, that in the numberless confessions about Christ which follow one another without system in the letters of Paul the reference is not to a diversity of many objects but to a diversity of the psychological reflections of the one object of religion. To this one object the confessor bears witness in a continually new variation of figurative words of similar meaning and often with the parallelism of prophetic emphasis. And it is our business to grasp the figurativeness, the ancient popular pictorial character of these testimonies." [37] The observation hits close to the fact. And the diversity becomes clear and simple to the common man just because it ex-

---

[37] *Paul, A Study, etc.,* pp. 166-167.

plains an experience already well known to him. Mysticism had already opened up an area of psychology and consciousness which Saul could approach from many angles and describe in various terms. The language of Saul is, however, descriptive rather than philosophical. His aim is to lead men into an experience of the spiritual fact, not into a knowledge in which the fact is revealed as an integral factor. The latter would lead almost at once to that academic disaster which almost always overtakes religion—the substitution of an intellectual comprehension of the facts of religion for an experience of the facts.

What is the experience in substance? The individual hears the gospel proclaimed; he believes the message to be the way of life; he accepts that message; he submits to baptism as a symbolical witness of his willingness to be, not submerged and lost in Christ, but exalted and recreated in Christ; then by the laying on of the Apostle's hands he receives the Holy Ghost, actual mystical contact with God with all its attendant manifestation of power. The old life is abandoned, and the new life of the new creature in Christ has become a fact.

Now just this simple spiritual experience must be made clear to those who hold to a legalistic notion of redemption and who have therefore a sense of guilt. It must be made to square with the Jewish background of final judgment. The guilt must be regarded as removed and the accusation quashed. The prisoner must be acquitted. Saul presents as the ground for acquittal a condition which he terms "faith." God through Christ and in Christ produces this faith, or persuasion leading to contact; by this contact, this state of being apprehended, this mystical experience of the Holy Ghost, the prisoner becomes a new creature and is "acquitted" of his past life and old personality. In a similar way the enmity between man and God is wiped out by God's acts of reconciling grace in this experience of Christ. The metaphor of the debtor views the grace, or the movement of God toward man, in this experience as a forgiveness of the debt involved in the selfish nature of the old life. And the figure of the slave pictures man as being redeemed from his slavery to the old life by his becoming a new creature. Thus the one mystic experience is variously described and made clear to those who already know something of it through previous religious training. The actual religious experience is in itself not nearly the involved and difficult matter the advocates of Paulinism have made it.

The new creature—the prisoner acquitted, the enemy reconciled, the debtor forgiven, and the slave redeemed or set free —enjoys all the privileges of the individual submerged in Deity. In other words, the Christian is in no sense behind the Buddhist in the deific favor he receives. At the same time he still possesses his individuality. And although at times the bond is psychically loosed so that he is fully aware of the presence of the old nature striving in him—he feels two forces at war in his nature, one unto life, the other unto death—he never wholly lapses into the old life. God renews him daily, or frequently; nothing can pluck him out of the hand of God or separate him from the love of Christ. Thus his life becomes a controlled life, the life of a bond-slave in Christ. He suffers for his cause, but the enmity is not against him but against his Master. His life is "lived unto God" and his sufferings are in the last analysis the sufferings of Christ who dwells in him. "Not I—but Christ," says Saul. He has risen above any adversity which may touch either his flesh or his spirit, for they are Christ's afflictions and Christ is able to bear them.

To the Jew Saul necessarily presented the Master of this slave as the one who should come. Messianism and the prophetic experience—Judaism in its hope and divine contact— are identified with each other in the person of Jesus. This Lord was in himself the very spirit of ideal Judaism in its great rôle of Servant in the divine task of saving the world.

Some one must be the leader in such an enterprise, some one must set the example and actually begin the great new Messianic kingdom of spirituality which should bring the world to God. This Jesus had actually done. He had borne his people's sins in his own body, and through his own personal sufferings had actually healed his people, for he had thus provided a way for their salvation.

This identification of Jesus with the Messianic hope of Israel required that Saul make some explanation of the kingdom of the Messiah. It is quite clear that he regarded his labors of the ministry as only a preparation for the second coming of the Lord. This would occur soon—soon enough that he hoped to see it. Jesus would come, inaugurate his Kingdom, and rule until he had put all things under his feet. When all things had been subjected, the Kingdom would be turned over to the Father who would be all in all. But along with this expectation, which is essentially Jewish in character, there was another idea which was Persian or Hellenistic. The individual would be preserved. Those who died before the establishment of the Kingdom would not perish but would go "where Christ is." This place "where Christ is" could scarcely have been the grave. And yet, in describing the actual coming of Christ, Saul says: "The trumpet shall sound and the dead in Christ shall rise first. We who are alive and remain at his coming shall be caught up together with them in the clouds. We shall be changed. This corruptible must put on incorruption." In such utterances it appears that the dead linger in their graves until Jesus comes.

Upon this point Deissmann says: "The Apostle's hope did not however dogmatically fix the time of this metamorphosis. At one time it tends toward the more Jewish and Pharisaic conviction of the resurrection: the dead will rest in their graves and will be awakened at the parousia of Christ and along with those who are still alive 'changed' into the spiritual. At another time his prophetic gaze is more Hellenistic and is directed towards the immortality of the soul:

> For we know:
> If our earthly tent-house be dissolved,
> We have a building of God,
> A house not made with hands,
> Eternal in the heavens.[38]

There is a lack of harmony in Saul's thinking at this point. Or, perhaps, the contradiction is from the nature of his communications—letters which presuppose much oral teaching in which the harmony may have been presented. The very fact that the two views are called to the attention of the Corinthian Church [39] would seem to indicate that such disharmony had been previously discussed and cleared up. And yet the very immediacy of the Messiah's coming would tend to put all such considerations in the background. "In Christ" or "with Christ" the individual was safe: "whether we live therefore, or die, we are the Lord's." Haste and enthusiastic preparation for the Lord's coming occupied the attention of these early converts. It was therefore reserved for a later age to criticize these assuring utterances and to make them into an eschatological problem.

The greatest difficulty encountered by Saul had its origin in the fact that he proclaimed a leader who had been crucified. To the Jew it was a stumbling block and a rock of offense. Their Messiah would conquer, not be put to death! To say that he had been crucified was to insult the Jew. And to the Greek such a teaching was preposterous. Man at death went to Hades; he did not walk in this world or have any power over events to come. The success of Saul's preaching shows that he was able to meet this difficulty from both angles and to

[38] *Paul, A Study, etc.*, pp. 217-218.
[39] I Corinthians xv. 51ff. and II Corinthians v. 1.

achieve among certain people the conviction that the crucifixion of Jesus was the occasion which established the power
and the wisdom of God.

How did he do it? He presents no metaphysical defense of
the doctrine of the resurrection, at least none that could be
termed conclusive. All his utterances upon the subject are
couched in the "mystery" terms of the religious experience of
his generation. They are understood by the people who hear
him because they express certain religious ideas and values
already well known. The resurrection of Jesus makes possible
the mystical experience of Him. While he was alive they saw
him with their eyes; when he died he was transformed, was
given a special form and a special body; he became like a
spirit, and was now to be known only by the spiritually
minded, or to whomsoever he wished to reveal himself. It was
necessary for him to die if his people were to have the joy
of this experience of him, for they could not of course have
this experience of Christ in the flesh. And he must die if the
"spiritual discernment" was to be made the central feature of
all religious knowledge. His disciples never so understood
Him, never surrounded him with his true atmosphere. He
was the One to come, but they thought he would be the ruler
of Judea, a kingdom like all the other kingdoms of this earth.
Life would, in their conception of his sovereignty, be as it had
always been—sinful, sordid, earthly, just life in another world
power. But he had come that they might have life more abundant. It was his purpose to exalt life, to lift it to the prophetic
pitch, to make it conspicuously spiritual. To do this it was
necessary for him to die and to be transformed. No real
knowledge of the kind of life he had come to reveal could be
gained by His followers until he had died and had appeared
to them in his spiritual form. All this is made clear in the
words of Jesus, "It is expedient for you that I go away: for if
I go not away, the Comforter will not come unto you; but if I
depart, I will send him unto you." The death of Jesus was an

essential step in revealing the nature of His kingdom and the type of existence man was to receive.

This mystic experience of the living Christ, of the Crucified, was not the result of the believer's imagination. The experience was to the disciples and others wholly external to any use of their own powers—completely a matter of divine grace; Jesus appeared to them. The appearance was the presentation of a concrete fact. At this level man came into contact with deity, with the highest meaning of Jesus, and with the fullest expression of his own being. Here was to be found the life that was life indeed. While Jesus was in the world he was the light of the world, but when he went away He became the light of eternity. Thus in suffering death he had become the perfect witness of the way of man's great possibility, the Captain of this Salvation made perfect through his suffering.

We may now read Deissmann's remarks with clearer understanding: "The following are Paul's convictions about the resurrection of Jesus. In them old Biblical and Pharisaic beliefs have amalgamated with the apostolic tradition under the influence of his personal experience at Damascus. It was the miraculous act of God and took place 'according to the scriptures' on the third day; it was identical with the exaltation and was the resumption of the spiritual life of Jesus in glory with the Father. It was not fleshly, but it gave to the Living One, probably by a process of transformation, a spiritual heavenly body. It was the conquest of death, and it did away with the puzzle of the cross." [40]

"According to the Scriptures." We experience much difficulty in finding just the Scriptures referred to. As we go over the citations offered by Saul we realize more and more that even this reference above depends upon a certain way of handling the Old Testament. We find that the passages in question in speaking of one thing have either intentionally or unintentionally spoken of other matters than the subject under

---

[40] *Paul, A Study, etc.*, pp. 199-200.

discussion. In other words, the passages contain an allegory; they have spoken of things to come in a figure. Without a knowledge of the type of exegesis then prevailing among Biblical teachers we might be put to much trouble to find Scriptural ground for these significant events in the life of Jesus. But with such knowledge—the point of view exercised by Philo and the translators of the Septuagint—we can find Scripture enough for the purpose. And incidentally, we have discovered the well from which Saul drank. As a Jew of the Diaspora he used the Septuagint almost exclusively and was therefore the heir of that Hellenistic tendency which expressed itself among the Jews of his time.

How difficult it has been for the soteriologists and Christologists to present the religious reality behind the cross! They discuss it from the standpoint of each metaphor Saul used. They try to present a reasoned Christian theology, a philosophy of the Christian religion, in which the cross is represented by a lifeless abstraction of no value to any one. In truthful moments they confess, "I know only this: for some reason and in some way Jesus died for our sins." In other words they know only what Saul has said, but have no knowledge of the mystic meaning his words contain. The "mysteria" of the cross thus becomes labyrinthine, mystery stretching on mystery, and to be greeted, because of the very confusion, with the cry that believes where it cannot prove, "O the depth of the riches, both of the wisdom and the knowledge of God; how unsearchable are its judgments and its ways past finding out!" But too frequently there is not enough appreciation of the "wisdom" to know that it contains judgment. A much more truthful exclamation would be, "O this stumbling-block of the cross, this foolishness, this utter mystery whereby we are saved!" Thus our eyes shine more often with the tears of defeat than with the tears of exultation and joy.

This assuredly could not have been the case with the early Christians. They experienced their proofs. They knew Him in whom they believed. They were by divine grace ushered into the presence of the Crucified, saw him, handled him, knew him. Whether or not we modern Greeks and Pharisees will care for these experiences does not matter. The men of the later Alexandrian Age did care for them, regarded them as the way to the presence of deity, made them the goal of all religious aspiration, and on this road of the inner life came to those consolations and liberties which lifted them above the privations and perils of their lot and made them victorious over Time and Death. Jesus, the Crucified, by the preaching of Saul became the Savior of the Gentile world.

To those who may retort that such a gospel is purely the product of an epoch, let me remark that Jesus *was* adapted to the Gentile world. He was presented to it in *its own religious language*, and he saved those who accepted him. If this Gospel is to be timeless we must seek to know our age well enough to make Jesus vital to its aspirations and the complete answer to its peculiar religious longing. A timeless gospel is one that serves each succeeding generation. "We have only to declare the gospel," say some. "It is the power of God unto salvation." All of which is more profoundly true than these enthusiasts can possibly understand. But those who have the sublime gift of a feel for history, and read in it the will of God, will not continue to be broken by falling over this stone. They will see in another blinding light the glorious superstructure of humanity redeemed and will know what to use as the head of the corner. Such was the gift which determined the method of Saul of Tarsus.

Here we leave him—wise, profound, sincere—gentle and tender as the Master he served, as fearless and as constant as he. He has blazed the way and revealed the spirit which must guide all those who seek to take part in this ministry with him. The way will be hard, and at times the spirit will be endangered by the studied cruelties and gross practices of men, but at the end is a crown of life. If Derbe will not receive us, let us go on to Lystra; at last comes a bright sword and the great release. It is still the chief merit of a servant that he be faithful. And for such there is a place prepared and set in order. This election to eternal habitations we must make sure.

CHAPTER XI

MAHOMET

Ameer Ali, Syed, in his book, *The Spirit of Islam*, says: "At the dawn of the seventh century of the Christian era, in the streets of Mecca might often be seen a quiet thoughtful man, past the meridian of life, his Arab mantle thrown across his shoulders, his tailasan (scarf) drawn low over his face; sometimes gently sauntering, sometimes hurrying along, heedless of the passer-by, heedless of the gay scenes around him, deeply absorbed in his own thoughts—yet withal never forgetful to return the salutation of the lowliest, or to speak a kindly word to children who loved to throng around him. This is al-Amin, 'the Trusty.' He has so honorably and industriously walked through life, that he has won for himself from his compatriots the noble designation of the true and trusty. But now, owing to his strange preaching, his fellow-townsmen are beginning to look suspiciously upon him as a wild visionary, a crazed revolutionist, desirous of leveling the old landmarks of society, of doing away with their ancient privileges, of making them abandon their old creeds and customs." [1]

Mahomet, whom Ameer Ali thus describes, is an Arab poet who has had a somber childhood. His father, Abdullah, shortly after his marriage to Amina, went on a trading expedition to Gaza, in Palestine, and on his way home became ill at Medina and died there before his wife or any of his friends could visit him. Shortly after this event Mahomet was born in Mecca and was, according to the custom of the upper classes, given immediately into the care of a nurse. His foster-mother,

---

[1] Ameer Ali, Syed, *The Spirit of Islam*, pp. 1-2.

Halima, took him away to her home in the mountains of Taif. Here in the fresh cool air of the uplands he remained for five years and grew sturdy and well favored in both mind and body. At the end of this period he was taken to his mother in Mecca. Soon afterward the widow took him with her on a visit to his father's tomb in Medina. While returning she sickened and died by the wayside, leaving her son to the care of a slave-girl. This girl brought him back to Mecca and gave him to his aged grandfather. For two years the child was shown every kindness, and then his grandfather died, passing him on to an uncle, Abu Talib, a rich and influential chief.

In consequence of all this unsettled condition in his earlier years, Mahomet's education was neglected. He was not taught to read and write, and these deficiencies were not made up in his new home. In all other respects he was treated with the highest consideration. He was given a seat at his uncle's table, was taught the use of arms, and was permitted to accompany the uncle wherever he went. Thus he learned the condition of much of the country, for his uncle engaged in numerous trading expeditions to distant cities.

In such surroundings and circumstances Mahomet grew up into a handsome young man. He was of serious and grave deportment, given to silence and meditation, and evidenced a dependability and industry which set him apart from others of his age. Perhaps his silence and meditative turn of mind were due partly to his later occupation and his lack of education. He was a shepherd at twenty and roamed the hills and valleys alone with his flocks. He could not read or write and was thus shut up to the broodings and imaginings of his very active and gifted mind. But his temperament was also largely responsible for his gravity and silence. Had he been ever so well educated he would have spent much time, very probably, in pondering the things he read. And he would have written

down the poems which he now composed and stored up in
his heart.

At the age of twenty-five he was chosen by a wealthy widow
named Kadijah to take charge of a caravan which she was
getting ready to send to Syria. He knew the route well, for he
had traveled over it some years before with his uncle who had
gone there on a trading expedition. Perhaps the young shepherd had shown even then that honesty, adaptability, and
special aptitude for trading which caused the widow to select
him. And perhaps there may have been already another reason
in her mind. At any rate, when he returned a year later
eminently successful and having by his shrewdness added
greatly to the wealth of his benefactress, he was rewarded
beyond his greatest expectations. Kadijah negotiated through
her sister a proposal of marriage, for she had fallen in love
with her handsome camel-driver.

Before the year closed Mahomet and Kadijah were married. She had been married twice before and her rich husbands
had died, leaving her all their property. At the time of her
marriage to Mahomet she was forty years of age, very beautiful, and one of the richest ladies of the land. In spite of the
fact that Mahomet was only a little over twenty-five years of
age their marriage was a very happy one. Gilman in his book
The Saracens describes Mahomet at this period: "His wide
chest and broad shoulders were surmounted by a long and
finely molded neck, and a massive head, from which looked
out a frank, oval face, marked by a prominent aquiline nose,
large, restless, and piercing black eyes, over which long, heavy
lashes drooped, and a bushy beard fell upon his breast." His
grave and thoughtful manner, his unusual intelligence and
fine physique, made him a commanding figure. In his new
position of wealth and influence he seemed quite at home, and
there was no feeling among his acquaintances that his marriage to Kadijah was in any way improper.

To be sure the discrepancy in the ages of the two was not

an unusual thing in Arabia, for it was the custom for the son to inherit the wives of his father, his own mother alone being excepted. But Mahomet had in a moment advanced from a position of comparative poverty to one of great wealth. With this wealth he also gained a place of considerable influence, and became a very important man in the city. His natural dignity, his great courtesy and kindness, and his hearty greeting to all who saluted him, rich and poor alike, showed that there had been no real change in the man. Thus neither at home nor abroad was there anything to mar the happiness of him who was to become a few years later one of the world's great leaders.

For the next few years he engaged in travel to distant places for commercial reasons. His trading expeditions were unusually successful and he added materially to his already considerable wealth. In time he gave up his active merchant life and turned his energies to religious interests. No doubt his serious and thoughtful frame of mind compelled him to feel that, as a man of considerable influence in Mecca and the surrounding country, it was his duty to help the people to a higher and better social plane. At his time of life he could not help but see the evils of society and know their cause. His deep love for mankind and his general pity toward all unfortunates caused him to ponder the causes of human suffering and evil almost constantly. And his intelligence of a high order helped him to devise a way by which the social condition of Arabia could be remedied.

In remote antiquity a temple was built at Mecca which tradition ascribed to Abraham. This temple, the Kaaba, continued to be the most holy and sacred of all the temples of the Arabic peoples. It contained three hundred and sixty idols, one for each day of the year, which were grouped facing the great idol of the god, Hobal, carved in red agate, the two gazelles of gold and silver, and the image of Abraham and his son. Each year the tribes came to Mecca to visit this shrine and to kiss the black stone which was believed to have fallen from heaven. Tradition declares that this stone was originally pure white. The Arabs affirm that it wept so much over the sins of men that it became black. J. J. Poole says that the stone is now reddish brown, or black, because it has been handled and kissed by tens of thousands, yea, millions, of devotees during the hundreds of years. It was perhaps originally embedded in the walls of a building, the Kaaba, around which the temple was built.

Mahomet's uncle, Abu Talib, was the guardian of this stone and took an important part in the worship. Thus the later prophet had every opportunity to be well acquainted with the religion of the Arabs. Mecca stood at the center of the commercial activity of the peninsula. The caravan routes passed out from it like the spokes of a wheel. Thus it was enabled to gather to itself the wealth and culture of the neighboring countries. It is said that from the nature of her situation her people became the carriers of the world's trade and that her prosperity excelled even that of Babylon. From Mecca caravans went to Byzantine, Persia, Yemen, Syria, India, and Alexandria. Mecca was the clearing-house for all the rich products of these countries. Commodities other than the articles of trade naturally made their way to this great metropolis. All the luxurious habits of the East came in with the merchants from many lands. Thus the vices of the neighboring empires began to show their effect upon the people of Mecca. Slave-girls from Persia and Greece sang and danced and served the sensual desires of the metropolitan population. The Meccans became passionately addicted to drinking, gambling, and licentious festivities. No voice in the city urged a more righteous course than that of seeking the joys of the present life.

During this period preceding the reforms of Mahomet, polygamy was practiced to an unlimited extent. The widow, other than the son's own mother, passed to the use of the son upon his father's death. Female infants were buried alive by all the tribes. There were numerous idols, sacred stones and trees, and holy places at which the worship was chiefly phallic. The majority of the tribes, however, were given to fetishism. Animals, trees, inorganic nature,—the gazelle, the horse, and the camel, the palm tree, and pieces of rock and stone were held in adoration. Some few of the more intelligent men revolted from the gross obscenities and materialism of the time and hoped for a Deliverer to come who would abolish such practices.

At Ukaz, a three days' journey from Mecca, the annual fair was held. During the sacred month of Zu'l-ka'da, when all vendettas and tribal feuds were suspended, the tribes went up from all parts of Arabia to this great national affair. Here trade and commerce were feverishly carried on; the poets sang and competed with one another, and actors came disguised from the avengers of blood to recite and to win the applause of the people. Ameer Ali, Syed, says: "But there was another side to the picture. The dancing women, like their modern representatives the almas and ghawazin of Egypt, moving from tent to tent, exciting the impetuous son of the desert by their songs and their merriment; the congregation of the Corinthians, who did not even pretend to the calling of music; the drunken orgies, frequently ending in brawls and bloodshed; the gaming tables, at which the Meccan gambled from night till morning; the bitter hatred and illfeeling evoked by the pointed personalities of rival poets, leading to sudden affrays and permanent and disastrous quarrels, deepened the shadows of the picture, and made a vivid impression on the orphan child of Amina." [2]

During this fair an insult was once offered to a woman of one of the tribes which resulted in what was called the Sacrilegious Wars, being so called because they took place in the

---

[2] Ameer Ali, Syed, *The Spirit of Islam.* p. 11.

sacred month when the shedding of blood was forbidden. In the interval between the first and second of these wars we learn that Mahomet traveled with his uncle to Syria and there witnessed a spectacle of social misery and degradation that never faded from his memory. It was this shadow of human misery and shame which Ameer Ali, Syed, wishes us to believe cast over the mind of the thoughtful Mahomet the spell of silence and gravity. The circumstances of his earlier years and these spectacles of degradation no doubt had a deep effect upon the highly impressionable youth. But it was the nature and temperament of the man which rendered him one who could be thus influenced. Perhaps in any case he would have been grave and thoughtful, but reared in such surroundings he would be doubly so.

Yet, strange as it may seem, it was only gradually that Mahomet began to be possessed with the burden of his people. Perhaps as he grew more rich he had more opportunity to realize how very unfortunate was the condition of the poor. Perhaps also his freedom from personal anxiety and need gave him time to think of other things than merchandise. At any rate, he began gradually to withdraw from active commercial pursuits and to give his time more and more to social and religious meditation. So intensely did he dwell upon these subjects that he would often fall in a trance. But it was not until he was beyond forty years of age that he experienced a call to prophetic duties. It had been his custom to spend some time each year in worship and thought in a cave on Mount Hira. Here he would pass whole nights in communion with the unseen and all-pervading God. At last a voice seemed to come from the earth and stones about him and to call him to fulfill the task that God had laid upon him.

Ameer Ali, Syed remarks concerning the call of Mahomet and the visions which attended it: "The mental visions and the apparitions of angels at these moments were the bright, though gradual, dawnings of those truths with which he was to quicken the world into life. Often in the dark and benighted pathway of concrete existence, the soul of every great man has been conscious of unrealized yet not unseen influences, which may have led to some of the happiest achievements of humanity." [3] All this is, to be sure, only an attempt to evade some of the worst features surrounding the call. Ameer Ali, Syed, feels that the modern mind will discredit the reality of the envisioned angels and will therefore substract from the worthiness of the revelation to an equal degree. But the Christian world must, in all honesty, admit that until within the past generation the highest conversion to Christianity was looked upon as being necessarily attended by similar phenomena. And the witness of many converts causes us to gloss over the possibility of such happenings even today. No outright denial of their possibility exists among us. But we have come to believe that the revelation is the important thing, no matter how it happens. To the man who thinks and broods over a problem the light will be most likely to come. And as his mental and emotional tension increases, the possibility of crisis is augmented; the whole man leaps for joy when the solution arrives. We probably ought to change Ameer Ali's words to read, "The mental visions and the apparitions of angels at these moments were the bright images with which a highly wrought imagination clothed those truths which burst suddenly upon the seeker." To many souls they come objectively, especially if there has been long wrestling and intense effort.

Having noted these facts about the intense religious experience one will quite readily grant the truth of Ali, Syed's, further remarks: "From Samuel, that ancient Seer, wild and awful as he stands, deep in misty horizons of the Past, to Jesus in the wilderness, pondering over the darksome fate

---

[3] *The Spirit of Islam*, p. 16.

of his people and the magnitude of his work, listening to the
gentle accents of the God of Truth,—from Jesus to Mohammed in the solitude of his mountain retreat, there is no break
in the action of these influences." [4] One might even go further and extend the influences to embrace a number of celebrated figures in both medieval and modern Christianity. The
"influences" are only psychological, the result of emotional
strain and physical discipline; they can occur to our common
humanity in any age or nation. But instead of being a witness
to the credibility of our "gospels," they perhaps have almost
nothing to do with them. The so-called visions are symp-
tomatic of the condition of the seer, not of the validity of the
message. The message must find its highest credential in
its application to the abuses and unrighteousness which fire
the brooding mind of the seer. Thus a prophet is truly a
prophet not because he has seen angels, but because he has seen
a gospel.

A great deal of misguided opinion about revelation must be
abandoned at some time—when we have learned to think
straight enough to do it. And in the highly rhetorical quotations which Ali, Syed, supplies to buttress his arguments at
this point, there is more rhetoric than truth. For instance:
"The Father of Truth chooses His own prophets, and He
speaks to them in a voice stronger than the voice of thunder.
It is the same inner voice through which God speaks to all of
us. That voice may dwindle away, and become hardly audible;
it may lose its divine accent, and sink into the language of
worldly prudence; but it may also from time to time assume
its real nature with the chosen of God, and sound in their
ears as a voice from heaven." [5] Stripped of its rhetoric, this
says merely: "We all have the capacity to conceive righteous-

---

[4] *The Spirit of Islam*, p. 16.

[5] Quoted from Dean Stanley's Lectures on the *History of the Jewish
Church*, Part i, Lect. 18, p. 394.

ness. We can lose this power, or we can develop it. When it is developed there are times when it achieves so much that it appears to have been the voice of God."

Again: "The natural relations of Mahomet's vast conception of the personality of God with the atmosphere of his age is the only explanation of that amazing soberness and self-command with which he entertained his all-absorbing visions; it could not have been accidental that the one supreme force of the epoch issued from the solitudes of that vast peninsula round which the tides of empire rose and fell. Every exclusive prophetic claim in the name of a sovereign Will has been a cry from the desert. The symbolic meaning given to Arabia by the withdrawal of the Christian apostle to commune with the power above flesh and blood, in Mahomet became more than a symbol. Arabia was itself the man of the hour, the prophet of Islam its concentrated word. To the child of her exalted traditions, driven by secret compulsion out into the lonely places of the starry night, his mouth in the dust, the desert spoke without reserve." [6] If we were simple enough to believe that a mere place has anything to do with the sensitive psychological, or mental, make-up which gives rise to the prophetic rôle, we might not be able to escape the absurdity of the above quotation. But we find that "every exclusive prophetic claim" has come only from a man; any place where he could think quietly and continuously has always been "desert" enough for him. Of course, there is nothing "accidental" about the issue of the supreme voice of any epoch; there is the juxtaposition of the need and the human nature which is able to meet it. The vast penetration of Mahomet's genius into the atmosphere of his age is the thing which accounts for his self-command as well as for his success. If Johnson had said this he would have come nearer the truth.

Ameer Ali tells us that "Whilst lying self-absorbed, he

---

[6] Quoted from Johnson, *Oriental Religions*, p. 561.

(Mahomet) is called by a mighty Voice, surging like the
waves of the ocean, to cry. Twice the Voice called, and twice
he struggled and waived its call. But a fearful weight was
laid on him, and an answer was wrung out of his heart.
'Cry!' called out the Voice for the third time. And he said,
'What shall I cry?' Came the answer, 'Cry—in the name of
thy Lord!'

"When the Voice had ceased to speak, telling him how
from minutest beginnings man had been called into existence
and lifted up by understanding and knowledge of the Lord, who
is most beneficent, and who *by the pen* had revealed that which
men did not know, Mohammed awoke from his trance, and
felt as if the words spoken to his soul had been written on his
heart. A great trembling came upon him, and he hastened
home to his wife, and said, 'O Kadija! What has happened to
me?' He lay down, and she watched by him. When he recovered from his paroxysm he said, 'O Kadija! he of whom
one would not have believed it (meaning himself) has become
either a soothsayer or one possessed—mad.' She replied, 'God
is my protection, O Abu'l-Kassim (a name of Mohammed,
derived from one of his boys), He will surely not let such a
thing happen to thee, for thou speakest the truth, dost not
return evil for evil, keepest faith, art of a good life, and kind
to thy relations and friends. And neither art thou a babbler
in the market-places. What has befallen thee? Hast thou seen
aught terrible?' Mohammed replies, 'Yes.' And he told her
what he had seen. Whereupon she answered and said, 'Rejoice, O dear husband, and be of good cheer. He, in whose
hands stands Kadijah's life, is my witness that thou wilt be
prophet of this people.' Then she arose and went to her cousin
Waraka, son of Naufal, who was old and blind, and 'knew
the Scriptures of the Jews and Christians.' When she told him
what she had heard, he cried out, 'Holy, holy! Verily this is
the Namus al-akbar who came to Moses and Jesus. He will

be prophet of his people. Tell him this. Bid him be of brave heart.' " [7]

There is no reason to doubt that this is a correct account of what actually took place. Mahomet had been resisting his vision, and continued to do so as long as he could. It finally overwhelmed him, forced him to admit its veracity and sublime character. Worn out by his meditation, its obligations seemed like a voice that thundered in his brain. And when he finally ceased to resist it, it flowed through him with all its pent-up wisdom and power. His own, Kadijah's, and Waraka's interpretation of the experience is just the thing the psychology of that age would have said of it. To them the character of the accompaniments determined the validity of the vision; to us the effect of the vision on social conditions becomes the last word in any test looking toward prophetic merit. Mahomet's worth rests not on the Voice but in the social betterment his teaching achieved. And it is safe to say that if it had come more quietly, as no doubt it did at first, it would have contained the same merit. That it would have convinced him, or any one else in his age, without the accompanying Voice (a mere convention of the prophetism of that age) is, of course, quite another matter. We who are accustomed to take our truth as it comes, and who seek truth for truth's sake, are able to dispense with the ecstasies and the voices. And in the most sober and self-contained modern atmosphere Mahomet is safe enough,—He is indeed the Prophet of his people.

Even the assurances of Kadijah seem not to have been enough to completely convince Mahomet. He continued to hold his peace when he went abroad. But his abstraction and mental unrest showed that he was more than ever engaged in conflict with the doubts and hopes which alternately wrung his soul. Upon one of his walks about the city he met Waraka,

---

[7] *The Spirit of Islam*, pp. 17-18.

Kadijah's cousin. The old man said, "I swear by Him in whose hand Waraka's life is, God has chosen you to be the prophet of this people; the Namus al-akbar [8] has come to you. They will call you a liar, they will persecute you, they will banish you, they will fight against you. Oh, that I could live to those days! I would fight for you." He kissed Mahomet's forehead in token of adoration. The declaration on the part of the man "who knew the Jewish and Christian Scriptures" brought comfort to the distressed Mahomet, but still he waited, although he now sought to know the further will of God.

He had not a great while to wait. The Voice came again, saying, "O thou, enwrapped in thy mantle, arise and warn, and glorify thy Lord." This second command came, like the first, after a long period of prayer and meditation, when Mahomet was almost exhausted in mind and body. Once more he hurried home to the comfort and reassurance of his wife, vainly seeking to escape the overwhelming Presence. Now at last he was sure of his call, and sure also of the nature of his message. It was his solemn duty to free his people of the bondage of idolatry. And he felt sure of final success for the Presence had assured him that in the future he would see the people of the whole earth hastening to accept the true Faith.

Mahomet began very cautiously to declare his message. It involved such a revolution in both religious doctrine and practice that it would have been dangerous for him to speak openly. He began with those nearest to him. Kadijah was the first to believe in his revelation and to abandon the idolatrous worship of her people. Then Ali believed in him. With his wife, and his cousin Ali, he was accustomed to go into the desert around Mecca to worship the God of all nations. It is said that not long afterward they were all surprised in the attitude of prayer by Abu Talib, the father of Ali. He asked what this strange religion was. Mahomet replied, "It is the religion of God, of His angels, of His prophets, and of our ancestor

---

[8] Namus al-akbar is the divine messenger.

Abraham." Then he called upon Abu Talib to accept the new faith, but the father of Ali declared, "I cannot abjure the religion of my fathers." But he swore an oath that he would while he lived not permit any one to injure Mahomet. Then turning to his own son the old Semite, after questioning him, said, "Well, my son, he (Mahomet) will not call thee to aught save what is good, wherefore thou art free to cleave unto him."

All this tells us much regarding the character of Mahomet. An impostor could not very well have begun his prophetic labors with his own family. They of all people would be most likely to know every imperfection in him. That they knew, and yet believed in his message, is the very highest proof of his integrity. His sincerity and goodness are beyond question. It is of course quite possible that he deceived himself and that the genuineness of his self-deception helped to deceive those nearest him. But the probabilities are very much against such a view of him. In both prophetic convention and in the character of his revelation, he met every test, his teaching met the divine requirement of exalted righteousness and the human need of the hour.

But it was the whole tenor of his previous conduct which was able to win his wife and cousin and to secure the respect of Abu Talib. Had his life been other than exemplary he could not so easily have convinced them that he had been chosen prophet. The man who had gained the title of "The Trusty" had continued to live a life of honor. The prophetic claim, therefore, did not present anything discordant with all that had gone before.

Just what his life was during the first fifteen years after his marriage to Kadijah we can only surmise. He began gradually to retire from active commercial pursuits and to engage in religious interests—introspection, communion, and meditation. He appeared in public only when his position as a man of wealth demanded it. His public acts are therefore very few,

but the few are very significant for our purpose. After the
death of Abd ul-Muttalib, Mahomet's uncle, who had charge
of the Kaaba sanctuary, authority in Mecca reverted more to
the ancient manner. The Arab, through personal attachment
to some individual, might achieve a temporary condition of
solidarity and stable government; but he was an inveterate
individualist, a free lance who was his own law and protector. [9] He kept his oaths until death ended them, but at all
times he was the judge of his own acts. With the death of
Abd ul-Muttalib old vows ended and only the general duties
of kinship operated in Mecca. Members of the tribe of the
Koreish were safe enough, but strangers were robbed and
oppressed. To restore the safety and order enjoyed under
Abd ul-Muttalib, Mahomet and the chief families of Mecca
bound themselves with an oath to defend every person, Meccan
or stranger, bond or free, from any wrong within Meccan
territory. This league was called the Confederation of Fuzul
and continued in effect during the first half-century of Islam.
At another time when a dispute arose among the people during the rebuilding of the Kaaba, Mahomet intervened and
averted almost certain bloodshed.

Two other acts, with the above, contain about all we know
of these quiet years of the prophet's life. His uncle Abu Talib
had tried to maintain the old position of his family and had
thus greatly depleted his fortune. Mahomet proposed to Abbas,
the brother of Abu Talib, that they each adopt one of Abu
Talib's sons. Abbas agreed, and took Ja'far; Mahomet took
Ali, and gave him an education. When Zaid, son of Harith,
was brought a captive to Mecca and sold into slavery to a
nephew of Kadijah he was finally given to Mahomet. The
future prophet promptly set Zaid at liberty. This kindness so
touched Zaid that not even the pleadings of his own father
could move him to leave Mahomet.

It is these acts of charity, mercy, and justice which indicate

---

[9] Cf. Gibbon, *Life of Mahomet*, pp. 25-45.

the nature of Mahomet's life and reveal the character which could inspire the whole-hearted respect and confidence of those nearest him. His quick sympathy with human suffering, his generous response to every need, and his active efforts on behalf of justice for all men show that he has added to his reputation of trustworthiness a record of unusual kindness. The record therefore explains why Ali and Zaid will believe in him, and will also account for the friendliness of Abu Talib to the faith he cannot accept. In an age of ignorance, wars, feuds, cruelty, and injustice, Mahomet will be almost irresistible to those who come to know him intimately.

He worked quietly for over three years, feeling that it was best to gain a fair number of believers before attempting any public ministry. The Koreish enjoyed their prestige over the other tribes by virtue of the fact that they were the keepers of the Kaaba and the supporters of the prevailing polytheistic religion. Any appeal to the people as a whole would be met by the resistance of the vested interests. Even if his message should appeal to the conscience it had nothing to fill the public treasury or to supply the honor the tribe enjoyed among the surrounding Arabs. But after three years he realized, from the number of converts that he had made—only thirty—that no considerable reformation of the desert tribes could be brought about unless he prosecuted his work publicly and boldly.

He therefore addressed himself openly for the first time to the Koreish. He called the people to him on the hill of Safa. In his sermon on the mount he boldly declared the enormity of the crimes of his people, spoke of the follies of idolatry, and warned them of the fate which had overtaken those nations which ignored their prophets and had continued to live in sin. He asked them to give up their idolatrous practices and to live in faith and love and purity. His hearers scoffed at him and his teaching, but went away greatly alarmed because of the highly revolutionary character of this movement which he had begun in their midst. If he should succeed, the old worship would be doomed and the prestige of the Koreish, as well as much of their profit, would be destroyed.

There was now no course for Mahomet to pursue but to appeal to the strangers, and in this he was largely frustrated by the alarmed Koreish. When the pilgrims began to arrive for the seasons of worship at the Kaaba the Koreish sent out sentinels to warn them of the dangerous teaching of Mahomet. But as is always the case the warnings only served to whet the curiosity of many, and they made special efforts to hear the new teacher. Mahomet addressed them with earnest and fiery eloquence, proclaiming a lofty morality and a pure conception of deity which profoundly impressed all who heard him. Though not many accepted the faith, all went home to tell the story of this strange orator who had counseled them to give up the religion of their ancestors.

The persecution of the prophet now became studied, intense, and continuous—so much so that Abu Talib wrote a poem denouncing the Koreish and declaring that he and one other family would defend Mahomet with their lives. About the same time the chief of the Yatrib wrote a letter counseling leniency. "An honorable man has adopted a certain religion," he said, "why persecute him? for it is only the Lord of Heaven who can read the heart of man!" The prospect of being embroiled in conflict both at home and abroad served to temper somewhat the nature of the persecution. Children, and the worst characters about the city, were encouraged to follow Mahomet and torment him. His places of devotion were strewn with thorns. But in the midst of all his afflictions the prophet never wavered from his purpose.

As the persecutions continued and the malice of the Koreish increased, the kinsmen of Mahomet gradually drifted to his defense. Strong and brave men, like Hamza, were converted. Meanwhile Mahomet's preaching grew more bold and more denunciatory. He addressed himself to unbelievers in scathing terms:

"They were like unto one who kindleth a fire, and when it had thrown its light on all around him, God taketh away the light and leaveth him in darkness and they cannot see."

"They are like those who, when there cometh a storm-cloud of heaven big with darkness, thunder, and lightning, thrust their fingers into their ears because of the thunder-clap for fear of death. God is round about the infidels!"

The vividly pictorial character of Mahomet's preaching filled the people with awe and fear. The leaders of the Koreish became more and more alarmed, for they realized that serious trouble was ahead. This movement meant the loss of profit, prestige, and even nationality. It must be arrested at all costs. Consequently a system of persecution was decided upon. Each family was to torture its own members who were suspected of having attached themselves to the prophet. Mahomet escaped because of his powerful relatives, but many others were thrown into prison, beaten, and openly tortured before the people with awe and fear. The leaders of the Koreish bespite of every persecution. Then the Koreish approached Mahomet and sought to bribe him with offers of honors if he would abandon his preaching. The prophet declined, calling upon those who had approached him to repent and telling them to do whatever seemed best to them.

This defiance was met by increased persecutions, and the followers of Mahomet, upon the advice of the prophet, fled to Abyssinia. The Koreish, determined to stamp out the faith, sent envoys to the king of Abyssinia asking that the exiles be returned to them. The king sent for the exiles and asked, "What is this faith for which you have abandoned your former religion?" The Mohammedan historians record that Ja'far, son of Abu Talib, replied: "O king, we were plunged in the depth of ignorance and barbarism; we adored idols, we lived unchastely; we ate dead bodies, and we spoke abominations; we disregarded every feeling of humanity, and the duties of hospitality and neighborliness; we knew no law but that of the strong, when God raised among us a man, of whose birth, truthfulness, honesty, and purity we were aware; and he called us to the unity of God, and taught us not to associate anything with God; he forbade us the worship of idols; and enjoined us to speak the truth, to be faithful to our trusts, to be merciful, and to regard the rights of neighbors; he forbade us to speak evil of women, or to eat the substance of orphans; he ordered us to fly from vice, and to abstain from evil; to offer prayers, to render alms, to observe the fast. We have believed in him, we have accepted his teachings and injunctions to worship God, and to associate nothing with Him. For this reason our people have risen against us, have persecuted us in order to make us forego the worship of God and to return to the worship of idols of wood and stone and other abominations. They have tortured us and injured us, until finding no safety among them, we have come to thy country, and we hope that thou wilt protect us from their oppression."

This speech of Ja'far may not be authentic, but it is undoubtedly very similar to the one he made. It correctly pictures the superiority of Mahomet's program over the prevailing beliefs of the Koreish and other Arabs. And the fact that the envoys were practically rebuked by the Abyssinian king and sent home in confusion indicates that the best they could say for themselves convicted them of cruel intolerance toward the devotees of a loftier faith than their own. In any case, the speech itself is in all probability a very accurate summary of the prevailing conditions in Arabia and an equally complete statement of the new creed. Ameer Ali, Syed asks, "Can there be a better summary of Mohammed's work or his teaching?" The speech is very probably just that, and studiedly so—a Mohammedan Apostles' Creed put into Ja'far's mouth. However, the speech has its value for all students of Islam, for it presents the social condition and the prophet's method.

During the absence of the envoys, persecution continued with more direct insult and annoyance. Mahomet indeed was safe enough, but his followers were being constantly driven out of the city or made to endure all manner of afflictions. One day while sitting near the Kaaba in the presence of some of his enemies, he was heard to remark that as for the goddesses, Al-Lat, Al-Ozza, and Manah, "their intercessions might be hoped for with God." This was naturally interpreted as an offer of compromise, and his enemies hastened to declare their willingness to meet him halfway. We are told that Mahomet did not make this statement himself, but that while reciting some verses belonging to the fifty-third chapter of the Koran he repeated, "And what think ye of Al-Lat, Al-Ozza, and Manah? the third besides." An idolater knowing that a denunciation was to follow hastened to supply, "They are exalted damsels, and their intercessions may be hoped for with God." Mahomet did not contradict him and thus the impression went abroad that the prophet had uttered this statement, or had permitted it to be uttered, as a part of his revelation.

That Mahomet momentarily allowed the matter to stand as a means of rescuing his followers from persecution seems probable. But he was quick to see that safety was being purchased at the price of the sacrifice of his whole mission. Ameer Ali, Syed, says: "When Mohammed learnt what had happened, he immediately proclaimed the words, 'They are nought but empty names, which you and your fathers have invented.' This is the version given by Mohammedan historians and traditionists."[10] But the shame and remorse which Mahomet felt often, and which he referred to a number of times in his ministry, seem to indicate that he at least allowed the impression of compromise to go abroad.

---

[10] *The Spirit of Islam*, p. 34.

Of this Lane-Poole says: "Western biographers have rejoiced greatly over 'Mohammed's fall.' Yet it was a tempting offer, and few would have withstood it. And the life of Mohammed is not the life of a god, but of a man; from first to last it is intensely human. But if once he was not superior to the temptation of gaining over the whole city, and obtaining peace where before had been only bitter persecution, what can we say of his manfully thrusting back the rich prize he had gained, freely confessing his fault, and resolutely giving himself over again to the old indignities and insults? If he was once insincere—and who is not?—how intrepid was his after-sincerity! He was untrue to himself for awhile, and he is ever referring to it in his public preaching with shame and remorse; but the false step was more than atoned for by his magnificent recantation." [11]

The fall of Mahomet is perhaps no greater than the fall of Elijah, after his victory on Mount Carmel, when he fled like a frightened rabbit from the threats of Jezebel. It all shows the effect of a law which is coming to be recognized in modern times: there is a close proportional relation between weariness and moral failure. Good mental and physical health accompany good morals. Worn out by days of worry and anxiety we might expect a mere human being to show some tendency to yield, just a little. Adjustment to environment is also one of the first laws of life. Mahomet was only a man, and was the first to recognize whatever wrong attached to his so-called lapse. And whereas his condemnation of the goddesses had been only implied before, he left no uncertain impression of his attitude toward them in his recantation.

Persecution naturally burst out with redoubled fury; and the idolaters, believing that the prophet had shown the weakness in his make-up, decided to try to bring pressure upon his uncle Abu Talib. They requested Abu Talib to prevent his

---

[11] *Studies in the Koran*, Introduction, p. xlix.

nephew from preaching, and were answered by him courteously at first. When Mahomet persisted, they came a second time
to his uncle and were not slow to show their impatience. "We
respect your age and rank," they said, "but our respect has
bounds. Either prevent him from so doing, or take part with
him, so that we may fight until one of us is exterminated."
They departed after delivering their ultimatum, and Abu
Talib sent for his nephew and asked him to give up his preaching. Mahomet replied that he would not desist until God's
cause was manifested, though he die by the hand of an assas-
sin. He turned away desolately, for he felt that now his uncle's
protection would be withdrawn. But his uncle recalled him
and swore not to abandon him ever.

Matters had obviously come to a crisis. Abu Talib appealed
to the kinsmen of Mahomet to defend a distinguished member of their family. The appeal was generously responded to,
and this family loyalty, together with the conversion of Omar,
a prominent and powerful warrior, caused no little alarm
among the Koreish. With such men as Hamza, Abu Bakr,
and Omar to defend the faith the enemy thought it best to
delay the decisive blow, and the followers of Mahomet grew
bold enough to perform their worship in public.

The report of the envoys, who had now returned from
Abyssinia, put the idolaters into a frenzy of anger. They
formed a league against the clan of Hashim and Muttalib for
the purpose of exterminating it, and bound themselves with a
solemn document which they deposited in the Kaaba. The
proscribed clan was composed of more idolaters than Mussulmans, and the league had the effect of increasing the numerical
strength of the followers of the prophet. The entire clan
abandoned their homes and resorted to the quarter occupied
by Abu Talib. This section of the city was on the eastern out-
skirts and was strongly protected by rocky walls. In this
strong position the clan dwelt with Mahomet for the next
three years.

Some of the chiefs began to be ashamed of their injustice toward their fellow idolaters and moved for a reconciliation. The pact was finally dissolved and the entire clan of Hashim and Muttalib went back to their homes in the city. But the semblance of peace was of short duration, for both Kadijah and Abu Talib died soon afterward. Mahomet thus deprived of his strongest protector seemed now to be at the mercy of the Koreish. He decided to try some other field of labor and journeyed at once to Tayef to begin, as he hoped, a more fruitful period of labor. The people of Tayef thought him crazy and drove him out of their city.

Discouraged and with many wounds, Mahomet returned to Mecca and lived there for a time in retirement, preaching only occasionally. Only during the period of the pilgrimages did he work actively, and then wholly among the strangers. This change of policy gave him a measure of security. One day he encountered six men from Yathrib and invited them to hear him. They listened, were deeply impressed, and became his proselytes. When they returned to their own city they spread the news of the new prophet who had risen to call all men to God and to heal the feuds and wars that had lasted in Arabia for centuries. The next year they returned with another six men who were likewise pledged to the religion of Mahomet. When these went back to their homes they took a disciple of Mahomet with them to teach them the complete doctrines of the prophet.

At the time of the annual pilgrimage the next year, seventy-fice converts repaired to Mecca with the caravan of idolatrous Yathribites to invite Mahomet to their city. The idolaters of course knew nothing of this. That night the seventy-five met with Mahomet and renewed their covenant. They were seen by a Meccan who spread the news in the city. The Koreish in a body sought the Yathribite caravan and demanded the disciples of Mahomet. They naturally could not be found and the caravan was allowed to depart. Mahomet, fearing that all his followers in Mecca would be massacred, sent them out of the city by twos and threes until all were safely on the way to Yathrib. When the Koreish heard what had happened they set a watch upon Mahomet's house to see that he did not flee until he could be brought to trial. It was decided at last that he should be assassinated by a number of men who should strike him at the same time so that no one family would be liable to the vengeance of blood. The assassins gathered about the house to wait until dawn, when the prophet would leave his room. Mahomet arose secretly, dressed Ali in his garments and had him take his place in the bed. Stealing out at one of the windows, the prophet made his way to the house of Abu Bakr and together they fled unobserved from the city.

They reached the hills south of Mecca and concealed themselves for several days in a cave. A tradition says that when the furious Koreish instituted a search for the prophet they came to the very cave in which he was hidden. But a spider had covered the entrance with its web. It was thought by the pursuers that Mahomet had not had time to enter the cave before the web had been woven. They did not search the cave and the man they sought was saved from certain death.

On the evening of the third day the fugitives left the cave, procured two camels, and by unfrequented roads sought to reach Yathrib. A price had been put upon Mahomet's head and many horsemen were scouring the country searching for him. At one time a fierce tribesman caught sight of the two fugitives and quickly overhauled them. Abu Bakr cried out, "We are lost!" But the prophet replied, "Be not afraid. God will protect us." When the idolater came near his horse reared and fell. Awed by this event the pursuer quickly sued for forgiveness and requested a token of pardon. Abu Bakr is said to have given the pardon inscribed on a piece of bone. Without further adventure the prophet and his companion reached Yathrib. Here they were soon joined by Ali, who had fled on foot from Mecca and had made the journey safely by traveling at night.

When Mahomet arrived the two Arab tribes composing the population of the city, the Aus and Khazraj, were enjoying a peace which had been concluded between them only after many years of destructive warfare. The two tribes at once rallied to the standard of Islam. The prophet effaced the old distinctions and divisions by giving to all alike the title of Ansar (Helpers). His followers who had fled from Mecca were called Muhajirin (Exiles). Both Exiles and Helpers were linked together in a brotherhood, and a commonwealth was thus established. Yathrib changed its name to Medinat un-Nabi, City of the Prophet, and was known ever afterward as Medina, the center of early Islam.

In establishing his new commonwealth at Medina Mahomet drew up a charter which defined the rights of the Moslems among themselves and the rights of the considerable Jewish population which dwelt in the territory belonging to the city. The excellent and statesman-like character of this document caused Muir to call its author "the master-mind of his age." It provided for freedom of conscience and made justice and humanity its chief aim. It begins: "In the name of the most merciful and compassionate God, given by Mohammed, the Prophet, to the Believers, whether of the Koreish or the Yathrib, and all individuals of whatever origin who have made common cause with them, all these shall constitute one nation.

"The state of peace and war shall be common to all Moslems; no one among them shall have the right of concluding peace with, or declaring war against, the enemies of his co-religionists. The Jews who attach themselves to our commonwealth shall be protected from all insults and vexations; they shall have an equal right with our people to our assistance and good offices: the Jews of the various branches of Auf, Najjar, Harith, Jashm, Th'alaba, Aus, and all others domi-

ciled in Yathrib, shall form with the Moslems one composite
nation; they shall practice their own religion as freely as the
Moslems; the clients and allies of the Jews shall enjoy the
same security and freedom; the guilty shall be pursued and
punished; the Jews shall join the Moslems in defending Yathrib against all enemies; the interior of Yathrib shall be a
sacred place for all who accept this charter; the clients and
allies of the Moslems and the Jews shall be as respected as the
patrons; all true Moslems shall hold in abhorrence every man
guilty of crime, injustice, or disorder: no one shall uphold
the culpable, though he were his nearest kin."

The above provided against the possible event of sheltering
the lawbreaker under the law of kinship. A further provision,
which made the prophet the judge with jurisdiction over all
parties living under the charter, did away with the vengeance
of blood. A strong central government was thus set up and
one that was humane and tolerant toward all people who accepted the charter.

Mahomet now becomes the guardian of the lives and the
rights of his people. He is still the prophet, but the compact
by which he has established himself as the head of a State will
lead him into new and varied activities. The enmity of the
Koreish and others will involve him in the necessity of creating an army and in leading it to the defense of his city. And
the various groups under the charter with their several ambitions will compel him to exert a strong hand in securing
peace and safety. Thus we shall find him leading the men of
Medina upon the field of battle and, as a judge, condemning
certain of the traitors of his city to banishment or to execution.

And the new experiences began almost at once. The Koreish
upon hearing that he had taken control of affairs at Medina
raised an army and set out to destroy him and his followers.
Prompt action was necessary, for if left to his own devices
the prophet might rally tribe after tribe to his standard and

put an end to Mecca as the leading city of Arabia. Mahomet, we are told, had not yet received God's command to do battle to his enemies. But the presence of the Koreish in force no doubt served to hasten divine action, for, when the enemy had begun to lay waste the fruit trees and to scatter the flocks of the citizens of Medina, the prophet had already gathered a considerable force to meet the foe. He led forth his army, after solemnly invoking divine aid, and put the Koreish to flight with great loss. Many of the chiefs were slain; and Abu Jahl, the commander, was among them. Many prisoners were taken and all but two were treated with the greatest humanity.

When the prisoners were given their liberty and had returned to Mecca, the Koreish lost no time in renewing hostilities. They encamped near Medina and began again the work of destruction. Forced by the fury and enthusiasm of his followers Mahomet marched out at the head of a thousand men and began the battle. He had almost gained the victory when his archers, forgetting to cover the rear, allowed the enemy horse to fall upon the unprotected army of Medina. A disaster was averted only by the greatest heroism of Mahomet's troops. By a timely retreat to Mount Ohod the Medinite army escaped, leaving the Meccans too exhausted to press their advantage. After mutilating their slain enemies the Koreish retreated to Mecca.

The repulse of the Moslems in this battle served to encourage the Koreish to make a third attempt. After forming a powerful coalition they advanced with ten thousand men to lay siege to Medina. Mahomet could muster only three thousand defenders, the Jews refusing to take part with them against the coalition. A deep moat had been dug about the city and the defenders could not be induced to leave its protection. The siege continued for twenty days. Numerous attempts were made to cross the moat, but Mahomet was too untiring in his vigilance for the Meccans. The provisions of the besiegers ran low; the allies of the Koreish became discouraged; and when a storm of wind and rain overturned the tents, extinguished the lights, and demoralized the camp, the greater portion of this powerful army fled, leaving the rest to take shelter among the Jews of the vicinity.

Mahomet demanded an explanation of this treachery. The Jews refused to give it. Their stronghold was besieged and they were very soon forced to unconditional surrender. Their punishment was left to Sa'd ibn-Mu'az, who had been mortally wounded in the attack upon the stronghold. He was a fierce warrior and just the person to insist upon the strict laws of war. He gave sentence that the fighting men should be put to death and that the women and children should become the slaves of the Moslems. The sentence was carried out. This indeed contrasts greatly with the former leniency shown to prisoners of war, but we must remember that in this case the prisoners had been guilty of high treason against the commonwealth during a time of actual siege. The Moslems in this case merely exacted a penalty which would doubtless have been considered just by any other people of that age.

The other Jewish communities were eventually forced to leave the territory of Medina. Thus the coalition, which the Mohammedans assert was formed almost wholly through Jewish influence, was completely broken up. Forays continued against Medina for some time, but they were usually avenged by the Moslems.

It is interesting to note that the instructions of Mahomet to his captains who were setting out upon these expeditions were marked by unusual mercy. "In avenging the injuries inflicted upon us," he said, "molest not the harmless inmates of domestic seclusion; spare the weakness of the female sex; injure not the infant at the breast, or those who are ill in bed. Abstain from demolishing the dwellings of the unresisting inhabitants; destroy not the means of their subsistence, not their fruit trees; and touch not the palm." These commands were usually faithfully carried out—something entirely unheard of in all the annals of Arab warfare up to this time. The unusual clemency of Mahomet in sparing property, in protecting the weak, in liberating all prisoners except those who had severely injured the citizens of Medina, began to attract much attention. Thousands of people began to flock to Medina to learn more about this great and merciful leader.

About this time Mahomet began to long for his native city. The Kaaba belonged to the whole of Arabia and the Koreish were merely the custodians of the shrine. They had been given no authority to enforce an interdict against even an enemy, if he came without arms or hostile design and professed that his purpose was a religious one. When the season of the pilgrimage arrived the prophet announced that he would visit the Kaaba, and a large company of the Medinites joined him. When he came near Mecca he was met by the Koreish, who had sworn not to allow the followers of the prophet to approach the shrine. Mahomet, wishing to end the state of war which existed between Medina and Mecca, declared himself willing to agree to any terms the Meccans might stipulate. A treaty was thus made which provided for a truce of ten years' duration, the delivery of all deserters, the privilege of making alliances on the part of both parties, and the withdrawal of the Moslems until the following year, when they might visit Mecca and the shrine for three days.

The next year Mahomet at the head of two thousand men went to Mecca and performed all the rites of the lesser pilgrimage. The Koreish, noting the size of his army, withdrew, as a precaution, to the heights about the city and waited there for the three days to expire. Faithful to his part of the contract, the prophet withdrew at the end of the allotted time and returned to Medina.

There seems little reason to doubt that suspicion soon brought on a termination of the truce between Mecca and the Moslems. Some of the tribes in the vicinity of Mecca plundered the Bani-Bakr. They appealed to Mahomet, their ally, for justice, and he quickly assembled an army of ten thousand men for the purpose. Ameer Ali, Syed, says: "The reign of iniquity and oppression had lasted long at Mecca. The Meccans had themselves violated the peace, and some of their chief men had taken part in the massacre of the Khuza'a." [12] Stobart says: "After eight days through unfrequented roads and defiles, the army, swelled to the number of 10,000 men, halted and lighted their camp-fires on the heights of Marr-al-Tzahran, a day's march from the sacred city. The prophet had been joined on his march by his uncle Abbas, and on the night of his arrival Abu Sufian again presented himself and besought an interview. (He had previously appealed in vain to Mahomet not to proceed against Mecca.) On the morrow it was granted. 'Has the time not yet come, O Abu Sufian,' cried Mahomet, 'for you to acknowledge that there is but one God, and that I am his Apostle?' He answered that his heart still felt some hesitancy; but seeing the threatening sword of Abbas, and knowing that Mecca was at the mercy of the prophet, he repeated the prescribed formula of belief, and was sent to prepare the city for his approach." [13]

Seated upon his camel and dressed in a pilgrim's garb, Mahomet entered Mecca repeating some verses from the Koran. He approached the Kaaba, touched the Black Stone, and made the seven prescribed circuits. The custody of the key he gave to the family of Othman, while the cup of the well was given to Abbas, whose family still retains it. The idols in the temple were thrown down and destroyed. The Koreish stood about sorrowfully, powerless to prevent the desecration. Mahomet meanwhile announced, "Truth has come, and falsehood vanisheth; verily falsehood is evanescent." The very enormity of the act must have impressed the

---

[12] *Spirit of Islam,* p. 95.
[13] J. W. H. Stobart, *Islam,* pp. 173, 174.

idolaters with the truth of his utterance. They were therefore
ready enough to hear the sermon which immediately followed
and to give full assent to the victor's teaching.

The gradual submission of all Arabia followed the conquest of Mecca. Tribe after tribe sent envoys, or came in a
body, to make the old pledge which Mahomet had always
exacted of those who were to become his followers. A few
powerful tribes, however, made a final stand but were defeated in battle with the hosts of the prophet. The moral
effect of the submission of Mecca was such that no tribe
thought of continuing hostilities. Mahomet had come to the
end of his mission, and from that time on until his death
only the mere formalities of receiving the submission of the
many tribes composed his labors. After one more pilgrimage
to Mecca in the following year, and one final deliverance pro-
hibiting idolaters from entering Mecca, he was stricken with a
fever and died.

In the hour of approaching death he was serene and humble.
He had lived as a man of his age and of his nation, and when
he knew that death was near he set about his departure with
dignity and resignation. He presided at the public prayers
until within three days of the end. And one night at mid-
night he went to the cemetery to pray and weep at the
tombs of his friends. In his last appearance at the mosque
he addressed the assembly, saying, "Moslems, if I have
wronged any one of you, here I am to answer for it; if I owe
aught to any one, all I may happen to possess belongs to you."
A member of the congregation at once arose and claimed three
dorhems which he had given to a poor man at the prophet's
request. Mahomet paid the debt, saying, "Better to blush in
this world than in the next." Then he blessed his people and
took his departure from the temple. His strength failed
rapidly. In his last moments ejaculations of his faith escaped
him—prayers of penitence, thanksgiving, the joy of pardon,

the exaltation of the vision of Paradise and the glorious associates on high.

The judgment passed upon Mahomet's character varies among non-Mohammedan writers. He is called an imposter, a licentious libertine, a murderer, an unprincipled politician, a pathological case. McDonald in his *Aspects of Islam* declares that Mahomet, but for his infirmity, might have been a great poet. "He was a poet-Manque, and was unfitted for poetry by his prophetism. He was an unfortunate, not a humbug, a politician, or an unprincipled schemer. And because of his mental condition he became during the last ten years of his life selfish, contradictory, and evil." [14]

Neither the character nor the conduct of the man who founds a religion has much to do with the establishment of a faith, provided he is not too widely at variance with the accepted customs of his age. What the people think of him during his activity, and how truly his ideas approximate and exalt the dawning spirit of an age, constitute the solution of the mystery. He does not need to conform to the perfections of a later age, nor preach a perfect truth. He must be, in some respects, better than the men of his time and indicate a loftier truth than is generally known; but he need not achieve the ultimate in either truth or morals. Judged by his own teachings, and by the standards of his age and nation, he qualifies for leadership; but, in the light of generations of developed conscience and of elevated ideals of social justice, he requires readjustment, restatement, and reformation. Mahomet found his people in a condition very similar to that of the Hebrews in the age of the Wilderness sojourn. And if Moses because of the hardness of Israel's heart permitted a certain leniency, we should not condemn Mahomet for the same good sense. He could not begin with the developed morality and high religious thought with which Jesus began. And it is a mistake on the

---

[14] McDonald, *Aspects of Islam*, see pp. 46-76.

part of both Christians and Mohammedans to compare them, for between the two lies a thousand years of moral and religious progress. Mahomet is really a contemporary of Moses.

Since the days of Spengler and Taine we have made a halfhearted concession to the social condition as a factor in explaining the character of literature and law, but we are still rather obtuse in making our estimate of the ideals and labors of the great leaders of mankind. We assign them worth by the single standard of their abiding influence alone, and we forget that every leader is voice and product of his age. The fact that one of them may shape the future course of human endeavor through long ages does not prove that he will be of final advantage to the race. On the field of probability, where so many forces must be considered, we may well wonder if the completed story of history might not have been told in a better way. In the soul of the leader some ideas of his age have become consciously reconstructed and developed; but are they just the ideas that should appear when the pile is complete? The impossibility of giving a categorical answer to this question makes us wonder if, after all, the sole value of the leader, in the light of divine purpose, may not be to preserve the tradition of exaltation until the next prophet comes along. If that be true, a leader has probably discharged his entire obligation when he has helped his people to surmount the social and spiritual perils of his little day.

On the basis of such a view of the nature and function of leadership many present demands will not apply to men of the past. Thus it would be the height of absurdity to detract from Mahomet's worth because he does not meet the requirements for social leadership in the modern world. There is a growing tendency among Mohammedans to reinterpret the teachings of their master and to bring them up to date. And they are approaching the task with the good judgment and broadminded understanding the situation requires. They realize that each age must be judged by its own standards, and that a man, even when a prophet, cannot see all there is to know. These reformers are, however, meeting with all the resistance which every crystallized and long-established body of teaching opposes to change. It seems fairly safe to predict that the reforms will be achieved in time, that the demands of modern civilization will help to bring them about. If Mahomet were here, he would, in all probability, be the first to recommend reform. Even in his own day he reformed his teaching by designating certain passages of the Koran which must be forgotten in favor of later ones. And this practice signifies that the prophet kept his eye upon the social situation and resorted to those expedients which would insure success. The key to Mahomet's value is to be found, therefore, in the conditions of his age and people.

Viewed from his social situation, Mahomet's work takes on enormous proportions. A man who can begin with a state of perpetual warfare among a number of wild tribes and unite them, inspire them, and make them into a world-conquering power has wrought a work which cannot be disposed of with vilifications. And when all this is incidental to the promulgation of a religion, we may be very sure that he had a religion of no little merit. This is further attested by the reverence in which his followers and closest friends held him. To these primitive tribesmen he was a leader far in advance of their condition and was sincerely laboring to lift them to a level somewhere near the vision he beheld. He does not meet our ideal to-day in every particular. He comes out of a society antagonistic to our own, and his teachings at many points are below our notions of morality and justice. But to his own background and the generation composing it, he was a great reformer and leader.

The strength of his leadership resides in the fact that he taught a number of the greatest truths we know. And the items of the teaching which we cannot accept were so established in prevailing customs that they aroused no antagonism among his own people. In thus adopting old practices of Arabic tribal life, certain contradictions and partial reforms have marred the work of Mahomet from our point of view. But without these concessions it is highly probable that no amount of reform could have been secured. Even if the prophet had really felt the force of a loftier ideal, the exigencies of his situation might have prescribed the half-step he took. There is a great deal of difference between the amount of truth a man may teach and the amount he may infuse into customs and institutions. And this fact, so often ignored or misunderstood, has usually expressed itself in that mutual contempt with which the theologian and the practical statesman have regarded each other. Mahomet may not have been a great statesman, but, after all, he was a practical statesman of sorts,— enough at least to realize just how much reform he could accomplish. And his large achievement makes us discount the criticism of idealists so far removed from the Arabia of Mahomet's time.

The great outstanding truth which Mahomet taught his disciples was the unity of God. He is reported to have said that of all the verses of the Koran the most valuable and important one is, "God, there is no God but He, the Living, the Enduring." But the same truth is presented in no uncertain terms in every Surah of the Koran. In the 112th Sura, one of the earliest, this conception is presented in more detail: "Say thou, He is God alone, God the eternal; He begat not, nor was He begotten; nor hath He any equal." Undoubtedly the prophet is aiming here at the doctrine of the Trinity which he knew in the forms of Christianity around him, as well as at the current polytheism of his own people. W. St. Clair-Tisdall says: "Muhammad from the beginning of his claim to the prophetic office showed himself to be irreconcilably opposed to polytheism in whatever form, and to be the bitter enemy of all idol-worship. And if ever iconoclasm was needed in the world, it was needed then. Not to speak of the shameful spectacle which the Christian Church in almost every part of the world then presented in this respect, the ancestral Temple at Mecca contained 360 idols, one for every day of the Lunar year. Besides these the planets and other heavenly bodies were worshipped, and almost every Arab tribe had contributed its own local deity to help to fill the building which, though still retaining its ancient appellation of 'The House of God,' had become a pantheon in which even 'Christian' idols were adored.

"Although great faith is placed in the efficacy of charms, talismans and the like, and great reverence—almost if not quite amounting to worship—is paid to holy places, yet the worship of idols has never been able to gain an entrance into the religion of the Mussulmans." [15] This aloofness from idolatry is primarily preserved by a fundamental conception of God's nature—there is a distinct chasm between the Creator and his creation. In fact the gap is so wide that man, though absolutely dependent upon God and completely determined by Him, never enters into that union and communion with Him which characterizes certain mystic phases of Christianity.

The prophet also taught that God had revealed Himself to man. Indeed man cannot know God or His will except through divine revelation. But Mahomet, like many Christians, narrowed both its scope and its process. To the Mohammedan true revelation had to do with Mahomet; and while Adam, Moses, Seth, Abraham, and Jesus all received revelations, their value lies in the fact that they all believed in Mahomet and prophesied of him. Many Christians believe that revelation is primarily concerned with prophecies of Jesus and of his Gospel. Surely there is much more to be revealed. Man truly does not live by bread alone, but he cannot dispense with bread. Great natural truths regarding the order and character of all creation have their place in undergirding the

---

[15] *The Religion of the Crescent*, pp. 17-19.

spiritual and are vitally concerned with the well-being of humanity. No great spiritual people can afford to ignore the so-called secular knowledge. In this field there is also revelation, and only the narrowest bigotry will deny it.

As to the process of revelation, or inspiration, it seems that Mahomet taught that God spoke directly through him in giving the Koran. At any rate, the present position of the Mohammedan teacher is that not only the subject matter of the Koran but also the very words of all the prophets were "sent down." In other words, God dictated them to the prophet through the angel Gabriel. All this is very valuable for both hope and morals until we face a situation in which the revelation so-called is in error, or outmoded by the conditions of a later age. In a situation in which progress in both righteousness and social development requires a modification of the revelation, we discover that the theory is a distinct misfortune, for the whole process of development must wait upon further revelation. Often it is not forthcoming, or the theory which determines the way in which it must come will not admit it. No doubt much revelation is by theory utterly out of caste with devout Mohammedans just as it is with some of our most conservative Christians.

But the very strictness with which the lines of the canon are held precludes the possibility of introducing further discrepancies into the teaching in any religious group. In this, of course, there is a decided advantage when piety may so easily be mistaken for creative genius. And yet, the "bitter-enders" often hold out stubbornly when the whole ocean of loftier truth has overflowed them. A cross-section of the faith of any religious group will show the successive inundations crystallized and distinct, a conglomerate composed of many curious little pebbles of spiritual history. The antidote becomes at last a bane. Mohammedanism has repeated the everlasting story of sanctity versus progress, of beliefs too sacred to be revised.

The theory of the origin of the Koran is further supported

by the statement (by Mohammedans) that the prophet was illiterate. The purity of the Arabic in which the Koran is written, and the eloquence and beauty of its language, would, however, tend to create some doubt of this affirmation. But the followers of the prophet reach from this evidence a wholly different conclusion: Mahomet could not have written it; therefore, it is a miracle. Arabic is the language of heaven; thus the Koran, dictated by God, would necessarily be characterized by just the literary excellencies it possesses. There are, however, an abundance of logical and moral difficulties which will prevent this conclusion from becoming acceptable to the Occident. Holiness has become inseparably associated with deity in the Western mind—too much so for us to believe that the Koran originated wholly without human agency. Yet it is just the possession of a book which is supposed to have been spoken by a divine voice that proves a source of strength to the religion of Mahomet.

Another source of the strength of Islam is in the obligation to pray. With the followers of Mahomet, prayer is not primarily a privilege but a duty which must be faithfully discharged. Five times each day the call to prayer is heard from the minarets of the mosque—in the morning before sunrise, at noon, before the sun sets, during the twilight after sunset, and when night has commenced. The muezzin cries, "Allahu akbar!" "God is most great," which he repeats four times in a loud voice. Then in a lower tone, "I bear witness that there is no God but God, I bear witness that Mahomet is the Apostle of God." After repeating each clause twice, he continues in a loud voice, "Come to prayer, come to prayer! come to the Refuge! come to the Refuge! God is most great, God is most great! There is no God but God!"

The Mohammedan now takes with him his prayer-carpet wherever he goes; and at the hour of prayer he spreads it upon the ground, kneels upon it or prostrates himself with his face turned toward Mecca, and recites the set prayer in Arabic, the language of heaven, the language in which God speaks in revelation. After the formal prayer, the prayer of obligation, the worshiper is permitted to use his own language and to ask God for anything he needs.

The custom of thus praying frequently and regularly each day, and the privilege of asking for any individual need at each hour of prayer, serves to keep the faith a living issue. But the practice also makes for extremes. The most pronounced hypocrisy and the most fervent fanaticism exist side by side. There are those, no doubt, who are seeking in all sincerity for spiritual peace, for a rational faith, for high and great truth, and for a righteousness in conduct which may be divinely approved. But there are thousands who rest their fate upon the mere fact that they have fulfilled the obligation.

A magic power is thus ascribed to the act of prayer. The fanatic trusts that by more frequent prayer and by certain pious attitudes and practices—by self-inflicted flagellations and by the repetition of long passages of the Koran—to secure for himself a holy character and a spiritual calm which will make for perpetual exaltation. On the other hand, the worldly man hopes by his regularity and faithfulness in fulfilling the strict letter of the obligation that all will be well with him. Salvation is thus in the pious act.

Lane says of the Mohammedans of Egypt: "The utmost solemnity and decorum are observed in the public worship of the Muslims. . . . Never are they guilty of an irregular word or action during their prayers—they appear wholly absorbed in the adoration of their Creator." [16] Of this St. Clair-Tisdall remarks: "Nor does it become any of us too hastily and uncharitably to judge whether this seeming devotion is or is not heartfelt. May we not rather find comfort in the thought that God is no respecter of persons; but that in every nation he that feareth Him and worketh righteousness is acceptable to

---

[16] *Modern Egyptians*, Vol. I, p. 120.

Him?" [17] The real question here is not one of sincerity or lack of it, but of the final social results growing out of the system so solemnized. If hypocrisy, fanaticism, bigotry, non-coöperation, and social wrongs are accelerated or permitted by the system, no amount of solemnity or sincerity can quite make up for the errors thus encouraged. Compassion and tolerance are never out of place, to be sure, but surely the comfort derived from the vaporings of pious tom-fooleries is almost as great a foe to real spiritual progress as any other type of religious error. But it is a rare person indeed who can balance justly his emotions and his common sense.

The whole question of prayer needs to be examined critically if it is not to prove a perpetual stumbling block to religious advance. With adoration of the deity and dependence upon Him, there is little ground for complaint, provided the deity is of the right sort. But what does the prayer solemnize? And what sort of social condition is it which is regarded as divinely approved when we come back from our devotions? The whole weakness of prayer lies in the fact that it so frequently sanctifies more errors than truth. Prayer, therefore, because it is regarded uncritically, is undoubtedly one of the most vexing problems any reformer can face. It resurrects a thousand ghosts that have been laid and lets them stalk forth again. It takes the place of logic, justifies the suppliant's contentions and wishes, worthy or unworthy, hallows him and all his, and provides a mighty breast-work to resist both error and enlightenment. One of the mightiest factors for the preservation of Islam or any other faith is, therefore, the prayer life of the people.

Another source of Islam's strength resides in its doctrine regarding a future life. The Koran teaches that there will be a resurrection of the dead, a Judgment Day, a Paradise prepared for the good, and a Hell for the reward of the wicked.

---

[17] *The Religion of the Crescent*, p. 42.

No religious system perhaps has provided such tortures for the unfaithful: "They who believe not shall have garments of fire fitted upon them, boiling water shall be poured upon their heads, their intestines shall be dissolved thereby, and also their skins; and they shall be beaten with maces of iron. So often as they shall endeavor to get out of Hell because of their anguish of torments, they shall be dragged back into the same, and their tormentors shall say unto them, 'Taste ye the pain of burning.'" [18] Regarding Paradise the Koran says: "Paradise is promised to the pious, and therein are rivers of incorruptible water, and rivers of milk, the taste whereof changeth not, and rivers of wine pleasant unto those who drink, and rivers of clarified honey, and therein shall they have plenty of all kinds of fruits, and pardon from their Lord. Moreover they shall receive beauteous damsels as wives, having fine black eyes, and complexions like rubies and pearls. The reward of good shall be good." [19]

As soon as one dies he must try to cross the bridge of Sirat which is as narrow as a hair and as sharp as a sword. Across this bridge which spans the abyss of Hell the righteous pass with ease and find themselves quickly in Paradise. The wicked, however, fall headlong into the regions of fire to undergo excruciating torments. "There are in Hell seven stages, the lowest of which is reserved for hypocrites, who, though with their lips professing to be Muslims and to believe in God and His 'Prophet,' yet wrought deeds of infidelity." Moslems believe that any person having the least atom of the true faith in his heart will, after suffering in Hell for a time, find an entrance into Paradise and thus be free of any further torment.

A further doctrine which adds greatly to the strength of Islam is that of predestination. Nothing happens, we are told,

---

[18] Sura 22.
[19] Cf. Sura 37.

either for good or bad but as God wills it or permits it. Men ought therefore not to grieve too much because of the joys and comforts they miss in the present world, or to exult too much in the good fortune that comes to them. In battle the faithful, if victorious, will be rewarded in this world, and in case of defeat or death they will get their reward in the world to come. Thus the Mohammedan soldier became filled with a fanaticism which knew no fear. He went into battle knowing that he would be rewarded and that God would not desert his cause. Convinced, therefore, of his safety and his call to do battle in a holy war, he swept away his foes. Upon this article of faith the great Mohammedan conquests were secured and maintained for centuries.

The teachings of Mahomet were well calculated to unify the many tribes of Arabia and to make them fearless in the face of any danger which might threaten the future of the State. There could be no more feuds, no more private acts of vengeance. This provision eliminated the quarrels which had kept the tribes in constant turmoil for centuries. There could be no more tribal gods, protectors of a small group or a village. There was no God but God. This provided against the growth of distinct religions and cultures within the nation and the misunderstandings, prejudices, and hatreds which separated the members of the same race. Mahomet gave the people a common faith and destroyed all that drove them apart. The loftier ideals of Islam commanded the mind and conscience of the more thoughtful Arabs, while the doctrines of predestination and rewards provided just the hope, and the indifference to personal pain, which a conquering race must possess.

That the teaching of Mahomet is bone and sinew of the Arabian situation is apparent as the centuries pass. The doctrines which were pointedly designed to reform, unite, and preserve were by necessity just the views and policies which could have succeeded in bringing centralization and nationality out of the anarchy of Arabian tribal conditions. And so directly does Mahomet deal with Arabia in all he advocates that it is rather difficult to believe that he ever even remotely dreamed of world-conquest. The unity of Arabia—a strong Arab nation—that was his goal spiritually and politically. But as always happens when a vigorous people unites and ceases to spend its vigor within itself, the strength turned outward. The power thus united had to find something to do. Mahomet perhaps did not foresee that the strong semi-military state he was creating to unite his nation when its task had been achieved, would become all the greater and would have no further local work to perform. The new state would inevitably advance to a place among the nations.

Furthermore, a cessation of the devastating wars within materially increased the population. The ancient custom of burying alive the female children had also been prohibited. These practices, cruel as they were, no doubt kept the population down to that volume which could be supported by the desert. The country was already populous to the point of saturation, and the very difficulty of maintaining an existence in this barren land had led to the wars in question. When a neighboring tribe could no longer plunder its neighbor, this means of a livelihood could not be followed. The new economic situation and the rapidly increasing volume of the population made overflow inevitable. An Arab horde erupted from the desert to the north and east. It was opposed; wars followed from one pretext or another; the soldiers of Islam were supplied with a creed which made them invincible; conquests followed to fire the imagination and whet the greed of a naturally poverty-stricken people; and the vast human engine which Mahomet had built rolled on its relentless way.

That the desert Sheik whose dream of a united Arabia started all this can be thought of as consciously planning the conquest of Asia and Africa, is of course absurd. Asia he may have known in a vague sort of way, for he had been to Syria; but Byzantium, Babylon, Persia, and Egypt must have been dim fabulous regions to him. What would he have said if by any chance he could have seen in one of his visions the palaces of Bagdad, Cordova, and Granada? Would he have been content to mend his own clothes, prepare his own food, and live in the simplest dwelling? He dressed the part of the prophet of his own people, and no doubt was constantly surprised at each new accession to the State he had erected. And if the views of certain Occidental writers be correct, the power he was able to secure turned his head. He became a despot with the function of prophecy to support his every whim, often to cover up his perfidy and licentiousness. Perhaps it was better for both Islam and the world that he was spared a vision of the Alhambra. He might have deified himself; and that, considering the errors and temporal character of his teachings, would have been very unfortunate indeed.

It has been said that his teachings were well adapted to the building of great empires, but not so well calculated to preserve them. This in a word very accurately gauges the vigor of Mahomet's system. But if the prophet had continued to live simply and had resisted the temping visions which approved his licentious desires, Islam might have had a finer story to tell. The example of the prophet could not be emulated legally, but with the convenience of divorce he could be surpassed. And as casuistry and technicalities developed among the commentators and caliphs, even the semblance of restriction to desire was removed. The empires were conquered, amazingly well organized, administered with genius and liberality. Art, science, literature, and commerce flowered in splendor. But the heaven on earth with couches and gardens and dark-eyed damsels without number made the leaders too tender for the privations and herculean labors which keep an empire in existence. A few generations of ease and the strength and courage of Islam passed to the women. Thus the mother of Boabdil rebukes her weeping son, "You may well weep like a woman for what you could not defend like a man!" Islam reformed may yet make a bid for power, but it will keep what it gains only so long as its heart is virtuous and sound. Alas that the prophet should have had so many visions in his later years!

But perhaps if Mahomet had not himself yielded to his sensual desires and thus have left an example to corrupt his followers, his doctrine of determinism would have sufficed to accomplish it. Epicurus himself lived an exemplary life of self-denial and virtue, but his doctrine of happiness as the chief end of life was used to defend the escapades of his disciples. The teaching of Lao Tze has been wrested from out its proper position to defend the magical popular religion of the Taoists of China to-day. And among Moslems the legalist view predominates, yet is checked short of its penalties by the doctrine of determinism. A man must pray, for it has been commanded. One need not love God or take pleasure in prayer, but if he fulfills the command he has an opportunity to be saved. Of course, one may not be saved, for there is nothing in God's character to compel Him to save any man. God's will, in Mohammedanism, is God's whim. The value of prayer has been stated by the prophet in a question, "If there be a river at the gate of any one of you, in which he bathes five times a day, will there remain any defilement on him?" He was answered, "No dirt will remain on him." Mahomet said, "Then that is what the five prayers are like; by means of them God wipes out sins." [20] But sin is thought of as a disease for which man cannot be held greatly responsible. God is merciful and compassionate and will not punish a man very severely for being ill. And besides, God has fated man to do as he does. At the root of the matter God is Himself the Author of man's sinful acts. Furthermore, God is the Author of both good and evil and there is nothing inconsistent with His nature when He causes man to commit sin.

This kind of reasoning shows us how almost any act may

---

[20] Mishkat, *Kitabu's Salat*, sec. 3, p. 50.

be justified. A man must keep his covenants and obey the commandments; but if he should fail, it is God who is responsible. St. Clair-Tisdall reports that a Maulavi said: "We confess that we are sinners and have done wrong, but although we are obliged by our reverence for God to say this, yet if we go back to the root of the matter God is Himself the Author of our sinful acts. It is not reverent to say that He has lied or stolen or murdered, and we confess that *we* have done so. Yet after all the fault is not ours; God is the Creator of both good and evil." [21]

A strict determinism amounts to this in any system where it occupies a prominent position. Even Presbyterians have borne the stigma of an ultra-Calvinism—infants in Hell not a span long. Mahomet may have ended as Paul the Apostle so often does—with divine control and human freedom imperfectly defined. Such inchoateness always proves among the weak a source of much confusion as well as untruth and positive evil. There is not enough incentive to be righteous, and we behold the most flagrant sinners defending their immoralities by both good logic and good theology. A religious reformation which ends in this condition needs to be reformed again, let its place of origin be what it may, Arabia or Geneva.

But a reformation should be a true reformation, not a mere gesture, or only an echo of some shibboleth long outmoded by the exigencies of a later time. The Protestant Reformation came all too near being no reformation of fundamental ideas. As a gesture it was pronounced in two ways: it substituted the infallibility of the Bible for the infallibility of the Pope; and it put its fate in the hands of majorities rather than in true liberty of conscience. In the first case it reformed nothing, for the shift of infallibility had almost as many evils as merits. There was a change in the mechanism, origin, and execution of the control, but the spirit of man was bound by concepts

---

[21] W. St. Clair-Tisdall, *The Religion of the Crescent*, pp. 87-88.

which held as effectivity as papal restriction. Religion returned to Apostolic disorganization but did not escape the very legalism which Jesus labored so much to avoid. And no man realizes the true significance of the religious ferment to-day, which is sometimes called Modernism, when he fails to see that it is a revolt against the iron-clad legalism of Protestant infallibility. It is not that the Bible is no longer the guide to faith and practice. The whole trouble is that Protestantism has been hellenized, subjected to philosophical refrigeration in the days of Calvin and Luther, so that defending the faith has become only a matter of keeping theology away from the light and heat of Biblical criticism. Philosophical method is proper enough in any age; but no philosophical construction has ever proved to be for long of vital consequence to the human spirit.

In the second case the liberty of the Protestant has been surrendered to the denominational group. Voting majorities allocate to themselves the right to prescribe for the individual conscience. And Eck forced Luther to admit that final authority could not rest in the Council! Protestantism now passes by in serried ranks clad in the neat-fitting, bright-colored denominational uniforms, but the conformity is only apparent. Within is all manner of ecclesiastical ambitions, political aims, and differences of private opinion. One wonders at times if the uniformity thus secured is not bordering upon a lie to the Holy Ghost. Strait is the gate and narrow is the way that leads between the Scylla of religious anachronism and the Charybdis of atheism; few indeed pass through to the open sea of honest individual salvation.

Mohammedanism, like Christianity, has also had its season of reformation. And its reformation came, like our own, after a period of rationalism. Indeed reform always has its roots in a season of thinking on great fundamental human problems. First, there is the social change, for good or evil, which creates the problems. Second, there is the attempt to solve the problems thus created. And finally, there is the inevitable clash between the religious doctrines and the solutions thus derived. Mohammedanism possessed both the social solution and religious readjustment which would meet the Arabian situation; but when the followers of Mahomet had prosecuted a generation of conquests, the exigencies of a prosperous empire demanded the expansion of implied religious truth, the intellectual liberty which alone could achieve that atmosphere which would stimulate creative labor, and the correction, or insulation, of certain doctrines which opposed the necessary steps in the religious and social policy. All these steps were taken, with the result that some of the most brilliant and progressive nations of history came to be.

Ameer Ali, Syed,[22] tells us how this reformation came about. Abu Huzaifa Wasil bin 'Ata al-Ghazzal, a man of great mental powers, thoroughly versed in the sciences and traditions, differed from the Imam on a question of religious dogma, and was forced to withdraw from the lecture-room at Medina. He at once founded a school of his own, Ahl-ul-I'tizal (Dissenters), which soon rivaled the school at Medina. "The general rationalism of his school enlisted the loyalty of the strongest and most liberal minds. Proceeding upon the lines of the Fatimide philosophers, and appropriating the principles which they laid down and the ideas to which they had often given forcible expression, he formulated into theses the doctrines which constitute the basis of his difference from the predestinarian schools and from Patristicism generally. For several centuries his school dominated over the intellects of men, and with the support of the enlightened rulers who during this period held the reins of government, it gave an impetus to the development of national and intellectual life among the Saracens such as had never been witnessed before. Distinguished scholars, prominent physicists, mathematicians,

[22] *The Spirit of Islam,* pp. 414-415sq.

historians—all the world of intellect in fact, including the Caliphs, belonged to the Mu'tazilite school.

"Men like Abu'l Huzail Hamdan, Ibrahim ibn Sayyar an-Nazzam, Ahmed ibn Hait, Fazl al-Hadasi, and Abu Ali Mohammed al-Jubbai, well read in Greek philosophy and logic, amalgamated many ideas borrowed from these sources with the Medinite conceptions, and impressed a new feature on the philosophical notions of the Moslems. The study of Aristotle, Porphyry, and other Greek and Alexandrian writers gave birth to a new science among the Mu'tazilas, which was called Ilm-ul-Kalam, 'the science of reason (logic),' with which they fought against the external as well as the internal enemies of the Faith,—the non-Moslems who assailed the teachings of Islam from outside, and the patristic Moslems who aimed at the degradation from within. . . . A careful comparison of the Mu'tazilite doctrines will show that they were either word for word the same as were taught by the early Fatimides, or were modifications of those doctrines induced by the requirements of a progressive society, and partly, perhaps, by the study of Greek and Alexandrian philosophy."

Ameer Ali, Syed, is correct in assigning the motives for the reform. It was directly "induced by the requirements of a progressive society." The political and social conditions of the empire determined the type of problems which should be presented to the thinkers of that generation. Thus the philosophers and rulers pushed forward into an atmosphere of thought which had many affinities with Greek and Alexandrian philosophy. Thus just these affinities growing out of the social situation dictated the study of Alexandrian thought. The conviction that this philosophy was the correct one, and the social situation, demanded the correction of the predestinarian doctrines in the interest of human freedom in both thought and action.

As often happens, the warrant for the reform rested upon only a portion of the teaching of the founder instead of the whole teaching. This opened the way for debate, for political striving, for jealousies, and for persecutions. The conservative party had upon its side the traditions, the history of interpretation, and many actual sayings of Mahomet to support it. The liberals had the results of liberty, some truth, progress, and an intellectual age to support their views. They were compelled to oppose the traditional interpretation and to seek a ground for their movement in the words of Mahomet. And they had to select from them, ignoring many sayings which were undoubtedly hostile to their position. Just here we encounter the weakness of every reform which tries to press the past into terms that will serve the present; the needs of the present are too obviously forced upon the past teaching. Dogmatists, bigots, and fanatics are always quick to see and to take advantage of this weakness. Thus reform seldom triumphs without secession from the parent church.

In Islam the controversy continued with varying fortunes for each side for more than a century. Then Ibn-Hanbal appeared to denounce learning and science and to proclaim a holy war against Rationalism. He was eloquent and vehement, and had great influence with the masses of the ignorant Moslems. The lawyers whose power depended upon their influence over the ignorant masses made common cause with him against the philosophers and scientists. He was finally imprisoned because he had fulminated riotings and general disorder. When he died shortly afterwards, and before he had gained his freedom, he was followed to his grave by one hundred and forty thousand men and women. About all that Ibn-Hanbal therefore really accomplished was a tightening of the lines of the two parties.

Soon afterwards Mutawakkil came to the throne. "The Rationalists were the directing power of the State; they held the chief offices of trust; they were the professors in colleges, superintendents of hospitals, directors of observatories; they were merchants; in fact, they represented the wisdom and the wealth of the empire; Rationalism was the dominating creed among the educated, the intellectual, and influential classes of the community. Sifatism was in force among the lower strata of society, and most of the Kazis, the preachers, the lawyers of various degree were attached to it. A cruel, drunken sot, almost crazy at times, Mutawakkil had the wit to see the advantage of an alliance with the latter party. It would make him at once the idol of the populace, and the modern Caliph of the bigots. The fiat accordingly went forth for the expulsion of the party of progress from their offices under the government. The colleges and universities were closed; literature, science, and philosophy were interdicted; and the Rationalists were hunted from Bagdad." [23]

An inquisition was instituted with a College of Jurists to hunt out all heresies. The literature of the day was closely examined and the smallest taint was sufficient to cause any book to be committed to the flames. The authors of such books were put to death or subjected to excruciating tortures. And yet the Rationalists were not exterminated. Now and then they would gain a season of triumph over their enemies and the cause of enlightenment would be secure again.

Thus for five centuries the Rationalists assisted Islam in the intellectual development of her empire. Then a reaction set in and all too soon philosophy and science were put beyond the pale of Islam. St. Clair-Tisdall in commenting upon Ameer Ali, Syed's work says: "When these heretics (the Rationalists) lost their political power and orthodox Muhammedanism again asserted its authority, the brilliant but short period of intellectual growth and progress in Muslim lands swiftly passed away. It is unfair, therefore, to attribute to Islam results which ensued from the cultivation of Aristotelian philosophy and

---

[23] *The Spirit of Islam*, pp. 439-440.

Grecian science, and which disappeared for ever when the true spirit of Islam reasserted itself." [24]

It is scarcely proper to thus deny to Islam all right to development and progress. The rival claims of Romanists and Protestants to possess exclusively the spirit of Christianity would indicate that the same situation probably existed between the rival parties in Islam. Reforms are usually brought about by the faithful, not the unfaithful. In any event the highest intellectual life within Mohammedan countries was achieved by men who probably would have deeply resented the charge of heresy. Their loyalty to the Koran and the prophet is enough to indicate the elasticity and vitality of Islam. It is a religion which is capable of much expansion and which can be stretched to afford room for a highly intellectual civilization. When a social situation is built up which transcends the dogma of the prevailing religion there are two ways of saving religion: the dogma may be reformed, or expanded, to suit the need of the times; the social situation can be made to disappear. Islam has the distinction of having tried both in turn, and of having been equally successful in each undertaking. And it is worth noting that a living religion cannot be so surely pigeon-holed in any of its various stages of life as St. Clair-Tisdall does it. The true spirit of Judaism is just what it is to-day; its true spirit has been somewhat different, at certain points, in the past. In fact, true Judaism has usually varied with the problems and fortunes of the Jewish people. It has never been so true in any stage that it has refused to make those modifications of its popular thought which were necessary to permit it to live. Evidently the same liberty must be given to Mohammedanism, or to any other religion. To regard only that which has not evolved as being true is to make everything heretical but primordial Chaos. But, of course, St. Clair-Tisdall would not go quite so far as

[24] *The Religion of the Crescent*, Appendix B, p. 242.

to say that the act of creation was heresy. He would rather, like many another religious thinker, take his jumps of progress as he wants them—perhaps without any relation to law or reason. When he sees the wheels of miracle he perhaps believes that he is looking at the uninspired, the heretical.

A comparison of the results of the reformation within Islam and those which have followed upon the return to tradition would seem to establish beyond a doubt that Mahomet aimed at his time too directly to give us a timeless gospel. It is possible, to be sure, to demonstrate that the teachings are for all time, but such a demonstration would be only a reformed Arabic society of the prophet's time. Between the Arabia thus achieved and the glory of Granada, or Cordova, there is much to give the educated Mohammedan food for thought. Thus progressive men in Mohammedan countries are finding the traditional position unfavorable to their best instincts and desires. They are prevented, both by popular feeling and their own convictions, from questioning the prophet's authority. The only method of gaining relief is to so interpret the Koran that there will be no fundamental opposition to modern ideas. And this interpretation is now upon the way. Whether or not the venture will succeed will depend upon the breadth of territory covered by the movement. A united Islam can bring it about. Otherwise the reformers will repeat the story of the Moors in Spain.

We may sum up the work of Mahomet in the words of J. W. H. Stobart: "That he did through evil and good report, under mockery and persecution, persevere with unfaltering steps in winning his countrymen to a better life and a more spiritual belief, no one can deny, and for this all honor is due to him who dwelt in a light so much brighter than the thick darkness around." [25] The chief fault in Islam is to be found in the fact that its code of ethics falls below that of Chris-

[25] Stobart, *Islam*, p. 229.

tianity, yet is regarded as final and irrevocable. This doctrinal position which supports the permanent nature of the Koran provides a guarantee that the Moslem will not return to idolatry, but it presents on the other hand an almost insuperable barrier to progress. Should the leaders succeed in intellectualizing the statements of the Koran, so as to favor progress, and set up again an educated and scientific order, there would still be large masses of the people who would take the Koran just as it reads, or as they read it. And this abiding conservative element would very probably greatly outnumber the intellectuals. Such a situation would afford the bigot or the opportunist just the situation he would find most helpful to his ambitions. The demagogue and the gifted ignorant leader could seize the reins of government and defeat the party of reform. Only the most watchful care, the most vigilant propaganda, and a long line of powerful and progressive leaders can ever deliver Islam from this danger.

And yet it may all come peaceably and quickly, for it is becoming increasingly clear to many Mohammedans that the prophet spoke only for his own time. As soon as his code of morality became the law of Arabia his people were ready for another and a better prophet. But Mahomet unfortunately believed that he was the last of the prophetic line—an item of faith which has caused trouble at other times in the world's history. He solved his own problems and those of his generation, but he left relatively untouched the social and religious questions which have sprung from the complexities of the modern world. Wherever religion and morality have achieved conceptions of conduct purer and loftier than those Mahomet taught, Islam can make no headway except by force of arms, and that instrument of regeneration has now passed definitely from her hands. Perhaps as soon as the Western world brings to the desert its vast mechanism for comfort and progress the reform will come quickly. And how much of the prophet it will leave, only the future can determine.

CHAPTER XII

Conclusions

Our study of the conditions which the saviors of mankind sought to meet leads us to conclude that the social and religious programs of deliverance follow a rule like that to be met with in the biological realm: there is no universal system except within the particular ones. This universal, however, cannot be thought of as being constituted only of the similarities and likenesses to be met with in all redemptive gospels. Such a construction would be desiccated, bloodless, abstract, and out of touch with human life. It would be only an intellectual graph, a picture devised by the logical imagination. While it is possible to make such a construction and to find it exceedingly useful in handling the materials involved, we must remember that we have devised something which has only an academic value. And if by the pressure of persuasion and social authority we should contrive to start an order of society in accord with our new system, we should discover, even if our venture persisted, that we had achieved only another particular. In other words, our highest knowledge is but a fragment of the human story, no matter how much we may hallow it. Furthermore, in any attempt to make knowledge perform its proper function in meeting the problems of human life, we inevitably discover that we are dealing with a special segment of humanity. Thus in both statement and application we are compelled to make our gospel only another special expression of mankind's thought and experience.

Such findings are rather devastating to the hope of securing universal knowledge or the universal application of that knowledge. No matter how exactly we may fit our program to a single generation of mankind, we discover that we are at variance with the genius and needs of the generations which follow. In some cases our ideas are lofty, too lofty in fact ever to meet vitally the line of actual human experience. In other cases our construction will fall below the line of developing conscience and the new generation will cast upon us a patronizing glance of kindly and amused tolerance or one of withering scorn. Thus, if we could live long enough, we should hear our greatest redemptive constructions described as "impracticable," "old-fashioned," and "quaint." Our fate springs from the fact that we have selected only one possibility out of the many which the past implies; we have found ourselves confronted with new and unique social conditions and with a unique generation of mankind. If the race had remained constant to its groove we might have framed a gospel for its future, but it has not done so. Without any adequate background, and without any discoverable biological cause, the new generation arrives and our social predictions go the ways of oblivion.

It therefore becomes increasingly apparent that only the most local and concrete significance can be accorded the several social and religious programs of history. Their sole worth resides in the very definite time-limit of the generation to whom they were addressed. They may have a faint meaning for the generations to come, but that meaning will grow more and more faint as generation follows generation. The point of actual, vital contact with human destiny is to be found in the social state which prompted their construction. They had then an indispensable function to perform in the social rehabilitation of the generation in question and assisted in the solution of the problem of national or racial survival. They cannot prescribe for the succeeding generations who seek to make the most of their special genius.

Any social condition which we may seek to import from

the past will therefore prove intolerable when, by the constant change of human nature through biological differentiation, a generation with an entirely different genius arrives. And the more completely we adapt religion to the peculiar needs and temperament of any given generation, the more certainly will our doctrines be modified by the social and religious leaders of to-morrow. To seek to perpetuate a system of thought which is ill-adjusted to a later generation is to erect a hindrance to the free self-expression of the new individuals who appear upon the scene. If the difference in temper between the man and his heritage of ideals be slight, conformity may follow; the bondage may not be greatly felt. But if that difference be marked, either of two possible results may ensue. First, the faith may be loyally defended in word, but practically denied in personal conduct—the individual will be inconsistent enough to order his life unconsciously along lines which are more congenial to his nature in spite of his loyal public utterances. His life will be a doing contrary to all he says. The other result arises from clearer thinking and more down-intellectual honesty; that is, a definite break with the old order will be publicly avowed and a new régime, one more in accord with the fundamental nature of the new generation, will be advocated. It will be recognized that the old has gradually become incompetent, uncongenial, and hostile. Thus by inner necessity the new individual will be compelled to work out his own destiny and to escape by his own skill the dangers he will encounter. Our most learned prophets of the past can give him only the most general advice.

It is to be noted also that all established religions tend to become theological, abstract, crystallized into given modes of behavior, and divorced from the realm of normal human experience. The power and the guardianship pass to a special group which administers religion according to its own views and purposes. Religion degenerates into a tool of the rulers, or, if free, has no vital instruction for the actual problems of life. This chasm widens as biological differentiation proceeds upon its way and as humanity continues to pyramid its intellectual gains. Then if no freedom of conscience and action be permitted a revolution is sure to follow. Both the government and the religious hierarchy find themselves face to face with determined enemies. And whatever may be the first fortunes of the revolt, change must come unless the revolutionists perish. One way to end reform is to kill those who have the inner need for it—a method which has been tried more than once in the world's history. But it is rather difficult to dispose of a whole generation, and any show of mercy will make victory for the conservatives only a temporary condition. The next generation will demand an even greater reform.

All revolutions are not equally well managed, to be sure, and many have failed. Poor generalship, the unwisdom of admitting abuses worse than the ones for which a cure is proposed, lack of a clear and proper appraisal of the existing situation in the formation of the remedy, and the selfish and unprincipled character of the leaders have given to the enemies of progress a power not in the nature of their cause. Furthermore, leaders are mortal, and they are likely to be cut off before their reforms are accomplished and without even a remote possibility that they shall be followed by competent successors. Add to this the unwieldy and stubborn force of habit and the faint-heartedness and stupidity of mankind, and we have a reason for the failure of the social group to go forward surely and steadily upon its course.

In addition to the natural strain brought about from changes within the group, through the arrival of new and different personalities, there is oppression and interference from conquerors and unwise rulers. Governments imposed upon a people arrest the attempt to achieve spiritual and social destiny of the indigenous type. And at just this point we discover why a popular revolution is always, at its roots, indistinguishable from popular religion. The drive, the motive power, is in the inner spiritual need of the revolting individuals. Their war-cry is the cry of the whole man for his birth-right of spiritual self-expression. Personal liberty is, therefore, the most sacred possession of the individual, for it means room to live his own peculiar life. And yet it is true that those who make the most frequent demand for this freedom are prompted more in their course by moral degeneracy and perverted selfishness than by any lofty feeling of spiritual restraint. It is a wise government that can detect the genuine cry of spiritual hurt, and a wise people that knows when it has a worthy cause for revolution. The form of government perhaps does not matter so long as it fits the man who gives it obedience, for any government manned by statesmen wise enough to awaken the imagination of the individual and stimulate him to seek the fulfillment of his noblest life is the right government for the moment.

The fundamental at-oneness of patriotism and religion, of social and spiritual necessity, determines the function of all true redemptive measures. Liberty must be guaranteed or it will be taken. Control must give both room and stimulation, must "unbind the prisoners" and indicate a Way, must educate and restrict, must carry enough inspirational ballast to hold the ship steady until the next generation can take the wheel, and must be wise enough to know when to insist and when to revoke its laws. In attempting to exercise permanent authority, inspired and infallible gospels have seldom fared better than secular and uninspired ones. They have been contravened, ignored in practice, reformed in the heat of passion and by means of bloody wars, and sometimes lost in the shuffle of striving races and nations. One discovers that only that system lives which serves the new individual in achieving the life which is most congenial to him. When his vision is restricted and his aspirations thwarted, he will walk out of the holiest temple and turn his steps toward a more helpful shrine.

Religion must therefore advocate a theory of human conduct which will secure the most wholesome measures of personal freedom and provide at the same time a way of gaining the highest social and spiritual expectation which the age it seeks to serve can know. Its holiest deliverances will be described as holy or true only when they so approximate the *Zeitgeist* as to make articulate the deep and vaguely felt aspirations of a people then alive. And a particular religious system will persist only so long as its recommendations serve these individual needs. When it fails to do this it ceases to be the religion of the people and becomes the refuge of the recluse, the shibboleth of the fanatic, the tool of the human beast of prey, the solace of the esthete, and for the masses only a kind of burial insurance. It has no value for toiling men, for it answers none of their questions and gives no aid in their labor of self-realization.

Religious control, therefore, like that of true government, must provide room for spiritual self-expression. In both doctrine and ethics it must set its deliverances by the roadside to point out the Way for those who are making the journey of self-realization. It must understand that the road itself may be changed; that it may be laid out over entirely new regions; that it may wind about or be shortened for the convenience and happiness of the travelers. The advocates of decalogues and inspired deliverances must remember the practical character of their wares; they must not forget that a religion that has signally served the needs of mankind in the past is too completely adapted in its final form to be scientific, to point as the crow flies or as the magnetic needle functions. A scientific religion will indicate the shortest way and will face directly toward the goal. Practical religion always gets down to earth; studies the terrain, the art of road-construction, and the mechanics of getting the race forward. It brings into existence a half-dozen practical arts. There is, therefore, necessarily a distinction between the statements of scientific religion and the laws of the practical spiritual life. A failure to recognize this difference and to keep the two divisions to their rightful place has brought about many bloody chapters of history. In an art there is all room under the rules for individual expression; and the genius of the individual working through the rules has given us our most splendid artistic achievements. In fact, art is enriched by the marks of individuality.

How difficult it is to frame a scientific religion we have already noted. Only the most general jurisdiction can be granted to any of its recommendations. Honesty, virtue, truthfulness, monogamy, worship of the deity, justice, coöperation, peace—all these find their place in such a statement. But in the art of living, in the application of the recommendations, latitude must be given for individuality and for the dead weight to be supported. The mortal must not be given an impossible burden. The determination of the nature of the cardinal principles must not be made the goal at the expense of the man. And the more we study them the more we realize that they are only the most general concepts—that they find their real concrete force only in specific instances of human intercourse. And the more complex society becomes the more impossible it is to apply the lump-judgment of dogmatics. Scientific religion, therefore, serves more as an ideal, a basis of recall, the ground principle of regeneration, a means of keeping the race going in the right direction. It merely points out the region to which we should move.

All truly great religions have recognized the priority of individual needs over doctrinal statements—yes, over the logical necessities of religious systematics. The Sabbath is made for man, no matter about its holy character as a day blessed and hallowed by God. But all great religions have not lost sight of the subordination of the individual to the welfare of the race or nation. There is a place where the individual ceases to be of primary consideration, and that point is reached when further privileges of freedom and self-determination would oppose the highest interests of mankind. Just here sets in the obligation of sacrifice and the application of the principle: individual rights must be checked by the higher interest of the general good of all. Heretofore society has administered this profound law with a facility too great to have come from any worthy knowledge of the man in question or of the ideals which ought to determine the future of the state. Fumbling cruelty and injustice, with irreparable loss to the race, have often characterized the proceedings; and administrative function has been too exact to be just, too dogmatic to be wise, too hallowed to recognize the subtle differences of peoples and of individuals upon whom it passes judgment. And when it turns in mercy to the individual it degenerates too often into unwholesome sentimentality and takes no account of the true issue involved—the right of the individual to persist for the good of all men to-morrow. Religion and government have here their general principle—a scientific one—but perhaps the most difficult law to administer properly that man has ever conceived.

It is just at this point that we encounter the need for, and the function of, the leader. Call him statesman, prophet, religious founder, or social expert, his task is to guide humanity through its vexing problems to self-preservation and to the benefits which should accrue to it from the highest service of every person coming into this world. As these leaders appear and contribute their visions, the level of life rises. But a study of present conditions will reveal how unfinished is all our wisdom; how meager and inadequate is the sight of all our seers; how childish and incompetent is the administration of the light we already possess; how vague is the realm we call "the spiritual"; how unconscious of his selfishness is every man alive; how shallow is the veneer of civilization; how little we know of the problems that have confronted the race in the past; and how much of contradiction and uncertainty marks the prophecies of our wisest men when they venture to tell us the story of To-morrow. Under such circumstances, how could we even imagine that the final word has been spoken upon any human question? We must have leaders, an increasing number of them as we multiply and crowd the earth. And as we grow into such proportions as to swell our problems to a size never before encountered in history, we shall need inspired and self-sacrificing men. If we are to secure these and receive a saving help from their services we must educate our people, for only in this way shall we develop leadership and be wise enough to follow it. How many times we may yet need to be saved, and from what far-reaching dangers, may be sensed somewhat in the causes, results, and subsequent reverberations of the most recent European Armageddon. There is in such episodes enough to make any thoughtful man know that these leaders should come quickly.

INDEX